AMERICAN
CULTURAL CRITICS

EXETER STUDIES IN
AMERICAN AND COMMONWEALTH ARTS
GENERAL EDITOR: RICHARD MALTBY

AMERICAN CULTURAL CRITICS is a volume in Exeter Studies in American and Commonwealth Arts, a series produced by AmCAS, the Centre for American and Commonwealth Arts in the University of Exeter. Other volumes in the series include APPROACHES TO THE AMERICAN MUSICAL, edited by Robert Lawson-Peebles; REPRESENTING OTHERS: White views of Indigenous Peoples, edited by Mick Gidley; LOCATING THE SHAKERS: Cultural Origins and Legacies of an American Religious Movement, edited by Mick Gidley with Kate Bowles.

AMERICAN CULTURAL CRITICS

edited by

DAVID MURRAY

UNIVERSITY
of
EXETER
PRESS

First published in 1995 by
University of Exeter Press
Reed Hall, Streatham Drive
Exeter, Devon EX4 4QR
UK

British Library Cataloguing in Publication Data
A catalogue record of this book is available
from the British Library

ISBN 0 85989 404 5

Typeset in Monotype Plantin
by Exe Valley Dataset Ltd., Exeter

Printed and bound in Great Britain
by BPC Wheatons Ltd, Exeter

Contents

Introduction

David Murray

In 1976 Alan Trachtenberg published *Critics of Culture*, a collection of the writings of American intellectuals focused around the 1920s, among them Van Wyck Brooks, H.L. Mencken, Waldo Frank and Lewis Mumford. Trachtenberg identified a "spirit of change"[1] which these figures both expressed and promoted. He found this spirit most clearly amongst artists and intellectuals, who combined dissent, in the form of a rejection of the gentility and falseness of the current American culture, with an optimism about change and the future. But in a characteristic American gesture, this embracing of change was seen as allowing a re-engagement with the most fundamental American values rather than a rejection of them. As Trachtenberg puts it "they thought of themselves as inheritors of an American tradition."[2] The source and ground of their criticism of their society was an idea of America exemplified and invoked in a figure such as Walt Whitman. For this group, the flowering of a cultural revolution was directly related to social criticism, and celebration and criticism could co-exist. In addition the recognition of this change was itself part of a quest for power. Trachtenberg identifies this group as the first figures to establish themselves as "professional nonacademic intellectuals—not specialists or experts in particular fields but synthesizers, interpreters, evaluators."[3] The role of critic of culture allowed at least a temporary resolution of "the tension between their dissent and their affirmation."[4]

The figures discussed in the present collection are not so easily grouped, either chronologically (they range mainly from the 1930s to the present) or in their ideas, but the case for using the umbrella term cultural criticism has become even stronger, as the use of the term culture itself has become more pervasive and inclusive. The range of figures and disciplines represented here, while making no claim to be comprehensive, gives some sense of how the idea of culture has become both more diffuse and more crucial to the ways in which intellectuals and writers articulate their relation to American society in general.

If for Trachtenberg's chosen figures the role of cultural critic could bridge contradictions within their views of America, this was at least partly because of the slipperiness of the idea of culture. In critiquing what they saw as the snobbish and inappropriate cultural values and expressions of the "genteel tradition," these critics were not rejecting the idea of culture, but changing its terms. By invoking a national culture they could imply a more representative, less hierarchical entity, but this view still retained the idea of culture as a sort of "better self" of society, rather than a neutral or anthropological use of the term to refer to the whole range of customs and practices of a society. In this way *authentically* American culture was itself a critique of the shortcomings of current America, just as the Constitution and Bill of Rights could be seen as both an expression of America's values and the severest critique of its practices. The critic's knowledge and expertise made him or her a guardian and explicator of the fundamental values, and also an arbitrator of just which cultural expressions are the genuine article. Thus, while one sort of hierarchy might be rejected, there was still a strong if imprecise sense of the authentic and the inauthentic.

These issues continue in only slightly modified form in the later arguments over high and low, or elitist and popular culture, which run like a common thread through so many otherwise opposed positions. One of the clearest conservative expressions of the argument for culture as something dependent on hierarchy can be found in the arguments for a specifically Southern culture which developed in the wake of the publication of *I'll Take My Stand*[5] in 1930, and are associated with the Agrarians. Michael Kreyling's essay traces the development of these ideas through founding figures such as Allen Tate, but focuses on the work of a later defender and refiner of the idea of a Southern culture, Richard Weaver (1910–63). The defence of a Southern cultural tradition may, as Kreyling shows in his treatment of Weaver, invoke a distinctive mystique of history and place, but what it shares with the New York intellectuals of Hugh Wilford's essay is a suspicion of the philistine mass brought into being by the social developments associated with modernity. Wilford focuses on Philip Rahv (1908–73), who, with his poor Jewish immigrant background, his engagement with communism and with the cultural avant-garde through *Partisan Review*, and his later Cold War accommodations with America and its institutions, is in many ways exemplary of the New York Intellectuals. Nowhere is this more so than in the way his views on the independence of the artist and intellectual as guardian of cultural values and high culture come to involve him in positions of cultural and political conservatism. As Rahv's own career shows, the move from social critic to celebrant is possible, and perhaps even facilitated by the congruity of right and left positions on the necessity of a hierarchy of culture.

There are, of course, clear differences between right and left about the causes and the inevitability of cultural, as well as social inequality. The example of F.O. Matthiessen (1902–50) demonstrates just how misleading it would be to equate a concern with what is now canonical and "high" culture with political conservatism. Best known now as a literary critic and establisher, through his *American Renaissance* (1941),[6] of the canon of major nineteenth-century American literature, Matthiessen is sometimes wrongly associated with a New Critical orthodoxy. In fact, as Richard Bradbury's essay insists, Matthiessen's radical politics not only involved him in opposition to McCarthyism and to the prevailing Cold War intellectual climate, but also informed both his view of American literature, where he traces a tradition of radical democratic thought ignored or effaced in more conventional criticism, and his view of the social and political responsibilities of the critic.

Susan Sontag (1933–), too, attaches great importance to the role and responsibilities of what she calls the writer-intellectual. Her work has developed many of the concerns of the earlier New York Intellectuals without following their political direction. As well as being a novelist and director of films and plays, her critical focus has included the avant-garde and the popular. As Liam Kennedy's essay points out, Sontag's intellectual trajectory from the 1960s has involved tackling subjects ranging from Camp, the Cuban Revolution and photography to cancer and AIDS. Kennedy argues that this role of free-floating cultural critic or generalist has been thrown into question with the decline of a left-liberal idealism in America, and he places Sontag in the context of other cultural analysts such as Christopher Lasch.

What allowed the strange coalition of right and left over mass culture was partly the long tradition within Marxism of aesthetic debate. This tradition has been unwilling to sacrifice the category of art as a privileged term, arguing that art is endowed with formal capacities that allow it to transcend or at least critique the everyday values of the society which produced it. Running from Trachtenberg's earlier generation of culture critics through the Marxists of the 1930s to the contemporary conservative lamentations about cultural standards, we can see a view of art as the highest product of a society, and a view of those who produce and interpret it as key figures in the society. There are other ways of talking about culture, though, as Michael Wood's essay on Stanley Cavell (1926–) shows. Cavell's integration of literary and film criticism with his philosophical work has made him an intellectually impressive figure, but his argument for American culture as not linked with intellect opens up another angle on the relation of cultural *expression* to the wider aspects of society. His claim for the "wild intelligence of American popular culture" as found in film in particular, involves taking very seriously the idea of a culture which is possessed by America without being acknowledged as such, and whose distinctive quality is its apparent absence. Wood shows how Cavell links this both with Emerson and with ordinary language philosophy, in order to explore the position of culture in a democratic society.

So far the figures discussed have all been recognizably cultural critics in that they have dealt with the manifestations of culture in the *arts*, even if they have raised questions about the adequacy of that manifestation. There is, though, a much broader view of culture, which brings into focus a rather different set of intellectual figures as culture critics. The sheer range and diversity of the work of Lewis Mumford (1895–1990) takes him beyond his criticism of the arts in the nineteenth century to architecture and town planning and a comprehensive philosophy of modern civilization itself in his monumental study of the development of Western cities. Clive Bush's essay presents him as pioneer cultural historian and critic and throws into relief his explorations of the idea of community through a comparison with the English proponent of the Garden City movement, Frederic Osborn. Their correspondence, as Bush presents it, offers a useful reminder of the rich international nexus of political ideas within which Mumford operated, in which the practical as well as intellectual aspects of community and culture were explored.

Running parallel with Mumford, the move from defining culture as the production and maintenance of a higher artistic realm to seeing it as the general practices of a society or group was made more generally possible by the development and adoption of the anthropological use of the term. In this context, the influence of Franz Boas and his followers in America earlier in the century went well beyond their own academic field. A book like Ruth Benedict's *Patterns of Culture*[7] is a continuation of the Boasian approach to cultures as entities to be understood in their own terms rather than judged. But her work is characteristic of a large number of "culture and personality" studies in relating other cultures to contemporary American culture, even if only implicitly. From the 1930s onwards, these studies were recognized as having a political dimension in the wider public world outside their professional field. Helen Carr's essay brings together two widely influential figures, Margaret Mead (1901–78) and Karen Horney (1885–1952), to show how their use of anthropology and psychology to analyze the cultural construction of gender in America was inevitably a critique of American society and its cultural values.

Just as Margaret Mead's explorations of other cultures' ways of dealing with sexuality and growing up were seen as addressing real concerns in contemporary American society, so Erik Erikson's (1902–1994) psychoanalytic studies, best known through his *Childhood and Society* (1950),[8] touched a responsive chord at a popular as well as academic level by demonstrating the interplay of the personal and the social or cultural. Lawrence Friedman's essay on Erikson points to the importance of the interdisciplinary climate in which he could operate, and in which his work on psychoanalysis and the life-cycle were inextricably linked with his long-running engagement with American culture. It is the insistence on the complexity of the political and cultural implications of pyschoanalysis, and specifically of Freud's work, which gives the work of Philip Rieff (1922–) much of its critical edge. In his essay on Rieff, Jerry Z. Muller shows just how interlocked his account of Freud and his critique of modern America are. For Rieff, the influence of Freud himself has been "the catalyst of a new cultural sensibility," in which the emphasis on the therapeutic and the self has increased to the detriment of ideas of authority and society. Rieff's conservative scepticism about the promise of individual autonomy connects with a more general critique of American society as made up of lonely atomized narcissists rather than full social beings. This analysis is shared by left cultural criticism but it also stretches back at least to de Tocqueville. What makes the historian and cultural commentator Garry Wills (1934–) so interesting, in Stephen Whitfield's account of him, is precisely his prolonged engagement with these issues through an exploration of the meanings and the power of liberalism in America. That exploration ranges from a discussion of the founding tenets of the American political system in *Inventing America*[9] to detailed accounts of contemporary figures and movements, and utilizes Wills' talents as both historian and journalist.

If, as Wills and so many others argue, the end of liberalism, in the sense of economic individualism, is already occurring, is it being replaced by any recognizable community ethic, or communal public space? The communitarian and utopian thinking invoked by Mumford in Bush's essay stressed the importance of the communal, as opposed to the private space, as an arena for intellectual activity as well as a literal part of the environment. If specialists like Mead or Erikson have been able to bring their expertise to bear in ways that have had general relevance, this has also required a place where they were heard and where genuine debate could take place. For the German émigré Hannah Arendt (1906–75), as Richard King's essay shows, this place was quintessentially the public space necessary for political activity to happen at all. In her longstanding engagement with totalitarianism, revolution and violence she explored many of the implications of modernity and straddled the transatlantic divide, but King shows how her controversial distinction between the political and the economic and social challenges both liberal and Marxist views.

Of course, one of the problems with the idea of a public space and public debate, especially one related to or guaranteed by political institutions, is that it may not be sufficiently inclusive or representative, even while claiming to be so. The role and responsibilities of what Susan Sontag referred to as "people who reason in public," as well as politicians, require some acknowledgement from the community at large that there is a significant public space, as well as a recognition of the status of intellectuals. This space, though, is one already affected by increasing awareness of the exclusions and discriminations of class, race, and gender which have been smuggled in under the idea of the representative or the public. Changes in media technology as well as social structures have allowed for a presentation or self-presentation of American culture which is much more various, with the presence of voices other than the white male ones of Trachtenberg's generation. The change from a general public to a series of publics nevertheless raises its own problems, and Ross Posnock's essay on black intellectuals examines the conflicting pressures for them of being exemplary within the general culture. As he shows, from James Weldon Johnson and Du Bois onwards, "the price of representative authority" has been keenly felt, and he traces opposing choices, and creations of representative selves by a range of contemporary figures.

While their minority status has ensured that Posnock's chosen figures are only too aware of the public nature of their representative selves, Russell Jacoby has lamented the more general loss of the public intellectual and the impoverishment of what he calls "public culture."[10] He sees the persisting influence and prominence of intellectuals who made their mark in the 1950s as evidence not so much of their brilliance, or of the dominance of a conservatism in intellectual life, but of the change in the role of the intellectual. He stresses the increasing specialization and institutionalization of academic and intellectual life, a theme taken up very fully in Foucauldian analyses of the relation of knowledge to power. When combined with interpretations of America as a postmodern society, the concern of such analyses with system and control rather than individual action can have the effect of presenting culture as an area of co-optation rather than critique or liberation. Thoreau's observation that to move society you need a fulcrum, a position outside from which to lever it, depended on an individualism which is now seen not to be available. The contemporary emphasis on the all-embracing nature of discourse, and the inextricable relation of knowledge to power, has tended to throw doubt on the capacity of criticism to escape the terms of society, as has the increased awareness of the institutional and disciplinary aspects of intellectual activities.

If in the past culture seemed the privileged access to a critique of society, in which the other more material and economic realms could be seen reflected, there was still the idea that there were other spheres and other ways of discussing society. The sociologist Daniel Bell (1919–) may have been at best premature in his description of *The End of Ideology* (1960), and his later work on the post-industrial society and what he sees as *The Cultural Contradictions of Capitalism* (1976) have often been seen as the expression of a conservative viewpoint,[11] but his demonstration of the increasing autonomy of the cultural sphere shares a great deal with the more Marxist analysis of Fredric Jameson (1934–). As Nick Heffernan's essay on the two men shows, the relation between Jameson's postmodern and Bell's post-industrial is both close and complex, but Jameson is not as prepared to discard the explanatory and analytic framework of Marxism, which maintains a sense of the primacy of something other than culture, or the ultimately emancipatory project of modernity. But Jameson's approach to the postmodern is untypical in its political emphasis. For most commentators, whether for or against it, postmodernity is characterized by the absence of grand narratives and by the triumph of the cultural realm over all others. Whether seen as the impact of the communication industry over production, or more generally as the disappearance of the political, culture appears as both the privileged, indeed the only, way of talking about society, and also as itself the problem, and this has given an added urgency to questions of culture and cultural criticism, and to their institutional manifestations.

One manifestation of this interest is the emergence of the new field, or the new name, of cultural studies. Whereas this book deals with particular intellectuals whose work has constituted a critique of American society or culture and, in most cases, whose special areas of expertise gave them a vantage point from which to comment, cultural studies would seem to offer a discipline in itself—yet one with serious internal contradictions which echo the ambiguities within the idea of culture itself. In their introduction to a huge collection of essays called simply *Cultural Studies*, the editors point to "a kind of double articulation of culture in cultural studies, where 'culture' is simultaneously the ground on which analysis proceeds, the object of study and the site of political critique and intervention."[12]

The question is whether cultural studies is to be a neutral umbrella term, describing a variety of not necessarily compatible approaches to cultural products, or whether it will retain the critical edge developed in British cultural studies, associated with Raymond Williams, Richard Hoggart and Stuart Hall. This approach involved assumptions about power and inequality and their key role in any discussion of cultural representation, informed by Marx and Gramsci. As it develops in America the same issues of power and representation can be seen across a broad spectrum of concerns over race and gender, but the idea of class all but disappears. At one level this no doubt reflects the different political vocabularies, but it may also be seen to reflect a larger move away from a Marxist basis. Thus, though cultural studies in America may still be seen as "left" by its practitioners and critics alike, what holds together the broad coalition is likely to be ideas of marginality rather than class.

The stance of marginality can, of course, be a powerful resource as well as a privation, and is one that we can see already employed by a number of figures in this book. It could be argued that in breaking down traditional communities and values, the experience of modernity both created the space for cultural criticism and gave a role to the free-floating intellectual, whose very marginality, or alienation as it was more likely to be described, was an asset. We need to be clear, though, about this position on the margin. With access to major publishing houses and journals, the marginality of the New York Intellectuals was of a very different order from that created by poverty and discrimination. For some groups, marginality itself has become an institution with its own power. The recognition of this problem can be seen in the soul-searching within cultural studies about the relation to the academy, and the awareness of the ease with which mere oppositionality can be co-opted and institutionalized. If in the past the figure of cultural credibility has been the apparently independent outsider-intellectual, the emphasis on marginality rather than alienation now brings with it the idea of conflicting groups and constituencies of interest contesting in the market-place for public attention. Here the idea of marginality can be part of a bid for power in a competitive battle to be heard. (Ironically, the claim to be marginal or "more marginal than thou" is a claim to authority even employed by those on the right who lament, in highly publicized books and articles, about their own silencing and marginalization by a tyranny of the politically correct.)

This returns us to the question of the public space in which intellectuals or cultural critics operate, and its relation to power. The increased awareness of the controlling power of the media, at the level of academic debate as well as mass circulation, and the importance of access from the margins may produce a healthy scepticism about the idea of free-floating criticism and the circulation of ideas, but it also throws into doubt the possibility of a neutral public space for ideas rather than for conflicting interest-groups. The upbeat and non-conflictual postmodern view of this might be that changes in the circulation of knowledge, combined with the end of the power of the "grand narratives" will result in a plurality of local knowledges and communities, without the need to totalize. More sceptical and materialist accounts would point to the inequalities of economic and political power which would need to disappear before such a dialogical free-for-all could take place. What is lost, according to these accounts, is the idea that culture plays off against a material base, and sceptics see the postmodern subsuming of all categories into the cultural as actually diminishing rather than expanding the power of cultural critique.

This collection of essays focuses on just some of those many American intellectuals who have addressed issues of culture and its multifaceted relation to politics and specific intellectual disciplines, and it would be perfectly possible to assemble another complete list of major figures not included here. While it would be impossible to do justice to the depth and diversity of the debate over cultural criticism in America over the last half-century, this collection aims to broaden the terms of that debate beyond concerns over popular versus high culture, and explore the ways in which a very diverse group of American Intellectuals, including some European émigrés in America, confront a common set of issues. These involve the continuing reaction to modernity and technology, the complex legacies of Marxism and of psychoanalysis, the re-examination of American founding principles and figures in conservative or liberal terms, and the changing role and nature of the media. They also bear witness to the continuing vitality and range of debate around culture in America.

Notes

1. Alan Trachtenberg (ed.) *Critics of Culture* (New York: John Wiley, 1976), p. 3.
2. Trachtenberg, *Critics of Culture*, p. 10.
3. Trachtenberg, *Critics of Culture*, p. 6.
4. Trachtenberg, *Critics of Culture*, p. 8.
5. Twelve Southerners, *I'll Take My Stand* (New York: Harper, 1930; repr. Baton Rouge: Louisiana State University Press, 1977).
6. F.O. Matthiessen, *American Renaissance* (New York: Oxford University Press, 1941).
7. Ruth Benedict, *Patterns of Culture* (London: Routledge & Kegan Paul, 1935).
8. Erik Erikson, *Childhood and Society* (London: Imago Publishing Co., 1951).
9. Garry Wills, *Inventing America: Jefferson's Declaration of Independence* (Garden City, N.Y.: Doubleday, 1978).
10. Russell Jacoby, *The Last Intellectuals: American Culture in the Age of Academe* (New York: Farrar, Strauss and Giroux, 1987), p. 5.
11. Daniel Bell, *The End of Ideology: On the Exhaustion of Political Ideas in the Fifties* (Cambridge, Mass.: Harvard University Press, 1988) and *The Cultural Contradictions of Capitalism* (London: Heinemann, 1979).
12. Lawrence Grossberg, Cary Nelson and Paula Treichler (eds) *Cultural Studies* (New York and London: Routledge, 1992), p. 5.

1

Southern Literary and Intellectual History in the Twentieth Century
The Agrarians to Richard Weaver

Michael Kreyling

> You can't understand it. You would have to be born there.
>
> William Faulkner[1]

To admit that you were studying the literary and intellectual history of the American South used to be an invitation to a joke; Mencken had the first and biggest laugh in "The Sahara of the Bozart."[2] What literature? What intellect? The collective IQ of the old Confederacy would not add up to a two digit number. And so on. Quentin Compson had the problem of trying to gag Shreve's laughter at the same joke and hold himself from joining in. Maybe, if the quintessential Southerner of twentieth-century fiction had laughed, he would be alive today. The study of the intellectual and literary history of the South, for most of the present century, has created divisions embodied in Quentin: schizophrenic—if not raving—minds struggling simultaneously to define a subject and defend it against a host of suspicious critics.

By the mid-1980s much progress had been made in bridging the chasm. *The History of Southern Literature* (1985)—with emphasis on the definite article—has established itself as the culmination of decades of embattled thought on the South inaugurated by the publication of *I'll Take My Stand* (1930).[3] Anthologies and readers, each with their own strong definition of Southernness, have, since the early 1950s, been spun off by the gradually evolving consensus of these fifty-five years. One can teach *Modern Southern Short Stories*, *A*

Southern Reader, *The Literary South*, the major Southern literary figure (William Faulkner), complete with the kind of axiomatic definition of Southernness that seems always to have been there. Not until the appearance of *The History of Southern Literature*, however, has the consensus seemed so free-standing, un-mortgaged. The genesis of that consensus on the definition is seldom questioned; like all first principles, it is assumed always to have been there and evident to all. There have been few, like Shreve, to doubt the miraculous birth of Southernness as a cultural constant.

The main lines of Southern literary and intellectual history have, nevertheless, been inscribed by the strong presence of the first principle, and by the cultural work that has established it. To borrow Isaiah Berlin's categories for the reasons humans study their history,[4] the guilds of Southern literary criticism and intellectual history are chiefly occupied by those who study the South from an ethical point of view: the history of thought and expression in the South provides a lesson in the difference between true and false value, a lesson that teaches that the South persevered in the central values of the western classical tradition from Plato through the confusion of truth and romantic will in the Enlightenment and into the present. These believers in the Southern consensus discern patterns in its history leading to a single ontological meaning: Calhoun's defeat in the Nullification controversy is repeated in the Civil War, and in the conquest of the South by industrialization in this century. History is from moment to moment; the South is always. This pattern is often projected backward in time, linking the South to medieval Europe (ruined by "the rise of the middle class") and to classical Greece and Rome (ruined by various tribes of barbarians). Perhaps the most ambitious, and revealing, of these excursions into the cultural past, were the fanciful and posthumous genealogies of Robert E. Lee that traced his blood through King Arthur all the way back to Jesus Christ. Thus, the history of the South is essentially greater than American history; it surpasses history itself as a vessel of meaning.

Few, it seems, inquire of "the South" how in the present century it became such powerful collateral, powerful enough to back individual books and a fully-equipped academic field. How did "the South" grasp and hold the capital "S"?

The process began with the construction of "the South" in and around the Agrarian manifesto *I'll Take My Stand* (1930). This story has been told and analyzed many times, usually under the assumption that "the South" was there as the object of the volume of essays before the twelve Southerners began to write, that it called them into articulation like a breath of inspiration. An extension of the origin story brings "the South" one step further into the work of Richard M. Weaver, a student of the first generation of South-builders, who bridged the gap between the South as it was variously understood by the titans of the 1920s and 1930s and the South fully-fitted for use in the discipline of literary and intellectual history. Weaver, an undergraduate at the University of Kentucky in the late 1920s, a graduate student under John Crowe Ransom in the 1930s at Vanderbilt, and a doctoral student under Cleanth Brooks at Louisiana State University in the early 1940s, combined the faith of those who say "the South" as an ethical and ontological constant above history with dedicated work in the archives of Southern intellectual culture: its obscure fiction, periodical essays, all-but-forgotten writers. Weaver's major works in this cause are his posthumous *The Southern Tradition at Bay* (1943; 1968) and his *Southern Essays* (1987).[5]

In his study of Southern intellectuals and their work, *The War Within: From Victorian to Modernist Thought in the South. 1919–1945*, Daniel J. Singal prefaces his main argument with a caveat that illustrates the slippery immunity of "the South" as a first principle in the discourse of literary and intellectual history: "To write the history of thought accurately, to avoid the large-scale reifications—such as the 'American Mind'—that have plagued the discipline so often in the past, we must concentrate on individual thinkers as the first step toward our more thematic treatments."[6] The process of reification in the social history of thought is nothing if not surreptitious. If such ideologically loaded terms as "American Mind" have "plagued the discipline" of intellectual history, so has the central term "the South," accorded a kind of immaculate ideological birth. Singal and others, like Fred Hobson in *Tell About the South: The Southern Rage to Explain*,[7] proceed with their "thematic treatments" as if "the South" were unmediated and constant in all contexts. It seems to be necessary at this stage in the discourse of "the South" to cloud the customary transparency of the term, to challenge its neutrality. Hobson's title, borrowed from Shreve's hectoring of Quentin Compson in *Absalom, Absalom!*, supposes that "the South" possesses the ontological fixedness that gives shape and meaning to a discourse that might, troublingly, contain a large portion of self-reference; the South might have invented the South, then treated it as an onto-logical constant prior to thought. When Quentin, the Southerner, mutters to Shreve, or to no-one in particular, "You can't understand it. You would have to be born there," he is interpreted to have established the ontology of "the South": not an "it," a thing among many things to be grasped by the human faculties of analytical intelligence, but a "there," a pre-condition for any kind of thought at all. Quentin in vain argues the superiority of faith over Shreve's narrative improvisation.[8]

It was just such a distinction between an image (the South) immune to human play and improvisation and human manipulation of life and value that shaped the thinking of the small group of Southern conservative thinkers who planned *I'll Take My Stand* in the late 1920s. The 1920s seems to have been a propitious time for thinking aloud about the production of culture. Karl Mannheim's *Ideology and Utopia* was first published in German in 1929, the crucial year the Southern Agrarians worked to assemble and publish their manifesto. Mannheim studies "the sociology of thought" rather than thought itself, and he is especially interested in the formation of intellectual elites, self-formed social groups "whose special task it is to provide an interpretation of the world."[9] Mannheim's work provides useful general guidelines for the re-thinking of the history of the formation of "the South":

> This type of thought [that of professional intellectual elites] does not arise primarily from the struggle with concrete problems of life, nor from trial and error, nor from experiences in mastering nature and society, but rather much more from its own need for systematization, which always refers the facts which emerge in the religious as well as in other spheres of life back to given traditional and intellectually uncontrolled premises.[10]

The survival in power of the particular group takes precedence over empirical data; cultural power, not "the search for truth," is the primary motivation for intellectual production. The group that names the system therefore controls those who seek entrance or maintenance within it. The group that establishes the most resilient "traditional and intellectually uncontrolled premises" ("there" rather than "it") wins the sweepstakes. Southern intellectual history, in the present century, began or resumed—post Mencken—as much concerned with the formation of an elite as it was with the description of a cultural thing.

"In the battle of ideas," wrote Irving Babbitt, chief of a rival elite and arch-enemy of the first twentieth-century cadre of Southern intellectuals, "as in other forms of warfare, the advantage is on the side of those who take the offensive."[11] Babbitt and his humanist cohorts had seized the advantage in a battle of ideas that might, in

Norman Foerster's clarion call, define the "needs of America as the dominant world power and inadequate model of civilization in the twentieth century."[12] The campaign of the humanists, fusing ancient Greek, Confucian, and Christian philosophies against Romantic naturism percolating below in human instinct, and enthused, revealed religion above, had made great progress in the public mind of the 1920s while those who would take arms against it were writing poetry and publishing *The Fugitive*.

Donald Davidson was at Yaddo in upstate New York in the summer of 1929 when he found out about the progress of the humanist offensive. He wrote to John Crowe Ransom sounding the alarum: "It seems that More, Babbitt, and other humanists are about to bring out a symposium on Humanism in America . . . and this is expected to give their movement a concrete source to expand from."[13] Work on the Agrarian symposium, as yet untitled, had not progressed so far. Allen Tate, the driving force, was in France on a Guggenheim Foundation fellowship. Davidson feared that the advantage of surprise had been lost, but he saw another Southern quality that, if exploited, might even up the contest:

> the lack of these humanists is their failure to have intimate touch, to be really a coherent body. They can only write and hope vaguely, whereas we, though constituting a group of less majestic proportions, really form a unit of mutual understanding and actively are in touch with a specific Cause.[14]

Davidson's reconnaissance captures the Southern intellectual movement early in its formation as concerned chiefly with "its own need for systematization" in a struggle between intellectual elites for cultural advantage. The South, early in the process, appears as the "Cause"; actual concrete historical circumstances are less important than the power of "intellectually uncontrolled premises" to bind an order of individuals into a group that is almost religious. Both the humanists and the inchoate group of Southern reactionaries were "looking for a new set of controlling ideas capable of restoring value to human existence," a gospel.[15] The meaning of history for the humanists, dissolved into terms like poise, self-control, moderation, had less appeal than securing power in the present. They disappointed some potential followers because they saw no use in social action; they were Emerson's heirs. Although the Southerners originally seemed to be more interested in the possibility of reform, an encounter with history, their movement ultimately moved away from programme and towards belief.

There was a second offensive, closer to home, that pressed the Nashville group to clarify its rules of warfare. Howard Mumford Jones, then (the late 1920s) a professor of English at the University of North Carolina in Chapel Hill, had approached both Davidson and Ransom in the summer of 1929 for advice and contributions to a symposium he was to edit for UNC Press. The working title was "Culture below the Potomac," a phrase reminiscent of Mencken's poisonous prepositions in "The Sahara of the Bozart," which relentlessly place Dixie "under" and "beneath" and "below" the culturally dominant North. Although Jones and Davidson had corresponded cordially, and although Davidson eventually wrote an essay on trends in modern Southern literature for the UNC volume (published as *Culture in the South* in 1934 with W.T. Couch as editor),[16] there was not much more than formal politeness between the two men and their camps. In a letter to Tate, Davidson showed the other face of the movement, its tendency to exclusiveness and internal systematization:

> But I also enclose a copy of a letter from Howard Mumford Jones which just reached me and is self-explanatory. It upset me!
>
> You will see, after reading it, what is before us. If Jones, whom I like and respect in many ways, put his scheme on foot, the "progressive" note will be accented very much, I greatly fear. You can imagine, for instance, what a man like Odum would have to say about the negro question. For us, the issue is: Will we let the Progressives (some of whom are "immigrant" Southerners) capture the field and walk off with public opinion [?] But they have great strength on their side—prestige, resources, etc. They can get eminent contributors. They may even cut the ground out from under us.[17]

The rhetoric of battle, perhaps Davidson's favourite, suggests that dialogue was not his goal. Although the progressive Southern symposium was delayed several years, the threat of it triggered in Davidson a reaction to control and define the South as subject.

Tate, still in France, was not blasé. He agreed that Jones was indeed a "Yankee" who had adopted "Southernism as a means to academic preferment," and added that he (Tate) was full of energy for the Southern cause.[18] With a sense of arriving belatedly on the field, Davidson, Ransom, and Tate rushed *I'll Take My Stand* to completion. With latter-day Puritans like Babbit to the right of them, and imitation Southerners like Jones to the left, there was little room to manoeuvre. Enemy emplacements in the form of symposia and anthologies dotted the intellectual landscape. Such close quarters bequeathed to the Southern intellectual elite a defensiveness towards foes and a strictness with one's comrades in arms. The snide hostility of Mencken's tirade in 'The Sahara of the Bozart' had metamorphosed into a formidable intellectual opposition.

Tate's call for strictness in the ranks was due in large part to his sense of being outnumbered and outhustled. In any case, the crisis as it appeared late in 1929 was tailor-made for him, for he had made his debut as an international literary and cultural critic in T.S. Eliot's *Criterion* that July with an attack on the philosophy of the New Humanists, "Humanism and Naturalism." Tate's charge against Babbitt and his followers was that their thought lacked "a living centre of judgement and feeling."[19] "Until this center is found," Tate continued, "and not pieced together eclectically at the surface, humanism is an attempt to do mechanically—that is, naturalistically —what should be done morally." Shrevean improvisation, the eclectic piecing together of meaning, was the sign of error regardless of the meaning espoused. The crucial assumption underpinning Tate's thought, an assumption he injected into full ideology as it took form, was that the centre was an entity to be "found." "The South" was to become this objective correlative for Tate's opposition to modern and progressive modes of thought.

More than any of his comrades in the Southern reactionary movement, however, Tate knew that he was implicated in the creed of the enemy. He knew that in thinking about the One, the centre, he could not be sure it was also outside human thought. Not until his conversion to Roman Catholicism in the 1950s, perhaps, was Tate sure that the object of his belief was indeed prior to and beyond human thought and construction. The act of violence he called for in *I'll Take My Stand* is an act of intellectual violence, a sort of self-maiming: one simply overleaped the limits of human thought, sure through faith of landing in the moral centre. "The South" was Tate's centre until he found one he believed to be absolute.

For Davidson and his friends at home, Tate had a full-scale plan of battle worthy of Stonewall Jackson, whose biography he had written a few years earlier. Tate projected the "formation of a society, or an academy of Southern *positive* reactionaries made up at first of people of our own group," the recruitment of an auxiliary of "inactive" members from professional classes outside academia, a constitution that "should set forth, under our leading idea, a complete social, philosophical, literary, economic, and religious system," and an eventual publication to promulgate the group's agenda.[20] Tate's zeal was not for the second coming of the South in concrete historical terms, for his own self-consciousness was more nuanced than those of his colleagues. Hints had arisen a few years earlier when he and Davidson exchanged letters on Tate's long poem "Ode to the Confederate Dead." Davidson had complained, "your *elegy* is not for the Confederate dead, but for your own dead emotion, or mine (*you* think)."[21] Tate did not disagree: "my attempt is to see the present from the past, yet remain immersed in the present and committed to it. I think it is suicide to do anything else."[22] The programme he espoused would likewise be aimed at the present: "this programme would *create an intellectual situation interior to the South*. I underscore it because, to me, it contains the heart of the matter."[23] In brief, Tate was originally more interested in the formation of an elite than in the contents of its programme.

Tate also supplied a tentative table of contents for the book; his controlling idea was that the Agrarians could recoup through intense coherence what they stood to lose through tardiness. Like Stonewall, he might pull off a lightning march and salvage the battle. Nothing less than cultural survival was at stake: "for this end we must have a certain discipline; we must crush minor differences of doctrine under a single idea."[24]

The "single idea" and the "intellectually uncontrolled premises" were never specifically named: you could not understand it; you would have to be born there. A few months later, as he became more familiar with the character of Davidson's belief in the single idea, Tate clarified and retreated from the crusading rhetoric and the implied belief:

> There is one feature of our movement that calls for comment. We are not in the least divided, but we exhibit two sorts of minds. You and Andrew [Lytle] seem to constitute one sort—the belief in the eventual success, in the practical sense, of the movement. The other mind is that of Ransom and Warren and myself. I gather that Ransom agrees with me that the issue on the plan of action is uncertain. At least I am wholly sceptical on that point; but the scepticism is one of hoping to be convinced, not by standing aside to watch the spectacle, but by exerting myself. In other words, I believe that there is enough value to satisfy me in the affirmation, in all its consequences, including action, of value. If other goods proceed from that, all the better. My position is that since I see the value, I am morally obligated to

affirm it. That sounds pretty grand, but I can think of no other phrase.[25]

Tate could see the "it" and the "there," the practical and the myth; to his mind the South ran on both tracks, was party to both kinds of discourse. As he acknowledged to Davidson, his position was neither easy to explain nor readily susceptible of quick and fervent belief. His position lay somewhere between the hallowed silence of the Davidsonian view and the concrete historical view of the "progressives." Tate tried to explain the differences and to hold them in intellectual suspension in his essay for *I'll Take My Stand*. In *Who Owns America?*, the sequel to the Agrarian volume, Tate tried more explicitly to turn the concrete-historical, property and exchange, into the metaphysical; by his own admission, he failed.[26]

Whereas the "progressives" habitually described the South in objective terms, as distribution of income, as agricultural zones, as races and classes, as census and tax figures, the Agrarians preserved a seeming tactical advantage by never submitting their single idea to the scrutiny of history. For example, essays that eventually appeared in *Culture in the South* consistently positioned the South as an historical phenomenon like many others; culture in the South supposed that the South had little or nothing to do with the culture itself. In his preface to the volume of thirty-one essays, William Terry Couch, who had replaced Jones, set the tone for the whole volume by taking for granted that "the fundamental issues in southern life. . . are much the same as elsewhere."[27] The Agrarians could absorb criticism of their own volume by consoling themselves that those on the outside did not understand and made foredoomed efforts trying to, but ranking the South on an historical par with every other place and time as an object of professional study was anathema. Rupert Vance's essay treats the South as a set of circumstances susceptible of improvement by "regional planning,"[28] and Broadus Mitchell (the *bête noire* of Davidson who could think of no more appropriate punishment for him than "hanging"[29]) made the bold assertion: "Our religion, letters, laws, arts, social amenities, and race relations are all functions of our economic life."[30] Reductive statements such as this understandably made the Agrarians disinclined to attribute much merit to the volume or the agenda on which it was built.

Howard Mumford Jones, who surrendered "Culture Below the Potomac" when he moved from Chapel Hill to Ann Arbor in 1930, had already taken opposing intellectual and literary ground in an essay in Stringfellow Barr's *Virginia Quarterly Review*, "Is There a

Southern Renaissance?,"[31] before the Agrarian manifesto appeared. His answer to the question in his title was negative, but his means of arguing to this verdict are more revealing, perhaps, than the verdict itself. Jones contrasts the theological underpinnings of the Northern (i.e. Puritan) literary culture and those of the South. He can find no evidence that the South could ever come up with a cultural renaissance since it could not match the vigorous intellectual life created by generations of New England Puritans from Bradford to Emerson. And in a subsequent essay, "The Future of Southern Culture,"[32] Jones faintly praised the neo-Confederate wing of Southern intellectuals for the power of their manifesto, yet held their feet to the fire of concrete historical circumstances by consistently admitting Negro slavery, the continuing race problem, and such real-life conditions as single-crop agriculture as liens on the myth. Jones enlisted under Stringfellow Barr's critical banner: "the apotheosis of the hoe" was a pretty myth but left out too much history for intellectual safety.

The Agrarian intellectuals were not very effective in rebuttal, for they were loath to submit the vision to reasoned discourse. Davidson's negotiations with Jones over his essay for the UNC volume, "The Trend of Literature: A Partisan View," provide a case in point. Jones accepted Davidson's work before he left the project to Couch, but he had some reservations: "My main—indeed, my only—quarrel with it is that I seem to go around in a circle since you nowhere explicitly state what it is you mean by the Southern quality of Southern literature."[33] Davidson stood fast, refusing to be drawn into the trap of definition: that trap would force him to lower (as he saw it) Southernness to the level of historical data. His essay as published is quite certain what is not Southern about the literature under survey: social satire, propaganda, Faulknerian decadence, Cabellian whimsy. He is opaque as to what is Southern: it would be hard to pick out definitely Southern characteristics in any given number of Southern poets, but it would be equally hard to prove that they are un-Southern.[34] The single idea would be known to initiates, those born into the knowledge, and would confound those outside the circle. To explain Southernness, Davidson argued, "would require a second essay,"[35] a project he had no intention of undertaking.

When Richard M. Weaver came to Vanderbilt for a Master's degree in 1932 (he had applied for a fellowship to North Carolina and been turned down), the fervour of the Agrarian movement was in metamorphosis. The soldiers in the Cause were beginning to think of life after the crisis. Tate, the envy of his friend Davidson, had always been able to turn down the polemic and turn up poetry in an instant. That flexibility now became a goal of Davidson's: "And how I do envy you that you can still turn to poetry, again and again, and let all your feelings out; while I remain stopped-up, raging speechlessly when I should be raging in verse."[36] Personal and professional hardships seemed to dog Davidson's tracks. Soon he became disenchanted with the movement because it seemed to be the cause of so many disappointments: "We like to think of ourselves as crusaders; in our minds' eye, we can see ourselves doing a kind of Pickett's charge against industrial breastworks, only a *successful* charge this time. But we don't actually do the crusading."[37]

By 1937, Davidson longed to get back to "the literary side."[38] Pseudo-Confederates like Couch seemed to possess the field. Ransom, always too cool and intellectually distant for Davidson's taste, was on the brink of moving to Kenyon and into literary criticism. Dissatisfaction with the way Vanderbilt's administration had managed the negotiations with Ransom left Davidson with a sense of estrangement from his institution. The burdens of the Agrarian cause were made even more onerous when Seward Collins, whose *American Review* had served as a pulpit for the Agrarian order, gave Grace Lumpkin an interview in which he proclaimed, "Yes, I am a fascist," and dug the grave deeper by stating that both Jews and Negroes were troublemakers who deserved segregation.[39] Even Tate, as much as he felt the need for an organ of public discourse, wanted to put some distance between the Cause and Collins. But damage had been done. What fatigue and low professional nourishment had not weakened in the Agrarian intellectual fibre, the loose lips of Seward Collins had sunk. By the end of the 1930s, the Southern intellectual movement faced a more formidable opponent than Mencken's derision: it was in the pits of political incorrectness.

Richard Weaver's entrance upon the scene coincided with the turn into literature and away from destructive polemics. Like most of the Agrarian initiates, Weaver cared less for history than for ideology; unlike them, however, he knew more of the actual intellectual history of the South before the twentieth century. And unlike his elders, Weaver was neither poet, novelist, nor literary critic. He could not turn from disputation to literature. He was a rhetorician and debate was his way of life.

From the generation of the fathers in the late 1920s and 1930s to Richard Weaver in the 1940s, and until his death in 1963, the work of Southern intellectuals had been to lift the South out of what

Mannheim calls the "concrete problems of life" (where Shreve's improvisatory mode of explanation seems as good as any other stab at meaning), and to place it on the pedestal of myth. Lewis Simpson, sympathetic with the desire for the first principle and sceptical at the same time, recognizes this act of thought in an essay on the work of Richard Weaver: "In fiction and in poetry in the most complete signification of the term—a vision of the South had emerged which defied the meaning of the history of the South more fundamentally than reasoned discourse has the capacity to do."[40] In Weaver's work, the process by which vision cast out history in the discourse of the South was fulfilled. The process was both intentional and unconscious, for Weaver recuperated several of the significant themes and tropes of the argument of *I'll Take My Stand* and used the general programme of that symposium on specific political and cultural "problems." Unlike the original twelve, who usually professed to dislike confrontation, Weaver the debater sought it deliberately.

Like Paul following after the Messiah, Weaver was an apostle too late for the original calling. *I'll Take My Stand* had been planned, written, and published while he was an undergraduate at the University of Kentucky (1928–32), and still, by his own account, under the baleful spell of the progressive, liberal heresy. In his twenties after the crash of the stock market, Weaver later confessed, he lived by the false creed of liberalism. Such delusions, he implies in his memoir "Up From Liberalism," were natural. The national economic and social structures had been shaken by the Great Depression, and academic men flocked to the new political correctness: "science, liberalism, and equalitarianism."[41] This was, as Paul might have called it, the philosophy of the age, promulgated in classrooms, textbooks, lectures, and essays. Weaver looked back on this philosophy as the worn-out tide of humanism, and like Tate before him made a debut, of sorts, in his Master's thesis under Ransom with an attack on humanism.

It was Ransom's influence in the mid-1930s that pushed Weaver to begin to acknowledge the feet of clay on his modern, liberal idol. "I had tried some of the Leftist solution and had found it not to my taste," Weaver wrote, "it was possible that I had been turned from the older, more traditional solutions because they wore an antiquarian aspect and insisted upon oppositions which seemed irrelevancies in the modern context."[42] The "older more traditional solutions" increasingly answered the modern problems as Weaver saw them. The past assumed the character of the One and the present slid into the chaos of the Many.

Weaver's sense of historical time loosened as he began to assemble a narrative from traditional times to the modern. The fourteenth century marked, for Weaver, the last pinnacle of metaphysical clarity: the five centuries since had been a long decline into an empirical wasteland. In classic conservative fashion, Weaver jettisoned the future and embraced the past, erasing from historical significance the times (middle-class and mercantile) that had given him birth and character.[43] Weaver also entered into a sense of history that dispenses with the "it" and conceives of meaning in history as the struggle between two ideas (unity vs. multiplicity) perennially at odds under the guise of the ideal and the local.

Weaver did in fact find himself intellectually at Vanderbilt, for his Master's thesis contains in embryonic form many of the ideas and attitudes he later refined. "The Revolt against Humanism" is Weaver's first major swerve away from his liberal youth. The essay traces the fall of the ideal from Protagoras, the first mind in the West to be corrupted by the empirical, to Henry Adams, thence to Weaver's own mentor, Ransom, the man of courage who took up "the hated word 'orthodoxy' and defended it."[44] In Ransom's return to the unity of the Platonic tradition, Weaver found his path.

Weaver left Vanderbilt with an MA in 1934, and eventually took a position teaching English at Texas A&M College Station, Texas, which was ripe for missionary work: "I encountered a rampant philistinism, abetted by technology, large-scale organization, and a complacent acceptance of success as the goal of life."[45] After a couple of years parched by the "naturalism" of Texas, Weaver was ripe for conversion. His calling so closely parallels that of Saul (Acts 9: 3–19) that it deserves full quotation:

> I recall very sharply how, in the Autumn of 1939, as I was driving one afternoon across the monotonous prairies of Texas to begin my third year in this post it came to me like a revelation that I did not have to go on professing the clichés of liberalism, which were becoming meaningless to me. I saw that my opinions had been formed out of a timorous regard for what was supposed to be intellectually respectable, and that I had always been looking over my shoulder to find out what certain others, whose concern with truth I was beginning to believe to be not very intense, were doing or thinking. It is a great experience to wake up at a critical juncture to the fact that one does not have a free will, and that giving up the worship of false idols is a quite practicable proceeding.[46]

He turned the car around and headed for Baton Rouge, where, perhaps, Cleanth Brooks, like Ananias in Damascus, was having a dream that a man named Weaver had need of his teaching.

Weaver went to Louisiana State University to study the Southern literary thought and expression of the nineteenth century. With his dedication to a Platonic orthodoxy and his aversion to rationalism, he meant to find a "reified" Southern Mind unfettered by particular circumstances. "The study and appreciation of a lost cause," he wrote retrospectively of that decision, "have some effect of turning history into philosophy."[47] Turning history into philosophy, the Many into the One, could only be accomplished under the sign of an ideal unity, a Platonic dream, such as Weaver predicated of the South: "that unified and preponderating mind"[48] which Weaver believed he had found not only in the South but prior to it, not so much *in* historical events as hovering above.

Weaver's doctoral dissertation, written under the supervision of Brooks, carries the title "The Confederate South. 1865–1910: A Study of the Survival of a Mind and a Culture" (1943). The aim of the work is to document the "cultural and spiritual unity of the South as it revealed itself after the Civil War."[49] The work was unsuccessful in finding a publisher in Weaver's lifetime; it went out to university presses a few years after W.J. Cash's *The Mind of the South* had cornered the market. It was posthumously published in 1968 under the title *The Southern Tradition at Bay*, with an introduction by a still-unreconstructed Southerner, Donald Davidson, who must have recognized some of the ideas and relished the rhetoric of battle.

Weaver's book is an amalgam of polemic and scholarship, history and ideology. He profiles the inchoate Mind of the South that operated as the template for the individual minds and temperaments of the contributors to *I'll Take My Stand*. That is, he goes before them into post-bellum Southern intellectual life to identify the culture of the fathers' fathers. Like Plato rather than Protagoras, Weaver finds an ideal—the South as a poetic constant—to serve as the measure of human social and literary endeavour. *The Southern Tradition at Bay* asserts the existence of an intellectual culture in the South based on community, tradition, and the persistence over time of a "metaphysical dream."[50] Unlike many other historians of Southern thought, who generally channel Southern history through the agonistic minds of Faulkner or Warren (Woodward is a good example), Weaver routes his study through the *kerygma* of the Agrarian message. He thus helps Southern literary study, already formalistically sophisticated and historically linked to the culture of modernism, to mark a history generated by a trans-historical ontology in "the South" as idea. The Agrarian group left us some pointers in thematic readings of literary works, but barely the minimum of literary history. Weaver leaves us with the history and the paradigm that invests it with meaning.

Weaver himself seems to have been just the intellectual hybrid, scholar-crusader, to undertake the work: rhetoric was his lance, and he was prepared to fight to the death and to flourish in defeat. In his "Introduction" and "Epilogue" to *The Southern Tradition at Bay*, Weaver sounds the alarum as Davidson had when he saw the Humanist host:

> I should list first of all the fact that the South, alone among the sections, has persisted in regarding science as a false messiah. This by itself indicates that the Southern tradition has a center of resistance to the most powerful force of corruption in our age. While the western world has gone after false gods it [the South] has clung, often at the cost of scorn and insult, to its lares of the field. More concretely, it has not, in the same measure as "progressive" sections of the country, become engrossed in means to the exclusion of ends.[51]

Critiques of the programme inherent in *I'll Take My Stand* had already made it clear that many Southerners had gone the way of progress happily. And even Davidson, the hardest and most resolute soldier of them all, was convinced (in 1938) that the battle had been lost, and he himself left dismembered on the field like Ransom's Captain Carpenter. He was already prepared for retrospective and memorial rituals.[52]

Weaver, who had had no first-hand experience of the battles Davidson remembered, opened a new front. If particulars had always been the bane of the image of the South, then he would argue strenuously that particulars had nothing to do with the metaphysical centre anyway. The mind of every genuine Southerner was the mind of the South. That single mind, however, had not grown out of local conditions, Southern or American, but had been carried through history and deposited in the Confederate South as part of an essential sequence in time. In his "Epilogue," Weaver reveals this essential sequence and its relationship to the South: "That the fall of Rome, the dissolution of medieval Catholicism, the overthrow of Napoleon, the destruction of the Old South were purposeful and just are conclusions that only the tough-minded will question."[53] Lewis Simpson chooses this passage as "a summary moment" in Weaver's meditation on the mind and culture of the South.[54] By ranking these four historical moments together, Weaver argues in favour of the trans-historical importance of the South: the fall of Rome to the barbarians lost the world of the West its tradition of civil and domestic piety; the destruction of medieval Catholicism by middle-class reformers cost the West its metaphysical moorings and a model for a social hierarchy; the overthrow of Napoleon and the Jacobin takeover in France gave the Enlightenment the political foothold it needed in world history. The defeat of the South summed up the history of the tragedy of the Western, Christian ideal, and conferred instant longevity and authority on the South. By Weaver's reconfiguration of history, the South was now part of a meaning far older than any that could possibly be claimed by mere American history. Defeat in the Civil War meant the demise of "*the last non-materialist civilization in the Western World*,"[55] a fortunate defeat in that it promoted the South from phenomenon in history to ideal above it.

As Weaver underscored that line, re-thinking the meaning of the history of the West, that civilization was in the midst of its second major war of the century: a war that would confront its survivors with the facts of technological genocide by the eventual losers, and a technological apocalypse in the arsenal of the winners. The South, as Weaver imagined it, had a powerful ideological part to play in the cultural rebuilding of his time, the re-defining of good and evil in the aftermath of the Second World War.

Most of Weaver's "Southern essays" are situated in this ideological milieu. Like the Agrarian manifesto, they are immediately aimed at a local political and ideological opponent. The impassioned supporters to whom Weaver aimed his message—"sons of the Confederacy" bound by a particular regional and class piety, to paraphrase George Core and M.E. Bradford in their preface to *The Southern Tradition at Bay*—comprised a conservative, white, male South which, at least since the years of the Agrarian movement, had thought of itself as a cultural elite whose increasingly difficult mission was to remind the South of a culture it was both losing to outside forces and willingly giving up. Weaver the conservative philosopher was, to this group and cause, the Southern Aquinas. His Southern essays constitute the Southern *Summa*.

Weaver's first published essay establishes the line of reasoning that runs consistently through all of his work. "The Older Religiousness in the South" was published in *Sewanee Review* in 1943, just before Allen Tate assumed the editorship. The essay also bears the marks of strong influence from Tate's essay on Southern religion in *I'll Take*

My Stand. Consciously or not, Weaver was following the track of the battles that had preceded him.

"Religiousness" is a carefully chosen term, for it refers to an attitude or temperament rather than to a body of doctrine, to the idea of religion rather than to the social history of a particular sect. Weaver intended such a distinction, as his essay gradually reveals. A body of doctrine, offering propositions for assent or for dispute, invites rational examination and discourse. That, in turn, exalts reason over religion, and the decay of faith inevitably follows. Weaver's point is that such rational religion (doctrine rather than faith) is a Northern vice: Emerson and Unitarianism made "assent a matter of intellectual conviction," and persuaded an individual "to explore principles,"[56] rather than to submit will and intellect to "that general respect for order, natural and institutional, which is piety."[57] Belatedly attacking a foe who had left the arena, Weaver dismissed Babbitt's humanism as nothing more, in this context, than the spirit of Puritanism without the religious trappings. Southern society, by virtue of its innate religiousness and its comparative laxity as to doctrine, presented a more stable and natural society than any New England might boast. "The necessity of having some form of knowledge which will stand above the welter of earthly change," Weaver wrote, "and bear witness that God is superior to accident, led Thomas Aquinas to establish his famous dichotomy, which says, briefly, that whereas some things may be learned through investigation and the exercise of the reasoning powers, others must be given or 'revealed' by God."[58] Weaver, echoing Tate's horse-power example in "Thoughts on the Southern Religion," advanced a similar Thomist dichotomy: on one side (the side of earthly change) he put the "egotistical and self-willed people"[59] of the Puritan tradition; nearer to God he put the South. Southern history was, in Weaver's strict view, the history of God's true religion on earth: "And when that army [Lee's Army of Northern Virginia] went down in defeat, the last barrier to the secular spirit of science, materialism, and pragmatism was swept away."[60] History cast out metaphysics when Grant accepted the sword of Lee. And metaphysics, Weaver's whole body of work strongly insists, is the only deserving foundation for culture and art. The Emersonian North, pace Howard Mumford Jones, has less claim to a meaningful culture the more it mixes reason with piety. Weaver not only imitated his elders in intellectual work, he also fought the old antagonists over the old ground.

Weaver's subsequent essays continue to argue that human history made a fatal wrong turn when it crushed the Confederate South. He was scrupulous in maintaining, however, that the metaphysical dream of history had not been touched. In his wartime and Cold War Southern essays, he continued the ahistorical mapping of Southern ideology upon contemporary terrain. Albert Taylor Bledsoe, an ante-bellum Southern intellectual, theologian and lawyer appeared, to Weaver, the perfect model of resistance to the "pragmatic liberalism" that had done so much damage to the West since the French Revolution. History was merely the riot of accident; essences remained unmoved. Bledsoe's pro-slavery arguments merely needed a simple updating for use in the growing desegregation turmoil of the late 1940s. The cultural improvisers dismantling discrimination could not answer the essential argument: except with force, and that only highlighted the correctness of Weaver's stand.

In yet another Southern essay of the time, "Southern Chivalry and Total War," Weaver argued the position that the proper corrective to the horrors of the Second World War was to be found in the institution of Southern chivalry—or would have been had the Union armies not annihilated it. Bound to his Platonic unity, Weaver found the enemy of 1861–65 to be the enemy of 1939–45: "It scarcely needs pointing out that from the military policies of Sherman and Sheridan there lies but an easy step to the total war of the Nazis, the greatest affront to Western civilization since its founding."[61] Nor was it the Union military leadership alone who fell into Weaver's relentless paradigm. Since Southern society, in its fundamental forms, is a feudal organization, it stands as the antidote to Nazism. The middle-class society of the urban North is, to Weaver, a much more frightening spectre than the slave system of the South:

> The Nazi movement has been sponsored by the lower middle class, and all of its so-called innovations are but projections of the middle-class mentality . . . And total war [as perfected by Hitler and Sherman] is a typical middle-class concept because this class, with its materialistic bias, is unable to see that there is involved in war anything other than complete destruction of the enemy, so that, as the popular thought has it, we won't be at the expense of having to do this again.[62]

Had the critics of the Agrarian manifesto attempted to tar them with fascism because of Collins' loopy interview? Weaver was now on the scene to turn the tables, to link fascism, the middle class, and the heroes of the Grand Army of the Republic. In his Southern essays specifically, as in his other work generally, Weaver completed the South out of an original design his elders had shelved.

Richard Weaver's historical sense, always selective, seems to have been eventually smothered by the bell jar of his Southern ideology. Although he meant such statements as "But a nation is made what it is by its past; there is no identity without historicity,"[63] his own commitment to the "metaphysical dream" of the South permitted him to eliminate unfavourable aspects of "historicity," matters of fact that tended to mar the shapely contours of the myth. He was, according to Hayden White's convenient definition, a metahistorian. Data was always of less importance to Weaver than ideology, the "set of prescriptions for taking a position in the present world or social praxis."[64] The South was not of "the present world of social praxis" and essentially never had been. It was the legitimate successor to the ontological and moral authority husbanded in the "Platonic-Christian tradition," the enhanced but essential South in which Richard Weaver took his stand.

From the first deliberate and concentrated work of the twelve Southerners in the late 1920s to the work of Richard Weaver in the 1940s and 1950s the route of a conservative Southern intellectual history runs true. This is not the only intellectual history to be derived from the Agrarian source, but it is the truest to its intellectual genesis. Louis D. Rubin represents another column, a liberal intellectual and literary history of the South, with greater debts to Thomas Wolfe and W.J. Cash, greater allowance for African-American cultural expression, a greater generosity of interest in finding consensus in a diverse South. The circumstances under which the liberal "tradition" in Southern intellectual and literary history was invented, and the formula by which it was reconciled with the elder and more conservative source, are parts of another story. Weaver insisted on a purer line of descent, and the intellectual project he furthered found its philosophical apotheosis in the vision of Eric Voegelin, for whom history was a more or less "adequate symbolization" of a presence transcending human reality. In the Preface to Order and History, Voegelin asserts a paradigm into which Weaver and the conservative tradition of Southern intellectual history snugly fit. Simply add "the South" to the societies herein acknowledged: "For the great societies, beginning with the civilizations of the Ancient Near East, have created a sequence of orders, intelligibly connected with one another as advances toward, or recessions from, an adequate symbolization of truth concerning the order of being of which the order of society is a part."[65] Deep in its cultural cortex, the mind of the South insists upon oneness with the whole that surpasses the part.

Notes

1. William Faulkner, *Absalom, Absalom!* (London: Chatto & Windus, 1960).
2. H.L. Mencken, "The Sahara of the Bozart," in J.T. Farrell (ed.) *Prejudices: A Selection* (New York: Random House, 1955).
3. Louis D. Rubin *et al. The History of Southern Literature* (Baton Rouge & London: Louisiana State University Press, 1985); Twelve Southerners, *I'll Take My Stand* (New York: Harper, 1930; rep. Baton Rouge: Louisiana State University Press, 1977).
4. Isaiah Berlin, *The Crooked Timber of Humanity: Chapters in the History of Ideas*, ed. Henry Hardy (London: John Murray Ltd., 1990), pp. 49–50.
5. Richard M. Weaver, *The Southern Tradition at Bay: A History of Postbellum Thought*, eds. George Core and M.E. Bradford, foreword by Donald Davidson (New Rochelle, N.Y.: Arlington House, 1968); Richard M. Weaver, *The Southern Essays of Richard Weaver*, eds. George M. Curtis III and James J. Thompson Jr. (Indianapolis, In: Liberty Press, 1987).
6. Daniel J. Singal, *The War Within: From Victorian to Modernist Thought in the South, 1919–1945* (Chapel Hill: University of North Carolina Press, 1982), p. xiv.
7. Fred Hobson, *Tell About the South: The Southern Rage to Explain* (Baton Rouge: Louisiana State University Press, 1980).
8. Faulkner, *Absalom, Absalom!*, p. 378.
9. Karl Mannheim, *Ideology and Utopia*, trans. Louis Wright and Edward Shils (New York: Harcourt, Brace, 1959), p. 10.
10. Mannheim, *Ideology and Utopia*, p. 11.
11. Norman Foerster (ed.) *Humanism amd America: Essays on the Outlook of Modern Civilization* (New York: Farrar and Rinehart, 1930), p. 44.
12. *Humanism and America*, p. xvi.
13. Davidson to Ransom, 5 July 1929, Donald Davidson Papers, Vanderbilt University Library (hereafter DDP).
14. Davidson to Ransom, 5 July 1929, DDP.
15. *Humanism and America*, p. vi.
16. W.T. Couch (ed.) *Culture in the South* (Chapel Hill: University of North Carolina Press, 1934.)
17. *The Literary Correspondence of Donald Davidson and Allen Tate*, eds. John Tyree Fain and Thomas Daniel Young (Athens: University of Georgia Press, 1974), p. 228.
18. *Literary Correspondence*. p. 231.
19. Allen Tate, *Reactionary Essays on Poetry and Ideas* (New York: Charles Scribner's and Sons, 1936), p. 139.
20. *Literary Correspondence*, pp. 229–30.
21. *Literary Correspondence*, p. 186.
22. *Literary Correspondence*, p. 189.
23. *Literary Correspondence*, p. 230.
24. *Literary Correspondence*, p. 230.
25. *Literary Correspondence*, pp. 240–41.
26. Herbert Agar and Allen Tate, *Who Owns America?: A New Declaration of*

Independence (Boston: Houghton Mifflin Co., 1936). See also *Literary Correspondence*, p. 295.

27. Couch, *Culture in the South*, p. vii.
28. Couch, *Culture in the South*, p. 38.
29. *Literary Correspondence*. p. 289.
30. Couch, *Culture in the South*, p. 80.
31. Howard Mumford Jones, "Is There a Southern Renaissance?" *The Virginia Quarterly Review* 6 (April 1930), pp. 184–97.
32. Howard Mumford Jones, "The Future of Southern Culture" *Southwest Review* 16 (January 1931), pp. 141–63.
33. Jones to Davidson, 7 October 1930, DDP.
34. Couch, *Culture in the South*, p. 207.
35. Davidson to Jones, 21 October 1930, DDP.
36. *Literary Correspondence*, p. 262.
37. *Literary Correspondence*, pp. 276.
38. *Literary Correspondence*. p. 302.
39. Grace Lumpkin, "'I Want a King'" *Fight Against War and Fascism* (February 1936), n.p.
40. Lewis Simpson, "The South and the Poetry of Community," in Lewis P. Simpson (ed.) *The Poetry of Community: Essays on the Southern Sensibility of History and Literature* (Atlanta: Georgia State University Press, 1972), p. xvi.
41. Richard M. Weaver, "Up From Liberalism" *Modern Age* 3 (Winter 1958–59), p. 32.
42. Weaver, "Up From Liberalism," p. 23.
43. Cf. Mannheim, *Ideology and Utopia*, p. 35.
44. Richard M. Weaver, "The Revolt Against Humanism."
45. Weaver, "Up From Liberalism," p. 24.
46. Weaver, "Up From Liberalism," p. 23.
47. Weaver, "Up From Liberalism," p. 25.
48. Weaver, "*Southern Tradition*," p. 30.
49. Richard M. Weaver, "The Confederate South, 1865–1910: A Study in the Survival of a Mind and a Culture," Ph.D. Louisiana State University, p.v.
50. Weaver, *Southern Tradition*, p. 40.
51. Weaver, *Southern Tradition*, pp. 30–31.
52. *Literary Correspondence*, p. 51.
53. Weaver, *Southern Tradition*, p. 388.
54. Simpson, *Poetry of Community*, pp. xv–xvi.
55. Weaver, *Southern Tradition*, p. 391.
56. Weaver, *Southern Essays*, p. 136
57. Weaver, *Southern Essays*, p. 135.
58. Weaver, *Southern Essays*, p. 142.
59. Weaver, *Southern Essays*, p. 136.
60. Weaver, *Southern Essays*, p. 146.
61. Weaver, *Southern Essays*, p. 169.
62. Weaver, *Southern Essays*, p. 196.
63. Weaver, *Southern Essays*, p. 251.

64. Hayden White, *Metahistory: The Historical Imagination in Nineteenth-Century Europe* (Baltimore: Johns Hopkins University Press, 1973), p. 22.
65. Eric Voegelin, *Order and History: Volume One, Israel and Revolution* (Baton Rouge: Louisiana State University Press, 1956), p. ix.

2

The Agony of the Avant-Garde
Philip Rahv and the New York Intellectuals

Hugh Wilford

Philip Rahv was born in 1908 to poor Jewish parents at Kupin in the Russian Ukraine. After moving with his family between Austria, Rhode Island and Palestine, he settled in the United States, on his own, at the age of fourteen.[1] Following a period spent working as an advertising copy-writer in Oregon, he drifted eastwards, fetching up in New York City shortly after the Wall Street Crash where, unemployed and destitute, he joined the Communist Party. In 1933 he helped launch the *Partisan Review*, a party magazine devoted to the publication of "revolutionary literature." Over the course of the next three years, however, he and William Phillips, a fellow editor, grew so frustrated with the communist literary programme, and so perturbed by reports of events in Stalinist Russia, that they eventually resolved to quit the party and relaunch their magazine on an independent footing, with a dual commitment to non-sectarian Marxism on the one hand and the highest cultural standards on the other. This was to prove a winning formula. In addition to attracting regular contributions from New York-based intellectuals similarly disenchanted with Stalinism, the "new" *Partisan Review*, which made its first appearance at the close of 1937, also won the support of a number of established American and European critics and writers. By the mid-1940s *Partisan Review* was generally recognized as "the most stimulating and satisfying magazine of ideas and literary expression now being published in the United States."[2] Meanwhile Rahv had earned a considerable critical reputation in his own right, as an author of trenchant, synoptic essays about American literary history, most notably "The Cult of Experience in American Writing" and "Paleface and Redskin," and as an authority on the modern European novel.[3] In 1957 he was appointed to a professorship at Brandeis University. This did not prevent him from continuing to pursue a high-profile career as a literary mandarin within New York's cultural media (in 1965 the *New York Times Magazine* voted him one of "The 97 In-Most" members of Manhattan society).[4] When he died in 1973, the *Times Book Review* carried an obituary on its front page, acknowledging his achievements as a critic, and describing *PR* as "the best literary magazine in America."[5]

What are we to make of this Horatio Alger-like rise from obscurity to celebrity? First of all, it is important to understand that Rahv's career was not *sui generis*; rather it was typical of a broader pattern of historical experience. During the Great Depression many New Yorkers of Jewish immigrant stock aspiring to careers in such intellectual professions as university teaching and publishing found themselves unemployed. Lacking institutional affiliations, these young intellectuals were forced to lead a free-floating, bohemian existence on the margins of American society, Given their situation, it is hardly surprising that some of them began to experiment with intellectual modes of protest and dissent. Marxism illuminated the causes of the economic crisis which had so disrupted their lives and, moreover, offered the prospect of a radical transformation of the society which had marginalized them. Not only that, the Marxist-Leninist concept of a theoretical vanguard, a cadre of "professional revolutionaries" charged with the task of raising proletarian consciousness, equipped them with an ideal model of intellectual community, one which assured them a leading role in the revolutionary future. Finally, membership of the American communist movement provided them, in their state of institutional exile, with practical benefits of the kind normally provided by institutions, such as access to publishing outlets, in the shape of party magazines. By 1937, however, a sizable faction had grown disillusioned with the example of Soviet Communism (and correspondingly sympathetic with the fate of the exiled intellectual Trotsky), and had decisively broken with the party's Stalinist leadership. The New York Intellectuals—as these anti-Stalinist Marxists later became known —rallied around the relaunched *Partisan Review*, which in return performed a number of quasi-institutional functions on their behalf. Besides the obvious one of publishing their writings, it helped to define and validate their particular intellectual values and concerns, and opened up channels of communication with other intellectual groups. By virtue of his ascendancy at *PR*, Rahv became a dominant figure within the New York Intellectual community. Alfred Kazin characterized him as the Intellectuals' "master of ceremonies" their "Doctor Johnson."[6]

There were other traditions of dissent from bourgeois civilization available to the Intellectuals besides Marxist-Leninism. During the late 1930s and early 1940s Rahv and other members of the *PR* circle began to depict themselves as a cultural avant-garde, heirs to the great modernist tradition bequeathed by the novelists and poets of the 1910s and 1920s. The messianic suffering and loneliness of the alienated modern artist seemed to them to correspond with their own experience of marginalization. Rahv might just as well have been recounting the history of the Intellectual community when he described the modernist movement in the following terms:

> The avant-garde has attempted to ward off the ravages of alien-
> ation in a number of ways: by means of developing a tradition of
> its own and cultivating its own group norms and standards,
> by resisting the bourgeois incentives to accommodation, and
> perforce making a virtue of its separateness from society.[7]

Consequently much of the Intellectual community's energy was devoted to a critical celebration of the artistic accomplishments of the modernist movement. The Intellectuals now regarded their main duty to be not so much the creation of a revolutionary situation as the protection of modernist literature from the contaminating influences of both capitalism and Stalinism. This is not to say that they advocated a withdrawal from politics into aestheticism or mysticism. In 1947 *PR*'s editors responded to criticism of their political coverage by vigorously asserting the necessity of "engage-ment" and fiercely denouncing the quietism of "the Genteel Reader."[8] In the same issue Rahv used a review of a book by Arthur Koestler as a platform to attack the "yogis," Western Intellectuals like W.H. Auden who, traumatized by the horrors of the recent political past, had sought spiritual consolation in transcendent religions.[9] Rahv and his colleagues still regarded themselves as political radicals. The modern-ist cultural tradition, they reasoned, implicitly negated "the bourgeois spirit;" by seceding from society in order to protect and nurture that tradition, they were, therefore, performing a radical role.[10]

This attempt to synthesize the paradigms of the revolutionary vanguard and the cultural avant-garde, to modulate the conflicting doctrines of engagement and aestheticism, was only partly successful: certain contradictions were never resolved. *PR*'s editors frequently denounced "leftist" literature, fiction which embodied a vulgar

Marxist aesthetic, in the belief that ideology, which they defined to mean abstract political theory, tended to distort, to falsify representations of lived experience.[11] Quite apart from the theoretical problems of this conception of the relationship between ideology and experience, the editors' valorization of non-political literature was in fact contradicted by their own critical practices. Throughout the 1940s they consistently championed ex-radical novelists like Arthur Koestler, George Orwell and Lionel Trilling, whose fiction explored such political themes as the breakdown of revolutionary movements and the rise of the totalitarian state. Rahv described Koestler as "both the poet and the ideologue of the homeless radical;" he reckoned Trilling's novel *The Middle of the Journey* was "a daring work and a first rate piece of writing;" his review of Orwell's *1984* was a hymn of praise.[12] Similarly, although by 1942 he had come to believe that literary critics should abjure "metaphysical commitments" and achieve "aloofness from abstract systems,"[13] Rahv continued to employ Marxist concepts in his own critical writings. His 1946 *PR* article, "Concerning Tolstoy," is a case in point.[14] Although it contains elements of psychoanalytic theory and existentialist philosophy, the conceptual framework of this essay is basically Marxist. Rahv argues that the key to understanding Tolstoy is to view him as "the last of the unalienated artists."[15] Whereas other writers of his age were affected by the capitalist division of labour, and succumbed to either commodity or art fetishism, Tolstoy's origins in the pre-capitalist class of the Russian peasant-patriciate protected him from the worst ravages of alienation, and enabled him to carry on creating art in a productive interchange with nature. "Concerning Tolstoy" is a highly imaginative, one might also say prophetic venture in Marxist literary criticism. Not only does it echo Gyorgy Lukacs' writings about realism and reification, passages of it are reminiscent of formulations by later Marxist critics, such as Raymond Williams' concept of "residual ideology."[16]

The Marxist intellectuals who most obviously invite comparison with New York Intellectuals are the Critical Theorists of the Frankfurt School. The two groups had much in common: Jewishness, anti-Stalinism, allegiances to modernism, a desire for autonomy from the organized communist movement, a sense of exile in America, and pride in their marginal status. The Frankfurt School's journal, the *Zeitschrift für Sozialforschung*, was strikingly similar, both in tone and content, to the *Partisan Review*. In spite of its title, the *Zeitschrift* was concerned less with social research than with Marxist theory and cultural criticism. Individual members of the two groups resembled one another. Philip Rahv's counterpart in the Frankfurt School was Max Horkheimer. Both men possessed outstanding entrepreneurial talents, an inclination towards political cautiousness, and great strength of personality, which they used to dominate their respective intellectual communities.[17]

During the 1940s the thinking of Rahv and his colleagues on PR's editorial board and the Critical Theorists developed along broadly similar lines. Both arrived at a profoundly pessimistic view of the political future, and came to conceive of the cultural avant-garde as the last refuge of revolutionary consciousness.[18] The Frankfurt School Theorists believed mature capitalist society to be a seamless totality in which contradictions between productive forces and relations had effectively been abolished. Rahv and his colleagues likewise regarded the United States as a mass society, vulnerable to periodic unrest in the shape of nativist uprisings but incapable of proper social revolution. The Intellectuals distinguished between "low-brows" and "middle-brows," but insisted on viewing both as passive consumers of banal, stultifying mass-produced cultural forms.[19] Throughout the 1940s PR's editors became increasingly convinced that autonomous intellectuals like themselves represented the only surviving progressive force in society. As this conviction grew, they displayed a growing interest in such individualistic traditions of thought as existentialism and psychoanalysis.[20] Meanwhile the Critical Theorists, engaged in research into the roots of political authoritarianism, also eschewed "structural factors, particularly class factors" in favour of "analysis of subjective dispositions and attitudes."[21] Finally, the two groups shared the same tastes in literature, valorizing German Expressionism above other modernistic literary genres. The Theorists' view of the plight of the individuated personality in the face of bureaucratic control was directly influenced by the turbulent, anxious art of the Expressionist movement, and in particular by the novels of Franz Kafka.[22] During this period PR's editors published more original work by Kafka than by any other European modernist. Moreover, their extremely dismal notion of the condition of the modern artist—which Rahv defined in terms of "obsessive introversion," "jealously maintained privacy" and a "bent toward the obscure and morbid"—was clearly generalized from the example of Kafka.[23] Other Marxist aestheticians valorized different modernist genres: Cubism for Brecht; Symbolism for Benjamin. The fact that the Intellectuals and the Theorists shared a taste for Expressionism must surely be related to their common state of political despair.

Confined to the margins of American society, the New York Intellectuals had resourcefully constructed a usable tradition for themselves from the elements of Marxism and modernism, one which privileged marginality. In the meantime, however, the marginal phase of their group history was drawing to a close. The recovery of the American economy during and after the Second World War allowed for the gradual re-expansion of cultural institutions. absorbing the intellectual surplus. New career opportunities opened up to the Intellectuals in the universities and culture industries. Ironically, the knowledge of modernism which they had acquired during the period when they had been denied institutional employment suddenly came to possess an unexpected institutional utility. This was the period when previously disreputable works by modernist poets and novelists were incorporated in academic canons, and publishing houses began to merchandize experimental literature for a growing suburban market. By 1960 the Intellectuals had acquired the status of literary celebrities, writing introductions for new editions of modern classics, fronting bookclubs, and holding prestigious posts at elite universities.[24] Throughout all this they were undoubtedly aided by their proximity to the metropolitan headquarters of the leading American publishing houses and other literary media, and by the United States' historic lack of a cultural "establishment," a single institutionalized intellectual formation capable of dominating high cultural discourse and regulating high cultural production comparable to Oxbridge and Bloomsbury in Britain.

This was also, of course, the period when anti-communism became a cardinal principle of US foreign policy. In much the same way that cultural institutions searching for new literary texts to teach or sell had discovered a use for the Intellectuals' knowledge of modernism, so the American state now found a purpose for their record of independent and militant anti-Stalinism. During the 1950s government operatives engaged in a propaganda campaign against the Soviet Union secretly recruited several Intellectuals in an effort to open a cultural front in the Cold War. In this semi-official capacity the Intellectuals concerned travelled abroad to lecture European and Asian audiences on the folly of neutralism in the struggle between the Superpowers, and to help edit literary magazines with a pro-American and anti-Soviet orientation.[25] To sum up, then, the Cold War witnessed the *institutionalization* of the New York Intellectual community. As Rahv himself put it in 1952, "the long spell of prosperity that America has enjoyed since the War . . . has at long last effected the absorption of the intellectuals into the institutional life of the country.[26]

Quite understandably, the New York Intellectuals were gratified by this turn of events. Their new relationship with American institutions was reflected in their writings from this period, which generally expressed affirmation of existing social and political arrangements in the United States. The most famous (or notorious) example of this affirmative tendency dates from 1952, when *PR* published a symposium entitled "Our Country and Our Culture." The purpose of this symposium, the magazine's editors explained, was "to examine the apparent fact that American intellectuals now regarded America and its institutions in a new way . . . [and] now feel closer to their country and its culture."[27] All of the intellectuals who participated in the symposium agreed that such a reconciliation had indeed taken place. Lionel Trilling, for example, believed that "avowed aloofness from national feeling is no longer the first ceremonial step into the life of thought." Moreover, most reckoned that this reconciliation was a positive development. Intellect, argued Trilling, "has now associated itself with power as perhaps never before in history, and is now conceded to be itself a kind of power."[28]

This optimism was not, however, shared by all, especially not the younger symposiasts. Norman Mailer felt obliged to remind his fellow intellectuals that "the great artists—certainly the moderns— are almost always in opposition to their society, and that integration . . . has been more conducive to propaganda than art."[29] This, broadly speaking, was the view of two other young contributors, C. Wright Mills and Irving Howe. What is less often remembered about "Our Country and Our Culture" is the fact that *PR*'s editors also registered objections to the conciliatory mood they had detected in American intellectual circles. After voicing his preference for American democracy as opposed to Soviet totalitarianism, Rahv attacked those intellectuals who either tolerated or supported "the vicious antics of a political bum like Senator McCarthy." He also felt qualms about recent cultural developments in America, in particular the prolifer- ation of mass cultural forms which had occurred since the war. As he admitted, intellectuals could do little to stem the growth of mass culture, but they could at least "keep apart and refuse its favors."[30]

Like other Americans who had experienced a sudden and dis- orientating improvement in their material fortunes since the end of the war, the New York Intellectuals were haunted by the fear that they might lose their status as rapidly as they had acquired it. The new popularity of the causes they had long championed, anti- Stalinism and modernism, filled them with apprehension. As Rahv observed, the anti-Stalinist socialists of the 1930s "had played a vanguard role in that they were the first to discern the totalitarian essence of the Soviet myth." With the advent of the Cold War, however, this minority cause had "virtually become the official creed of our entire society."[31] What role could anti-Stalinist intellectuals play now? The same question could well be asked of the old literary avant-garde. The academicization and commodification of modernism had, according to William Phillips, "created a new intellectual bureaucracy" of pseudo-experts "ready to challenge the authority of the old elite."[32] Realizing the dangers of their own position implied by the success of anti-Stalinism and modernism, the Intellectuals stridently insisted on the uniqueness of their knowledge, even as others began to share it. Rahv strove to distinguish his brand of anti-communism from other variants of that ideology prevalent at the time, such as the "cultural vigilantism" of unscrupulous politicians like McCarthy, or the confessional millenarianism of recent converts like Whittaker Chambers.[33] Similarly, he denounced middle and low-brow cultural technicians, as well as such postmodernist literary tendencies as the Beat movement.[34] He tried, in short, to protect his intellectual patch.

However, the main cause of the anxiety from which the Intellectuals suffered in the Cold War era had to do with their self-definition as an avant-garde. Like other modern intellectual movements, they believed passionately in the doctrine of independence, in the intellectual's sacred obligation to remain detached or aloof from society. In their own case, this meant independence both from institutions and from counter-institutions, radical organizations such as the Communist Party. Although many of their other beliefs changed drastically in this period, their faith in the doctrine of independence never wavered. Yet how was it possible to reconcile this faith with their new relation to the institutions? For, as William Barrett remarked, "when avant-garde becomes the Establishment, one is led to question whether it does not thereby lose its own raison d'être."[35] In the Cold War era the Intellectuals were confronted with a choice between two sorts of success: one sort defined by themselves to mean the maintenance of intellectual independence, and another sort more conventionally defined to mean institutional recognition, social prestige, and so on. The constant necessity of choosing between these sorts of success caused them considerable anxiety. After interviewing several Intellectuals around the time, the critic Al Alvarez formed the impression that "the shift from alienation to status . . . induced in most of them . . . a profound unease."[36]

Still the drift towards the institutions was very difficult to resist.

The rise in the cost of living associated with the postwar economic boom had made it practically impossible for the Intellectuals to subsist on earnings from occasional jobs, as they had done previously. Moreover, New York City itself had become a less hospitable environment for bohemian intellectuals like themselves.[37] There were other, even more irresistible historical forces at work as well. The Intellectuals supposed that the relationship between the avant-garde and the culture industries was one of straightforward opposition. This was not, in fact, the case. Ever since the 1920s the latter had looked to the former for fresh ideas, new designs, and so on. Modernism's "forms lent themselves to . . . the commercial interplay of schools, styles and fashion so essential to the market."[38] By assuming an avant-gardist identity, the Intellectual community had also acquired the function of the "research and development arm of the culture industry."[39] Viewed in an even wider historical context, the Intellectuals' institutionalization appears as inevitable. It is by now a sociological commonplace that the modern state's need for scientists, educators and propagandists has resulted in the professionalization of the Western intellectual. In America the implications of this development became apparent during the First World War, when university professors volunteered their services as patriotic rhetoricians.[40] The CIA's recruitment of the New York Intellectuals for the cultural Cold War must surely be regarded as a manifestation of the same phenomenon. It finally remains to mention a more particular, more intimate threat to the Intellectuals' independence, their ethnicity. As immigrant or second generation Americans, the Intellectuals were powerfully motivated to achieve status within the dominant ethnic culture. The Depression deflected them from their assimilationist trajectory. Later, when the national economy revived, and the assimilation of minority groups regained momentum, they enjoyed vastly improved social opportunities. The urge to take them was very strong.[41]

No other New York Intellectual had a greater personal stake in the doctrine of independence than Philip Rahv. During the 1930s he had been the most ardent of revolutionary vanguardists; afterwards he became a dedicated cultural avant-gardist. Throughout this period he had made it his business to provide institutionally unaffiliated intellectuals with a "home," a "sanctuary," in the shape of the *Partisan Review*.[42] Naturally, therefore, he was opposed to any move by the Intellectual community in the direction of the institutions. Besides offending his belief in the sacredness of independence, such a move also threatened to rob *PR* of its quasi-institutional function as an avant-garde community centre—and *PR* "was an extension of his personality—one might almost say, of his body."[43] Nevertheless, Rahv was not impervious to the trappings of success, conventionally defined. In fact his acquaintances remember him as being an extraordinarily ambitious man. Mark Krupnick, for example, suspects that although "his cultural style was [that of] a nineteenth-century Russian intellectual . . . his social aspirations were as American as a Dreiser hero's."[44] In this respect Rahv personified the contradiction which shaped the history of the New York Intellectual community, that is the conflict between the Intellectuals' assimilationist impulses and their self-imposed obligation to remain detached from American society. Indeed, Rahv is often portrayed in memoirs by New York Intellectuals as an archetypal figure, embodying the dilemma of an avant-garde as it underwent institutionalization.[45] According to William Phillips, he "was a symbolic figure, an insider and an outsider at the same time."[46]

Rahv's relations with the publishing industry were paradigmatic of this contradiction. During the 1950s he became a sort of broker for New York publishing houses engaged in the marketing of experimental or "high-brow" literary production. Among the writers he introduced to Dial Press in this role were Randall Jarrell, Robert Lowell and Allen Tate.[47] He appears to have relished and excelled at the business of literary reputation-making and fashion-setting. While carefully cultivating Saul Bellow, for instance, he deliberately neglected a less successful Chicagoan writer of Bellow's generation, Isaac Rosenfeld.[48] His letters to Lowell and Tate reveal a fascination with an intricate knowledge of the workings of the publishing industry. Yet despite his fondness for literary gossip and machination, Rahv evidently entertained misgivings about what he described as "commercialized letters."[49] Judging by the abruptness with which he terminated his association with Criterion Books, he felt little personal affection for the publishers who employed him.[50] After surveying the literary scene in 1953, he commented:

> (New York) is overrun by publishers and their assistants, all drearily searching for the best sellers. The old time literary life— with its proud autonomy, absorbing gossip, and keen expression of personality—now belongs to the historical past.[51]

Although he moved in the most powerful of American literary circles, Rahv never fully assimilated to the dominant gentile culture. His "awkwardness and his detachment from his body" reminded William Phillips of his own immigrant father. He never shed his Ukrainian accent, and looked, according to Delmore Schwartz, who nicknamed him "Philip Slav," "like the Paris Commune."[52] Despite the unparalleled success of his literary career, Rahv remained in many ways the most marginal of the New York Intellectuals.

The chief agent of the Intellectual community's institutionalization was of course, the university. As a result of his disrupted and peripatetic childhood, Rahv had hardly any formal education at all. He was an autodidact, and proud of the fact. According to one acquaintance, he regarded American universities "as just glorified high schools."[53] As the Intellectual community he had helped create was academicized, Rahv provided a half-laconic, half-anguished commentary. In 1949 he himself began to teach university summer schools and the odd course in New York. "Everybody on *PR* is now teaching," he wrote to a friend, "which shows you how far things have gone.[54] Eight years later he left New York to take up his appointment at Brandeis. "The Zeitgeist has got me down," he remarked wryly. "There's no escaping it."[55] William Barrett, a former colleague on *PR*'s editorial board, found it impossible to visualize Rahv outside of downtown Manhattan: "It was strange to think of him entering into the professorial world, stranger still to think of him being extricated from the milieu of these New York streets where he seemed so eminently to belong."[56]

By the time of his move to Boston, Rahv had for all intents and purposes quit *PR*'s editorial board, although his name continued to appear on the magazine's masthead. In 1963 William Phillips made arrangements to move *PR* from New York to New Jersey, into offices owned by Rutgers University. Rahv made several frantic attempts to sabotage Phillips' plans. He was unsuccessful and the move went ahead.[57] These events caused considerable dismay amongst believers in the doctrine of intellectual independence. According to one observer, "Some have likened *Partisan Review's* move to Rutgers to Rocky Marciano's retirement; the old fight game as we know it is dead."[58] This, presumably, is why Rahv tried to block the move. The suburbanization and academicization of *PR* signified to him the final stage of the institutionalization of the New York Intellectuals.

The last years of Rahv's life were not, as one might have supposed given the amazing success of his career, tranquil or happy ones. His second wife died tragically in a fire at his Boston home, and a third marriage ended in divorce. A new magazine, *Modern Occasions*, launched in 1970 in very promising circumstances, ceased publication after only two years. By then Rahv himself had reached, as Mark Krupnick puts it, "a kind of psychic dead-end."[59] The emergence of the New Left had caused him to expect a revival of the old tradition of autonomous dissent. Before long, however, he had realized that the radicalism of the 1960s had little in common with the sort of vanguardist revolutionary politics he had espoused in his youth. Increasingly isolated from his friends, preoccupied with obscure literary vendettas against "'trendies' and 'swingers'," and dependent on drugs to treat various illnesses, he became "a wrathful, disappointed old man entirely given over to destructiveness . . . The 'kids' had let him down; so had America; so had History."[60]

The decline of the intellectual tradition to which Rahv belonged was not, as has often been alleged, the result of a collective failure of will, a clerical treason, although of course in some individual cases faint-heartedness or opportunism may have played a part. The accommodation of institutionally unattached, "public" intellectuals in the period after the Second World War was rather a matter of *normalization*. The formation of the New York Intellectual community had been in the first place a kind of historical accident. The Great Depression interrupted the three hegemonic processes which should have obviated the need for such a community: the consumerization of American society, the professionalization of intellectuals and the assimilation of ethnic minority groups. When the United States entered a period of unprecedented prosperity in the 1940s, these processes resumed with a greater degree of rapidity and intensity than ever before. The Cold War era was "a profoundly hegemonic moment" in American history.[61] The New York Intellectuals' chances of remaining independent in this age of cultural and political settlement, of severing "the ties of class and body and institutional affiliation,"[62] were non-existent. Even the proudly marginal émigré Critical Theorists of the Frankfurt School were institutionalized during this period.[63]

If Rahv and his fellow Intellectuals are to be accused of error, it should be for assuming that it was possible or, for that matter, desirable to detach themselves from American society. Considering the circumstances in which they found themselves in the 1930s, their affiliation with the tradition of autonomous dissent was understandable. In the years after the war, however, it became increasingly apparent that such a code of intellectual practice was no longer practicable. Given the changes that had occurred in American society, it was only to be expected that the doctrine of independence to which the Intellectuals had sacrificed themselves should be overtaken by a "new grammar of dissent," one which rejected the "hard, guilt-ridden school of cultural maturity" and "vanguardist structures of political authority" in favour of "the values of

community, liberation, and personal empowerment."[64] Perhaps
Irving Howe provided the most fitting epitaph to Rahv's career when
he wrote of the New York Intellectuals:

> The New York writers came toward the end of the modernist
> experience, just as they came at what may yet be judged the end
> of the radical experience . . . One shorthand way of describing
> the situation . . . is to say *they came late*.[65]

Notes

1. For further biographical detail, see Andrew James Dvosin, *Literature in a Political World: The Career and Writings of Philip Rahv*, diss., New York University, 1977.
2. Benjamin Ray Redman, review of *The Partisan Reader*, ed. William Phillips and Philip Rahv, in *Saturday Review of Literature* (28 December 1946), p. 18.
3. Philip Rahv, "Paleface and Redskin" *Kenyon Review* 1 (1939), pp. 251–56; "The Cult of Experience in American Writing" *Partisan Review* 7 (1940), pp. 412–24.
4. Sherman L. Morrow, "The In Crowd and the Out Crowd" *New York Times Magazine* (18 July 1965), pp. 12–13.
5. Quoted in William Barrett, *The Truants: Adventures Among the Intellectuals* (New York: Doubleday, 1982), p. 2.
6. Alfred Kazin, *Starting Out in the Thirties* (London: Secker, 1966) pp. 159–60. A list of persons identified as New York Intellectuals would include, besides Rahv and Phillips, the following: Lionel Abel, William Barrett, Daniel Bell, Saul Bellow, Elliot Cohen, Leslie Fiedler, Paul Goodman, Clement Greenberg, Sidney Hook, Irving Howe, Alfred Kazin, Irving Kristol, Mary McCarthy, Dwight Macdonald, Norman Podhoretz, Harold Rosenberg, Isaac Rosenfeld, Meyer Shapiro, Delmore Schwartz, Susan Sontag, Diana Trilling, and Lionel Trilling. The best researched account of *PR*'s break with the Communist Party and its early years as an independent publication is Terry A. Cooney's *The Rise of New York Intellectuals: Partisan Review and its Circle* (Madison: University of Wisconsin Press, 1986).
7. Philip Rahv, "Our Country and Our Culture" *Partisan Review* 19 (1952), pp. 309–10.
8. "A Note on the Genteel Reader" editorial, *Partisan Review* 14 (1947), pp. 106–8
9. Philip Rahv, "Testament of a Homeless Radical" *Partisan Review* 12 (1945), pp. 398–402.
10. See Philip Rahv, "Twilight of the Thirties" *Partisan Review* 6:4 (1939), pp. 3–15.
11. See Philip Rahv, "Proletarian Literature, A Political Autopsy" *Southern Review* 4 (1938–39), pp. 616–28.
12. Rahv, "Testament," p. 398; letter to Lionel Trilling, 30 August 1947, Lionel

Trilling Papers, Butler Library, Columbia University; "The Unfuture of Utopia" *Partisan Review* 16 (1949), pp. 744–47.

13. Philip Rahv, "On the Decline of Naturalism" *Partisan Review* 9 (1942), p. 484.

14. Philip Rahv, "Concerning Tolstoy" *Partisan Review* 13 (1946), pp. 420–32.

15. Rahv, "Tolstoy," p. 432.

16. See Raymond Williams, *Marxism and Literature* (Oxford: Oxford University Press, 1977), pp. 121–27.

17. See Lewis A. Coser, *Refugee Scholars in America, Their Impact and Their Experiences* (New Haven and London: Yale University Press, 1984), pp. 90–101. Despite these similarities, there was surprisingly little personal contact between the Intellectuals and the Theorists during the period of the latter's residence in New York City. This might partly be explained by social and cultural tensions arising from differences in ethnic origins: whereas the Intellectuals' roots lay in Eastern Europe's Jewry, the Theorists were mostly German-speaking Jews.

18. Theodor Adorno and Max Horkheimer conceived of the "auratic," "hermetic" avant-garde as a "progressive" social force precisely because it had attained some independence of a "totally administered" society, and thus represented one of the few remaining sites of potential resistance to the "instrumentalized rationality" of corporate capitalism. See the "Culture Industry" chapter in Theodor Adorno and Max Horkheimer, *The Dialectic of Enlightenment* (New York: Herder, 1972).

19. For an example of *PR*'s editors' extreme political and cultural pessimism in this period, see William Barrett, "The Resistance" *Partisan Review* 13 (1946), pp. 479–88. According to Barrett (after 1945 an associate editor of and frequent contributor to *PR*), political and cultural conditions in the United States approximated to an "occupation." The heroic refusal of the last remnants of the avant-garde to surrender their "authentic" culture to the insatiable maw of the culture industries was like the determination of a "resistance" movement not to "collaborate" with the occupying enemy.

20. See, for example, William Barrett, "Dialogue on Anxiety" *Partisan Review* 14 (1947), pp. 151–59, and William Phillips, "Dostoeovsky's Underground Man" *Partisan Review* 13 (1946), pp. 551–61.

21. Coser, *Refugee Scholars*, pp. 96–97.

22. Early in his intellectual career Theodor Adorno spent two years (1925–26) in Vienna, during which time he came into close contact with the avant-garde enclave surrounding the Expressionist composer Arnold Schoenberg. This experience was "pivotal . . . for [his] education as an aesthetic and social thinker," and particularly "important in forming his notion of available forms of 'negation' in late bourgeois society." Eugene Lunn, *Marxism and Modernism: An Historical Study of Lukacs, Brecht, Benjamin and Adorno* (Berkeley: University of California Press, 1982), pp. 196–98.

23. Rahv, "Twilight," p. 12.

24. Previously only small firms like New Directions had taken an interest in experimental, avant-garde writing; now major houses such as Random House and Viking, Harcourt, Brace began to move into the "high-brow" market. Anchor Books, a subdivision of Doubleday, specialized in republishing and

marketing books by New York Intellectals for a college audience. The Intellectuals' movement into academic employment is impressively documented in Stephen A. Longstaff, *The New York Intellectuals: A Study of Particularism and Universalism*, diss., UCLA, 1978, pp. 387–92. As one literary historian has remarked, somewhat sourly, the typical Intellectual was, after the 1950s, "a professor without a PhD." Grant Webster, *The Republic of Letters: A History of Postwar Literary Opinion* (Baltimore: John Hopkins University Press, 1979), p. 240.

25. See Christopher Lasch, "The Cultural Cold War; A Short History of the Congress for Cultural Freedom" *The Agony of the American Left* (New York: Vintage, 1968) for a partisan yet extremely valuable account of these developments. Peter Coleman's *The Liberal Conspiracy: The Congress for Cultural Freedom and the Struggle for the Mind of Postwar Europe* (New York: Free Press, 1989, is more detailed but less stimulating.

26. Rahv, "Our Country," p. 306.

27. Editorial, *Partisan Review* 19 (1952), p. 282.

28. Lionel Trilling, "Our Country," pp. 318, 320.

29. Norman Mailer, "Our Country," p. 301.

30. Rahv, "Our Country," pp. 307, 310

31. Rahv, "Our Country," pp. 307–8.

32. William Phillips, "The American Establishment" *Partisan Review* 26 (1959), p. 113.

33. See Philip Rahv, "The Sense and Nonsense of Whittaker Chambers" *Partisan Review* 19 (1952), pp. 472–82.

34. The Beats suffered what Morris Dickstein has described as an "Olympian putdown" at the hands of *PR*'s editors. In his memoirs William Phillips claims that he had wished to extend greater recognition to the Beats, but was prevented from doing so by the opposition of Rahv. Morris Dickstein, *Gates of Eden: American Culture in the 1960s* (New York: Basic, 1977), p. 6; William Phillips, *A Partisan View: Five Decades of Literary Life* (New York: Stein, 1983), p. 219.

35. Barrett, *Truants*, p. 159.

36. A. Alvarez, *Under Pressure: The Writer in Society, Eastern Europe and the U.S.A.* (Baltimore: Penguin, 1965), p. 117.

37. See Russell Jacoby, *The Last Intellectuals: American Culture in the Age of Academe* (New York: Basic, 1987), pp. 27–53, for an account of the consequences for "public intellectuals" of the decay of New York's public utilities and the gentrification of the traditional quarters of Bohemia which occurred in the postwar period.

38. Raymond Williams, *The Politics of Modernism: Against the New Conformists* (London: Verso, 1989), p. 35.

39. Thomas Crow, quoted in Casey Blake, review of *How New York Stole the Idea of Modern Art: Abstract Expressionism, Freedom and the Cold War*, by Serge Gilbaut, and *The Romance of Commerce and Culture: Capitalism, Modernism and the Chicago-Aspen Crusade for Cultural Reform*, by James Sloan Allen, *Telos* 62 (1984–85), p. 216.

40. The most famous instance of protest at the quietism of the American universities during the First World War is Randolph Bourne's 1917 essay

"The War and the Intellectuals." Randolph Bourne, *War and The Intellectuals: Essays by Randolph Bourne and Others, 1915–1919*, ed. Carl Reseh (New York: Harper and Row, 1964). See also Carol S. Gruber's *Mars and Minerva: World War 1 and the Use of Higher Learning in America* (Baton Rouge: Lousiana State University Press, 1975).

41. Alexander Bloom's *Prodigal Sons: The New York Intellectuals and Their World* (New York: Oxford University Press, 1986) takes as its main theme the assimilationist dimension of the Intellectuals' history.

42. Alan Lelchuk, "Philip Rahv, The Last Years" in Arthur Edelstein (ed.) *Images and Ideas in American Culture: The Functions of Criticism. Essays in Memory of Philip Rahv* (Hanover: Brandeis University Press, 1979), p. 212.

43. Barrett, *Truants*, p. 29.

44. Mark Krupnick, "He Never Learned to Swim" *New Review* 2:22 (1976), p. 37.

45. See Barrett, *Truants*, p. 69, and Irving Howe, *A Margin of Hope: An Intellectual Autobiography* (London: Secker, 1983), p. 159.

46. Phillips, *Partisan View*, p. 279.

47. Randall Jarrell, letter to Allen Tate, 4 April, 1945, in *Randall Jarrell's Letters: An Autobiographical and Literary Selection.*ed. Mary Jarrell (London: Faber, 1986), p. 124; Philip Rahv, letters to Robert Lowell, 2 and 16 January, 1946, Lowell Papers, Houghton Library, Harvard; Rahv, letters to Allan Tate, 12 and 24 January 1953, Tate Papers, Firestone Library, Princeton.

48. Bloom, *Prodigal Sons*, p. 291; Barrett, *Truants*, p. 112.

49. Philip Rahv, letter to Allen Tate, 19 February 1952, Tate Papers.

50. Phillips, *Partisan View*, p. 271.

51. Philip Rahv, letter to Allen Tate, 19 February 1952, Tate Papers.

52. Phillips, *Partisan View*, pp. 278–79; James Atlas, *Delmore Schwartz: The Life of an American Poet* (New York: Farrar, 1977), p. 98; Barrett, *Truants*, p. 222.

53. Lelchuk, "Philip Rahv," p. 205.

54. Philip Rahv, letter to Morton Dauwen Zabel, 10 October 1950, Morton Dauwen Zabel Papers, Newberry Library, Chicago.

55. Philip Rahv, letter to Allen Tate, 7 February 1957, Tate Papers.

56. Barrett, *Truants*, p. 12.

57. Phillips, *Partisan View*, p. 264.

58. Charles Newman, "Concerning the Little Magazines" *Carleton Miscellany* 7:2 (1966), p. 62.

59. Krupnick, "He Never Learned," p. 34.

60. Krupnick, "He Never Learned," pp. 38–9

61. Andrew Ross, *No Respect: Intellectuals and Popular Culture* (London: Routledge, 1989), p. 56.

62. Ross, *No Respect*, p. 223.

63. During the Second World War, Leo Lowenthal and Herbert Marcuse worked for government agencies, Marcuse for the Office of Strategic Services, the precursor of the Central Intelligence Agency. In the years after the war those Critical Theorists who remained in the United States obtained full-time, permanent acadamic posts, mainly at Columbia and Brandeis.

64. Ross, *No Respect*, pp. 221–22.

65. Howe, *Margin of Hope*, p. 151.

3

F.O. Matthiessen's "Devotion to the Possibilities of Democracy" and his Place as an American Intellectual

Richard Bradbury

Although I had been aware of Matthiessen's work from my undergraduate studies of American literature, nothing had especially
marked him out for me from a number of other critical writers until
I embarked on a desultory study of McCarthyism in between trying
to juggle the demands of my first temporary and part-time contract
against the pressing needs of the year of the National Union of
Miners' great strike in Britain. Although the two events were not
contemporaneous, my subsequent recollection has conflated Margaret
Thatcher's speech on the enemy within with my reading of Eric
Bentley's *Thirty Years of Treason*. It was here, for the first time, that I
found a powerful connection to Matthiessen. At the start of that
monumental book, Bentley quotes from Alvah Bessie's collective
obituary to the victims of McCarthyism which contains the following
line:

> Francis O. Matthiessen, Harvard professor and renowned
> critic, suicide following accusation by J.B. Matthews before a
> Massachusetts legislative committee that he was a Communist-
> front member.[1]

My response, perversely, was an immediate excitement. Here was
an academic, one of those people who wrote the books I read and
taught but who occupied a world somehow detached from that which
I inhabited beyond the university; an academic who was at the very
least engaged with the immediate political processes of his time in the
way that my support for the beleaguered miners made me feel
connected to my time. Here, I felt, was one of those very few people

who appeared to some degree to live in both of the worlds I inhabited. The importance of this was that the more dominant model I had been offered for dealing with this felt split between literary and cultural criticism, and political activism, was to hold the two worlds apart from each other and vacillate between the two. Nevertheless, this didn't offer any satisfactory long-term solution to the feeling that I was constantly bifurcated in my efforts to remain loyal to both sets of concerns.

Here, however, with the discovery of Matthiessen's commitments, was an academic who had crossed the divide and appeared along-side many another more famous radicals as a serious opponent of McCarthyism. There would be another route to this discovery; namely, by ceasing to regard Matthiessen as a one-book wonder and looking at the whole of his work. What that would reveal would be the eclecticism of method which produced both *American Renaissance* and *Translation: An Elizabethan Art*. It would also reveal an intellectual whose literary concerns ranged from Sarah Orne Jewett to Henry James to T.S. Eliot to Theodore Dreiser, and many more besides. And these were the writers with whom he was sufficiently concerned to write full-length studies. We could also remember his work as an editor and anthologist, which gave readers access to so much neglected work. If we move beyond his books to other writings, then an even greater heterogeneity of concern emerges. One of his least-remembered (because un-collected) pieces is a vigorous defence of striking miners in New Mexico in 1934. The breadth of his personality, which I think of as the embodiment of his ideas, is most succinctly described in the recollections of him published in the *Collective Portrait*.[2] Here, friends and colleagues range across his qualities but time and again they return to the idea that it was the combination of his enthusiasm for his academic work in tandem with his commitment to democracy which made him so remarkable. Indeed, his work at one fundamental level demonstrated and demon-strates that it is possible to find ways of healing the split between academic work and political involvement. What that necessitates, however, is a change of terms; away from thinking of Matthiessen as an academic and towards regarding him as an intellectual.

The distinction between academic and intellectual was a theme common to several thinkers of the immediate postwar period, from Paul Baran's distinction[3] between intellect workers (those who worked on the production lines of the educational factories and accepted the demarcations set up by the managers) and the intellectuals (those who in their every effort challenged that compartmentalisation of thought), to Sartre's better-known separation of the two kinds of thinker. The lines of division which these formulations generated during the immense postwar growth of higher education in the USA could almost act as a chart with which to describe the development of the university as an institution in the last fifty years. Of course the situation has changed profoundly since these theories first appeared, but the types still exist as the articulation of different pedagogical and political discourses within the institutions. The recent shift from literary to cultural studies could be seen as another expression of the difference between the two orders of activity.

In a broader historical context, one of the clearest parallels between 1935–50 and 1975 to the present is the way in which Marxism was/has been "discredited" as both a means of explanation and as a guide to action. On both occasions an ideological offensive has sought to sweep away all credibility from the ideas of Marxists; it was not enough to confirm an intellectual institutional dominance against them, they had also to be discovered in the most unlikely places by the more fervent paranoids of the right and then humiliated with accusations of philosophical failure and the temptation to totalitarianism.

In this, the most effective rhetorical strategy has been to lasso all Marxisms together under the rubric of Stalinism and then use the crimes of Stalinism as a means to condemn both the perpetrators and their victims, especially those who for years fought a battle to defend Marxism against the bastardizations of Stalinism. Matthiessen's very tentative efforts to argue a case for the intellectual importance of Marx were greeted with howls of derision and distaste which became increasingly strident as the Cold War was engaged. At the same time disbelief and a rhetoric designed to invalidate the very project greeted the idea that an intellectual had any place in the world of politics (that discourse of division) at a time when consensus was rendering public debate increasingly bland. Democrat and Republican became virtually indistinguishable as commonsense and pragmatism replaced the (very few) ideological differences between the two parties with a rhetoric of consensus and conformity. The response of all too many of the dissident academics—especially those concerned with the study of literature and culture—was a flight from commitment and the public arena towards an increasingly grotesque fascination with the rhetorics of selfhood. Those few who retained an attachment to work in the discredited realms of the social were subjected to ridicule and a constant suggestion of either naiveté or vulgarity.

Whilst Matthiessen was never to my knowledge accused of

vulgarity, the charge of naiveté was repeatedly levelled at him both during his career and by those who chose to abuse him after his death. As a tool of derogation, of course, that word is especially useful because its simple employment seems to absolve the prosecution of the responsibility to define its terms. In this way anything which steps beyond the boundaries of commonsense (that which Gramsci called the everyday employment of the ideas of the ruling class) can be attacked without the need for any substantive debate. So, Matthiessen's late vision of a democratic socialist Europe was ridiculed as postwar liberalism chilled into the late 1940s, and this generalized to a campaign against any liberal ideas in his work as the rise of neoconservatism strengthened. But it is also important to see that his work went beyond liberalism in some crucial respects, two of which are particularly relevant to the present essay.

In the early pages of *American Renaissance* Matthiessen, knowing the scope of the work before his readers, sees the need to define his terms so as to provide some clear routes into the long march ahead. In the context of the late 1930s, leading up to 1941, one of the terms most open for debate, most available for employment by many divergent factions, was democracy. For Matthiessen, as for many others, it was clear that this term needed a clear definition of its content in order to move its usage beyond rhetoric. Matthiessen's insistence on the connectedness between political and economic democracy, first, puts his thinking beyond liberalism—which reproduces the conservative commonsense belief in the separation of the two—and, secondly, made explicit the roots of the author's interest in the period from (roughly) 1840 to 1860. This was the period in which the always-present contradictions between politics and economics, between ideology and materiality, within US civil society became strained to breaking-point. Matthiessen begins his discussion by referring approvingly to Emerson's value "for those who believe now in the dynamic extension of democracy on economic as well as political levels,"[4] but it is clear that even in the 1850s this was becoming a forlorn hope rather than a prediction of the immediate possibilities of the future. It is useful to hold on to this idea though, not least because it informs later sections of the book in a way which is obscured by regarding the text as a series of disparate essays rather than conceived as a whole, and also because it is an idea which recurs in Matthiessen's later thoughts and actions.

At the very least, the recognition of a clear connection between politics and economics opened up the problematic yet fruitful rapprochement between Matthiessen and Marxism which led to the agonized scepticism about the Second World War and to his insistence throughout the war on the continued existence of an economic class struggle within the United States, even as the trumpets of the war for political democracy were being blown especially hard. This position put him at some distance not only from liberalism, but also from the Communist Party of the United States (CPUSA) and its fellow travellers who abandoned their post-Stalin/Hitler pact anti-war position and collapsed into an acceptance of the argument that the war was unproblematically a war against fascism after the invasion of Russia; a position which lead to a refusal to support domestic civil rights struggles of any kind.[5]

The text of *American Renaissance*—presumably finished during this period, given that the book was published in April 1941—bears the marks of this struggle of ideas, even in the finished form before us today, as Matthiessen returns again and again to this question of the nature of democracy. In his discussion of Thoreau's contribution to contemporary social thought he begins by focusing on, and praising, the clarity with which Thoreau saw the damaging effects of the division of labour within industrialization. As Matthiessen moves on to Thoreau's limitations as a political activist and theoretician, though, there appears a footnote which makes clear the weakness of an anti-capitalist argument rooted in an agrarianism and which quotes at length from the writings of Marx and Engels on the division of labour within bourgeois society. In itself, the direction of this objection makes clear the distance between Matthiessen and such other "anti-capitalists" as T.S. Eliot and the Fugitive poets—whose solution to the problem of the damaging effects of the division of labour was wholly regressive.

Furthermore, the quotations from Marx and Engels are taken from a French translation of the original text of *Die Deutsche Ideologie*. This seems to me to indicate an ambiguous attitude towards the ideas being quoted, when it should have been possible to provide either his own translation or a reference to the original in the *Gesamtausgabe*.[6] Much clearer evidence of this ambiguity, though, comes in his opening remarks about Emerson. Here, as he shapes Emerson to his needs, he reproduces an entry from the journals in which Emerson makes a connection between the extension of democracy and the development of a national American literature.

> What is good that is said or written now lies nearer to men's business and bosoms than of old. What is good goes now to all. What was good a century ago is written under the manifest belief

that it was as safe from the eye of the common people as from the Tartars. (The Universal Man is now as real an existence as the Devil was then. Prester John no more shall be heard of.) Tamerlane and the Buccaneers vanish before Texas, Oregon territory, the Reform Bill, the abolition of slavery and of capital punishment, questions of education, and the reading of reviews; and in these all men take part. The human race have got possession, and it is all questions that pertain to their interest, outward or inward, that are now discussed, and many words leap out alive from bar-rooms, Lyceums, Committee Rooms, that escape out of doors and fill the world with their thunder.[7]

The place of this passage is clear, not simply as an indication of the extension of American literary nationalism but also of the democratic nature of that extension. This is indicated by his references in the pages before this quotation to the writers who "speak for the people and protest against the corruptions and tyrannies of monarchy."[8] There is also an element here of the continuing Emersonian theme of the democratization of individuality and the individualization of democracy.

All of which makes the incompletion of the quotation still stranger, for Emerson continues:

When I spoke or speak of the democratic element I do not mean that ill thing vain & loud which writes lying newspapers, spouts at caucuses, & sells its lies for gold, but that spirit of love for the General good whose name this assumes. There is nothing of the true democratic element in what is called Democracy; it must fall, being wholly commercial.[9]

I admit that I have emphasized my point by cutting off the quotation at the word commercial, in order to make clearer my point that a good part of Emerson's objection to democracy is to the absence of economic democracy. Nevertheless I think that it is clear that by quoting in the way that he does, Matthiessen is revealing a conflict between his desire to defend the tradition of radical democratic thought which he saw in nineteenth-century writing, and an equal desire to maintain some distance between himself and the ideas of that radical democrat, Karl Marx. Even at the end of the "Red Thirties", even at the brink of the alliance of the United States with Stalinism (overwhelmingly perceived at the time as the heir of Marxism) and the subsequent if brief flourishing of American Stalinophilia, crossing that intellectual frontier too vigorously carried obvious penalties.

Lastly, Matthiessen's decision to concentrate on the *anni mirabili* of 1850—55 came primarily from his recognition of the huge flowering of artistic (specifically literary) activity in this period but that concentration carried with it—especially for a writer with Matthiessen's methodological and social commitments—the obligation to engage with the debates on the nature of democracy in which his subjects were themselves immersed. For Matthiessen, the Christian socialist, these debates revolved around the two poles of "a firm conception of the relation of man to society and [of] the nature of good and evil."[10] The two elements come together most dramatically in his discussion of the "latent economic factor in tragedy"[11] as it appears in the work of Melville in a chapter entitled "The Economic Factor." But throughout the book, Matthiessen returns repeatedly to the idea that democracy as an ideal contains both the political and the economic, and also resolves the question of the relationship of the individual to society.

Nevertheless, the charge of naiveté was given weight by the difficulties Matthiessen seemed to face in his political and philosophical attempts to formulate *concrete* positions with which to underpin his critical practice, and these difficulties flowed from his inability or refusal to clarify certain crucial questions. Perhaps the three most important of these were, in ascending order of practicality and immediate application: the relationship between materialism and idealism which in his particular case focused on his religious beliefs; the identification of the primary mechanism of fundamental social change in capitalism; and the role and function of Stalinism in the years from 1935–50. In each of these examples his work contains major vacillations and contradictions which are only partly explained by the historical specificities of the period.

The thread which draws these apparently disparate theoretical and practical issues together is a belief in the commonality of humanity, a category which ultimately subsumes all differences beneath itself and which is most clearly expressed in Matthiessen's opening words to the 1947 Salzburg Seminar at which he spoke of the importance of "the chief function of culture and humanism, [which is] to bring man into communication with man."[12] This, combined with his evident belief in the essential goodness of those attending the seminar despite the political affiliations of some which he would, surely, have found obnoxious, marks out a role for culture as the expressive medium through which a set of (universal?) truths about the condition of humanity are best articulated because it probes beyond what is, in the final analysis, the unessential material of historical specificity. At the same time, though, the force accorded to that historical matter is somehow undiminished: it is not a thin veneer easily removed but rather the immensely knotty and difficult grain which interweaves the essential. In this light, Melville's wrestling through specificity towards universality without recourse to platitude is given significant priority as *Moby Dick* becomes, arguably, the key text of *American Renaissance*.

In the same vein of difficulty and contradiction, his attitude towards the mechanisms of social change are never articulated in unproblematic form. On the one hand, the almost patrician attitude of the Thomasite Socialist Party (of which he had briefly been a member in the 1920s) met the Stalinism of the postwar Eastern European Communist Parties in their common belief that they could visit socialism (in whatever form they conceived of it) upon a more or less unwilling but certainly passive working class. On the other hand, he retained a faith (and in this case that is the best word) in the desire and ability of ordinary people to change the world in which they lived. Hence, one of the motives behind supporting Wallace's presidential candidacy appeared to be the connection to the mobilizing capacities of the New Deal (an aura which accrued to Wallace through his association with the Roosevelt presidency). Hence, also, the confusions about the operations of Stalinism in Eastern Europe in the postwar years as it attempted to exploit the credibility it had earned by being part of the leadership of the resistance in order to construct regimes in its own domestic interest. With the perfect vision of hindsight, it is very easy to mock any idea that Stalinism represented any progressive qualities. However, in the context of a war-devastated Europe, a state which had achieved substantial economic growth during the 1930s and operated through a set of political practices which still seemed somehow connected to the Russian Revolution, was capable of commanding at least qualified support from a range of people far beyond the confines of the CPUSA and its fellow-travellers.

In any case, Matthiessen's progressivism would have seemed to flow down broadly the same channels as the Stalinist project in the postwar years, certainly not in any easy fashion, as his often tortuous attempts to formulate a political relationship to Stalinism as an international phenomenon demonstrate, but in sufficient proximity to ease the task of the red-baiters who turned their gaze in his direction. What is clear from the comments on Stalinism scattered through the pages of *From the Heart of Europe* is that he was not the morally calloused and/or profoundly naive creature that the contemporary reviewers of the book portrayed, but rather someone who was wrestling with the difficult questions of social change. For instance, his sympathetic remarks about the broad tradition of "socialism from above" were seized upon by hostile critics in order to condemn him as a fellow-traveller. At the same time, though, his arguments about the distance between Lenin's thought and Stalin's practice and his praise for the Trotskyist Vincent Dunne, which would have set him at some considerable distance from the CPUSA, were swept under the carpet of Irving Howe's review. As, indeed, was the insistence I have outlined earlier on the relationship between political and economic democracy. The vituperative qualities of this review still come through very clearly in the accusation that Matthiessen suffered from "an advanced case of calloused moral imagination."[13] The irony here is that Matthiessen's comment on ex-Trotskyists summarizes succinctly Howe's own career, when he writes that after their apostasism, they produced "little more than sterile though heated debate, followed by a wearied disillusionment with all politics on the part of many who believed that they stood farthest on the militant left."[14]

However, the more serious "sin" of the casting of doubt on the wonders of contemporary American capitalism proved to carry so much greater weight in the years of the accelerating Cold War as to obscure the sophistications of Matthiessen's thought. Indeed, the refusal to be simplistic seems, ironically, to be precisely the root of the accusation of naiveté. In short, Matthiessen had an agenda which had very little coincidence with the developing postwar intellectual dominant framework, in which his concerns were either marginalized or "refuted".

This is in some ways clearest in a lecture he gave in 1949 entitled "The Responsibilities of the Critic." Here he set out to summarize his views on the role of the critic in a fashion which drew its inspiration, if not its tendency, from Matthew Arnold. In the course of this lecture, Matthiessen stresses repeatedly the responsibilities, duties and awarenesses of a literary intellectual in the political and social climate of 1949. He begins with acknowledging the impact of, especially, T.S. Eliot on the nature of criticism. By bringing the demand for a rigorous attention to the structures and textures of language into the study of literature, Eliot marginalized belletrism and replaced it with "a more serious and exacting body of work than we had previously witnessed in this country."[15] But having acknowledged the debt owed to this revolution in literary study, Matthiessen points out that it contains within itself a tendency towards self-absorption: "we have come to the unnatural point where textual analysis seems to be an end in itself."[16] Unnatural, because the responsibilities of the critic, the first duty of any thinker, is to be in the fullest possible contact with the world in which they live.

The lecture returns to this argument several times until the conjunction of intellectual and political responsibilities is quite clear. Intellectually, the avoidance of sterility in the discussion of literature comes through the understanding of the social roots of literature and of its connections to other forms of knowledge. The walls which divide knowledge into closed gardens need to be removed, and replaced with a conception of knowledge as a field across which the critical intelligence can range, making connections between points of analysis: "It is hard to conceive of a good critic of literature who does not have an alert curiosity about other fields and techniques."[17]

Having argued this double point, about the interconnectedness of literature and society and the forms of knowledge required to grasp both, Matthiessen delivers the sentence at the heart of this credo: "The series of awarenesses which I believe the critic must possess lead ineluctably from literature to life, and I do not see how the responsible intellectual in our time can avoid being concerned with politics."[18] "Ineluctably" carries the baggage of all those failed theories which attempt to prise the two apart—whether in disappointment or malice—in its connotations of the irresistibility of the idea. Later, Matthiessen will also argue that "judgement of art is unavoidably both an aesthetic and a social act."[19] This formulation is, I would argue, a move beyond the practical, but theoretically eclectic, solution to the relationship between aesthetics and social thought offered in *American Renaissance*.

The logical conclusion of this argument, for Matthiessen, is to recognize the importance of the work of Marx and Engels in arguing for the connectedness between phenomena. In 1949, after the sackings of college staff for their attachment to socialism had already begun, Matthiessen described in detail his intellectual debt to Marxism. I quote it in full here not only because it is apposite to my argument about Matthiessen's conception of democracy but also because, given the context of nascent McCarthyism in which it was written, it is an astonishingly candid, indeed even disingenuous and perhaps naive, statement. It is also, clearly, a gesture of great principle of which many others found themselves incapable.

> Emerson held that a principle is an eye to see with, and despite
> all the excesses and exaggerated claims of the Marxists of the
> Thirties, I still believe that the principles of Marxism—so much

under fire now—can have an immense value in helping us to
see and comprehend our literature. Marx and Engels were
revolutionary in many senses of that word. They were pioneers in
grasping the fact that the industrial revolution had brought
about—and would continue to bring about—revolutionary
changes in the whole structure of society. By cutting through
political assumptions to economic realities, they revolutionized
the way in which thinking men regarded the modern state. By
their rigorous insistence upon the economic foundations underlying any cultural superstructure, they drove, and still drive,
home the fact that unless the problems rising from the economic
inequalities in our own modern industrialized society are better
solved, we cannot continue to build democracy. Thus the
principles of Marxism remain at the base of much of the
best social and cultural thought of our century. No educated
American can afford to be ignorant of them, or to be delinquent
in realizing that there is much common ground between these
principles and any healthily dynamic America.[20]

While there is nothing startling original in this orthodox outline of
the strengths of Marxist theory it is both remarkable for the moment
at which it was written and also in many ways typical of the
ambiguities of one of the dominant trends within wartime and
postwar US Marxism—namely, the Communist Party's attempt to
define communism as twentieth-century Americanism. In this they
were attaching themselves to more widely-based attempts to re-define
the national culture as a radical tradition which had been led astray
by upstart conservatism.

Most notable though, is Matthiessen's insistence on the connection between economic and political democracy, and the connection
between that and cultural production. At both stages of this
argument, there is a crucial emphasis on the idea of participation.
Here, especially, there is emphasis on the critic's active contribution
to cultural production by adopting the role formerly occupied by
Shelley's poet as the unacknowledged legislator of the society. In
1949 there are clear ways in which there is an argument rooted in
both perceived strengths and actual weaknesses.

This conception of participation is also at the heart of the objections levelled at the mass media. Matthiessen begins by attacking the
passivity engendered by this form of cultural consumption. Again,
this is familiar stuff for the time of writing if we have read Dwight
Macdonald's jeremiads from the same period, but Matthiessen does

not stop here. He has, if nothing else, learned from Marxism that phenomena are dialectical and goes on to argue that the mass media are also an expression of both "our immense potentialities and continual corruptions."[21] This phrase also, of course, carries within it echoes of a religious conception and as such demonstrates the proximity of the two modes of thought in *practice* in his work.

These disparate threads of argument are gathered together by the recognition that "Man becomes free, not by realizing himself in opposition to society, but by realizing himself through society." The critic, the intellectual, the thinker, have a responsibility—to both their society and to themselves—to be involved in the fullest possible fashion in the life of the world as they live in it. He had already introduced William James as an exemplary thinker, and now he introduces Christopher Caudwell as another. If James was exemplary by virtue of the quality and range of his thought, Caudwell's qualification is that he combined the roles of thinker and man of action in almost archetypal fashion. Not only that, but the nature of his death and the contemporary descriptions thereof have the ring of martyrhood.

Furthermore, given that the latter part of the lecture was about the dual themes of constructing a usable past and the relations between America and Europe, the independent Marxist thinker killed whilst fighting in the good war in Spain becomes an important figure shadowing the final pages of the text. Because it is in these pages that Matthiessen begins to construct a usable past based on the idea that: "What makes the art of the past still so full of undiscovered wealth is that each age inevitably turns to the past for what it most wants, and thereby tends to remake the past in its own image."[22] This usable past, then, consists of two major elements. First, the figures whose works are exemplary and, secondly, interpretations of the writings of the past which makes those texts work in the present. The fashion in which these texts were made to work now becomes the crucial question, and the answer to that is informed by the whole of Matthiessen's conception of the function of culture within a democratic society. That, in turn, is informed by his understanding that: "The extension of our sense of living by compelling us to contemplate a broader world is the chief gift that literature holds out to us."[23]

As Edward Said has written on the propositions of this essay, "its seeming unproblematic ontological simplicity is most unlikely to reappear today."[24] This proposition, in its turn, is born out of a perception that Matthiessen's theoretical and political positions were naive. That perception rests in the contemporary separation of intellectuals from political activity and this is a situation generated not by the inexorable march into postmodernity, but by a set of specific historical factors. Factors which are contingent and, therefore, open to change.

Nevertheless, on all three of the counts outlined earlier—the relationship between materialism and idealism, the identification of the primary mechanism of fundamental social change in capitalism, and the role and function of Stalinism in the years from 1935–50—Matthiessen's thought and writing attempted to embrace the contradictions coming from the different social discourses which combined to shape the intellectual territory of his life. At no point was there a drive towards reductionism or simplicity for its own sake. This can easily be characterized as incoherence but it seems to me that its roots lie in that drive for inclusion which I have already remarked upon. Beyond the various ways in which this was formulated, it is important to see that the material roots of that thinking lie in the belief that the operation of the mind and the logical explanation of an argument alone are sufficient as mechanisms for the resolution of conflicts both intellectual and social, and that position, in turn, comes from the social position occupied by intellectuals and (even more by) academics.

Perhaps even more importantly, this conception of the intellectual's function is at a huge distance from the consensual thinking which began to dominate intellectual life, especially literary theory, in the postwar years. Although Matthiessen contributed to the volume which has come to be seen as the centrepiece of this literary history, Robert Spiller's *Literary History of the United States*, it would be over-hasty to lump his work in with those who subsequently went to some lengths to establish their distance from, and lack of respect for, his writing. It is also disingenuous to claim that because his work was subsequently claimed by the consensual establishment as their own, this is the only available reading of (especially) *American Renaissance*. The grand gesture in this dominant approach was the severance of author from text. The more pervasive effect of this manoeuvre was, and is, the removal of the idea and practice of contextualisation from any crucial or even important role in the processes of reading. An enormously important part of that contextualisation would always mean a reading of the conflicts from which the text is produced. In the case of *American Renaissance* that would involve understanding Matthiessen's reading of his own loyalties to literary criticism and history, to the nation state and socialism, as deeply contradictory and problematic.

Whatever detailed and important disagreements and criticisms I may have with his particular choices and formulations, I continue to find the image of the Harvard professor standing on Boston street corners collecting solidarity funds for striking Chicago meat packers beguiling. It is also a snapshot of a recurrent theme in Matthiessen's life: the attempt to put it all together and make sense of the connections.

He is so surprising. The manifest pleasure he gained from working with literature connected to the epiphanic moment when he got drunk with the Hungarian immigrant workers to whom he had been teaching English, and that connected to the difficult processes through which he passed in order to learn pleasure in his sexuality. The parts of his life interconnected, not in some simplistic fashion by which all the practices of his life became unproblematic, but because he attempted to deny the existence of barriers between the different forms of human activity. This attempt was, clearly, mediated by the historical moments of writing and littered with blind spots which it is necessary for us to interrogate if we are not to replicate those weaknesses in our work, but the presence of this interconnection appears in startlingly clear fashion when one reads the widest possible collection of his work. An example of this would compare the absence of any reference to Whitman's sexuality in *American Renaissance*—something much remarked upon since the appearance of the volume of letters to his lover Russell Cheney—to a letter written to Cheney in 1924 when, in order to explain his developing feelings towards the latter, Matthiessen quotes at some length from Whitman. It seems, furthermore, that the interconnectedness of the elements of his life meant that when disasters combined he was particularly stripped of defences: Russell Cheney's death, the defeat of Henry Wallace's presidential campaign, the worsening international and domestic atmosphere, the abuse heaped on *From the Heart of Europe*, all came together in a short period and pushed Matthiessen towards his suicide. Yet even in death he made provision for the continuation of the tasks he saw as important by leaving in his will the money which in large part made possible the survival of that influential journal, *Monthly Review*, in its early days.

Themes repeat but with each repetition our engagement seems somehow more difficult, because the arguments had seemed resolved; we thought we had settled the old arguments. That history does, *does* repeat itself is a hard lesson.

If for nothing else, Matthiessen's argument about the American renaissance and the works which constituted its core will be remembered for its predictive power—he was after all one of that crucial group who both literally and conceptually moved Melville's works on to the shelves of American literature. That growing swell of opinion during the 1930s about key texts culminated in *American Renaissance*, which took both its weaknesses and its strengths from both sides of the ideological and methodological divide within literary critical discourse. By so doing Matthiessen attempted to weld the concerns and critical procedures of the two camps into a single contiguous unit in which equal weight fell upon all parts of the sentence with which he summarized his method: "An artist's use of language is the most sensitive index to cultural history."[25]

Seen from this perspective, Matthiessen is not the looming father figure standing over the birth of American studies as a discipline, who shakes his head disapprovingly at any suggestion of the inclusion of— for instance—Harriet Beecher Stowe or Susan Warner into the canon of great works. He is, rather, the last bastion of a brief progressivism which found itself able to agree about canonical texts with later generations. If he was that patriarch I have described above, then his thinking about texts (as opposed to the texts about which he was thinking) and his critical methods would have been inscribed into the institution as acceptable and indeed definitive practices.

What happened, however, was two-fold. First, the ground on which he had chosen to make his stand was accepted as *the* ground and the texts for which he argues in *American Renaissance* did become the canonical texts of (at least) the next twenty-five years. At the same time, though, his choices were increasingly deprived of their critical and political power by being elevated to the status of classics. That the texts he chose to discuss took on this canonical status has often obscured the fact that his arguments about, and judgements of, these texts are at some distance from later readers.

The same can be argued about his methodology. At the simplest level, the appeal to a democratic tradition which seems to me to be central to the opening "Method and Scope" section of the book ceased to be quoted by almost everyone who made reference to the book during the 1950s. The distance between the liberal and conservative conceptions of democracy and Matthiessen's under-standing of the term, rooted as it was in a practical understanding of class politics and a theoretical language based on mid-nineteenth-century radical democratic ideas culled from sources as divergent as Emerson and Marx, was too great to be ignored and so was set aside almost as though it were not there in the text. There is, in this method of reading Matthiessen, a patronizing streak which wishes to save him from his politics. Furthermore, the appeal to the formation of a community of scholars–a cry which has echoed repeatedly through the writings of American radicals of many a hue when they have turned their gaze towards the university—became a utopianism when placed alongside the massive postwar extension of American higher education.

Beyond that, the appeal to a literature of democracy which had not been simply an academic position when the book was completed in the spring of 1941 as the Western world slid into a war against fascism, is set in a form which asks "Are you using such gifts as you possess for or against the people?"[26] The focus of the intellectual concern has also become a yardstick by which to assess the quality of one's citizenship, and must have been a clear statement of purpose which positioned its author on the side of anti-fascism and in favour of a democracy which needed no more than that appellation to be potentially fatal to its proponent.[27] Of course, by making the statement as vague as it is in "Method and Scope" and by leaving its religious overtone unchallenged, Matthiessen was also placing himself within that upsurge of populism which almost completely overwhelmed the voices of (more radically ideological) dissent during the march to the Second World War. But by 1950 that phraseology would sound very different to the ears of J.B. Matthews, chair of the Massachusetts Committee of HUAC, and the linking of democracy with the people would be produced as evidence of fellow-travelling. Such were the rapid motions of history and language during these years. Beyond that, though, the book had its stated purpose gradually eroded by an absence of reference to it. It is clear why that should be so. In the postwar years, the critic who argued that "the true function of scholarship as of society is not to stake out claims on which others must not trespass, but to provide a community of knowledge in which others may share"[28]—the drift of which appears profoundly utopian even to one who agrees with the sentiment—and who, furthermore, made no secret of his continued adherence to socialist ideas had to suffer one of two fates: banishment into the wilderness or the adjustment of his ideas to a point at which they appear innocuous. Matthiessen had the misfortune to have a particularly effective combination of the two wielded against him.

From the Heart of Europe has never been reprinted since its first edition in 1948. Neither has *The Responsibilities of the Critic*. Gradually, what was a contested reputation[29] became the source of useful quotations for essays about the use of symbols by Melville *et al*. New Criticism's rise to becoming the orthodoxy of literary study involved, first, severing the connection between "the poem itself" and its "extra-literary" context and then, when this severing was completed, re-instituting an anodyne version of contextualization which claimed to have no positionality. By 1964 Leslie Fiedler ambiguously called *American Renaissance* "that astonishingly non-academic critical work"[30] but didn't bother to get the volume's title correct. Indeed, by the time Russell Reising wrote *The Unusable Past* in 1986, Matthiessen had become the author of "the first study of American literature to apply New Critical analytic tools to American writing as a whole."[31] That he employed the techniques of close reading to attempt to open up texts precisely in order to reveal the social contents is lost here beneath a symptomatically loose use of terminology and a determination to precipitate Matthiessen into the camp of the self-reflexive theorists.

Matthiessen's work, then, has been the subject of many readings in recent years which have attempted to discredit him as a useful source for studying American literature and culture; readings which have attempted, in one way or another, to situate him as part of the critical establishment. He has been rendered as the father figure who must be displaced in order to release the newly discovered feminine powers of sentimentality, the patrician whose work had no feel for the world around him, the more or less willing dupe of liberalism, the self-denying gay critic who denigrated homosexuality as pathological.[32] Of these four broadly-drawn positions, I wish to reject the first two and accept some elements of the latter pair, and in doing so I will attempt to draw this essay to a conclusion by outlining my own position.

Matthiessen, in my understanding, was not the start of an interpretation of American literature so much as the attempt to synthesize an older progressivist thinking about content with an obviously superior "internal" method for critical reading in which matters of form are the primary concern. The texts which this eclecticism identified as the core of the tradition of nineteenth-century American literature were accepted as canonical by subsequent generations of critics but they found very different content within the texts, and that which was evacuated was a sense of the social as profoundly determining and as determined by the needs of the critical reader. As the conditions which had made this synthesis possible were replaced by a growing sense of the distance between literary text and non-discursive reality, the method became unrepeatable. The richness which marks the interplay between critical methods in Matthiessen's texts is replaced by a critical discourse which is, at its worst, enfeebled by its inability to imagine positions beyond the boundaries of the liberal consensus. In this context, much of what Matthiessen actually wrote becomes literally unreadable and even more commonly unread. When this happens, what is left is the conventional shell of a literary critic whose choices and commitments have been erased.

The Matthiessen I would argue for is the complicated and deeply contradictory figure I have attempted to adumbrate in this short study, and the greatest compliment we can pay to him is to engage with his work as the inscription of his complexities—certainly, by exposing the weaknesses and contradictions within his methods and judgements in our intellectual engagements, but also by assenting to the definition of the intellectual which he represented in his life's work.

Notes

1. Eric Bentley, *Thirty Years of Treason* (New York: Viking, 1971), p. xix.
2. The *Collective Portrait* initially appeared as a special volume of the *Monthly Review* in October 1950 and was then published as a book with the title *F.O. Matthiessen (1902–1950) A Collective Portrait* (New York: Monthly Review and Henry Schumann, 1950).
3. Paul Baran, *The Longer View: Essays Toward a Critique of Political Economy* (New York: Monthly Review Press, 1969) edited with an introduction by John O'Neill.
4. F.O. Matthiessen, *American Renaissance* (New York: Oxford University Press, 1941), p. 4.
5. See Martin Glaberman, *Wartime Strikes: the Struggle Against the No-Strike Pledge in the UAW During World War II* (Detroit: Bewick Editions, 1980), pp. 67–68, for one of William Z. Foster's more lurid defences of the CPUSA's positions, quoted from the October 1941 issue of *The Communist*.
6. From which Stanley Hook had made his own translations five years earlier for *From Hegel to Marx: Studies in the Intellectual Development of Karl Marx* (London: Gollancz, 1936).
7. Ralph Waldo Emerson, *Journals of Ralph Waldo Emerson 1820–1872* vol. IV (Boston & New York: Houghton Mifflin, 1910), pp. 94–95. The sentences enclosed in brackets have been elided in Matthiessen's quotation, *American Renaissance*, p. 13.
8. Matthiessen, *American Renaissance*, p. 93.
9. Entry from Emerson's journal dated 23 September 1836. Quoted from *Selected Writings of Ralph Waldo Emerson*, ed. William H. Gilman (New York: New American Library, 1965), p. 63.
10. Matthiessen, *American Renaissance*, p. 316.
11. Matthiessen, *American Renaissance*, p. 400.

12. F. O. Matthiessen, *From the Heart of Europe* (New York: Oxford University Press, 1948), p. 13.
13. Irving Howe, "The Sentimental Fellow-travelling of F.O. Matthiessen" *Partisan Review* 15: 10, p. 1127.
14. Matthiessen, *From the Heart of Europe*, p. 80.
15. F.O. Matthiessen, "The Responsibilities of the Critic", reprinted in *The Responsibilities of the Critic* (New York: Oxford University Press, 1952), p. 4.
16. Matthiessen, *Responsibilities*, p. 5.
17. Matthiessen, *Responsibilities*, p. 8.
18. Matthiessen, *Responsibilities*, p. 10.
19. Matthiessen, *Responsibilities*, p. 14.
20. Matthiessen, *Responsibilities*, p. 11
21. Matthiessen, *Responsibilities*, p. 9.
22. Matthiessen, *Responsibilities*, p. 17.
23. Matthiessen, *Responsibilities*, p. 17.
24. Edward Said, *The World, the Text, and the Critic* (London: Faber, 1983), p. 162.
25. Matthiessen, *American Renaissance* p. xv.
26. Through a lengthy quotation from Louis Sullivan, quoted in *American Renaissance*, pp. xv–xvi.
27. Remember, for example, Karl Wittfogel's use of pseudonyms to publish articles about oriental despotism in Germany as it slid into Nazism at the beginning of the 1930s.
28. Matthiessen, *American Renaissance*, p. xx.
29. The details of which I have outlined in my forthcoming monograph on Matthiessen and Muriel Rukeyser.
30. Leslie Fiedler, *Waiting for the End* (Harmondsworth: Penguin, 1967), p. 161.
31. Russell Reising, *The Unusable Past* (London: Methuen, 1986), p. 170.
32. Whilst there are, of course, no individual texts which articulate these precise positions, a reading of the relevant sections in the following would give the reader a sense of the prevailing tone of the discussions. Jane Tompkins, *Sensational Designs* (New York: Oxford University Press, 1985); William Cain, *F.O. Matthiessen and the Politics of Criticism* (Madison WI: University of Wisconsin Press, 1988); Donald Pease, "Melville and Cultural Persuasion" in Sacvan Bercovitch and Myra Jehlen (eds) *Ideology and Classic American Literature* (Cambridge: Cambridge University Press, 1986).

4

Susan Sontag
The Intellectual and Cultural Criticism

Liam Kennedy

Writing in 1969, *Partisan Review* editor William Phillips observed:

> More than any other writer today, Susan Sontag has suffered
> from bad criticism and good publicity. If she could be rescued
> from all her culture-hungry interpreters, it might be possible to
> find the writer who has been made into a symbol. This is no
> longer easy because a popular conception of her has been rigged
> before a natural one could develop—like a premature legend . . .[1]

Not much has changed in the last twenty-five years, at least in so
far as Susan Sontag's name would seem to carry with it explicit
intellectual, cultural and political connotations for many. "The
standard picture" in the late 1960s, Phillips noted, "is that of the up-
to-date radical, a stand-in for everything advanced, extreme and
outrageous."[2] The picture has taken on some new emphases over the
years, but whatever the reworkings of this popular conception, all
testify to the teasing implication in Phillips' comments: if Sontag did
not exist, American intellectual culture would have had to invent her.
In a sense it has invented her. Sontag has been made into not one,
but many symbols: "The Evangelist of the New," "Miss Camp,"
"The Dark Lady of American Letters," and most recently (and a sign
of the critical times) one of "The Last Intellectuals." Sontag's
intellectual role and contribution to American cultural criticism
cannot be easily prised apart from such popular conceptions. Her
intellectual trajectory from the early 1960s to today has been a highly
public one—she is probably the best-known and most widely read
intellectual of her generation. To study her writings today is to

encounter an illuminating critical history of changing conceptions and conditions of public intellectual life in America.

If there is an intellectual role that Sontag has self-consciously performed it is that of the generalist or, in her own phrasing, "writer-intellectual."[3] Her free-ranging studies of thought and culture are not the work of a systematic theorist, and she has consistently disavowed academic and scientific theorizing. Her essay subjects are strikingly diverse, including essays on happenings, Camp, science-fiction films, pornographic literature, the Cuban Revolution, photography, fascist aesthetics, cancer and AIDS. (She is also a novelist, short story writer, film director—features and documentary—and director of plays.) Sontag has explicitly endorsed the generalist model, acknowledging influences, both American—Paul Goodman and Harold Rosenberg—and European—Walter Benjamin and Roland Barthes. In her 1966 introduction to the American edition of Barthes's *Writing Degree Zero*, she asserts "Only if the ideal of criticism is enlarged to take in a wide variety of discourse, both theoretical and descriptive, about culture, language and contemporary consciousness, can Barthes plausibly be called a critic."[4] For Sontag, intellectual generalism requires this widened conception of "criticism;" it is an ideal of criticism she believes is best met by the writer-intellectual who eschews critical schools and specialization—working on the assumption that "no position should be a comfortable one or should be easily held."[5] Sontag's notion of generalism is at one with an insistence upon autonomy, and in this she implicitly endorses one of the most prevalent twentieth-century conceptions of what an intellectual is: a free-floating commentator on the general culture, unaffiliated to specific interest groups or institutions.[6] I want to look more closely at some of the assumptions which attend Sontag's self-conception as a free-floating generalist; throughout this essay I shall be concerned with the recent history and politics of this intellectual role.

While Sontag has long been recognized for her ability to provoke and generate ideas, this is often taken to support rather than question the "standard picture" of her as a connoisseur of novelty. Morris Dickstein, for example, charges that she has "grown adept at provoking controversy with sensational formulations on sensitive issues."[7] I have no wish to vindicate Sontag's work as above such reproach, but I view Dickstein's dismissive comment as indicative of knee-jerk critical reactions to her work. Sontag's avant-gardism is often a deliberate form of provocation—I shall be considering how she formulates and situates such provocations—but we should also recognize how this operates as a reflexive practice of *clarification*. In her most challenging cultural essays—those in *Against Interpretation*, *On Photography*, and *Illness as Metaphor*—she works to clarify, that is to organize afresh, particular cultural assumptions. Of *On Photography* she has stated that she was attempting to "organize what everybody knows," to lend a distinctive pattern to common feelings about photography.[8] This project of clarification illuminates a good deal about Sontag's (intellectual) assumptions and values.

Clarification modulates the characteristic movement in her essays from a particular subject outwards to more general cultural issues. An interrelatedness is sought between the ostensible subject and others from a wider cultural or political context. Often, Sontag looks not so much to run these connections to conclusions as to rub subjects off against each other to see what might synthesize, what might fall away, and where following a certain idea might lead. (As we shall see, in practice this is not at all arbitrary, but it is open-ended and a further irritant to those who would decry her lack of intellectual seriousness and programme.) This urge to clarify has encouraged Sontag to champion certain critical values—the sceptical, the dialectical, the negative—and to elevate ideas to the highest intellectual currency. Her essays often seek to animate ideas presented by her subject and to juxtapose them with related ideas. When she proclaims that "thought is a kind of excess," and celebrates the "dramaturgy of ideas" in the writings of others, she explicitly announces what is clear enough even in a casual reading of her texts: a fascination with the volitions, imperatives and even imperialism of thinking. It is no accident that Sontag should find herself most at home with the essay form, self-consciously manipulating its provisional and performative features, using it to "try out' ideas.[9]

In outlining these features of Sontag's intellectual outlook and approach, I have isolated her somewhat from social and political contexts. It is tempting to view Sontag as some sort of maverick intellectual figure, largely self-formed and swayed by little more than her tastes and prejudices. I want to argue, on the contrary, that her ideas and self-conception as an intellectual generalist are very much grounded in a specific intellectual culture—that of New York from the 1950s to the present. While she has clearly been influenced by her European tastes, the critical consciousness expressed in her writings shows her to be most closely affiliated with New York intellectual culture.

When Sontag entered the New York intellectual scene in the early 1960s she was already intimate with the writing habits and arguments of the grouping around *Partisan Review* known as the "New York

Intellectuals."[10] Irving Howe has noted this grouping's urge to address contemporary issues in their writings: they were critics, he observes, who "found a way to pay attention to a particular text and also comment on the larger cultural context in which these texts had appeared."[11] Stylistically, these critics shared a preference for the essay form to convey their concerns. They developed, in Howe's words. "a characteristic style of exposition and polemic . . . The kind of essay they wrote was likely to be wide-ranging in reference. It is a kind of writing highly self-conscious in mode, with an unashamed bravura and display."[12] These intellectuals had a strong sense of European cultural models, not merely as a fact of ethnic inheritance (many were of Jewish immigrant background) or incorporation, but of self-chosen dialogue and identity—in this they often articulated a cosmopolitan sense of culture. The mid-century writers have often been viewed as "public intellectuals," a definition which signifies their tendency to utilize a relatively jargon-free public idiom and address a broadly educated audience.

While I believe Sontag's work owes a good deal to this New York intellectual model, it has also existed in tension with it during a period in which this model has come to be widely viewed as anachronistic. As we shall see, Sontag's intellectual role has taken on a symbolic importance in relation to major transformations in New York intellectual culture in the last thirty years. The changing conditions—social and conceptual—of intellectual activity should not be ignored when the questions are posed: who is the intellectual?; from where and to whom does s/he speak? Sontag is certainly alert to the contexts in which she writes and speaks. She has stated: "people who reason in public have—and ought to exercise—options about how many and how complex are the points they want to make. And where, in what form, and to what audience they make them."[13] In order to examine how she has herself exercised such options I have selected two key texts to focus my concerns: *Against Interpretation* (1966), a collection of essays on varied cultural subjects; and *On Photography* (1977), essays on aesthetic and political consequences of "photographic seeing." With this very selective approach I do not aim to offer a balanced survey, though I shall comment on other texts, nor to offer a detailed exegesis of these two texts. I want to look at these particular texts so as to consider how they address particular cultural moments, how they inscribe an intellectual role, and how they relate to the "standard picture" of Susan Sontag.

I

The twenty-six essays in *Against Interpretation* were written between 1961 and 1965 and cover a wide range of cultural concerns. These include general essays on aesthetics and contemporary culture as well as essays on philosophy, anthropology, literary criticism, film, theatre, religion and psychoanalysis. The title of the collection comments significantly on its contents; as a statement of intent and position it does some justice to the fairly consistent line of argument in the essays. In her title essay Sontag explains that she is not opposed to interpretation *per se*:

> I don't mean interpretation in the broadest sense, the sense in which Nietzsche (rightly) says, "There are no facts, only interpretations." By interpretation, I mean here a conscious act of the mind which illustrates a certain code, certain "rules" of interpretation.[14]

What she *is* opposed to are established interpretative discourses—especially those of American literary, film and cultural criticism—which she believes are governed by pre-established rules and apply familiar categories to the "objects" of interpretation. In many of the essays in *Against Interpretation* she seeks to challenge the nature and function of this form of interpretation, while attempting to formulate "a descriptive, rather than prescriptive" critical vocabulary. What she seeks to produce is a demystifying metacriticism which will "expose and clarify assumptions underlying certain judgements and tastes" and will be autocritically attentive to its own procedures (AI, p. viii).

"Against Interpretation" adopts a manifesto-like approach to argue the merits of a formalist aesthetic and denounce "the modern style of interpretation [which] excavates and as it excavates, destroys; it digs 'behind' the text, to find a sub-text which is the true one" (AI, p. 6). In the essays which follow this lead, Sontag shows herself particularly drawn to texts and "temperaments" that have proved resistant to readily available interpretative templates. In many of these essays she demands recognition of this resistance. In her essays on "new formalists" such as Alain Resnais, Jean Luc Godard, and Nathalie Sarraute she focuses on a poetics of impersonality: "The typical formula of the new formalists of the novel and film is a mixture of coldness and pathos: coldness enclosing and subduing an immense pathos" (AI, p. 237). Sontag advocates taking "pleasure" in the formal challenges of the new novel and film, a corollary of her view that "the sensory experience of the work of art" should not be taken for granted (AI, p. 13). A similar view underlies her appreciation of sensual imagery in Jack Smith's film *Flaming Creatures* and Peter Weiss's play *Marat/Sade*. Of the former she writes:

> There are no ideas, no symbols, no commentary on or critique of anything in *Flaming Creatures*. Smith's film is strictly a treat for the senses . . . It is not in the knowing about, or being able to interpret, what one sees, that the pleasure of *Flaming Creatures* lies; but in the directness, the power, and the lavish quantity of the images themselves (AI, p. 229).

In her final essay, "One Culture and the New Sensibility," which suitably frames the collection with "Against Interpretation" in echoing the concerns and the polemical tone of the introductory essay. Sontag casts her view across the contemporary art scene in America to identify a "new sensibility" in the arts which is impersonal, parodic and self-reflexive. Referring to Andy Warhol, John Cage, William Burroughs and others, she contends "they are changing the ground rules which most of us employ to recognize a work of art" (AI, p. 298).

Against Interpretation is littered with very deliberately staged provocations. Sontag writes with both a constant awareness of the contexts of American cultural criticism and readership she works within (while many of the essays are on European subject matter, they all appeared in American journals and clearly address an American audience) and a self-consciousness about the rhetorical character of her avant-gardism. This latter concern is implicit in her diagnostic tone and efforts to formulate a fresh vocabulary with which to "describe" avant-garde texts, but it is occasionally explicit as when she comments on the emergence of the new novel entailing "a commitment *to all sorts of questionable notions*, like the idea of 'progress' in the arts and the defiantly aggressive ideology expressed in the metaphor of the avant-garde," and goes on to suggest that critics may have to encourage such notions "by all sorts of *seductive and partly fraudulent rhetoric*" (emphasis added, AI, p. 103). Sontag wears her own commitment to avant-gardism lightly, yet finds that this "partly fraudulent rhetoric" serves a useful critical strategy which she never openly announces: that of serving notice on the intellectual tenure of her American, and in particular New York, predecessors.

Many of the essays in *Against Interpretation* specifically address "critics," demanding or entreating that they recognize new aesthetic and cultural developments. Sontag consistently indicts American cultural criticism (though she rarely names individual critics) as "provincial" in outlook, lacking an understanding of either the new French formalism or "new sensibility" in America. In her essay on Nathalie Sarraute she refers to "the great flowering of literary criticism in England and America in the last thirty years" (the New Criticism) only to point up its inability to adequately engage the contemporary non-realist novel (AI, pp. 102-3). In an essay on Norman O. Brown's *Life Against Death* she argues that "in America, the twin subjects of eroticism and liberty are just beginning to be treated in a serious way" (AI, p. 257). Such comments display a heightened concern with the critical contexts in which texts are being received and interpreted in America. At certain points in her essays this concern is revealed to have a thoroughly localized and even agnostic impetus.

In "One Culture and the New Sensibility" Sontag articulates one of her key critical claims for her own programme: "A new non-literary culture exists today, of whose very existence, not to mention significance, most literary intellectuals are entirely unaware" (AI, p. 298). The reference to "literary intellectuals" repeated throughout this essay (and sporadically elsewhere) is significant as it indicates a particular kind of intellectual figure Sontag is positioning herself against. For Sontag, the literary intellectuals are obsessed with differences between "literary" and "scientific" cultures and "continue to cling to literature as the model for creative statement" (AI, p. 298). I believe Sontag has in mind a quite specific grouping of literary intellectuals—her New York contemporaries and their postwar predecessors. This becomes clearer when we recognize that her complaint is in part with intellectuals who use literature mainly as "texts, or even pretexts, for social and cultural diagnosis" and clearer still when she notes that the new sensibility arts have challenged "many established distinctions within the world of culture itself," including "(a favourite of literary intellectuals) 'high' and 'low' culture" (AI, p. 297). In the 1940s and 1950s New York intellectual criticism paid considerable attention to such perceived cultural dichotomies as "avant-garde" and "kitsch," or "high culture" and "mass culture," validating new hierarchical vocabularies such as "high-brow," "middle-brow" and "low-brow," or "High-Cult," "MidCult" and "MassCult".[15] Sontag's essay provocatively engages these concerns and forms of New York cultural criticism still prevalent in the early 1960s. She argues for a "[contemporary] grasp of our present cultural situation;" one which will recognize "the pan-cultural perspective on the arts that is possible through the mass reproduction of art objects" (AI, p. 296). Barriers between high and low come to seem artificial in light of this "pan-cultural perspective" which she believes is shared by "many younger artists and intellectuals" (AI, p. 303). Her argument for a need to embrace positively the changing social conditions of contemporary artistic practices is overly sanguine about the new relationship between artists and mass reproduction (and seems forced in its efforts to be dialectical), but it gains a polemical energy from its attack on "literary intellectuals" and implicit recognition of how socially negligible canonical modernism had become in America.

With this essay and *Against Interpretation* as a whole Sontag distanced herself from some of the most prominent lines of cultural and political concern in the New York intellectual world. As well as undermining the high culture seriousness and prurience of fellow intellectuals—"Notes on Camp" offers a famous example, where she remarks that "one cheats oneself, as a human being, if one has respect only for the style of high culture, whatever else one may do or feel on the sly" (AI, p. 287)—she consistently questions the "humanist" concerns of critics who view art as "a vehicle of ideas or of moral sentiments" (AI, p. 300). and in her opposition to interpretation as "excavation" lampoons the depth hermeneutics of Marx and Freud—the gods-who-never-quite-failed of the postwar New York Intellectuals. None of this is to seriously challenge my earlier association of Sontag with the New York model of the free-floating intellectual—she is speculative, given to provocative generalizations, comfortable with the essay form, wide-ranging in reference, and cosmopolitan in outlook—but there are distinct differences. All of these features are marshalled towards clarifying diverse cultural assumptions and practices which are largely alien to an earlier generation of intellectuals. Sontag's modernist cosmopolitanism, for example, is not that of a Lionel Trilling or Irving Howe who looked to the Russian novel or to the "political" modernists such as Arthur Koestler and Andre Malraux.[16] Sontag is persistently drawn to the more iconoclastic areas of European modernist thought and aesthetics: the asceticism of Simone Weil; the shameless abjection of Jean Genet; the suffering of Cesare Pavese; the "complex modern pessimism" of Claude Levi-Strauss; and the sensory stimulation of the Artaudian theatre.

Sontag's anti-literary bias also sets her apart. It is important not only to the new sensibility essay but to the collection as a whole. Of twenty-six essays only four deal exclusively with literature or literary criticism. While the postwar New York Intellectuals exhibited a generalist thrust, they were predominantly literary intellectuals, viewing literature as *the* medium through which to analyse broader contemporary issues. Thomas Bender has been one of the few critics to comment on these intellectuals' limitations in confronting visual and aural culture, finding them "terribly inexperienced with the culture of the eye and the ear" and suffering from an "almost puritanical fear of the seductiveness of the aesthetic pleasure" these organs might afford.[17] Throughout *Against Interpretation* Sontag probes the limitations attending a "literary" sensibility in an increasingly diversified and synchronically immediate cultural world. While she is by no means as optimistic about artistic innovations as the cultural democracy of her new sensibility argument implies, she appeared an original force in the 1960s in her speculative analysis of what she termed "the culturally over-saturated medium in which contemporary sensibility is schooled" (AI, p. 288).

In retrospect *Against Interpretation* may seem to offer little that was original, and indeed a close examination of Sontag's treatment of popular culture shows that she employed a gloves-on approach that signifies her own respect for high culture.[18] Yet her essays had a major intellectual and cultural impact in the mid-1960s beyond anything she could have either imagined or manipulated. That they did so owes a great deal to the dialectical charge of her writings as she worked across conventionalized boundaries tacitly separating literary and visual cultures, moral and aesthetic ideas, and intellectual and bodily pleasures. Reviewers were quick to identify her as an intellectual "swinger," a barometer of all that was radically chic in New York intellectual culture. In a review entitled "Swingtime," in the *New York Review of Books*, Robert Mazzocco found *Against Interpretation* a "trend-swept chronicle of cultural disturbances."[19] Others casually linked avant-gardism and gender: "The lady swings," wrote Benjamin DeMott in the *New York Times Book Review*, "She digs the Supremes and is savvy about Camp . . . She likes her hair wild and her sentences intense . . ."[20] Such popular images became fortified even as the implications of Sontag's writings were contested. While many dismissed Sontag as lacking in intellectual seriousness and programme, others claimed her for their own arguments or movements. Writing in 1968 Richard Gilman pictured her as "a representative advanced consciousness," an avant-gardist situated at the cutting edge of "the new" and so "able to discern what actually is coming to be born . . ."[21] For Gilman, and for many since, Sontag was the avatar of an emergent postmodern culture.

Those more parochially interested in New York intellectual culture quickly recognized the challenge Sontag posed to the critical hegemony of her predecessors and their more devout followers. While many sniped at her avant-gardism in reviews and asides in cultural essays, it was Irving Howe who provided the most damning commentary when he allotted Sontag a demonic role in his history of the New York Intellectuals. In a lengthy essay, which appeared in *Commentary* in 1968, Howe wrote a generally warm appraisal of "New York Intellectuals." Howe's essay was something of a valedictory as he argued that "the influence of the New York Intellectuals . . . is now reaching an end," opposed by and being replaced by "a rising younger generation of intellectuals: ambitious, self-assured, at ease with prosperity while conspicuously alienated, unmarred by the traumas of the totalitarian age, bored with memories of defeat, and attracted to the idea of power."[22] Howe denounced "the political-cultural style . . . the new sensibility" of this younger generation, believing it to signify "a new phase in our culture, which in motive and spring represents a wish to shake off the bleeding heritage of modernism . . ."[23] Howe goes on to name Sontag as a leading proponent of this new sensibility, finding it "both embodied and celebrated" in "a publicist able to make brilliant quilts from grandmother's patches."[24] To be sure, Howe names other intellectuals he identifies with this new sensibility—among them, Norman Mailer, Norman O. Brown and Marshall McLuhan—but Sontag is his prime target among "the younger generation" he believes mark the demise of the New York Intellectuals' influence.

By the end of the 1960s Sontag was, as William Phillips noted, "a stand-in for everything advanced, extreme and outrageous." For her own part, she claimed great surprise and even resentment at her avant-gardist celebrity. In a prefatory note published in the paperback edition of *Against Interpretation*, she remarked:

> I wrote as an enthusiast and a partisan—and with, it now seems to me, a certain naiveté. I didn't understand the gross impact which writing about new or little-known activities in the arts can have in the era of instant "communication." I didn't know—I had yet to learn, painfully—the speed at which a bulky essay in *Partisan Review* becomes a hot tip in *Time*. Despite all my exhortatory tone, I was not trying to lead anyone into the Promised Land except myself.[25]

Time and again in 1960s interviews Sontag sought to separate herself from the public image, stressing that her idea of the intellectual life was one of privacy, a life that is "reserved and contemplative."[26] Such a view is more than borne out by *Against Interpretation*, for all its breathless novelty. Among the essays Sontag's highest regard and a clear sense of identification is held for figures whom she believes have lived out an intense sense of intellectual vocation—an ascetic Simone Weil and a melancholy Claude Levi-Strauss. In the anthropologist Levi-Strauss she finds her prime modernist, a witness to the violent accretions of history he is also a "custodian": "Lamenting among the shadows . . . he acts out a heroic, diligent, and complex modern pessimism" (AI, p. 81). In the 1970s and 1980s a melancholic purview of modernity becomes a defining feature of Sontag's writings, but it is already present in her earliest essays, particularly in her assumption that modernism is in a late phase. If, in *Against Interpretation*, her thoughts on the contemporary American cultural scene often lighten this pessimism, they also announce it in surveying parodic and self-reflexive practices as the fallout of an exhausted modernism. Irving Howe could not have been more wrong when he aligned Sontag with "an impulse to shake off the burdens and entanglements of modernism." With a large dose of forced optimism and "fraudulent rhetoric" Sontag sought to revitalize her modernist heritage by emphasizing the aesthetic and ironic strain it had always held. And yet Howe was not simply wrong, for he recognized how the challenge Sontag posed to the seriousness and authority of his New York intellectual generation had been widely taken up. For Howe, as for so many of Sontag's "culture-hungry interpreters," she was the very face of the Zeitgeist.

II

Between 1973 and 1977 Sontag published a series of essays on photography in *The New York Review of Books*; in 1977 five of these essays, in revised form, were published under the title *On Photography*.[27] As with so many of Sontag's essays, those in *On Photography* are laced with contentious generalizations and impart a sense of embattled need to demystify and to warn. A major theme, upon which many variations are sounded, is her concern about the "predatory" nature of photography—a theme well supported by a distinctive vocabulary of keywords. Photography, she posits, "appropriates," "violates," "controls," "distorts," "anaesthetizes," "distances," "captures," "collects," and "colonizes." This concern with how photography acts upon the real weaves through all the essays, loosely connecting diverse ideas and arguments. I shall briefly outline her major complaints about particular aesthetic and political effects of "photographic seeing."

Firstly, Sontag contends that photography has an adverse aesthetic effect on historical understanding because it abstracts and fragments; in historical terms it destroys or at least encourages ignorance of context—the lived history in which events first took on meaning. "One of the central characteristics of photography," she observes, "is that process by which original uses are modified, eventually supplemented by subsequent uses—most notably, by the discourse of art into which any photograph can be absorbed" (OP, p. 106). The second major complaint Sontag offers—related to these comments on aesthetic transfiguration—utilizes the metaphor of tourism: "the camera makes everyone a tourist in other people's reality, and eventually in one's own" (OP. p. 57). Examining the middle-class origins of documentary photography she derides the "social adventurism" of treating "reality as an exotic prize to be tracked down and captured by the diligent hunter-with-a-camera" (OP, pp. 54–55). At another point the tourist metaphor takes on further political connotations when she comments on how "taking photographs has set up a chronic voyeuristic relation to the world" which makes it unnecessary for viewers to feel personally involved in what they see (OP, p. 15).

One of the seeming paradoxes—it is presented as a paradox, which invites speculation—Sontag comes at again and again is that "the medium which conveys distress ends by neutralizing it" (OP, p. 109). Her formulation of this paradox and speculations upon it indicate her anxiety about the effects of photographic images on moral response and historical understanding. This anxiety is made explicitly contemporary in the final essay, "The Image World," which pulls together many ideas from preceding essays. Views already established on the aesthetic distancing and chronic voyeurism of photographic seeing now take on a broad social import:

> Our very notion of the world—the capitalist twentieth century's "one world"—is like a photographic overview. The world is "one" not because it is united but because a tour of its diverse contents does not reveal conflict but only an even more astounding diversity. This spurious unity of the world is effected by translating its content into images. Images are always compatible, or can be made compatible, even when the realities they depict are not. (OP, p. 174)

This view of how the image world dissolves difference and conflict finds that the logic of capitalist society is fully compatible with that of photography—the "logic of consumption" (OP, p. 179). This argument is prefigured in an earlier essay when Sontag argues that people become ("through the camera") not only tourists but "customers" . . . of reality," and the reality that is packaged (or "framed") and consumed is one that blurs any distinctions between originals and copies (OP, p. 110). For Sontag, photography "does not simply reproduce the real, it recycles it," and she finds this recycling well suited to a capitalist society's needs: "The production of images also furnishes a ruling ideology . . . The freedom to consume a plurality of images and goods is equated with freedom itself" (OP, pp. 178–79).

On Photography evidences the hit and miss of speculative thinking as it moves between brilliant insight and banal generalization. Tempting as it is to engage Sontag's arguments, I want to ask questions of this text similar to those asked of *Against Interpretation*: from what intellectual position does Sontag write and whom is she addressing? To begin with the question of intellectual position, it is notable that *On Photography* quite self-consciously, if often obliquely, addresses her own intellectual past, revising some of her earlier views on aesthetic "ways of seeing" and on the "pan-culturism" afforded by mass reproduction.

Whereas in the early and mid-1960s Sontag pushed herself to some optimism about the "shock" value and "transgressive" impetus of the new sensibility arts, by the mid-1970s she is sharply critical of the value of such ideas in a post-industrial consumer society. This revisionism is clearly informed by her sense of a new historical situation in which the "logic of consumption" has rendered avant-garde strategies redundant. In a 1979 interview she is more explicit on this than she is in *On Photography*:

> There is really quite a close fit between avant-garde art and the values of the consumer society which needs products, constant turn-over, diversity, outrage and so on. The bohemian or radical artist's challenge of conventional bourgeois sensibility doesn't work any more. The consumer society is so sophisticated and so complex that it has broken down the lines between high and mass taste, between the conventional sensibility and the subversive sensibility.[28]

In *On Photography* Sontag expresses some ambivalence about the fate of the "subversive sensibility" in American culture, and offers some oblique comments on her own relation to it. When, in her second essay ("America, Seen Through Photographs Darkly"), she harshly critiques Diane Arbus's photography, we should recognize an autobiographical note. When she argues that Arbus's sensibility "is the sensibility of someone educated and middle-class who came of age between 1945 and 1955—a sensibility that was to flourish precisely in the 1960s," and goes on to identify Arbus with "the aesthetic's subversion, which the sixties was to make peculiarly its own," Sontag is taking a look at her own past. Yet, while identifying a common past she repudiates Arbus's project for encouraging "a pseudo-familiarity with the horrible" (OP, p. 41). In her repudiation of Arbus, Sontag seeks to distance herself from any easy identification with the "subversive sensibility" she was popularly identified with in the 1960s. Her attack on Arbus reflects a belief that the latter has helped undermine the kind of modernist "standards" she admired in *Against Interpretation*, in the "sensibilities" of Weil, Levi-Strauss and others (and, indeed, re-pledges herself to quite explicitly in the 1970s essays collected in *Under the Sign of Saturn*[29]). Sontag refuses the common view that Arbus was an artist "delving into her own entrails to relate her own pain," seeing her rather as "a photographer venturing out into the world to collect images that are painful" (OP, p. 40). Because Arbus's relation to pain is voluntary, Sontag denies it the authenticity of the moderns she admires; the implication is that Arbus's experience is always second-hand, never earned.

Sontag's views on Arbus are pivotal to her more generalized complaints with photographic seeing. Her anxiety about dissociation of feeling and knowledge in capitalist society is hardly a new intellectual anxiety, but it has a fresh impetus (historical and personal) in her text, which underlines not only her critical investment in high modernism but also her liberal politics. In *On Photography* she formulates this anxiety from within and addresses it to a particular audience, that of educated, left-liberal Americans. Again, it is in the essay on Arbus that this is clearest. When she argues that "Arbus's work is a good instance of a leading tendency of high art in capitalist countries: to suppress, or at least reduce, moral and sensory queasiness," she also notes that such art is "popular among sophisticated urban people right now: art that is a self-willed test of hardness" (OP, p. 40). The theme of "equivalence" in photographic seeing which runs throughout *On Photography* takes on a particular political cast in Sontag's commentary on Arbus when she observes: "making equivalences between freaks, mad people, suburban couples, and nudists is a very powerful judgement, one in complicity with a recognizable political mood shared by many educated, left-liberal Americans" (OP, p. 47). Sontag does little more to name this "political mood," nor does she so directly addresses it or her readership at any other point in *On Photography*, but what she is diagnosing and warning her readers against is a false pluralism which feeds off a too complacent response to the democratized alienation of "the image world." Her left-liberal audience is subliminally encoded in keywords and phrases, as when she warns: *our ability* to stomach [a] rising grotesqueness in images . . . works out not as a *liberation* of but as a *subtraction from the self*;" or again, in her rousing polemic against the politics of consumption in her final essay: "The freedom to consume a plurality of images and goods is equated with *freedom itself*" (emphasis added, OP, pp. 178–79). Liberty, self, plurality and freedom are watchwords of a liberal community. What *is* "freedom itself"? Sontag herself assumes her readers know.

In her concern with liberal values Sontag echoes many other American intellectual voices of the mid-1970s. Much intellectual writing of the period is characterized by a sensed "crisis of liberalism" and radical uncertainty about the parameters and functions of a public liberal culture. Such concerns are particularly clear in the work of intellectuals associated with New York—in the writings, for example, of Daniel Bell, Christopher Lasch, Harold Rosenberg and Marshall Berman.[30] Whatever their different positions along a liberal spectrum (from right to left) these intellectual critics, like Sontag, are all agitated by their sense of forces ranged against the autonomy of self and of culture. To be sure, the differences are striking and important; Bell and Lasch, for instance, are scathing on the perversity of the "subversive sensibility" as one of these forces, while Sontag sublimates this view to a more damning critique of the capitalist conditions which have neutered this sensibility by democratizing it. Yet, these intellectuals share similar assumptions about the need for individual (especially ethical) responsibilities to a community. Lasch's pessimistic analysis of the "narcissistic personality of our time" often echoes Sontag's views on "chronic voyeurism," as when he observes that: "avoidance of emotional entanglements and of 'judgemental' attitudes towards others reflects, at bottom, a narcissistic withdrawal of interest in the outside world. Other people matter only as they impinge on the self" . . .[31] Both intellectuals lament what Lasch terms "the devaluation of values" and "atomized individualism" of their culture.[32] In this they express not only a broadly liberal concern, but one that is much more narrowly intellectual.

Despite their different angles of approach to the ills of liberal culture, the intellectual values Sontag and Lasch share are evident in their intense concern for sceptical thought and rational discussion in America. For Lasch, the narcissistic sensibility corrupts "prevailing modes of thinking and perception" producing "intellectual apathy": "The social order no longer excites a passionate curiosity to understand it."[33] For Sontag, the image world defeats the very impetus to understand:

> Photography implies that we know about the world if we accept it as the camera records it. But this is the opposite of understanding, which starts from not accepting the world as it looks. All possibility of understanding is rooted in the ability to say no.(OP, p. 23)

It is what she perceives as the image world's threat to this urge to understand that Sontag is most sensitive to, as a threat to her own intellectual legitimacy. Several reviewers of On Photography complained that Sontag heaped too many social ills on photography. There is some truth in this, but I have preferred to ask why she should have done this. On Photography offers a displaced narrative of intellectual unease—a concern that the very conditions for critical intellectual thought (as Sontag understands this) are diminishing in America. In a 1975 interview, conducted during the period in which she was writing her essays on photography, Sontag asserts:

> We live in a culture in which intelligence is denied relevance altogether, in a search for radical innocence, or is defended as an instrument of authority and repression. In my view the only intelligence worth defending is critical, dialectical, sceptical, desimplifying.[34]

Where in the mid-1960s, she could take these intellectual values for granted, and indeed draw on them to test the limits of a public liberal culture and of high modernistic aesthetics, here, in the mid-1970s, she finds it necessary to defensively assert them.

Sontag's own "ability to say no" is the measure of how highly she values her role as a free-floating generalist. In a 1978 interview she proves sensitive to questions about her specialist knowledge of photography, yet confident about the values of generalism. The interviewer closely and repeatedly questions Sontag on how her interest in photography developed, probes her knowledge of the history of the medium, and suggests that the photography "community might question your commitment to the medium."[35] Sontag's response is to assert that such a complaint shows no understanding of "what the intellectual is." *On Photography*, she goes on,

> is not addressed to photography professionals. It is addressed to people who want to think about what's going on in the modern world . . . It seems to me the objections of the photographic community must be ultimately objections to some kind of free speculation . . .[36]

This is an illuminating exchange. The interviewer is sceptical about Sontag's lack of specialist credentials and so formulates the specialist's protective question: on what authority do you write or speak? For Sontag, the authority is self-evident, that of an educated and freely speculative mind ("I started [writing on photography] because I think about photographs a lot"[37]) Yet, Sontag's "free speculation" bespeaks specific cultural, political and critical values which play a major part in focusing her intellectual concerns and shaping her arguments.

III

"The deepest structure in the culture and ideology of intellectuals." comments Alvin Gouldner, "is their pride in their own autonomy."[38] In her writings and interviews Sontag evinces such a pride. Yet if Sontag has idealized the transcendent powers of the intellect, she has done so with a keen critical eye on cultural and political forces ranged against this idealism. As she came to suspect at the time she was writing *On Photography*, it is not easy to activate dissent or even assume the need for it in "a society that divorces public from private concerns (OP, p. 177). Much of Sontag's intellectual activity in the last fifteen years has her seeking to negotiate this perceived gap between the private and public. In *Illness and Metaphor* (1978) and *Aids and Its Metaphors* (1989) she has examined how metaphors of disease have distorted and simplified understanding of individual experiences and provided insidious rhetorical support for social and political policies. In the same period Sontag has become more politically active, especially with her involvement in collective intellectual responses to international issues of human rights and freedom of expression. From the mid-1980s as president of PEN American Centre, she has been particularly active in organizing support for Eastern European and Latin American writers. In such writings and protest activities she has sought not only to demystify but to influence cultural and political thinking. Sontag is not blind to idealism, nor to its timeliness. In a 1985 interview she comments:

> The way in which a certain kind of political idealism has been discredited and scorned makes the danger not that the intellectuals keep on making fools of themselves, formulating political opinions when they might not be as informed as they might be, but that they retreat and leave politics to the professionals.[39]

The discrediting of a left-liberal idealism in America in the 1980s and 1990s has had a major impact upon intellectual life, giving rise to a heavily politicized debate on the roles and functions of intellectuals. The question of "what the intellectual is" is not so easily determined as Sontag implies in the interview quoted above; the ideas of autonomy and responsibility which support the symbolism of the free-floating public intellectual are now widely questioned. Indeed, this model of public intellectual activity is now widely viewed as being in terminal decline, overtaken by the pressures of professionalization and academicization which have given rise to a "New Class" of intellectual specialists—technical experts, policy advisers and academics.[40] These pressures have certainly had a major impact in restructuring the intellectual field and redefining both the site (institutional) and sign (specialism) of intellect, but I do not believe the public intellectual has simply "declined" as a result. Rather, this intellectual role has changed greatly both in its objective functions and in the ideologies supporting it. A significant example, particularly relevant to New York's intellectual culture, is the emergence of a powerful neoconservatism. Neoconservative intellectuals such as Norman Podhoretz, Irving Kristol, Hilton Kramer, and Joseph Epstein have been prominent public intellectuals in the last twenty years, writing in a public idiom for an educated middle-class audience. However, their writings and political positions have signified a self-conscious effort to strip this intellectual role of its associations with an ethic of dissent or critical negativity. Hand in hand with the attack on regnant left educators who "politicize" learning, neoconservative intellectuals have sought to "deradicalize" the concept of intellect. A brief dip into the pages of *Commentary*, *The Public Interest*, or *The New Criterion* reveal this ongoing effort to denounce what Joseph Epstein has termed "the invasion of politics into culture."[41] Ironically, much of the rhetorical effort given to stemming this invasion is issued in clearly political tones.

At a time when "the retreat from liberalism" among American

intellectuals has threatened to become a widespread desertion, Sontag's efforts to connect private and public terrains of thought and issue have taken on a political symbolism. She has long been a favoured target of neoconservative censure. In a 1986 article in *The New Criterion*, Hilton Kramer castigates her as an aesthete "hopelessly in thrall to the winds of fashion" and ignorant of "political realities;" "neoconservatism," he concludes, "emerged from the turmoil of the Sixties to defend American democracy against the atrocious ideas of people like Susan Sontag."[42] Kramer's hysterical comments should not be taken to represent neoconservatism which is by no means a homogeneous intellectual movement. Yet, like many other neoconservatives, Kramer can speak loudly and with some confidence due to a surer sense of shared intellectual identity and purpose than that enjoyed by left-liberal intellectuals over the last twenty years. A major "strength of neoconservatism," as Daniel Bell has observed, is "its critique of the simplicities of liberalism and of utopian illusions"—a critique which underlies Kramer's comments on Sontag.[43] This is not to suggest that Sontag is "the last intellectual" of the dissenting, public type, though she is the most visible of her generation and a favoured critical target of neoconservatives who would cast her in the role of an unreconstructed "Sixties" radical.

Today, as she did in the mid-1960s, Sontag can sound highly ambivalent about the public role she plays. "Think of the things that I don't do," she comments in a recent interview,

> I don't appear on television. I don't write for any newspaper or magazine regularly. I'm not a journalist. I'm not a critic. I'm not a university teacher. I don't speak out on most public issues. If I wanted to play a pundit role, I would be doing all of these things. Still, the legend goes on. My life is entirely private. My interests are not those of a pop celebrity.[44]

As Sontag recognizes, "the legend goes on;" essentially, "the premature legend" William Phillips identified in 1968, which pictures her as a proselytizer of the new. I have sought to show that her responses to the new have been much more tentative and nuanced than the popular image allows. From her earliest writings she has cast herself as a generalist seeking "to expose and clarify the assumptions underlying certain judgements and tastes" (AI, p. viii). For many, this has been a project in avant-gardism; for Sontag, it has been a personal investigation of "what it means to be modern." Yet the personal is often made universal in her writings, a consequence of her own assumptions about "what the intellectual is." In her urge to "clarify" which issues are important to her, she has made of the self-conscious exploration of her own "sensibility" a mode of general cultural enquiry. As the aura of negativity which once characterized this intellectual outlook has been eroded publicly (and come to be distrusted by academic cultural critics) it still lingers on in the figure of Susan Sontag. No longer announcing an emergent critical voice, her work yet retains a potent residual element of high modernist theorizing which she has translated into a personal style of critical reflection and speculation. Sontag's intellectual generalism may support an outmoded form of critical analysis, but it can still be both timely and provocative in unsettling cultural and political complacencies.

Notes

1. William Phillips. "Radical Styles" *Partisan Review* 36:3 (1969). p. 388.
2. Phillips, "Radical Styles," p. 388.
3. Monika Beyer, "A Life Style Is Not A Life: An Interview With Susan Sontag" *Polish Perspectives* 23:9 (1980), p. 43.
4. Susan Sontag, "Preface" to Roland Barthes. *Writing Degree Zero* (Boston: Beacon Press, 1970), p. xi.
5. Susan Sontag, *A Susan Sontag Reader* (Harmondsworth: Penguin, 1983), p. 346.
6. See Philip Rieff (ed.), *On Intellectuals* (New York: Doubleday, 1969); Alvin Gouldner, *The Future of Intellectuals and the Rise of the New Class* (New York: Seabury Press, 1979).
7. Morris Dickstein, "Up From Alienation: The Case of the New York Intellectuals" *Revue Francais D'Etudes Americaines* 16 (February 1983), p. 45.
8. James Alinder, "An Interview with Susan Sontag" *Untitled* 14 (1978), p. 35.
9. See Graham Good, *Observing the Self: Studies in the Essay* (London: Routledge, 1987), Chapter One.
10. Sontag has commented in several inteviews on her early interest in the writings and concerns of these intellectuals. In one interview, she recalls: ". . . when I was a fifteen-year-old kid at North Hollywood High School, I discovered a newsstand on the corner of Hollywood and Highland that carried literary magazines. I'd never seen a literary magazine before . . . I picked up *Partisan Review* and I started to read 'Art and Fortune' by Lionel Trilling; and I just began to tremble with excitement. And from then on, my dream was to grow up, move to New York and write for *Partisan Review*." Roger Copeland, "The Habits of Consciousness" *Commonweal* (13 February 1981), p. 87.
11. William Cain, "An Interview With Irving Howe" *American Literary History* 1:3 (Fall 1989), p. 561.
12. Irving Howe, "The New York Intellectuals" *Decline of the New* (London: Victor Gollancz, 1971), p. 241.

13. Sontag, *A Susan Sontag Reader*, p. 332.
14. Susan Sontag, *Against Interpretation* (New York: Octagon, 1982; first published in 1966), p. 5. Further references are incorporated into the text, and abbreviated to AI.
15. This interest in distinguishing distinct cultural spheres was in part a defensive intellectual response to the impact on cultural production of mass-mediated forms of reproduction, in part a displaced anti-totalitarian concern to defend against an insidious assault on the mind. See Dwight Macdonald, 'Masscult and Midcult' *Against the American Grain: Essays on the Effects of Mass Culture* (New York: Vintage, 1962). For a critical summary of the mass culture debate, see Christopher Brookeman, *American Culture and Society Since the 1930s* (London: Macmillan, 1984), pp. 41–58.
16. See Richard King, "Up from Radicalism" *American Jewish History* 75:1 (September 1985), p. 82.
17. Thomas Bender, *New York Intellect: A History of Intellectual Life in New York City, from 1750 to the Beginnings of Our Own Time* (Baltimore: Johns Hopkins University Press, 1988), p. 256.
18. See Andrew Ross, *No Respect: Intellectuals and Popular Culture* (London: Routledge, 1989).
19. Robert Mazzocco, "Swingtime" *The New York Review of Books* 6:10 (9 June 1966), p. 24.
20. Benjamin De Mott, "Lady on the Scene" *New York Times Book Review* (23 January 1966), p. 5.
21. Richard Gilman, *The Confusion of Realms* (London: Weidenfeld and Nicolson, 1970), pp. 38, 30.
22. Howe, *Decline of the New*, p. 248.
23. Howe, *Decline of the New*, p. 255.
24. Howe, *Decline of the New*, p. 258.
25. Sontag, *Against Intepretation* (New York: Dell, 1978), p. viii.
26. James Toback, "Whatever You'd Like Susan Sontag to Think, She Doesn't" *Esquire* 70 (July 1968), pp. 59–60.
27. Susan Sontag, *On Photography* (Harmondsworth: Penguin, 1984; first published 1977). Further references are incorporated into the text, and abbreviated to OP.
28. Paul Brennan, "Sontag in Greenwich Village: An Interview" *London Magazine* 19:1–2 (April/May 1979), p. 98.
29. Susan Sontag, *Under the Sign of Saturn* (New York: Farrar, Straus, Giroux, 1980).
30. See, for example George Levine, "Our Culture and Our Convictions" *Partisan Review* 39 (1972), pp. 63–79; Daniel Bell, *The Cultural Contradictions of Capitalism* (New York: Basic, 1976); Christopher Lasch, *The Culture of Narcissism* (New York: Norton, 1979).
31. Christopher Lasch, "The Narcissistic Personality of Our Time" *Partisan Review* 44 (1977), p 18.
32. Lasch, "The Narcissistic Personality," p. 19.
33. Lasch, "The Narcissistic Personality," p. 18.
34. Sontag, *A Susan Sontag Reader*, p. 346.

35. Alinder, "An Interview With Susan Sontag," p. 34.

36. Alinder, "An Interwiew With Susan Sontag," p. 35.

37. Alinder, "An Interview With Susan Sontag," p. 35.

38. Gouldner, *The Future of the Intellectuals and the Rise of the New Class*, p. 33

39. Eileen Manion and Sherry Simon, "An Interview With Susan Sontag" *Canadian Journal of Political and Social Theory* 9:1 (1985), p. 13.

40. On the New Class, see Gouldner, *The Future of the Intellectuals and the Rise of the New Class*; Barbara and John Ehrenreich, "The Professional-Managerial Class" in Pat Walker (ed.) *Between Labor and Capital* (Boston: South End Press, 1979); Ross, *No Respect*. Some have lamented the "decline" of the public intellectual: see Russell Jacoby, *The Last Intellectuals: American Culture in the Age of Academe* (New York, Basic 1987).

41. Joseph Epstein, *Plausible Prejudices* (New York: Norton, 1986), p. 12.

42. Hilton Kramer, "Anti-communism and the Sontag Circle" *The New Criterion* 5:1 (September 1986), pp. 6–7.

43. Peter Shaw, "The Retreat From Liberalism" *The Virginia Quarterly Review* 62:3 (Summer 1986), p. 382.

44. Richard Berstein, "Susan Sontag, As Image and as Herself" *New York Times* (26 January 1989), C17.

5

Stanley Cavell
Must We Believe What We Say?

Michael Wood

Philosophy has often sought to place itself beyond culture, in Lionel Trilling's phrase, and Stanley Cavell has often placed himself at an angle to what philosophy has become. Does this angle remove him further, take him beyond the beyond, or does it bring him closer to culture? It brings him closer, I want to argue; it even makes him a cultural critic. A further question, inseparable from the first in this context, concerns the Americanness of Cavell's work. Is he, for example, not only an American who writes cultural criticism, but an American cultural critic, a critic of American culture?

The answers to these questions may seem so obvious as to need no argument. Leaving aside the question of whether philosophy ever could place itself beyond culture—on several understandings of both words, philosophy *is* culture, or a major expression of it, "the world of a particular culture brought to consciousness of itself," as Cavell says[1]—surely a philosopher who is so interested in literature and film and ordinary language must find himself more deeply sunken than most inside culture, without even a chance or a thought of getting out of it. This is true, and this situation, these interests, are an important part of the reason why Cavell matters as a cultural critic. But then culture has many meanings, the deeper inside it you are the less plainly or simply visible it becomes, and Cavell himself, following Heidegger and Wittgenstein ("philosophers for whom the obvious is the subject of philosophy"[2]), has taught us to think twice about the obvious; about what he calls "the difficulty of seeing the obvious, something which for some reason is always underestimated" (*Must We*, p. 310). "For some reason" is slightly disingenuous, a form of stalling or postponement—Cavell means he is not going to have this argument today. The reason the obvious is difficult to see is that it *is* obvious. We see it, but only in the blind, automatic way we see much of the unwoken life around us and in us. In this case, the obvious thought that a philosopher is a cultural critic may seem to hide the equally obvious thought that philosophy and cultural criticism are not the same thing.

Cavell is a professor of philosophy at Harvard, the author of seven books of philosophy, two books on film and a book on Shakespeare, although these separate designations are seriously misleading. There is plenty of philosophy in the film books—"film exists in a state of philosophy" is how Cavell puts it in *Pursuits of Happiness*;[3] "as though," he adds in *Themes Out Of School*,[4] "the condition of philosophy were its natural condition"—and films appear in the philosophy books. Shakespeare emerges alongside Wittgenstein in *The Claim of Reason*; alongside Wittgenstein, Beckett, Austin, Kierkegaard in *Must We Mean What We Say?* A good part of Cavell's career has been dedicated to marking out for Emerson and Thoreau what he sees as their proper, founding place in American philosophy —to showing what it is they founded, what has been there all the time since they wrote, the way the faces are in the tree in the children's puzzle Wittgenstein talks about.

None of this is to imply that there is no difference between literature and philosophy, an argument Cavell associates with Richard Rorty; only that there is no single difference, and that having a range of tastes is not the same as being indifferent to difference. Wittgenstein is everywhere in Cavell's work, and so is the particular, I want to say American inflection Cavell finds for the practice of ordinary language philosophy. Cavell is strongly committed to the idea that "words know something,"[5] that philosophy, as Mallarmé said of poetry, is made of words; and in an early essay he beautifully suggests that the clarity Austin sought in philosophy was to be had "through mapping the fields of consciousness lit by the occasions of a word" (*Must We*, p. 100). A parallel thought is that film, for all its engagement with narrative and its overlap with philosophy, is another, entirely specific medium, that its projections reach us through the agency of a camera and an industry. It is thus that Cavell can without contradiction insist on the philosophical preoccupations of film, and rather intricately remind us that we don't know Kant in anything like the way we know a Hollywood film (*Pursuits*, pp. 9–10). There have been shifts in Cavell's interests, from an emphasis on film as film, to borrow Victor Perkins' phrase, to an emphasis on film as part of the conversation of culture. But there are continuities beneath the shifts too—the cultural question was always there—and the shifts may be less clear to Cavell than they are to his readers, since in a recent work he answers a question about "film as such" by declaring five assumptions about America. I shall return to this moment.

I can leave Cavell's work on Shakespeare for another time, but I need to look at the connection he makes between philosophy and film, because much of what he has to say about American culture arises from that connection, or becomes ideally sayable there. What is "the condition of philosophy?" There are many such conditions, of course, but for Cavell the modern condition, the one that began with the birth of modern science and Descartes' attempt to stem the very doubts that were about to take over the world, would have to include scepticism, a radical (actual or professed) uncertainty about the existence of the world and of others. The point about modern scepticism, as Cavell says, is that it is groundless.[6] There are no grounds for it, and no grounds against it. What it represents is not a worry about the world and the others, which it knows are real enough. Even the solipsist, Wittgenstein says, expects the chair to be there when he sits down. Scepticism is worried about the grounds it can't find and can't have. It has discovered what Cavell calls the knowledge of ignorance,[7] the desperate difficulty of not knowing how we know. Most philosophers treat scepticism, thus defined, as a problem, and Cavell sometimes calls it that. But he doesn't think it is a problem, in the sense that it requires or could have a solution. It is a defeat, he says, which is "not to be solved but to be undone" (*Conditions*, p. 21). And not only a defeat, although undoing it would still leave us some way from anything that would ordinarily look like a victory. Wittgenstein's work, Cavell tells us, "finds its victory in never claiming a final philosophical victory over (the temptation to) skepticism, which would mean a victory over the human" (*America*, p. 38). "Nothing is wrong; everything is wrong. It is the philosophical moment" (*America*, p. 99).

We can't assert that we believe in the world, "as if 'The world exists' were one more belief among others, the world one more object among others" (*Disowning*, p. 8). But if we don't believe in the world, where is it, and what is our relation to it? Even Hume's interesting metaphor of scepticism as incurable doesn't get us close enough to the condition as Cavell sees it: "Skepticism, or rather the threat of it, is no more *incurable* than the capacities to think and to talk, though these capacities too, chronically, cause sorrow" (*America*, p. 54, Cavell's italics). Scepticism makes the world seem impossible for us, unsettles everything; it is the opposite of habit, it wakes phenomena into strangeness; we can't live with it. But without it we could live only the lives of automata, the familiar is ours because we could lose it at any moment, we are continually, and properly, struck by its strangeness. "The answer to skepticism must take the form not of philosophical construction but of the reconstruction or resettlement of the everyday" (*Quest*, p. 176). The recourse to ordinary language in philosophy is therefore not, in Cavell's view and practice, an apology for unexamined ordinariness, as if everything was all right before the philosophers got to it. It is an invitation to examine the ordinary with a philosopher's eye, to find there what philosophy cannot possibly find anywhere else. Cavell understands philosophy, he says, "as a willingness to think not about something other than what ordinary human beings think about, but rather to learn to think undistractedly about things that ordinary human beings cannot help thinking about, or anyway cannot help having occur to them" (*Themes*, p. 9).

There are many connections to film here. The patience and catholicity of the movie camera offer an interesting analogue to ordinary language, and what we might catch in it if we looked. Film routinely invites us to find the familiar pretty strange, and Hitchcock's films, for example, plant secrecy and suspicion everywhere: there is no dreary, nondescript street that could not hide a murder, and no lurid appearance that could not misrepresent the perfectly ordinary, or at least the innocent. "The uncanny is normal experience of film."[8] Film itself places, must place the viewer in one of the recurring postures of the sceptic. We look at a world we can't believe in and have to believe in. We may not believe in Scarlett O'Hara but we have to believe in Vivien Leigh. Yet how can we believe in either of them? They are two dimensional optical tricks, they live in an entirely different time and space from the one they are shown in.

> Film is a moving image of skepticism: not only is there a reasonable possibility, it is a fact that here our normal senses are satisfied of reality while reality does not exist—even, alarmingly, *because* it does not exist, because viewing is all it takes. (*World*, pp. 188–89, Cavell's italics) Because common sense is, and ought to be, threatened and questioned by the experience of film itself. (*World*, p. 212)

Is scepticism American? Not exclusively, of course. Is there an American scepticism? I think there is, but the topic is far larger than

I have space for. It will suffice as a marker, perhaps, if I say that "to inherit the philosophy of Europe," as Cavell puts it (*America*, p. 70) would mean, in America, to pursue that philosophy in the context of an intimacy with doubt, and a sense of how far doubt could go, which are quite alien to any culture in Europe. This indeed is how Cavell reads ordinary language: not as what's there but as what might not be, a recurring miracle. The reading Americanizes Austin wonderfully; what's odd is how lightly, and easily, Austin travels. It doesn't (need to) Americanize Wittgenstein, because he made it his troubled business to doubt, precisely, just what his various cultures did not doubt; and because there is more than one way of arriving at the miracle of the ordinary. But then this deep scepticism, American or Wittgensteinian, concerns culture too. Failing or not wishing to place her/himself beyond culture, a critic nevertheless regularly needs, as Trilling and Adorno also suggest in their quite different languages, to call culture to a sense of itself, to invite different regions of culture to speak up against a dominant or domineering voice, even to seem to be, however incoherently or ironically, against culture.

Seeking to think of Wittgenstein as "a philosopher—even a critic—of culture" (*America*, p. 52), Cavell begins by suggesting that "the idea of a philosophy of culture signals something quite fundamental . . . in Wittgenstein's teaching," but something also "not yet quite surveyable" (*America*, p. 31). This is to say that Wittgenstein's assorted remarks on culture, his immediately identifiable pieces of cultural criticism, are not for Cavell as interesting as those of Adorno or Hannah Arendt, "let alone . . . of Kafka or Freud, or . . . of Nietzsche or Marx." "Wittgenstein's remarks on so-called cultural matters . . . are primarily of interest because it is Wittgenstein who made them" (*America*, p. 31). This means they *are* interesting, but only in their own way. Any other cultural interest we shall have to find inside Wittgenstein's teaching, woven into it, part of its work.

Cavell goes on to show that culture for Wittgenstein, as for Emerson, is a matter of disappointment and compromise—*Philosophical Investigations* is a portrait of the deformations and ravages of a sophisticated culture, which includes philosophy's ancient claims of getting beyond culture. Wittgenstein is seen as "endlessly forgoing, rebuking, displacing philosophy's claim to a privileged perspective on its culture" (*America*, p. 73). It's not just that philosophy can't claim this privilege, the very idea that it should is one of its diseases. This is not to say that philosophy accepts culture—what would all that forgoing, rebuking and displacing be about if it did?—but to say that it understands, or seeks to understand, what collaboration in a culture means. Cavell's word for what is to be understood is consent, which in turn involves cost and regret, and other features and emotions. There is a difference between Wittgenstein and almost everyone else here, Cavell suggests, memorably figuring it in the difference between the child and the youth in respect of demands. *Philosophical Investigations*

> discovers or rediscovers childhood for philosophy (the child in us) as Emerson and Nietzsche and Kierkegaard discover youth, the student, say adolescence, the philosophical audience conscious that its culture demands consent; youth may never forgive the cost of granting it, or of withholding it. The child demands consent of its culture, attention from it; it may never forgive the cost of exacting it, or of failing to. *(America,* p. 60)

Here are demands that may be met or not met; and even when met may be harshly remembered. And of course both the child and the youth are more troublesome, more mindful of demands, than adults are; or than an old country is. The contentments of civilization have their turbulences too; the discontents don't get all the action.

Now the sense in which Cavell is a philosopher—even a critic—of culture is a good deal more visible and less problematic than the case of Wittgenstein as Cavell describes it. Cavell's overt remarks about culture are of great interest, and can usefully be quoted—this is not to say his thoughts about culture are not internal to his teaching, not woven into it, but that they surface more often and more clearly than comparable thoughts in Wittgenstein. *The World Viewed* begins by asking and worrying at the question "What reason is there to care about any radical criticism of one's culture?" (*World,* p. 3); *Conditions Handsome and Unhandsome* reminds us that Hollywood comedies and melodramas are "in conversation with their culture" (*Conditions,* p. 124), and that this conversation can be something of a mystery: how can these films have been so well liked and so long misread or underrated (*Conditions,* p. 105).[9] There is an interesting difficulty, though. What Cavell has openly to say about *American* culture often seems so familiar, so securely placed within the standard myth of what American culture is, that we do not immediately see the difference of what he is saying, his inflection or understanding of these familiarities. Another case for thinking about the obvious. Not to do this here would be rather like remembering the long ironic list of absences Henry James offers in his book on Hawthorne as a characterization of American culture, and forgetting what James says next. We might think, James dryly says, that without any of these things, America just has nothing. "The American knows that a good deal remains; what it is that remains—that is his secret, his joke, as one may say."[10] The sentence allows all kinds of implications: that what the American takes to be a good deal isn't much by any other standards; that he himself only know there is something, but can't say what it is; that he knows exactly what it is but he isn't telling anyone; that what there is is so peculiar that it will seem a joke to anyone else; that what remains *is* a wonderful joke, it's what the inexpressible freedom from all that European junk might mean if you didn't want simply to romanticize the backwoods.

Cavell seems often to be reiterating James' list of absences; to see American culture as an absence. It's important to note therefore that Cavell too has his secret, his joke. He certainly doesn't want to romanticize the backwoods, but he doesn't want to pretend they are Paris or Heidelberg either. What would it have been like—"from time to time I wonder," Cavell says, "or wonder if it makes sense to wonder" —for the American New Critics "to have had a literary-philosophical culture comparable to Heidegger's within which to write?"

> I do not credit Heidegger with a better touch for literature than Ransom's, or Kenneth Burke's, or R.P. Blackmur's, or Paul Goodman's, but the Americans compose their theoretical works in a kind of scrip, good for exchanges at the company store but worth next to nothing on the international market. (*Quest*, p. 67)[11]

Cavell goes on, obviously thinking of more recent developments in American (academic) criticism, to say it sometimes seems the only choice is between this "kind of private language" and the public but flattened language of whatever is fashionable. This is a working sense of what it might mean not to have a culture. Or not to *have* one.

Cavell calls it "a plain fact of history" that "we are, we still find ourselves, looking for the commencement of our own culture" (*Conditions*, p. 37). Another, perhaps more interesting way of figuring this condition is to ask "What it might betoken about a culture that its *founding* works are works of the fantastic?" (*Quest*, p. 183, Cavell's italics). The American distress is double, in Cavell's view, an initial poverty compounded by a wilful forgetting. The thinness of "our common cultural inheritance" means you can't talk about Kant in America without seeming abstruse. "But if one of the indisputably most important philosophical achievements of the modern era of Western civilization is not a piece of our inheritance, what is?" (*Pursuits*, p. 9). I hear Henry James' American murmuring, "A great deal," and asking perhaps whether an uninherited culture might not count for a lot too. "Compared with the philosophical culture of Schelling's audience," Cavell says, "Emerson's mostly had none;"[12] and Emerson's posterity doesn't even have Emerson. Cavell describes this as "the inability of American philosophy to inherit the writing of Emerson and Thoreau" (*Themes*, p. 188), and finds the fault continuing even in John Rawls, who through his comments on the Emerson-inspired Nietzsche prolongs "American philosophy's repeated dismissal, I sometimes say repression, of the thought of Emerson" (*Conditions*, p. 4). This may seem to restrict the quarrel to American philosophy, incapable of seeing the philosophical seriousness of writing which is happily enough treated as literature. But Cavell's quarrel is wider than this, a quarrel with his culture itself, since not seeing how philosophical Emerson is amounts to a refusal to read him, described as: "the inability of our American culture to listen to the words, to possess them in common, of one of the founding thinkers of our culture, Ralph Waldo Emerson, an inability which presents itself to me as our refusal to listen to ourselves, to our own best thoughts" (*Conditions*, p. 129).

Things are getting a little more complicated now, as the double use of culture in that quotation suggests. It's not that America has no culture, it's that it doesn't know the culture it has. That is its secret, its joke. It may also be, although I don't think Cavell wants to go as far as this, that not knowing its culture is the form its (considerable) culture takes. What if Emerson also founded, as he probably did, the culture's inability to listen to him? This would alter the meaning of the following remark:

> I take it for granted that their (Emerson's and Thoreau's) thinking is unknown to the culture whose thinking they worked to found (I mean culturally unpossessed, unassumable among those who care for books, however possessed by shifting bands of individuals), in a way it would not be thinkable for Kant and Schiller and Goethe to be unknown to the culture of Germany, or Descartes and Rousseau to France, or Locke and Hume and John Stuart Mill to England. (*Quest*, p. 27)[13]

I wonder if the basic assumption here is true, and I find the image of cultural possession questionable in all kinds of ways. I also take Cavell to be articulating an American romance of European culture rather than describing any recognizable European reality. Even so, there is a large difference between feeling you are dealing in an international currency and feeling you are not. And there is a difference between both of those feelings and the feeling that you don't have to bother. There is a still further difference between any of that and knowing—Robert Frost would be my prime example—that you are dealing in an international currency but have mischievously disguised it as scrip. The effect of such a move, once understood, would be to reinvent the idea of the international, to get it to include American stealths and ironies. It would also be to reinvent the idea of the American. Emerson and Thoreau would not be ignored in such a perspective, they would have been unfathomably internalized.

I am taking my cue from Cavell even when I seem to part company with him, since this is how I read his splendid reading of the rural Ralph Bellamy's boasting in *The Awful Truth*. Bellamy sings a song with Irene Dunne—"Home on the Range," which already lifts him into a parody he hasn't understood as such—then responds to her polite compliment by saying "Never had a lesson in my life. Have you?" She sings so well that she doesn't think having or not having lessons is an issue. Why wouldn't you want to be as good as you can be, and why would you want to be anything but casual about how good you are?

> And what is that terrible American pride in never having had a lesson? Is it different from taking pride in any other handicap? I suppose it is not worse than taking pride in having had a lot of lessons, or in being free of handicaps. Dan has an American mind. His ideology of naturalness with respect to human or artistic gifts is to be assessed against a continental ideology of cultivation (call it pride in lessons), attitudes made for one another. (*Pursuits*, p. 247)

There is an American culture which is merely a dream of the rejection of culture; it's also possible to find any culture and its rejection pretty funny. For—this is where I need to begin to turn this argument around, to find the joke—the Irene Dunne character is surely no less American than the Ralph Bellamy one, in mind or heart or style, and no less American than Robert Frost. You might look culturally unpossessed, to a European eye, if you had perfected the art of the throwaway—you might seem actually to be throwing culture away, or never to have had it.

And of course even supposed cultural poverty, if we accept the myth for a moment, has all kinds of advantages, as Cavell makes clear. It can't be bad to be still looking for the commencement of a culture. This is part of what Emerson means by regarding thinking as something still to be started in America, and a large part of what

Cavell calls, in his recent work, moral perfectionism. Culture is what we have, the way we are, inabilities and all; but it is also what we might have, the best we haven't yet known or thought. This is how Cavell interprets Emerson's and Nietzsche's "call for culture" (*Conditions*, p. 25), as an invitation to discovery, not to consumption (*Conditions*, p. 18). Similarly, although Emerson's audience "mostly" had no philosophical culture, this can't have been entirely a hindrance, since Emerson's "philosophizing was more advanced than Schelling's."[14] "Advanced" reminds us that "American intellectual time" is different.[15] Emerson writes "as if before the post-Kantian split between the German and the English traditions of philosophy— as if it need not have taken place."[16] It did take place, and is among the reasons why Anglo-American critics and philosophers had to rediscover Europe, and why Derrida so knocked them over. Cavell's implication is that if they had known how to read Emerson they wouldn't have been so surprised.

What is to be found in Emerson then is not some sort of raw American philosopher scarcely worthy of the name, and not someone without a history, but someone who writes a different philosophical history, finds his own relation to Descartes, say. This is what Cavell calls Emerson's "inheriting of philosophy . . . for America,"[17] and this is why it makes sense to speak of Emerson as "founding thinking for America—discovering America in thinking" (*Conditions*, p. 133). I find it oddly restrictive that Cavell should add "finding our own access to European thought," as if that were all finding or founding America was. He must mean, I take it, that Europe too, or a certain relation to Europe, is part of what America is, it isn't all home on the range. It is in this sense of course that Cavell himself is an American philosopher, and critic of culture.

There is a charming and generous instance of this movement in *Conditions Handsome and Unhandsome*, where Cavell reads Polonius' advice to Laertes as somehow doubling back out of cliché into an effective moral life. "To thine own self be true," the old fellow famously says: an instruction from the hackneyed heart of old Europe, which no European, I think, could flog into any semblance of urgency or even interest. It's not that Cavell doesn't see the lateness and the dreariness of the words, it's that he wants to give them a second chance, and he manages this without any effort at all. The phrase has become, he says,

> all but uncitable as its vulgarizing of good advice is vulgarly cited
> as good advice. But even here, or here concentrated, there is a

despairing and a hopeful way to respond: you can hear in it
redemptive words reduced to serving a server, used by a man lost
to experience, spoiled by his voice, or nonvoice; or you can hear
in the words the sound of the good heart making a momentary,
flickering way back, perhaps called back by the man's taking
leave of his son, reminded of his own youth, even into this cave
of convention. (*Conditions*, p. 18)

Lionel Trilling glosses the same words in *Sincerity and Authenticity*,
and the comparison is instructive, since it gives us another, more
pious American reading. Trilling sees Polonius as "not only senile but
small" in spirit, but then hears the famous phrase as escaping the
character and our understanding of him. Its "lucid moral lyricism"
stands free of any tangling interpretation, Polonius has "a moment
of self-transcendence, of grace and truth."[18] This is harder for the
European to take than Cavell's suggestion. There is a romance of the
self at work, as if truth to the self could only be appealing, as if there
could be no greater appeal; and to respond to this one needs to feel
the tug of several intertwined American mythologies. "With what a
promise the phrase sings in our ears!" Trilling says.[19] Polonius
transcends himself but only in the name of a Platonic idea of
selfhood. Cavell too is interested in self-reliance, in the particularities
of the changing self as it qualifies and questions the generalities of
culture, but his reading of the *Hamlet* passage requires only that we
resist our cynicism, believe there are good hearts in rotten kingdoms,
and human affections even in grovelling courtiers.

Thinking of Americans, Cavell evokes "our wild intelligence"
—"our capacity for bringing our wild intelligence to bear on just
about anything" (*Pursuits*, p. 10)—and also the "wild intelligence of
American popular culture" (*Conditions*, p. 13). "Wild" seems to
glance at another meaning of culture, i.e. not nature. It is a virtue of
American culture that it keeps (stifling, taming) culture at bay, and
there is something of this wildness in the reverse definition of the
American implied in Cavell's sudden, apparently casual naming
of the European in *Conditions Handsome and Unhandsome*. The
Emersonian vision ("the true romance which the world exists to
realize"[20]) is "an excruciating one for those who can call for it but
who cannot imagine themselves shaking their memories and starting
again; call them Europeans" (*Conditions*, xxi). Americans have more
(cultural) memories than they like to admit; and they don't keep
starting, they keep starting again, as if life itself was one of Cavell's
comedies of remarriage. But they do shake their memories, as

perhaps the Europeans can't; or they can imagine themselves shaking them, which may be enough to keep the romance of the world going.

It remains to make the identification lurking in Cavell's use of the words "wild" and "popular," to name the democratic cast of a culture which is always looking for its commencement, never (in theory) caught up in its monuments, and this is what Cavell does, with remarkable lucidity and completeness, in his essay "Naughty Orators." He is answering what he calls a general question about his interest in "film as such," but responds, seeming to forget his affection for Bergman, Buñuel, Resnais, Truffaut, Dreyer and countless other moviemakers, with a description of the ambitions of American culture. What's interesting is not only that this is an American response, a response of the American in Cavell, but that "America" is taken to be a sufficient response, a large enough answer to a question about the viewed world.

> I assume that movies have played a role in American culture different from their role in other cultures, and more particularly that this difference is a function of the absence in America of the European edifice of philosophy. And since I assume further that American culture has been no less ambitious, craved no less to think about itself, than the most ambitious European culture, I assume further still that the difference everyone recognizes as existing between American and European literature is a function of the brunt of thought that American literature, in its foundings in, for instance, Emerson and Whitman and Poe, had to bear in that absence of given philosophical founding and edifice, lifting the fragments that literature found, so to speak, handy and portable. Finally I assume that American film at its best participates in this Western cultural ambition of self-thought or self-invention that presents itself in the absence of the Western edifice of philosophy, so that on these shores film has the following peculiar economy: it has the space, and the cultural pressure, to satisfy the craving for thought, the ambition of a talented culture to examine itself publicly; but its public lacks the means to grasp this thought as such for the very reason that it naturally or historically lacks that edifice of philosophy within which to grasp it.[21]

There is much to question here, but much that is profoundly suggestive too, indeed much that helps to constitute an image of what a demanding cultural criticism might well be. For the moment, let me settle for trying to suggest something of the flesh Cavell character-

istically sees on these bones. The craving for thought is catered for
everywhere in American movies, although often by pretending, as
Cavell says, that there is nothing to think about. One of the most
interesting questions to be asked about American (and some other)
film is the one Cavell puts near the beginning of *The World Viewed*:
"how can it have been taken seriously without having assumed the
burden of seriousness?" (*World*, p. 15). But the genre Cavell calls the
comedy of remarriage does think quite openly about intricate
matters. It thinks fast, never lingers, but the sheer complexity of what
is being proposed often takes the breath away. In Cukor's *Adam's Rib*,
for example, a fond husband and wife, both lawyers, oppose each
other in court in a case concerning a woman who has shot and
wounded her unfaithful husband. The lawyers' marriage is indirectly
on trial, and survives, as many, perhaps most marriages wouldn't,
because both members of the couple have the wit and the grace and
the luck to make it survive. Both of them are right and both of them
are wrong about dozens of things. For instance: the wife is right to
suggest that justice and society side with men, and that even her
adorable husband is more of a chauvinist than he thinks he is; wrong
to send him up in the courtroom, to use mockery as an argument, as
if she didn't know and love him, and didn't respect him. The
husband is right to suggest that the law should not be confused with
sexual or any other politics, and that his wife is fighting a private
battle in public; wrong to think the law doesn't need such argument,
as if the personal had nothing to do with it, and as if marriages could
get along without testing.

The comedy of remarriage—Cavell discusses seven instances in
Pursuits of Happiness, mentions a few more—starts with a couple
who are already together, married or "married," who quarrel and
separate, and who get back together again, because they can't
actually imagine living with anyone else. "Put a bit more meta-
physically," as Cavell says,

> only those can genuinely marry who are already married. It is as
> though you know you are married when you come to see that you
> cannot divorce, that is, when you find that your lives simply will
> not disentangle. If your love is lucky, this knowledge will be
> greeted with laughter. (*Pursuits*, p. 127)

This is already pretty interesting as a view of marriage, but Cavell
also sees it, as the title of his book suggests, as an American allegory,
a story about "the fate of the democratic social bond" (*Pursuits*,
p. 193), or as he says elsewhere, "the thought that while America, or

any discovered world, can no longer ratify marriage, the achievement of true marriage might ratify something called America as a place in which to seek it" (*Themes*, p. 172). "This," Cavell adds, "is a state secret;" the state's joke, as one may say. It's not that society supports these marriages, or that the happy couples are (democratically) representative. On the contrary: Cavell sees Howard Hawks in particular, in *Bringing Up Baby* and *His Girl Friday*, as showing the pursuit of happiness, in spite of its place in the American pantheon of expectations, as "a standing test, or threat, to every social order" (*Pursuits*, p. 129). This is to see marriage, and America, as a cultural question rather than a legal or a political fact; a picture of possibility, a *pursuit*, a task for youths and children, of whatever age—"I see no need of it," Emerson says of aging[22]—or for anyone who believes that culture is consent and remembers that consent can be given and refused; and given and refused and given again.

Cavell has more recently been pursuing unhappiness, in a genre which he calls the melodrama of the unknown woman—*Blonde Venus*, *Stella Dallas*, *Showboat*, *Random Harvest*, *Now Voyager*, *Mildred Pierce*, *Gaslight*, *Letter from an Unknown Woman*—and which he "derives" from the comedy of remarriage, as one might derive a shadow from an object in the sun. He asks what happens when the conditions which make a love lucky are not met, and why this should so often be a question about women. This is a question not only for America, but in context it is an American question. I'm still not persuaded that the craving for thought is *well* catered for in these films, that it isn't more often flirted with and cheated, and I suspect it is the presence of particular prejudices which makes them work the way they do, rather than an overarching absence of philosophy. But I should like to be persuaded, because the question is important, and these films take it into otherwise neglected areas.

The importance of film and literature for Cavell is not that they are always "in the condition of philosophy," but that they display and require acts of imagination philosophy can't do without. The issue of ordinary language philosophy as Cavell understands it is: "one of placing the words and experiences with which philosophers have always begun in alignment with human beings in particular circumstances who can be imagined to be having those experiences and saying and meaning those words" (*Must We*, p. 270). I think the implication is who can be imagined not just anyhow but plausibly or coherently or sympathetically imagined, as if they were like us, however different they seem, and however brittle or fantastic their narrative context. The reach of the imagination itself in any particular case is of course a matter of circumstance as well as of individual gift or will; a matter of culture. The men and women in Cavell's remarriage comedies don't know how different they are from each other, don't even know how much difference matters. But they know how to imagine difference, and they know how to laugh, as Cavell says, "at the idea that men and women are different *and* at the idea that they are not" (*Pursuits*, p. 122, Cavell's italics). The achievement—the imagination and the laughter and the critic's and the viewers' responses to them—seems ordinary enough, but culture can take a long time to reach it; and they can lose it overnight.

Notes

1. Stanley Cavell, *Must We Mean What We Say?* (Cambridge: Cambridge University Press, 1976), p. 313. Further references to this book are taken up into the text, as *Must We*.

2. Stanley Cavell, *In Quest of the Ordinary* (Chicago: University of Chicago Press, 1988), p. 6. Further references to this book are taken up into the text, as *Quest*.

3. Stanley Cavell, *Pursuits of Happiness* (Cambridge, Mass: Harvard University Press, 1981), p. 13. Further references to this book are taken up into the text, as *Pursuits*.

4. Stanley Cavell, *Themes Out Of School* (San Francisco: North Point Press, 1984), p. 152. Further references to this book are taken up into the text, as *Themes*.

5. Stanley Cavell, *This New Yet Unapproachable America* (Albuquerque: Living Batch Press, 1989), p. 21. Further references to this book are taken up into the text, as *America*.

6. Stanley Cavell, *Disowning Knowledge* (Cambridge: Cambridge University Press, 1987), p. 3. Further references to this book are taken up into the test, as *Disowning*.

7. Stanley Cavell, *Conditions Handsome and Unhandsome* (Chicago: University of Chicago Press, 1990), p. 123. Further references to this book are taken up into the text, as *Conditions*.

8. Stanley Cavell, *The World Viewed* (Cambridge, Mass. Harvard University Press, 1974, 1979), p. 156. Further references to this book are taken up into the text, as *World*.

9. See also Stanley Cavell, "Ugly Duckling, Funny Butterfly: Bette Davis and *Now Voyager*" *Critical Inquiry* (Winter 1990), p. 218.

10. Henry James, *Hawthorne* (New York: Macmillan, 1967), pp. 55–56. The full list of absences is: "No State, in the European sense of the word, and indeed barely a specific national name. No sovereign, no court, no personal loyalty, no aristocracy, no church, no clergy, no army, no diplomatic service, no country gentlemen, no palaces, no castles, nor manors, nor old country-houses, nor parsonages, nor thatched cottages nor ivied ruins; no cathedrals,

nor abbeys, nor little Norman churches; no great Universities nor public schools—no Oxford, nor Eton, nor Harrow; no literature, no novels, no museums, no pictures, no political society, no sporting class–no Epsom nor Ascot!"

11. cf. *Themes*, p. 200: "You give up the effort to buy into intellectual currency and settle into the use of a kind of scrip, good for all the essentials the country store has to offer, but worth next to nothing on the international market. It is standing temptation for American literary theorists."

12. Stanley Cavell, "Psychoanalysis and Cinema: The Melodrama of the Unknown Woman" in Francoise Meltzer (ed) *The Trials of Psychoanalysis* (Chicago: University of Chicago Press, 1988), pp. 243–44.

13. cf. *Themes*, p. 18: "Emerson and Thoreau are the central founding thinkers of American culture, but . . . this knowledge, though possessed by shifting bands of individuals, is not culturally possessed."

14. Cavell, "Psychoanalysis and Cinema," p. 244.

15. Stanley Cavell, "Naughty Orators: Negation of Voice in *Gaslight*" in Sanford Budick and Wolfgang Iser (eds) *Languages of the Unsayable* (New York: Columbia University Press, 1989), p. 361.

16. Cavell, "Naughty Orators," pp. 361–362.

17. Cavell, "Naughty Orators," p. 345.

18. Lionel Trilling, *Sincerity and Authenticity* (Cambridge, Mass.: Harvard University Press, 1972), p. 3.

19. Trilling, *Sincerity and Authenticity*, p. 4.

20. Ralph Waldo Emerson, "Emerson" in *Essays* (New York: Macmillan, 1903), p. 373.

21. Cavell, "Naughty Orators," p. 372.

22. Emerson, "Circles" in *Essays*, p. 261.

6

The Person in Place
Lewis Mumford, Pioneer of Cultural Criticism

Clive Bush

We have to be more than wrights or authors merely; we must
organise our labour to orchestrate our thought. Hence it is that
each Renascence of Culture is the Story of a City.[1]

In his short fictional sketch, "Through the Abruzzi with Mattie and
Harriet," published in 1945 in *Europe without Baedeker: Sketches
Among the Ruins of Italy, Greece and England*, the American writer,
cultural historian and journalist Edmund Wilson describes his
American heroine driving through the mountain town of Aquila. For
her it is a relief from the war-torn and ruined Italy, the frustrating and
testy relations between the English and the Americans at a moment
of European imperial decline and American ascendency:

> The town looked as if it were constructed of hard planes of shade
> and light that made the most violent contrasts. Above white
> blinding side-walkless streets stood façades built of local stone
> that had a richness despite their austerity, with their juxtaposed
> orange and sepia, burnt sienna and café au lait, neutral liver and
> greenish grey, that made a double scale of colours, one darkened
> and cold, one glowing. The tall doorways were impressively
> hooded with heavy ornamental architraves, and the windows,
> well-proportioned and brown-shuttered, were capped with a
> variety of pediments that resembled, now triangular crests, now
> crowns with twin peaks, now coronets, and contributed to a
> standard of dignity that—surprisingly, she thought, in that
> mountain town—attained something akin to grandeur. It did
> seem queer and not quite comfortable to keep driving through a
> place of that size and never once to pass a corner drug-store or a

Woolworth's or an A. and P.; but Aquila had a unity and a harmony which made it seem all to have been built in one piece like those wasps' nests in the hills that had given her the creeps, but which here imposed themselves upon her and compelled her to respect and admire. This, she saw, was what architecture could do—not merely lay out a plan as at Washington, but dominate a whole city and actually provide the medium in which human beings lived.[2]

Wilson's fictional character views the city as a quasi-abstract cubist vision of overlapping planes, but simplified, perhaps more like a late painting by Georgia O'Keefe, into a suggested contradiction of colour relations seeking their own allegiances with shade and sunlight. It is haunted by another image, a more gothic and naturalistic image, of the wasps' nest: co-operating, yet threatening, natural and yet needing to be studied and complexly understood in spite of a first response which regards it as alienating and foreign.

It is that final image which gives a first clue to the tone and substance of the strengths of Lewis Mumford, the greatest cultural historian of twentieth-century America. Could the virtually useless word "organic" be re-deployed to find a new view of human activity in the world, in which the eroticized power structure of Christian morality and passivity undercut its doctrine of love, in which the narrowmindedness and abstractions of the specialized scientist made him or her useless in the life-world, in which the Darwinist cynicism of the capitalist gave the lie to claims of freedom of action, and in which the scientistic, materialist utopianism of the positivist Marxist excluded the real anxieties of real people in a common world? The scarcely post-Victorian gods of Mumford's youth seemed on the point of collapse. Christianity's view of nature as unredeemed, its repressive view of the person, its reluctance to view any aspect of the world in other than its own restrictive terms had been contested since Nietzsche. Its eternal life routines cynically only seemed to serve the suppression of the poor in spite of, and possibly because of, its injunction to charity. It failed the modern world's scientific advances, its scepticism, and its view of the relation between irrationality and power. Capitalism careened out of control, funding and sustaining the last imperialist acts of the European powers. Its alliance with technology fed two worlds wars, underpinned the multiply-deployed arms race, drained the world of vital resources, helped orchestrate the Cold War whose effects are now being reaped in the Balkanization of the old Soviet Empire and every large American city, and triumphed in the globalization of competition as ideology and practice, smashing all the traditional modifiers of its barbarity in its path: local and ethnic community, workers' organizations, and the hardly-won welfare state. Marxism's view of nature as scientifically approachable in endless combatative dialectical process was transferred by analogy to deadly historical facticity, and its view of the person, negotiable only as pawn in an abstract game of power, had failed to combat the "repressive desublimation" of the professionally managed consumer society.

Mumford, like Wilson, lived in a century of the failure of these ideologies. Whatever claims those with specialist and partial views of the world (city and town planners, professional Marxists, hopeful capitalists, art historians, historians of technology, literary critics) make on Mumford's works, no serious reading of Mumford is possible without understanding the sheer passion of his integrative vision. There are weaknesses, some serious, like the absence of a concrete sense of actual power struggles between finance capitalism and the workplace, and, to sceptical Europeans, the naiveté of both his Spenglerian rhetoric and his "can-do" American pronouncements.[3]

Like Edward Wilson, too, Mumford stood in the ruins of Europe. In addition he had lost a son in combat. In 1945 Mumford faced a moment of reassessment, during which time he produced one of his greatest and most unknown books, *The Condition of Man*.[4] Behind him he had at least two extraordinary works which had already brought him fame as one of America's most important thinkers.

Mumford had grown up in New York on the Upper West Side in a relatively homogeneous neighbourhood which was the "connecting tissue of the bourgeoisie" between the poverty of Amsterdam and Columbus Avenues and the rich who lived in the big apartments of Central Park West or "in the heavy, stone-encrusted mansions on Riverside Drive."[5] A shift down-town to College, to 14th Street brought him into contact with a very different New York to the upwardly mobile Russian and Jewish young who devoured baseball and books with equal avidity. Mumford was young enough to watch the Public Library and the Grand Central Terminal being built. He was fortunate enough, too, to go to a school which though dedicated to science and the mechanical arts also had a good English department. He was encouraged to write a play by, and first heard the name of Bernard Shaw from, Thomas Bates, "a rapt, brooding young man with a freckled face and a huge mop of carroty hair," but he remembered also the man who taught him forging: "a German blacksmith of the old school . . . his iron roses and scrolly leaves were our envy."[6] Then there was City College just as it opened with a mere 500 students, a moment as fleeting as it was precious with its committed and off-beat teachers before it succumbed to the usual gigantism: a process now killing off the best in English education.[7] In this rare and ideal city environment, Mumford got himself an education, between heady discussions about Spinoza and the streets themselves, where in addition to boyhood explorations he also knocked about as a reporter.

Then it was London and England. But the experience was dominated by one man. As Emerson went to England in 1833 to meet Wordsworth, Coleridge and Carlyle, with only Carlyle proving satisfactory, so Mumford, too, found his Sartor Resartus in the figure of Patrick Geddes, a loved and distrusted mentor whose fiery intellectual life and multiple passions were to prove a profound and decisive influence. Geddes was a maverick Scottish intellectual whose work grew out of the socio-biology debate of the late nineteenth century. Geddes had tried to put values of abundance, creativity, and appropriateness into a revised *conception* of nature. A modern ecological theorist Murray Bookchin has said: "Either we succumb to a heavy-handed dualism that harshly separates the natural from the social, or we fall into a crude reductionism that dissolves the one into the other." The problem is well stated though, as with Geddes, the relations between nature, mental activity, political life, and creative interaction is asserted via homeostatic analogies, rather than analysed.[8]

Greta Jones has given a concise description of Geddes' position and role in the late nineteenth-century socio-biology debate. He attacked the individualism and the calculus of self-interest of classical political economy, and tried to use biological models to replace the "iron law of competition" with the "golden rule of sympathy and synergy." Economics for Geddes became a function of a correct understanding of biology (he had been student of Huxley), and from this basis he defended the role of social reform and state intervention. The agencies were mainly voluntaristic except for urban planning. Jones remarks:

> The cure of urban problems he saw in terms of the treatment of an organic disease which if left untouched would be fatal to the organism itself. In his description of the function of social science Geddes used medical metaphors. Sociologists were like doctors attempting to cure certain ills which had arisen in the body politic.[9]

It leaves the question of agency untouched, of course, and from 1933 onwards homeostasis was to become the watchword of the reactionary sociologist.[10] Geddes himself opposed organized labour unions.

For Mumford, however, it was Geddes' charismatic teaching which encouraged not only the particular direction of Mumford's intellectual gaze but also its substance. He was also to contrive to make Geddes' notion of homeostasis more flexible, more open-ended, less politically obtuse. Commenting on Geddes' *Cities in Evolution*, Mumford declared that:

> Using his own self-education, through study and practical activity as a basis, Geddes sketched out the background the citizen needed in history and geography and travel, in economics, politics, architecture, sociology. Thus at that juncture in urban history, *Cities in Evolution* performed the most valuable service that any single book could have performed: it taught the reader, in simple terms, how to look at cities and how to evaluate their development. See for yourself; understand for yourself; act on your own initiative on behalf of the community of which you are a part. That summarized Geddes' message. From the moment I gathered the import of Geddes' words, I began walking through the streets of New York and planning excursions into its hinterland with a new purpose: looking into its past, understanding its present, replanning its future became indissoluble parts of a single process, a task for all citizens, not merely for professionals.[11]

The city became the great space of a historical drama of dynamic and inert processes. It needed some knowledge of most of the human and physical sciences in combination to understand it. In a sense Mumford fought against the tide: against the German Ph.D. driven professionalization of the American graduate programmes and against the untrammelled and minimally imaginative and minimally intelligent growth of the vast American conurbations, with the car-obsessed suburbanite creating rural devastation and urban chaos equally. It was against the mean streets of the city as described by a Dos Passos, an Upton Sinclair, a Sinclair Lewis, or a Theodore Dreiser that Mumford wrote with urgency, and in a very nineteenth-century American mode he looked to the European past to ransack the history of art, architecture, technology, literature and culture in his search for solutions.

Like Melville (and Mumford's book on Melville for its insight and energy is worth most of the tonnage of academic commentary since) Mumford pitted his wits against the "skilled destroyer." While lamenting Melville's refusal to take up the more liberating Whitmanian poetic, Mumford singles out a moment from the still-neglected *Clarel*:

> . . . Arts are tools:
> But tools, they say, are to the strong:
> Is Satan weak? Weak is the wrong?
> No blessed augury overrules:
> You arts advance in faith's decay:
> You are but drilling the new Hun
> Whose growl even now can some dismay;
> Vindictive in his heart of hearts,
> He schools him in your mines and marts—
> A skilled destroyer.

Mumford's comments stand for themselves:

> The ruthless sweeping away of human values, the sacrifice of the worker's welfare to profits, and of general well-being to a bleak efficiency, and, finally, the sweeping away of all the decencies of life in a bestial internecine warfare, aggravated by all the improvements in the arts: Melville saw all these things and perceived that a good part of the routine of education, work and patriotism could be called, not least in the "advanced" countries, a drilling of the Hun.[12]

It was the theme he was to develop in his most brilliant work, *Technics and Civilisation* of 1934. Here tactically Mumford used one of Marx's greatest insights, though mentioning him only briefly. Marx had said that: "Technology reveals the active relation of man to nature, the direct process of the production of his life, and thereby it also lays bare the process of the production of the social relations of his life, and of the mental conceptions that flow from those relations."[13] Mumford took up the challenge of describing that process in the same spirit: "In back of the development of tools and machines lies the attempt to modify the environment in such a way as to fortify and sustain the human organism . . . "[14] And to a degree Mumford was able to deploy and shift his key, but treacherous terms, of "environment" and "organism" towards a radical rethinking of technics and the city. He seized on the multiply-phased and open-ended, rather than on the deterministic and abstractly materialistic aspects of the Darwinian revolution to make an analysis of the machine and the city which reintroduced human agency, will, intelligence, subjectivity, choice and a sense of co-operative design in the service of community against capitalist *laissez-faire* and the abstract materialist fatalism of the new breed of Stalinist Marxists.

With clear debts to Max Weber he looked at the psychological effect of the mechanization of time and used his ecological image of the diversely functioning organism to satirize the destructive gods of the twentieth century: "The power that was science and the power that was money were, in final analysis, the same kind of power: the power of abstraction, measurement, quantification."[15] He charted with merciless accuracy Eliot's "dissociation of sensibility" following the scientific revolution, but with no sense of the poet's moping melancholy, quietist regret or nostalgia for some wisdom-laden, authoritative Episcopalian clerisy that never was. The achievement was the framing of the subject matter and the way of dealing with it. Historians notoriously write about the past without mentioning technology. Psychologists think the past reveals itself in unconscious dream. Sociologists look at the human condition in an eternal moment of structuralist revelation. Mumford was able to emphasize finite loss and change, investigate the nuances of psychological behaviour, look at pattern and structure as slow changing persistences in the apparently new, and write history by deploying all three at once.

Mumford's was a battle for ways of thinking. Mental processes were intertwined with the whole productive process. To cite but one example: the production of glass. Mumford describes the multiple effects from the transformation of indoor life, the development of the study of botany, the length of the working day, revolutions in astronomy, microscopy, chemistry, to more intangible effects like the very ability, visually, to put the world in a frame:

> The most powerful prince of the seventeenth century created a vast hall of mirrors, and the mirror spread from one room to another in the bourgeois household. Self-consciousness, introspection, mirror-conversation developed with the new object itself: this preoccupation with one's image comes at the threshold of the mature personality when young Narcissus gazes long and deep into the fact of the pool—and the sense of the separate personality, a perception of the objective attributes of one's identity, grows out of this communion.[16]

It is that kind of integrative thinking—the key question "what are all the effects"—that Mumford urges at the end of this work in his concept of the "dynamic equilibrium." It is what today we would call "holistic" thinking: increasingly important in developing ecological awareness. Politically, it sets itself against *laissez-faire*, against untrammelled free-market economics, against the progress neurosis, and against those imbalances of useless commodity production which now, in increasingly right-wing states in the Far East and the Pacific basin, tout a notion of "ordered society" which serves the paradise of endless productive growth. Their representatives these days appear on television to inform us that the "European" enlightenment notions of liberty are simply inefficient in a well-run state.[17]

It was in the search for models of a different type of "growth" that Mumford began researching the history of the city. *The Culture of Cities* came out in 1938 just years before the cities of Europe and Japan were to be devastated by the most terrible technological war in human history. The book was at once a great critique of and paean to the city in history. The city is seen integrated fundamentally with the countryside while its multiple periods and modes of life save it from single vision and the autocrat's gaze. The city is partially a fact of nature, escaping conscious will to a degree, but also modelled by human directiveness both consciously and unconsciously. It is a codification and museum of the collective mind. It is a stubborn and concrete physical fact of human habitation. It is disruptive and orderly. It concentrates power and intelligence for good and ill. The intellectual bases for the study were from every shade of historical political opinion and study: from the Catholic right-wing Le Play in France to the anarchist Kropotkin, to the English town and country planners with their roots in Owenite utopianism and Quaker factory building, and finally to Marx himself. Side-stepping the Victorian legacies of neo-medievalists like the gothic writers and William Morris, Mumford, like Henry Adams before him, looked at the staggering achievements of the eleventh, twelfth and thirteenth centuries. Mumford provided photographs of Verona, Dinkelsbühl, Rothenburg-an-der-Tauber and Segovia so that the reader could use the visual information as part of the text. Woven into the arguments are economic statistics, agricultural changes, the rise of early capitalist practices, and of course technological change.

Nor did Mumford, with his belief that leisure was the one thing in life that gave real dignity to human beings, neglect customs, games and the social rituals of the city. Like Henry Adams before him, there is always the implicit challenge to think through the contrast in terms of value with modernity. One would have wished Mumford another ten years of a long life for what would have been his inevitable attack on "postmodernism." We are invited to contrast the medieval iron-mongers sign with any modern commercial image or assess the relative values of the occasional extravagances of celebrations for a saint or emperor "with the permanent order of illumination used in Broadway or Piccadilly Circus."[18]

In spite of a Spenglerian tone, Mumford never sees inevitable decline in transition. The Swiss and Dutch are praised for success-fully negotiating the movement from the medieval world to modernity: "the problem of the federal unification of the corporate towns and the countryside was actually solved without undermining the political integrity of the urban unit . . . That the Swiss achieved unity without despotism or submission to the arbitrary forms of centralized authority shows that the feat was technically possible . . ."[19]

The baroque order is similarly scrutinized for its ambivalences: the delight in design and grand open planning together with its centralized and dictatorial controls, and the energetic rise of the bourgeoisie and their shopping street together with its predatory displays and confusion of wheeled traffic. Nor is humour lacking from Mumford's probing generalizations: "Privacy, mirrors, heated rooms; these things transformed full-blown love-making from a seasonal to a year-round occupation: another example of baroque regularity."[20] The Victorians are later criticized for doing it under the blankets even when they could afford to heat rooms, "thus reducing sexual intercourse to purely tactile terms."[21] The British notoriously still don't heat their bedrooms.

But in 1938 there is generally a more sombre mood. Gigantism precedes technological change. Megalopolis is simply worsened by technological advance. Mumford does not ignore the horrors of Dickens' Coketown. Huge transport and water schemes simply make the problem worse: "Except for the Inner Circle Railway in London, metropolitan subway lines have been almost uniformly built so as to throw an increasing load of passengers into the central district."[22] The costs are fantastic: "the double-decking of Michigan Avenue [in Chicago] cost sixteen million dollars a mile. These terrific costs put a serious curb on the wide reconstruction of the metropolis."[23] Good things do, however, survive. Mumford takes Spengler to task for the serious contradiction between his "romantic belief in the predatory carnivore and the historic facts of rural domestication and urbane culture."[24]

As he nears the end of his work Mumford, influenced by the American regionalists, and having traced the progress of some resistances to untrammelled growth, finds posts of the good. Paxton of Crystal Palace shows the promise of iron and glass, the planners of parks, Downing, Olmsted, Ruskin, have their place in the "re-ruralisation" of the city. But Mumford struggles to maintain these moments of resistance. Long before Virilio wrote short books with one idea, Mumford identified the city as a place of collective hysteria, and as a network of global cosmopolitan intersections which destroyed all sense of *local* space. The imperialist buildings, whether in Washington or Berlin, exhibit a growing war-bureaucracy exhibiting its power in "wide avenues, endless vistas of useless columns, and huge stadiums fit for martial exercises and games . . . children assembled for the singing of vainglorious national anthems, the crowds marching in parades, or the mob that assembles in the public square to behold, at a discreet distance, the leader of the state . . . A million scattered, bewildered individuals whom the rulers cajole, bully, and terrorize into a state of unity."[25] The obvious historical relevance of this statement in 1938 should not obscure the fact that Mumford clearly felt that the structural conditions were the same in London and New York as well as in Berlin.

The moment of *The City in History* was a black one, and along with it, a year later, came a powerful direct attack on fascism in *Men Must Act*. Those who accuse Mumford of political naiveté need to read moments like this:

> Having aided fascism in order to secure protection against 'bolshevism', the British Tories apparently believed that they could appease the irrational aims of the fascist states at the immediate expense of the smaller democracies in Europe and at the ultimate expense of Soviet Russia. Since their interest in democracy is decidedly Pickwickian, such a policy seemed to them, apparently, to involve no serious sacrifice or danger. This, I take it, is the origin of the non-intervention treachery with respect to Spain: likewise it accounts for the facile betrayal of Czechoslovakia.[26]

Already way ahead of American opinion, Mumford rounded on American isolationism in terms of a world fight for democracy: a democracy to which the British Tories gave lip-service, which Americans thought they already had, and which they thought could be preserved passively. After the war Mumford was the among the first to realize the qualitative change in the human world created by nuclear weapons and, from 1945 onwards, was a tireless activist for disarmament.

At a moment of defeat he turned his attention to a literal and figurative rebuilding. At the very end of *The Culture of Cities* he had outlined what he called "the social basis of the new social order." He began by rescuing Ebenezer Howard's work from eulogist and detractor alike and became a fierce advocate of forward intelligent urban planning. The Garden City movement was more than a thread in Mumford's thinking, it brought together many of the disciplines which he had argued must be kept together in a practical intellectual life.

The movement itself simply cannot be considered only in terms of its achieved results: most famously in England, Letchworth and Welwyn Garden City, and its successful, though mutated offshoots in the Garden Suburb—notably Unwin and Parker's Hampstead; and unsuccessfully and most infamously perhaps in that high cyclone fence "around a Radiant Garden City project adjoining Johns Hospital in Baltimore," caustically analyzed by Jane Jacobs in her tirade against the entire Garden City movement in her famous book, *The Death and Life of Great American Cities* of 1961.[27] In the last instance, and by much more than irony, Garden becomes Turf in the daily violence of inner city stress.

It is in Lewis Mumford's correspondence with Englishman, Frederick J. Osborn, disciple of Howard and practical Labourite activist who masterminded the development of Welwyn Garden City, that the tumultuous world of postwar planning is revealed by two highly intelligent men deeply involved in reconstruction. The Garden City movement and its problems, from technology to ideology, lay at the heart of their friendship, their agreements and differences. By way of refocusing Mumford's career after 1945, aspects of their correspondence will be used to illuminate the cultural nexus of problems they shared and discussed, problems which went far beyond architecture and the history of the city into Atlantic politics, literature and technological creep.

Perhaps one thing their correspondence showed was that the success or failure cannot be laid at the door of an idea alone. Popular response to the complex idea of the Garden City is itself to be explained. Hoodlums do not multiply because of a bourgeois pastoral idea, nor does virtue spring from the sentimentalized urban sidewalks of Jane Jacobs' yuppified Greenwich Village.

The Garden City is and was many things: a rare, actual localized success of city planning, a general failure as practice. But that failure was linked to deeper failures of capitalist economics and the complexities of the distribution of power from national to local levels. For the Garden City is not only a complex historical and ideological way of thinking about the world, but a matrix of contradictions which relate to social class, cultural history, economics, design, theories of agency in history, and even belief.

In a lecture given to the Town Planning Institute at Caxton Hall in April 1945, Osborn described the foreground to his own heritage via Howard. He cites a quotation from Ruskin which Howard had used in the 1902 edition of his book. Ruskin had (pace Jane Jacobs) a view of the city which combined the "clean and busy street" and the "open country without."[28]

Acknowledging that he is simplifying the prehistory, Osborn cites what he calls "the unique combination of proposals" that Howard employed from a diversity of sources. At Howard's door Osborn laid the innovations of functional zoning, prescriptions of maximum density, the planning of whole towns through a leasehold system, the neighbourhood unit, landscape as an integral part of urban design, consumers' co-operative ventures (at the time conceived somewhat in opposition to both state socialism and free-market economics) and co-operative agricultural production based on local markets. Osborn continued: "What is more important, he steered his way with amazingly shrewd judgement between ideological extremes, detecting where social control was essential and where individual freedom could be left free play." It was, of course, the imbalance between these factors that caused the failure of these schemes, aided and abetted by technological development. As Osborn explained: "What did the internal combustion engine and the electric motor do but vastly enlarge the noble company of carriage folk."[29]

Like Howard, Osborn was to insist on the house and garden ideal, and a major disagreement was to occur between Mumford. and Osborn over this point. Osborn ended his lecture by attacking the other urban ideal of his own time, modern, well-designed apartment buildings, which in his view were the result of an unholy alliance between the high density party—that is the speculative builder—the agricultural lobby and rural preservationists.

> Vienna became the beacon and tremendous efforts were made to evade the problem of land values and dispersal by substituting for the ideal of the private family house, the quite illusory ideal of a commercialised life with a luxurious apparatus of creches, nursery schools, common laundries, restaurants, work rooms, club rooms and whatnot.[30]

One might imagine that Vienna's Karl Marx Plaza would not have appealed to the liberal democratic Osborn. But there are more

complex aspects of this nexus of judgements, as his later account of
the Webbs indicates:

> The Webbs, as leaders of the Society, took trouble to push
> promising youngsters into positions where they would acquire
> influence. Without any resentment I fancy they had a touch of
> unconscious snobbery. But perhaps they were right to pick out
> men with a classy air in dress, accent and self-assurance. I was
> dowdy, spotty-faced, and pathologically diffident—obviously
> lower middle class and council school.[31]

Looking back on a rich career there was no obvious resentment, but
all his life Osborn inveighed against the bohemian set as anti-family,
anti-family house and garden, pro-flat-living, and out of touch with
the people. Mumford had rather a soft spot for bohemians and for
flat living.

Howard was for Osborn what Patrick Geddes had been for
Mumford. A similarly energetic personal advocacy, a utopian and
visionary streak, a distrust of organized labour and organized government, had characterized Mumford's mentor Geddes also. It made
Howard, in fact, a natural ally of Americans. Co-operative utopian
experiments have studded American social history from Shakers,
Owenites, Rappites and Mormons to the hippy communes of the
1960s and beyond, and there was a strong utopian strain in
Mumford's own make-up. From the seventeenth century the idea
of "The City on the Hill" was a profound ideological strand of
American social consciousness, persisting alongside the more visible
Jeffersonian and individualist pastoral ideal whose effects are still felt
in tax distribution systems which operate largely to the disadvantage
of the actual city down to the present time.

True to the utopian tradition, the Garden City was to be a place
of brotherhood and sisterhood in which science, art, culture and
religion were to flourish. A somewhat nebulous pantheistic spiritual-
ism characterized the country for the distinctly urbanized Howard.
Politically the town was to be an estate "legally invested in the names
of four gentlemen of responsible position and undoubted probity and
honour."[32] The freehold was to be inalienable and increments earned
were to be for the benefit of all. Not nationalization but urban
regionalization was to be the basis of the British quasi-socialist
approach to town planning. The economic arrangements were
pilloried by Shaw who said that if successful they would be successfully taken over, which is precisely what happened. The privatization
of Letchworth, in fact, was stopped only by act of Parliament, and

Welwyn itself was "successfully" sold off.[33] But as Beevers points out, Shaw did invest his money in both schemes because of his belief in socialism, thereby "revealing his confusion of mind."[34] I think that judgement is a little harsh. While few people ever spend their money rationally, the issues are far larger than the less-than-complex personality of Shaw, and as unsolvable as they still cry out to be solved. Only national or federal legislation can regulate what are essentially corporate economics. Co-operation at the local level could only be safeguarded by strong policies at the centre.

What Jane Jacobs did not realize was that Garden Cities were initially not a pastoral brainstorm of a patrician grass-and-trees urban designer, but a serious commonsense attempt at a socialist economics which was in fact so successful in economic practice that capitalists could not wait to take over the minimal, though successful results.

Howard did not like actual American cities, complaining of the monotony of the gridiron plan. His overall designs for country-wide planning of new towns about a common city reflected early American hopes for democracy. He named one of them Philadelphia and another Concord. And quotations from two great nineteenth-century American writers give less tangible clues to strands of thought which weave through both Osborn's and Mumford's writings. The first is from Hawthorne's *The Scarlet Letter*: "Human nature will not flourish, any more than a potato, if it be planted and re-planted for too long a series of generations in the same worn-out soil." And the second is from Emerson's "Essay on Art": "Beauty must come back to the useful arts, and the distinction between the fine and useful arts be forgotten."[35]

Both quotations, as Howard uses them, invite double-edged responses, and they point to major problems in different ways in the work of Osborn and Mumford. The first is how the "organic metaphor" works for a description of the human condition, especially when it relates simultaneously to a concept of human nature, a description of historical process, and a theory of design. For Hawthorne's story included a very dark vision of human history. The new town in his classic novel is a site where the first priorities are jails and cemeteries. Howard's use of the quotation out of context might justify new towns, but could not promote urban renewal to the same extent. Emerson's statement fruitfully attacks the association of art with aristocracy and would support the ideology of the arts and crafts movements, but it offers no defense against utilitarian claims on art such as are always being offered in typical attacks on non-useful art such as painting, literature, drama, sculpture, ballet, film and so on, and has no measure for the renewal of those values which cannot be precisely evaluated according to market or utilitarian principles.

If the correspondence between Osborn and Mumford did not exist it would have had to be invented. English, Scottish and American thought on utopias, city-planning, democratic values, political ideology at the personal and national levels had been entwined for two and more centuries. The debates reached a particular intensity in the last two decades of the nineteenth century. In the early years of the twentieth century, for example, while working on a farm near Milan, Michigan, the American poet Kenneth Rexroth, then scarcely out of his teens, recalled how he worked for the proprietors, "two old maids in their late sixties," with a "massive granite grandmother" of ninety-two. The three redoubtable Michigan women gave him the scientific romances of H.G. Wells to read alongside Labour Party pamphlets, speeches by Debs, tracts by Charles Kingsley, and Upton Sinclair's anthology of the literature of social protest from the Egyptians to Max Eastman called *The Cry for Justice*.[36] It is an indication of the times from which both Osborn and Mumford sprung.

In a sense both Osborn and Mumford admired what each thought the other lacked. Mumford admired Osborn's pragmatic, activist hands-on political activity. Osborn admired Mumford's intellectual range, the productivity of his writing, and his profound historical knowledge. Yet within shared interests and values their differences are as marked as their similarities.

They had met at Welwyn Garden City in 1932, but the correspondence did not begin until 1938 after Osborn had read *The Culture of Cities* of 1938. By the time he met Mumford, Osborn had been active as an English socialist, had been influenced by the ideas of Bellamy and Morris, educated himself through a mutual book-buying club, worked for the Independent Labour Party and the Fabians, and in 1912 had become the secretary and manager of the Howard Cottage Society at Letchworth on £150 a year. He had been a conscientious objector in the war that followed, hiding at one point in the British Museum library on Edgar Allan Poe's principle in the "Purloined Letter" that if you were obviously seen nobody would notice you.

Osborn published his most important work, *Green Belt Cities: The British Contribution* in 1946, and from then on kept up a steady stream of articles and lectures in relation to his work at the Town and Country Planning Association, some of which will be used here to provide one of the contexts for his correspondence with Mumford.

Mumford, on the other hand, had only just started to become

relatively famous with *The Culture of Cities*. He had been born early enough to enjoy that mild respite from Victorian capitalist disaster known as the progressive era. It matched the triumph of English political liberalism with Lloyd George. As with Osborn, and indeed Rexroth, it was a generation that remembered the naturalist and socialist writers of the generation of the 1890s, from Edward Carpenter to H.G. Wells. Mumford, too, lacked a formal education, and in 1918 he noted that:

> It is impossible to examine the biographies of the leaders in Victorian science and art without coming to the conclusion that they owed some part of their vigor and originality to the fact that they escaped a formal education. Tyndall, Mill, Spencer, Dalton, Faraday, Dickens, and Shaw were none of them university bred. For that matter neither were Plato or Aristotle![37]

Mumford had lived in a Greenwich Village very different from Jane Jacobs', that is, in the years of its real fame between 1900 and 1930. As Mumford said:

> . . . that was a neighborhood where one knew people by sight or could guess at them easily: Max Eastman, Michael Gold, Hugo Gellert, Walter Pach, John Sloan, Kenneth Hayes Miller, Thomas Hart Benton, Art Young, Clarence Britten, to say nothing of the swarms of writers, from Harold Stearns to Llewelyn Powys or Conrad Aiken.[38]

The experience was then very different from that of Osborn's in London. It gave Mumford a sense of how valuable a good, historical, slightly run-down area of a city could be in the way of creative community. For Mumford it was a time when the neighbourhood that Melville "skirted, when he walked to his customs' shed on Little Gansvoort Street," was still intact, and Albert Pinkham Ryder still prowled through at night. It was this experience that would distinguish him from Osborn: "My almost comic quarrel with F.J. Osborn over desirable urban residential densities rests on our different evaluations of urban space and human contiguity. Like the classic differences between Sergeant Cuff and the gardener in *The Moonstone*."[39] Nonetheless they shared in common that Wellsian energy, testing the available theories at a time when the world still looked as though it might be put right if you came up with a good idea: "one day a Spinozaist, now an anarchist, now a socialist, now a Ruskinian Tory, now a Shavian, now a Platonist, now a disciple of Samuel Butler, a Whitmanite, a Geddesian, or a Tolstoian."[40]

But in America these possibilities seemed to end abruptly in 1919, and in 1930 Mumford looked back on the period of "normalcy" which was one of the legacies of the First World War:

> There were oil wells to be stolen, stocks to be promoted, graft to be picked up, flimsy houses to be built, motor roads to be laid, vacuum cleaners and radio sets to be sold . . . I lived in a world committed to war, a world subjected to intermittent tremors of animosity and hatred . . . a world where the principal resources of modern industry—petroleum, rubber, lac, coal, steel, vanadium—were unequally parcelled out . . . This was a world where every important activity was on an international scale except international organization for political control.[41]

There is a political urgency in Mumford's writings and a sense of tragedy which is entirely absent from Osborn's. Mumford had written eight books by 1938 and these were immediately followed by *Men Must Act* (1939). There are critics of Mumford's moral fervour. But they are in my opinion mostly people who seem to have conferred on themselves oracular insights into what the masses want.[42] Mumford's strongest point is one with which he ends *Men Must Act*:

> We shall not achieve the necessary élan merely by comfortably holding out the prospect of a few extra hours to dawdle in or a few extra comforts to ease the busy grind, as democracy's highest reward. No one was ever moved to a mighty effort by the prospect of a suburban cottage and a safe job. There must be equity and justice in our economic life, not simply because an economy of abundance makes this easy; but because equity and justice are conditions for our spiritual health, whilst greed, class-exploitation, and callousness are signs of deep-seated social ailments. And so in every department of our life: unless the active *will-to-create* be present, we shall achieve neither security nor a society that is worth the effort needed to safeguard it.[43]

Mumford was always primarily concerned with the creative as the measure of work and the possibility of consciousness and meaning in a world which seemed to lack both. In that sense he is close to Marx. Alan Trachtenberg once cited Huizinga's idea of a "psychological terrorism," which bans "summarily" all terms like meaning and consciousness.[44] For Osborn the Garden City was a goal, for Mumford it was a only a prelude to wider and more multiple activity.

It is true nonetheless that the question of agency, however, is not always confronted in Mumford. Jean-Paul Sartre once commented, in the context of praising Mumford's *Technics and Civilization*.

> In his excellent book Mumford says: "Since the steam engine *requires* constant care on the part of the stoker and engineer, steam power was more efficient in large units than in small ones . . . Thus steam power *fostered* the *tendency* toward large industrial plants." . . . I do not wish to question the soundness of these observations, but simply to note the strange language— language which has been ours since Marx and which we have no difficulty in understanding—in which a single proposition links finality to necessity so indissolubly that it is impossible to tell any longer whether it is man or machine which is a practical project. We all feel that his language is correct, but also realise that we cannot explain or justify this feeling.[45]

Here Sartre gets to the heart of the weaknesses of Mumford's organicism. *Requires* obliterates the freedom and necessity issue and the question of agency; *fostered* buries the analysis of causality in some sort of strange, organic parenting; *tendency* invokes a kind of Aristotelian teleology which makes history into an absolutely fatalistic narrative. The tendency of cities is to grow in certain ways bearing marks of their origins against whose traces contemporary values can be measured. The thesis is basically an organicist and a moral-psychological one.

Yet what Sartre did not take into account was Mumford's audience. To anyone coming from a European intellectual tradition and reading Mumford for the first time, unacknowledged parallels with certain moments of Marx's writings on technology and industrial urban chaos are striking. His view of technology as exhibiting all the relations of human beings to nature and to themselves is a case in point. A letter to Osborn of 19 September 1945 gives some clues. Mumford writes:

> As to the tactical matter, of achieving socialism without using the word itself or waving all the banners that go with it, I am entirely at one with you. In any particular situation I am not merely ready to go as far as a socialist or a communist, but possibly a little further; but I do my level best to avoid prejudging the issue by using the current catchwords: the only time I lapsed from this, as far as I can remember, was when I used the term "basic communism" in *Technics and Civilisation*; and there I was more intrigued by the reference to basic English than to Communism

and I promptly redefined the word in a fashion to withdraw the allegiance of any communist.

Mumford further commented that Geddes used to say that the best thing to do would be to imitate the Catholic Church "keep one's purpose definitely in view but never announce it beforehand or boast of it afterwards."[46] Such Benjamin Franklin-style comments do not rebut Sartre's criticism, but they explain the renunciation of an explicit socialist language.

Nonetheless Mumford mentioned Marx thirteen times in *Technics and Civilization*, seven times favourably with the odd correction, and six times unfavourably where he rejected the historical predictions and replaces dialectical process with psychological evolutionism and a *diabolus ex machina* called "machine mentality." In fact Osborn and Mumford had common socialist reading: Marx, Henry George, Wells, the Fabians, Bellamy, and so on. A late exchange in their letters about Marxism showed them both influenced by Marx to the extent that they emphasized real dominance-submission patterns in history which could not be transcended by moralism, stoicism or a generalized sense of tragedy.[47]

In the 1950s Mumford expanded *The Culture of Cities* (1938) into *The City in History* where he emphasized the importance of the citadel-shrine from Uruk to Harappa. The dominance-submission pattern, evolving with kingship and concretized in the urban nucleus, is a theme which runs through his entire history of the city. Against Proudhon, for example, he argued that property was originally held by kings.[48] By the time of the medieval town, power shifts from a small number of protected producers to rival princes and he continues:

> In turn, the attitude of protection and submission, which ideally characterized superior and inferior under the feudal regime gave way to hostile expropriation on one side, with seething revolt and counter-challenge on the other: in short the class war, in which no quarter was expected or given—precisely in the classic sense that would have gratified Karl Marx.[49]

By the time megalopolis is reached, the semi-teleological argument of protection-submission patterns is binary rather than dialectical, fatalistic rather than synthetic, story-bound rather than interactive through overlapping fields, and shifts increasingly to the mono-causal, Spenglerian thesis that "mechanical processes had supplanted organic processes." Communism and capitalism were indistinguishable in their common goal of expansion, productive wastage, equally blinded by the fetishism of products, equally devoted in reality to protectionism, gigantism, and equally in thrall to an overvaluation of science and technology. Like the return of the repressed unconscious, the citadel returns in the form of a monopoly of power and knowledge, and the skyscraper, the material form of the abstractions of high finance, is its imperial locus: a mechanized, human filing cabinet whose sole purpose is extending its own height and bureaucracy.[50]

Orthodox historians would throw their hands up in horror at the implications of this narrative of the conspiratorial return of ancient powers in new guises. Yet Mumford is not, as some have argued, some kind of born-again Savonarola, for his moral perspectives do invoke the long-range past imaginatively and heuristically in a world of publicity and of short-term academic memory. The range of historical evidence again and again points to distinctions: the baroque forms of the grand design are better at Amsterdam than at Versailles. In *The Pentagon of Power*, Mumford uses his racy descriptions of the return of the gods of death and the machine from the Egyptians to Galileo to telling effect. Mumford never loses sight of the fact that our own moment in history has no special privilege in the trusteeship of a world which will survive us. His organic processes at best remain hypothetical analogies of historical investigation not reasons of history, with all the treachery and creativeness of possible exposition that that implies. At best the ecological models of birth, growth and death avoid the capitalists' social-Darwinist legitimations and the historical fantasies of positivist Marxism, at worst they evade the precise detail of historical clashes of power and over-estimate the individual's capacity to create change out of personal confidence.

Mumford in fact bears witness to the changes of his own lifetime, the professionalization of the middle classes with its careers and certifications, national examination systems, the rise of mass media, the accelerated pace of industrialization, spurred by a century of wars, the creeping cancer of the internal combustion engine and urban sprawl, the rapid expansion of global metropolitan living, the shrinking of physical personal space in a world where cemeteries are bulldozed for office blocks, the deteriorations of water supply, public transport systems, and the control by Kremlin or Pentagon of an integrated war and business economy to safeguard global power resources with a capacity for technological destruction which knows no ideology.

Mumford, in his later phase is as "pessimistic" as Henry Adams whom he quotes in *The City in History*: "Law . . . would disappear as theory or a priori principle and give place to force. Morality would become police. Explosives would reach cosmic violence. Disintegration would overcome integration."[51] If the "eighteenth-century" Henry Adams hurled the world of John Adams, Locke, the Encyclopaedists, Jefferson, Washington, Voltaire, Pascal and Patrick Henry at the Trusts and early twentieth-century capitalism, so Mumford hurls the world of late nineteenth-century idealism, of Emerson, Kropotkin, Geddes, Sombart, Spingarn, Weber, Howard, Wells, Morris and the short-lived period of effective parliamentary sovereignty at the world of twenty-first-century global mismanagement, international corporate power and almost inevitable ecological disaster.

It would not have surprised Mumford that the scholars cannot quite cope with this vision. Objectivity and the specialized discourses of historian, psychologist, literary critic, economist, sociologist, and anthropologist exclude the taint of moral judgement, for in the specialist's vision every fact, until proved otherwise, is discrete in more senses than one. Suspension of moral judgement is no longer an imaginative modesty while evidence is carefully sifted. It has become a total and totalitarian demand, a method become goal of a process it was designed only to aid. The reproduction of José Clemente's mural of the academic establishment in *The Pentagon of Power*, makes graphically clear the social consequences of the activities of those whom Allen Ginsberg called "The Scholars of War."[52]

Against contemporary chaos, as he sees it, Mumford has the utopian audacity to defend the Garden City vision of Howard. Never mind the question of density or flats versus the family house, Osborn and Mumford are closest when they think about the Garden City. Mumford defends Howard for his principles; for promoting new patterns of urban growth; for advocating a stable marriage between country and city. He is praised for his plea of human measure, his advocacy of limits to growth and agricultural belts, and his commitment to decentralisation. For Mumford, Howard was a practical engineer and inventor testing out a model at Letchworth. He left large areas for others to develop. Mumford acknowledges that Howard underestimated the pull of the metropolitan centre but he praised his idea of the "Social City," ten smaller garden cities surrounding a more metropolitan one providing the more expensive facilities for all. For Mumford the "Social City" is the forerunner of Clarence Stein's Regional City, and in his preface to Clarence Stein's book, *Toward New Towns for America* (1957), Mumford charts the

Anglo-American co-operation in new town design that began with Charles Harris Wittaker's and Frederick L. Ackerman's visits to England during the the First World War. Stein is particularly praised for something which Mumford does not really emphasize in Howard's work in *The City in History*: the need for the state and private sectors to work together in planning.[53]

Stein concluded in his article on Radburn that a "private corporation has only a gambling chance to carry through to completion the building of a city."[54] In contrast the Baldwin Hills Village of 1941 managed to get going on Federal Housing Agency loans and mortgages and the Reconstruction Finance Corporation and kept going for eight years until privatized by the New England Mutual Life Insurance Company of Boston.[55] Elsewhere Stein notes that the rental policy at Chatham Village (Pittsburg) during the depression enabled the residents to survive and plan their lives more flexibly than at sunnyside (New York) where mortgage policies called in by the lending companies created misery on a large scale. He concluded in words which would have to some extent horrified Osborn: "Experience at Chatham Village demonstrated, as compared with Sunnyside, the fallacy of the American faith, almost a religious belief, in what is called 'home ownership'."[56]

Mumford attacks the fashionable notion that Howard was a quixotic failure. The influence of Howard's ideas spread from Scotland to India, and its ideas were behind the British New Towns Act of 1946. Over half a million people lived in British new towns alone, and Mumford concluded: "The fact that the New Towns programme was abruptly terminated at the moment that searching criticism of its achievements and further experiments in the formal organization of new towns was needed, was a failure of the British political imagination, not a failure of the New Towns themselves, and still less a failure of the premises upon which they were built."[57]

Mumford and Osborn also corresponded on other areas of cultural concern. Their views on literature and art are broadly similar, but Osborn is more limited. While both men were influenced by Wells and Shaw, they could be extremely critical of much of their writing, and they both took a delight in parodying the Bloomsbury group, still beloved by the literary establishment in New York and London and whose classy influence is still in inverse proportion to its distinctly limited achievements.

Unlike Mumford, Osborn had little discrimination in actual twentieth-century art, though his social and political critique of the Bloomsbury group is accurate. Mumford describes himself as also an atypical member of his generation, having reached an early maturity owing to his days in the navy, but he adds "I too had grown up with Shaw and Wells, which is why I find the living corpse of the first even more repulsive than the repetitious mummy of the second."[58] Though Osborn's role as a Victorian fossil, as he calls himself, made him completely blind to what the great period of post-impressionism had actually achieved, his view of his English generation is politically acute: "Shaw claims to have learned what he did know from Webb: the answer to that is Webb's Soviet Communism, with all its credulous innocence. Voltaire was going somewhere; where is Shaw going? Does anybody know or care? Wells was going somewhere; it was to Totalitarianism, and he pushed on long after any sensible person could have seen it."[59]

The strange thing is that Osborn's acuteness here did not serve his growing conservative mood after the 1920s. His papers, notes and lectures give a fascinating account of his responses to the development of his particular variety of English socialism. For Osborn the battle was not strictly a materialist one, but one for minds and morals. It is curious that in the propaganda-sodden late twentieth century such a battle is at least as important as a materialist one. In fact of course the division is not a real one. Osborn was merely answering the simplistic materialist teleology of the Marxists of his day:[60] "I dislike the Materialist Conception [of history] not so much because of any scientific inaccuracy as because in practice it is misleading. It has the same effect on propaganda as determinism has on morals."[61]

In contrast Mumford, as an American, felt less bound to the apparently either-or parameters of the European debate for or against Marxism, or even socialism. Mumford typically diffuses his sources into a more synthetic set of propositions. This is partly because the political debate in the United States did not divide in the same way as in Britain in the first half of the twentieth century. There were radical Republicans and radical Democrats, there were conservative Republicans and conservative Democrats.

The ideological struggles in England were fuelled by historical class divisions and hatred which kept the country, as it still is, politically divided in a manner which is still, even with a rightist social democratic Labour Party, more obviously reflected in the division of parties. In the United States there are clear party divides but there, to a much greater extent, different groups coalesce around single issues to do with race, environment, abortion, the women's movement and so forth. The relation between the politics of single issues and party affiliation where power is traditionally managed is a major problem of the twentieth century in the face of global economic strategies. Mumford addressed publically questions of fascism, planning, the environment, the arms race and the Vietnam War, but he was not tied into the actual political process as a party activist in the same way that Osborn was. There is a sense in which he profoundly admired and was envious of Osborn's hands-on, home grown and practical approach to politics, still possible before the power of television killed the local political association.

Yet besides the obvious differences in political culture, Mumford was always the more imaginative intellectual in cultural terms simply because the perspective from the United States invited a more wide ranging focus. Mumford was an Anglophile (even dressing and sporting a moustache like an English colonel) but paradoxically he was more European than British because he was American. Like a character in an O'Neill play, he may have read Shaw and affected the bitter-sweet melancholies of a Dowson to enjoy his adolescent pains, but as a great writer on Melville and a contemporary of Pound and Eliot, it was the humanist tradition of the late middle ages, the Renaissance and the philosophers of the French Enlightenment, together with a crucial American freedom, like Emerson, *to choose his past*, that characterize Mumford's acts of synthesis. While British post-imperialist culture spiralled downwards into a mean-minded nostalgic provincialism (there are exceptions like the investigative, open-ended localism of say an E.P. Thompson or in Scotland of the internationalist yet locally-oriented Hugh MacDiarmid), Mumford could capitalize on an American tradition which in spite of a strong strand of political isolationism was still open to a range of external cultural patterns which stimulated, enriched and modified actual cultural production. In Whitman's words, "I will not make poems with reference to parts/But I will make poems, songs, thoughts, with reference to ensemble."[62] It is that very American thrust which characterizes Mumford's work as well. The poet Muriel Rukeyser was a close friend of the Mumfords and perhaps it is her words that best sum up this very American cultural perspective: "If we are a free people, we are also in a sense free to choose our past, at every moment to choose the tradition we will bring to the future. We invoke a rigorous positive, that will enable us to image our choices, and to make them."[63]

It was precisely the absence of that flexibility of choice, the wide-ranging openness, and a curmudgeonly devotion to singleness of vision that Osborn encountered in British planning. Osborn was politically up against the fact that Conservatives and Labourites had *idées fixes* about what constituted good housing and development. The problem was best put by Catherine Bauer whom Mumford cites in a letter to Osborn of 18 September 1945 on why younger architects and planners have "such a loathing for the very name and idea of the Garden City:"

> She interprets their reaction simply as snobbery: a combination of communist snobbery and old-fashioned upper class snobbery, which has affixed the label of "middle-class" to the Garden City idea. It is really a disgraceful kind of isolationism; and it shows, too, a curious effort of detachment from a significant national tradition, which made England, before 1914, the Mecca for every intelligent German and French architect or planner.[64]

Mumford, of course, had the luck to work at a time when Americans were also rediscovering the vitality of their own tradition. F.O. Matthiessen's *American Renaissance* of 1941, for all the generally-misinformed carping of contemporary critics,[65] was one among many moments which signalled that an American tradition had been reborn in contemporary terms, and showed a renewed pride in America's cultural past. Roosevelt's public works programmes meant not only landscarring interstate highways but also public libraries. Painters, writers and dramatists were being publically supported. American art was being revalued. Mumford was lucky to be able to count on a relatively high point of American idealism, both as a young man and then again in the 1930s. Unlike Osborn, he was not obliged to combat the structural sociological inanities of a Karl Mannheim at the London School of Economics nor his notion of a hypostasized "Society" as a military "necessity."[66]

Both Osborn and Mumford are generally less satisfactory on gender issues. Osborn's theoretical advocacy of the family unit in the Garden City undervalues seriously the widening roles of women. Here Jane Jacobs' view of the city and of daily family organization in less blissful isolation is more satisfactory. Further his call for "a revival of family idealism," in the 1940s and 1950s, would need a strong dose of Betty Friedan's critique of the "home-maker" image of the same period as a corrective.[67] It would also need the anthropologist's, the historian's, and the sociologist's insights into the huge differences in what the "family" actually means historically and culturally. His argument is not helped, in practical terms, by his invocation of the conservative Huxley's *Brave New World*, as a critique of fascist politics in relation to sexuality. He uses Huxley's satire on state totalitarianism as a blanket condemnation of all critiques of the role of the family. His view of the "family doctor" as social arbiter is problematic given a generation that has read Ivan Illich or Michel Foucault.[68] He is matched here by Mumford in *The Human Prospect*, who is in full flight from the nineteenth-century Strindbergian criticism of the deadening effect of the family on creativity and personal development. Mumford deliberately ignores a crucial difference between the family as ideology, and the family as *one* personal and practical way of creating a decent human space in an increasingly mechanized and anonymous world. Given the propaganda about German motherhood in a devastating world war scarcely ten years ended, and the McCarthyite right-wing advocacy of the American family as he actually writes these words, some, though not all, of his statements are unusually sentimentalizing.

Both men profoundly ignore the possibility that what is masculine and what is feminine in a world where women are really the equals of men might change out of all recognition. Mumford believed that women and men were relatively easily definable as different. For both men simplistic definition of biological role extended far too easily and quickly into cultural difference, a major fault of their organicist metaphors. For Mumford, the masculinist bias is self-evident in sentences like the following: "He who has dropped a seed into a garden or into a woman's womb is ready to fight for the right of that seed to grow and fulfil itself."[69] And Mumford's remarks about homosexuals as threatening the heterosexual norm mark him out not only as a man of his time, but expose serious flaws in his organicist ideology.[70]

If he was of the generation of Howard he had clearly ignored Edward Carpenter. Both Mumford and Osborn loved Whitman, but had clearly no understanding of the differing forms which comradely love might take. In fact Osborn ends one lecture on the family in which he says "motherhood is the most important occupation of all" with a brilliant paean to Whitman whom he says delighted in the "pluralism of the human scene."[71]

The contradictions are there, of course, in Whitman's own organic model of the American person and the republic, and indeed in his own painful self-deceptions where he claimed to have fathered seven children. He was exasperatingly coy about the subject of sex to the ever-persistent John Addington Symonds who was moved to comment that he "entertains feelings at least as hostile to sexual inversion as any law-abiding humdrum Anglo-Saxon could desire."[72]

Finally Mumford, from a culture where political radicalism has only rarely touched the mainstream, was a great deal more radical on the international politics of the postwar decade than Osborn who grew up in a country where a left of centre Labour Party has had real, though fleeting, power. As the international crises of the 1950s, 1960s and 1970s unfolded, their disagreements were manifest: over Britain's collusion in the development of fascism before the Second World War, which Mumford described in *Men Must Act*, over Suez, on the atomic bomb, and above all on Vietnam. Mumford became more activist and more radical on international politics as Osborn became more conservative, or at least manifestly held back on his agreement with Mumford.[73] To a degree Mumford was right when he said the main difference between them was one of "historical perspective." The American's always-pressing need to invent a cultural perspective out of what Henry James once called a "usable past" gave him a steadier view of his own times than Osborn finally had himself.

Mumford's search for dynamic equilibrium as a principle of cultural investigation, cultural action and personal discipline was profoundly American. If his "organicism" had its degree of obfuscation and political evasion, it also had merits which in *his practice* are more and more appreciated at the present time. With regard to architecture it enabled him to say:

> Buildings exist in a landscape, in a village, or in a city; they are parts of a natural or an urban setting; they are elements in a whole. The individual unit must always be conceived and modified in terms of the whole. This cannot be done by architects who have their nose on the draughting board, and who, in their own conceit, have no regard for the principle of neighborliness and no interest in the surrounding works of nature or man.[74]

In his revised and expanded *Culture of Cities* which he called *The City in History*, Mumford warned of the dangers of the integrative electronic, mass communications age. While men like Buckminster Fuller and Marshall McLuhan were celebrating their respective global villages, Mumford was warning: "Our civilization is faced with the relentless extension and aggrandizement of a highly centralized, super-organic system, that lacks autonomous component centres capable of exercizing selection, exerting control above all, making autonomous decisions and answering back."[75] The world of E-mail moves towards a destruction of local renewal and change. Against super-organicism Mumford returned to organicism, that defense of not being in touch with the whole in a necessary Whitman-like local "separation" which is the health of "adhesiveness."

Steady and clear sighted to the end, in *The Pentagon of Power* Mumford attempted to chart that path struck out at the beginning between biological necessity and technological pressure. Reviewing human history as a history of solar myth sustaining actual autocracy, successively destroyed through gigantism, he lashed out at the contemporary yet ancient vision on which the academy and the military-industrial complex was spending its money, that fantasy of centralized control articulated at the birth of modern science by Galileo's helio-centric universe:

> Beginning with artificial insemination and extra-uterine pregnancy (Muller), the automatic conditioning of the infant will start in his isolated and enclosed crib (Skinner); thenceforward learning machines (Skinner and others) operating in isolated cells without direct human contact will teach the growing child; one set of electron apparatus will record dreams for computer analysis and personality correction, while another will provide programmed information; constant bombardment of meaningless messages will massage the tribalized mind (McLuhan); large-scale automated farming operations under remote control will supply food (Rand); central station computers with the aid of robots will take charge of all domestic operations from menu planning and marketing to housework (Seaborg); while cybernetically run factories will produce an abundance of goods (Wiener); and private motor cars under automatic central control (M.I.T. and Ford) will transport passengers along superhighways to underground cities or alternately to asteroid colonies in space (Dandridge Cole); while centralized computers will take the place of national decision-makers, and a sufficient supply of hallucinogens will give every vestigial human being the ecstatic sense of being alive (Leary).[76]

Mumford excoriated the straight and counter culture simultaneously. His sense of the creative diversity that was being polarized into meaningless and programmed mass binary reactions was acute. Nor did he spare the young (and their manipulators) lobotomized by drugs and deafened by "popular" cacophony at levels which damaged the ear, and most modes of social communication. In the difficult times of the late 1960s and early 1970s he stood for political opposition to the gigantic centres of global power, for active choice, the local loyalty, scholarship and a profound and searching scrutiny of the achievements of the past among which to make those choices. In that sense he was truly American.

Notes

1. Patrick Geddes, "The Sociology of Autumn" (1895) repr. *Edinburgh Review* (Summer 1992), p. 36.
2. Edmund Wilson, "Through the Abruzzi with Mattie and Harriet" in *Europe Without Baedecker: Sketches Among the Ruins of England, Greece, and Italy* (London: Secker and Warburg, 1948), p. 69.
3. The only time I met Mumford, however, (September 1973—a terrible point in American history) he blamed himself for writing too many books and not becoming involved enough in the political process.
4. This work is ripe for revaluation. It is typically deemed a failure. See Colin Ward, "Death of a Great Outsider" *The Independent on Sunday* (28 January 1990): "*The Condition of Man* was a disappointment. Like many writers, he was better at discussing particular things than at embracing everything." This is utter nonsense. Not only is his estimate of the book way off target but Mumford's precise brilliance was that he did attempt, often extraordinarily successfully, to "embrace everything."
5. Lewis Mumford, "A New York Adolescence" first published in the *New Yorker* (7 December 1937), repr. in *The Human Prospect* (London: Secker & Warburg, 1956), p. 55.
6. Mumford, "Adolescence", p. 59.
7. See, for example, *The New York Times*, Real Estate Section, 12 September 1993, for an article headed "City Colleges Add $2 Billion In Facilities."
8. Murray Bookchin, *The Ecology of Freedom: the Emergence and Dissolution of Hierarchy* (Palo Alto, California: Cheshire Books, 1982), p. 27.
9. Greta Jones, *Social Darwinism and English Thought: The Interaction between Biological and Social Theory* (Brighton, Sussex: The Harvester Press; New Jersey: Humanities Press, 1980), p. 59.
10. For a discussion of this see Clive Bush, *Halfway to Revolution: Investigation and Crisis in Henry Adams. William James and Gertrude Stein* (London and New Haven, 1991).
11. Lewis Mumford, "Patrick Geddes" in *The Human Prospect*, pp. 105–6.
12. Lewis Mumford, *Herman Melville* (London: Jonathan Cape Ltd, 1929), p. 139.
13. Karl Marx, *Capital* I, introd. Ernest Mandell, trans. Ben Fowkes (Harmondsworth, Middx.: Penguin Books Ltd, 1976), p. 493n.
14. Lewis Mumford, *Technics and Civilization* (1934; repr. London: Routledge, 1946), p. 10.
15. Mumford, *Technics*, p. 25.
16. Mumford, *Technics*, p. 129.
17. I am thinking of the mass propaganda dished out on UK television in the first half of 1993 in which various Singapore establishment figures celebrated their American, Japanese and European-funded economic growth rate with attacks on what is left of the Western democratic process.

18. Lewis Mumford, *The Culture of Cities* (London: Secker & Warburg Ltd, 1938), p. 36.
19. Mumford, *Culture*, p. 69.
20. Mumford, *Culture*, p. 118.
21. Mumford, *Culture*, p. 202.
22. Mumford, *Culture*, p. 239.
23. Mumford, *Culture*, p. 238.
24. Mumford, *Culture*, p. 284.
25. Mumford, *Culture*, pp. 273–74.
26. Lewis Mumford, *Men Must Act* (London: Secker & Warburg, 1939), p. 14.
27. Jane Jacobs, *The Death and Life of Great American Cities: The Failure of Town Planning* (1961; repr. Harmondsworth, England: Penguin Books, 1964), p. 58.
28. Frederick J. Osborn, "The Garden City Movement: a Revaluation" given to the Town Planning Institute, Caxton Hall, Westminster, 5 April 1945 (Osborn Papers, Welwyn Garden City Library), p. 3.
29. Osborn, "Garden City", p. 7.
30. Osborn, "Garden City", p. 11.
31. Reprinted as Chapter 3 of Arnold Whittick's *F.J.O.—Practical Idealist: A Biography of Sir Frederic J. Osborn*, foreword by Lord Stewart of Fulham (London: Town and Country Planning Association, 1987), p. 18.
32. Howard, *Tomorrow*, pp. 12–13.
33. C.B. Purdom, *The Letchworth Achievement* (London, 1963), Appendix E. (London: Dent, 1963)
34. R. Beevers, *The Garden City Utopia: A Critical Biography of Ebenezer Howard* (London: Macmillan, 1988), pp. 77–78.
35. Quoted in Howard, *Tomorrow*, pp. 128 and 153.
36. *The Kenneth Rexroth Reader*, selected with an introduction by Eric Mottram (London: Jonathan Cape, 1972), pp. 42–43.
37. Lewis Mumford, *Findings and Keepings: Analects for an Autobiography* (London: Secker & Warburg, 1976), p. 27.
38. Mumford, *Findings*, p. 45.
39. Mumford, *Findings*, p. 45.
40. Mumford, *Findings*, p. 156.
41. Mumford, *Findings*, p. 204.
42. For example, Henry Pachter's sneering little piece in *Salmagundi* 49 (Summer 1980), pp. 69f.
43. Mumford, *Men Must Act*, p. 217.
44. Alan Trachtenberg, "Mumford in the Twenties" *Salmagundi* 49 (Summer 1980), p. 41.
45. Jean-Paul Sartre, *Critique of Dialectical Reason*, trans. Alan Sheridan-Smith, ed. Jonathan Ree (London: New Left Books, 1976), p. 159.
46. *The Letters of Lewis Mumford and Frederic J. Osborn: A Transatlantic Dialogue 1938–70*, ed. Michael Hughes (New York, Washington: Praeger Publishers, 1971), p. 166. All further references to this book will be cited as *Osborn-Mumford*. Mumford's comment on "communism" occurs on p. 403 of *Technics and Civilization* (New York and London: Harcourt Brace Jovanovich, 1934). The Catholic Church for Geddes was more than a shadow in the background.

Joseph Duffey points out that "Mumford's approach to the study of society was strongly influenced by the British sociologists, Patrick Geddes and Victor Branford. Geddes and Branford founded the *Sociological Review* in London, which Mumford edited in 1920. Their approach to social theory was strongly influenced by the writings of Frederick Le Play, prominent among the Catholic counter-revolutionary scholars in early nineteenth-century France. Le Play described culture as arising out of the interaction of three factors: folk, place and work, corresponding to the more general categories of organism, environment and function." See Joseph Duffey, "Mumford's Quest: The First Decade" *Salmagundi* 49 (Summer, 1980) p. 61.

47. *Osborn-Mumford*, pp. 278 and 280.

48. Lewis Mumford, *The City in History. Its Origins. Its Transformations and Its Prospects* (Harmondsworth, Middx.: Penguin Books, 1966), p. 129.

49. Mumford, *City*, p. 297.

50. Mumford, *City*, pp. 598f.

51. Mumford, *City*, p. 635.

52. Lewis Mumford, *The Pentagon of Power* (London: Secker & Warburg, 1971), plate 25. Allen Ginsberg, "Howl" in *Howl and Other Poems* (San Francisco: City Lights, 1956), p. 9.

53. Lewis Mumford, introd. to Clarence S. Stein's *Towards New Towns for America* (New York: Reinhold Publishing Corporation, 1957), pp. 13–14.

54. Stein, *Towards New Towns*, p. 69.

55. Stein, *Towards New Towns*, pp. 189–90.

56. Stein, *Towards New Towns*, p. 85. This notion of economic procedure developed from Howard is common to the Mumford circle. See for example Mumford's "Municipal Functions and Civic Art" in *From the Ground Up* (New York: Harcourt Brace and Co., 1956), p. 144.

57. Mumford, *City*, p. 594.

58. *Osborn-Mumford*, pp. 56–57, 61.

59. *Osborn-Mumford*, p. 174.

60. *Osborn-Mumford*, pp. 11, 14.

61. *Osborn-Mumford*, p. 31.

62. Walt Whitman, "Starting from Paumanok", Section 12, *Leaves of Grass and Selected Prose* ed. John Kouwenhoven (New York: Modern Library, 1950), p. 19.

63. Muriel Rukeyser, *The Life of Poetry* (New York: Current Books Inc, A.A. Wyn, Publisher, 1949), p. 20.

64. *Osborn-Mumford*, pp. 103–4.

65. See the special issue of *Democratic Vistas* I:1 (1992) devoted to this topic.

66. Osborn, "Notes on Karl Mannhein and Howard's philosophies," 1 May 1944.

67. See Betty Friedan, *The Feminine Mystique* (London: Gollany, 1963).

68. *Osborn-Mumford*, p. 23.

69. Lewis Mumford, "Culture of the Family" in *The Human Prospect* (London: Secker & Warburg Ltd, 1956), p. 278.

70. *Osborn-Mumford*, p. 370.

71. Osborn, "Planning for the Family," Town and Country Planning Association Lunch Meeting, 16 April 1942, p. 5.

72. Justin Kaplan, *Walt Whitman: A Life* (New York: Simon and Schuster, 1980), pp. 45–47.
73. *Osborn-Mumford*, pp. 8, 266–67, 400.
74. Lewis Mumford, "The Basis of Universalism" in Lewis Mumford, *Roots of a Contemporary Architecture* (1952; repr. New York: Dover Publications, 1972), p. 380.
75. Mumford, *City* pp. 645–46.
76. Mumford, *Pentagon* p. 227.

7

Coming of Age in America
Margaret Mead and Karen Horney

Helen Carr

In 1989, I found myself simultaneously editing a book of feminist criticism and organizing a festival to celebrate the bicentenary of the French Revolution. In the first essay in the book, Cora Kaplan suggested that 1989 marked twenty years since American second wave feminism had, as she put it, "taken off."[1] I was intrigued by this joint anniversary. Kate Millett, whose *Sexual Politics* was one of the events of 1969 that marked that feminist take-off, had in fact referred to what was happening around her as the second phase of the Sexual Revolution:[2] and, as we have shifted from speaking of women's liberation to analysing sexual difference, feminist theory in those twenty years has re-enacted the trajectory from Enlightenment certainty to postmodern fragmentation which so many recent theorists have traced in the last two hundred years.

In *Sexual Politics*, "woman" was as univocal a term as "Man" in the Declaration of Rights. The oppressor which Kate Millett denounced was patriarchy, present, she argued, in every civilization known to history. She ranged eclectically over French, English, German, Russian and American experience to illustrate the denial of human rights to women and to urge their need to abandon their chains, the outworn social conventions, particularly marriage, that enslave them. Women must use their reason to see through the falsity of patriarchal ideology, and refuse to accept their inferior place. Substitute Man for woman, monarchy for patriarchy, and the model is clear. Since then, that unified notion of womanhood has splintered. A gap between radical and equal rights feminists gradually emerged, as did the disparate emphases of lesbian and heterosexual feminists. Concern with differences, both sexual and cultural, has outweighed the earlier universalism. Feminism can no longer be seen unproblematically as an international movement. The question of white feminists' attitude to race and imperialism was raised first by Afro-Americans, and later by Third World women, whose most high-profile representative among American feminist theorists is Gayatri Spivak. Even the idea of a unified Western feminism has been shaken by a particularly unsisterly debate about the differences between Anglo-American and French feminist theory, which re-invoked all the post-Jamesian stereotypes of naive Americans and supersubtle Europeans.

I am not suggesting Millett deliberately modelled her manifesto on the French Revolution; her vocabulary is more directly indebted on the one hand to the Marxist reworking of the revolutionary agenda, and on the other to the powerful presence of Enlightenment ideals in US political language dating back to its own revolution. Millett's book is now generally dismissed for its angry naiveté, yet a comparison can be made with the language of revolutionary humanism adopted by Frantz Fanon and other black liberationists, to the later pained distress of their deconstructionist admirers like Homi Bhabha.[3] They both claim the language of inalienable rights, even if ultimately it is impossible to write of "woman" or "a black man" as an Enlightenment subject. It has not been chance that second wave feminism has been contemporaneous with the growth of post-modernism: both are theories which call into question the master narratives, and which deconstruct the possibility of absolute and unitary knowledge. The terms in which second wave feminism announced itself, the starkness of its opposition between male the oppressor, female the oppressed, were bound rapidly to fracture, because the language it drew on had already been used of class, race and economic oppression, in which, as members of privileged groups, some women were implicated. Millett evokes in her postscripts a vision of "women" united with blacks, gays and the poor to oppose patriarchy. Such gestures provoked the anger of black women in the United States, who pointed out that a coalition of "women" and "blacks" paradoxically left them not acknowledged twice but invisible.[4]

Millett's universalism was, in any case, a question of rhetoric rather than subject matter: although she claimed to be attacking worldwide patriarchy, she was really writing about the United States. The tension in her postscript between Enlightenment universalism and the confrontation of difference has played a crucial role in the history of American feminism. Such tensions were, and are, present in other Western feminist movements, but not so acutely as in the United States, founded on an Enlightenment ideology of equality which was in practice denied in so many ways. The uncertainty over the appropriate-ness of the Enlightenment heritage has been equally present in US campaigns for racial justice: slavery was, after all, the institution which for the nineteenth century embodied most strikingly the failure of the revolutionary ideals. Should the response be Martin Luther King's humanistic dream or Malcolm X's Black Power? American feminism, perhaps inevitably has had an intricate and often troubled relation with issues of race. Olive Banks, in her comparative study of American and British feminist history, suggests that the "main difference between United States and Britain . . . is the closer link between Socialism or Marxism and feminism" in the British tradition.[5] Perhaps this distinction needs extension: for US feminism, the question of race took the place of that link with socialism. While in Britain feminists constantly used the imagery and analogy of class oppression to understand the position of women, in the United States the comparison and metaphor for the position of women has much more often been that of racial difference.

Feminists were not unique in this association of race and sexuality: anxiety over racial difference has suffused American imaginative and intellectual life. The nineteenth-century biological and anthropological theories which underwrote the inferiority of the non-white races were applied equally to women: those who argued against these theories found the issues inseparable. The most radical rethinking of gender in American society to predate Millett's "second phase of the Sexual Revolution" was made in the context of opposition to racism and the analysis of cultural difference, through the work of the culture and personality school in the 1920s and 1930s. Were racial and gender characteristics fixed and biologically determined, or were they the product of cultural and environmental forces?

This debate is one still very much to the fore today, with those positions now better know as "essentialist" and "constructionist." Margaret Whitford in a recent article associates essentialism with Enlightenment thought, and constructionism with postmodernism.[6] It is a useful distinction, but the Enlightenment heritage is a complex one: it is constructionism, not essentialism, which has been associated with Enlightenment ideals of political equality, in the argument that there are no "essential" differences between human beings. Certainly in the last few years there has been an assumption among sophisti-cated and "politically correct" cultural critics that "essentialist" is bad and "constructionist" is good. But recently, even a deconstruc-tionist like Gayatri Spivak and a cultural materialist like Jonathan Dollimore have argued for the "strategic" use of essentialism by subaltern women or homosexuals in asserting their political identity and rights, and Diana Fuss has rightly pointed out the highly problematic way in which the word essentialism has been demonized.[7] In this article I want to re-examine its contrary term, and consider the strengths and limitations of these interwar American arguments for "constructionism," looking particularly at the work of two women who were both in different ways influenced by the culture and personality movement in American anthropology. Their analysis of the cultural construction of gender in American society is inevitably a critique of American society in general, and one, I want to argue, that needs to be understood in modernist rather than in postmodernist terms.

One of these women, Margaret Mead, has been not only frequently discussed but often denounced by both feminists and anti-feminists. The other, Karen Horney, has for a long time attracted interest from feminists for her early work, though generally seen as failing the cause in her later works, and her role as a cultural critic has remained largely unnoticed.[8] Mead wrote about American culture from the position of an insider, though constantly trying to see it in relation to other cultures. Horney only came to the United States in mid-life, and was fascinated by the difference between American and European culture. What they shared was a belief in the cultural relativism central to Boasian anthropology, and in the importance of cultural factors in the construction of gender roles. Both wrote some of their most significant work on gender in the context of the Nazis' forcible revival of traditional, polarized sexual roles. Mead was an anthropologist, though her master's thesis had been in psychology, and her later work much influenced by psychoanalysis. Karen Horney became a psychoanalyst after training as a doctor, but her psychoanalytic theories were greatly influenced by anthropology. They knew each other and each other's work. They both believed that the sexes should have equal political and educational opportunities, and to that extent could be called feminists: but if by feminist is meant someone whose primary commitment is to achieving such ends, they were not.[9] I shall focus here on their attitude to gender, and will not, of course, attempt a complete appraisal of their theories: yet it was because their concern was with cultural as well as sexual difference that they grappled with many of the same problems contemporary feminist theorists have come to face again.

Earlier American feminists had been overwhelmingly essentialist, though whether "strategically" so must be open to debate. In spite of the fact that in the nineteenth century American women had more social and educational freedom than their British contemporaries, in the United States representation of gender characteristics and roles was in many ways even more strikingly polarized, and the separate spheres more sharply defined, than in Britain. Many feminists accepted this, in particular the idea of women's moral superiority, and were more concerned to celebrate and practise womanly virtues, as mothers, philanthropists, and upholders of morality, than to pursue equal rights, at any rate beyond the vote. Unlike Britain, education and the arts were often regarded as best fitted to women: many of the universities and colleges that opened up in the West in the later nineteenth century had to be co-educational to gain students, as so many young men felt business and practical projects were more suitable life options for them.[10] The emphasis on the moral importance of women was, and perhaps still is, a vital factor in reconciling Americans' Enlightenment belief in the importance of every individual with the actuality of women's political inferiority. Even in the early twentieth century, many suffragists argued for the moral contribution that the women's vote would bring. In the 1920s and 1930s, political feminism was split by the dispute over whether its energies should go into the fight for the Equal Rights Amendment, or into "womanly" movements for peace and social welfare.[11] In a period of rapidly changing sexual mores, individual sexual liberation seemed more important to many educated women than social equality.

Margaret Mead's professional life coincided largely with the years that Kate Millett described as counter-revolutionary, the blank trough between the first and second phases of the sexual revolution. Growing up in a liberal, progressive home, coming to adulthood when an older generation had fought the battle for the vote and access to the professions, she had much in common with present-day post-feminists, welcoming the results of the movement, enjoying the freedoms they had gained, but unconcerned about further political change, and filled with optimism, indeed complacency, about her possibilities in life.

Both Mead's mother and grandmother had college educations, and both worked, though by no means continuously, after marriage. Both were involved in traditional caring "feminine" areas. Her grandmother had been a teacher, who went back to work when left a young widow with one child. Her mother was a social scientist, who, after marriage and five children, used her training mainly in good works, although she completed a study of local Italian immigrants while Margaret was growing up, giving her daughter an early training in cultural observation and tolerance. Margaret Mead herself, typical of the best educated women of her day as opposed to those of her mother's generation, applied her talents to a profession rather than to philanthropy.

Mead felt herself to come from a small enlightened enclave away from the mainstream of American life. As she wrote, she "took pride in being unlike other children and in living in a household that was itself unique." But at the same time she also longed to be part of that other ordinary world, wanting to have "every culturally normal experience."[12] Like some women liberationists' daughters, she would much have preferred frills and fluff to the sensible unisex clothes in which she and her brother were dressed. In Mead's account of them, her parents form a little paradigm of gender roles in the American professional middle classes of their day, which both parallels and contrasts with Virginia Woolf's depiction of her British parents as the Ramseys. Mead's mother, like Mrs Ramsey, was beautiful, self-sacrificing, concerned for her family and the needy: unlike Mrs Ramsey, she was formally educated, believed in education for her daughters, and was sure her system of values was superior to her husband's. Mead's father, like Mr Ramsey, felt he had never quite been as successful as he should: but, for Edward Sherwood Mead, that was only partially because he had not reached the top intellectually. He knew his wife was disappointed that, although a professor of economics at the University of Pennsylvania, he was never made an Emeritus. But the reason he never secured that academic honour was that, being still of the generation dogged by the feeling that educational matters were women's affair, he had dissipated a good deal of energy and family income on unwise ventures into the "real world" of business and finance. Margaret Mead lived at a time of transition, and her own adaptation of this pattern gave her immense confidence in her chosen path. Like her mother, she believed education was right for women, but she entered a world where education was no longer necessarily looked down on as effeminate, and where a full-time career was a possibility for a woman. She rejected her mother's self-denying moralism, but the impact of Freudianism and psychoanalysis on American intellectual life meant that her mother's world of child-rearing and family was in a new way fundamental to an understanding of society: for Mead's generation, sexuality, not economics, was the "real world." Many of her causes, racial tolerance, the happiness of children, remained the same as her mother's and grandmother's but she preached them to the nation, not just her family.

By the time Mead was ready to enter college, funds were low, and only clever manipulation by her mother got her there. Her one-year experience of a Middle American college appalled her. She smarted from her failure to be invited to join a sorority, and was made miserable by the unpopularity with male students that her academic success brought. She escaped to the liberal, metropolitan, women-only Barnard College in New York, deciding from then on to avoid the male antagonism that competing with men brought by working with women and on women's subjects.

Mead's sense of the divisions within American society, her ambivalence towards mainstream American culture, and her own feeling of otherness are vital threads in her work. American society had become increasingly multi-ethnic during the early years of the century, and 1924, the year of her MA, saw a new immigration act that attempted to stem the flow of non-WASPs into the United States. The 1920s became increasingly anti-Red, anti-black, anti-semitic and anti-foreign. Following in her mother's footsteps, Mead herself wrote her MA thesis on Italian immigrants in New York, showing the unreliability of the intelligence testing that branded them inferior to Americans. The anthropologists with whom she associated, such as Franz Boas and Ruth Benedict, were committed to opposing the prejudice towards the new ethnic minorities as well as the old. At Barnard she became once more part of the elite of writers, intellectuals, conversationalists, and critics of modern society with whom she felt at home. She shared their impatience with American middletown parochialism and ethnocentrism, but although she went marching on behalf of Sacco and Vanzetti, and enjoyed being castigated as a "communist moron," Mead herself was, as she later put it, a radical only in sentiment, not in ideology.[13] She accommodated herself to the contemporary realities of the position of women in academe, rather than attempting to change them: if she was critical of American competitiveness in situations where it damaged her, she went along with it untroubled in contexts where she shone. She was fired by the desire to record primitive societies before they disappeared, but she never criticized the forces that impelled that disappearance. She was an educator but never a revolutionary.

Margaret Mead entered American anthropology at the very beginning of the culture and personality movement. Boasian anthropology rejected the nineteenth-century ranking of races and cultural groups in a hierarchy surmounted by the peak of white male civilization, a theory of cultural evolution which saw so-called primitive cultures as stages on the way to American democracy, and races other than the Anglo-Saxon as developmentally stunted.[14] Boas and his followers believed non-Western societies had their own complexly developed social organizations. Until the early 1920s he had argued against the idea of a steady uniform evolutionary pattern chiefly through negative instances, especially by documenting the geographical diffusion of cultural traits. Just about the time Mead met Boas, he had decided that "diffusion was done."[15] It was time to ask more positive questions: if difference was cultural rather than racial, what different patterns of culture existed? In what ways are behaviour and consciousness different in different cultures, and why?

Like their contemporaries who were Marxists or psychoanalysts, these anthropologists believed that the personality was formed by forces below the level of consciousness, though they stressed unconsciously absorbed cultural norms rather than class ideology or the individual family experience. Like Marxists and psychoanalysts, they believed the true understanding of these unconscious forces would set humankind free, in their case, of "the shackles tradition has laid upon us."[16] Although Boas had at one stage joined the Socialist Party, Marxism was of much less interest to most of these anthropologists than psychoanalysis. Boas himself, always cautious, was dubious about psychoanalysis, at any rate in its Freudian form, partly because of Freud's embrace of nineteenth-century evolutionary anthropology, but also because Boas believed psychoanalysis evoked a "psychological determinism which left no room for accident."[17] All the same, many of his followers, including Mead, were intrigued by it, and attempted to bring psychoanalytic or psychologistic insights to bear on anthropology. Boas' first Ph.D. student, A.L. Kroeber, actually practised as a lay analyst. Culture and personality became the dominant school in American anthropology between the wars, in conscious opposition to the increasing racism in the Western world. Significantly, most of its adherents were either immigrants or women.

As George Stocking has said, this school was part of the "revolt from civilization" that characterized so many intellectuals of that generation, as well as modernist artists, some of whom were fleeing the USA altogether.[18] Levi-Strauss has suggested that anthropologists are always critics of their own society, and this is certainly true of this group.[19] The sense that "primitive cultures" were preferable to modern society underlay much of their work, given its most explicit expression in Edward Sapir's essay, "Culture, Genuine and Spurious," which both echoes Eliot's and Pound's sense of the dissolution and sterility of modern society, and foreshadows later laments like Fredric Jameson's on the "waning of affect."[20] Primitive cultures for these anthropologists had a wholeness, a coherence, that the modern world lacked.

Although Margaret Mead's own strong emotional response to the cultures she described could be antagonistic as well as admiring, her writing shows more missionary zeal towards the United States than any of her colleagues. Paradoxically, this zeal sprang from her greater faith, at any rate before 1945, in America's capacity to progress through the teachings of science towards democratic enlightenment. She always wrote, she claimed in later life, to help her fellow-Americans "better understand themselves."[21] Her depiction of American society is an apparently contradictory one: on the one hand fragmented and alienated, on the other coercively conformist; on the one hand, democratic, freedom-loving and individualistic, on the other, ruthlessly competitive, driven by fears of failure; on the one hand, a conglomerate of mutually incomprehensible cultures, on the other, unified by the American goal of personal advancement. Much of her later work is a direct anthropological view of American society, but even her first book, *Coming of Age in Samoa* (1928), had as its original subtitle *A Psychological Study of Primitive Youth for Western Civilization*.[22] In the work for which she has been most criticized by feminists, *Male and Female* (1949), she spends almost half the book on American gender roles.[23] As James Clifford has said, all her work was "a pedagogical, ethical undertaking," and its aim was the greater good of the American people.[24]

Social scientists in the United States had begun questioning fixed racial and gender characteristics from the beginning of the century, and undoubtedly the theory, if not the practice, that Mead learnt from her parents blended immediately with Boas' and Benedict's views. The dissolution of hierarchies at which Boas aimed inevitably included that of gender. Until the 1920s there had been few attempts by anthropologists even to document the lives of women or the care of children. Nineteenth-century anthropology assumed that women's lot was at its happiest in civilized societies, and indeed that one of the marks of civilization was partriarchy, with its supposedly high valuation of women (in practice, of upper-class women) who were held to be virtuous, gentle, and too delicate for manual work. By the 1920s, such a view of womanhood in itself had become distasteful to many. Western gender relations were compared with those of other cultures, not necessarily favourably. Mead, more than any of her fellow anthropologists, wrote about gender, and, more than any, reached a wide public audience. She introduced a generation of educated Americans to the idea that there was no uniform way of being a man or a woman.

Marilyn Strathern, today's most distinguished feminist anthropologist, credits Mead with first establishing the cultural variability and social construction of sex roles and stereotypes.[25] She sees the crucial text as Mead's *Sex and Temperament in Three Primitive Societies* (1935) in which Mead looks at three societies with contrasting patterns of gender relations, one where both sexes are what the West would call "feminine," one in which they are both "masculine," and one where the men are "feminine" and the women "masculine." It is less easy to realize now that her first and most famous book was in itself, in the context of her upbringing where women were either good or sexual, a challenge to her mother's generation's definition of womanhood, though it was also in a long line of celebrations of primitive, "natural" sex relations.[26] What horrified feminist critics like Betty Friedan and Germaine Greer about her postwar book and best seller, *Male and Female*, was that to them it appeared a return to both biological difference and American gender roles.[27]

Derek Freeman, whose attack on Maragaret Mead has provoked anthropology's most high profile row to date, criticized her work for exactly the opposite reason from the feminists. They were shocked because she paid undue attention to nature: he because she took too much account of nurture. In *Margaret Mead and Samoa: the Making and Unmaking of an Anthropological Myth* (1983), Freeman attacks the Boasian paradigm, or rather his version of it, with the kind of Oedipal rage that one might have expected to be expressed no later than the postwar years in which Boasian anthropology lost pre-eminence. So it is not surprising to discover that Freeman had brooded over his attack since that period, and its own underlying paradigm is that of the natural sciences in the 1950s, with their return to biology, to evolution, to unitary explanations, of which the favourite was aggression, typified by man the hunter, and to arguments for the innateness of traditional sex-roles.[28] Criticism of many aspects of Mead's work had already appeared, and by the time Freeman's book was eventually published the post-colonialist analysis of ethnographic discourse was beginning. There is ample scope for the deconstruction of Mead's work, and some of the vocabulary, if not the concepts, of such deconstruction enters Freeman's book. Rather than focusing on colonialism and the problem of representation, Freeman, Popperian and positivist, cites Mead's personal failings (which for him include her size, age and sex) or mistaken adherence to Boasian principles.[29] Although he reaches the point when he can say that his research shows that ethnographers' reports may not always be taken as empirical statements, the possibility that his own observations might have a bias is not one he countenances. Mead, it has to be said, did understand that representation was problematic. She knew that no two attempts to read a culture would ever be identical, because they would depend on the viewpoint of the observer. What she claims for her work is that it has a value in its unique record of one individual's perception, at one moment of time, not in its absolute truth. Freeman actually quotes this comment, but, characteristically, misinterprets it to mean the opposite of what Mead said.[30]

Mead's work has been hotly defended and debated since Freeman's book, with even one of her original feminist critics, Eleanor Leacock, rallying to her support. As it happened, a new and warmly sympathetic reading of Mead as an anti-essentialist feminist had appeared the previous year, in Rosalind Rosenberg's *Beyond Separate Spheres* (1982). Although he would not use the term, Freeman is arguing for essentialism, though he does not raise the question of gender, concentrating on the issue of adolescence and the Samoan temperament. He virtually ignores *Sex and Temperament* but quotes extensively from *Male and Female*, unlike those earlier feminist critics interpreting its theoretical orientation to be as committed as ever to the cultural construction of the personality. Freeman himself assumes both a universal human essence, which includes difficult adolescence and aggression as a basic principle in human nature, especially in male sexuality, and also an essential nature for the Samoan people, which allows for no alteration through colonial impact or the passage of time, or differences between different groups. As Lowell Holmes and others have pointed out, Mead did her research in the 1920s in a remote island in American Samoa, while he draws mainly on evidence from the 1960s, in an urban centre in Western Samoa.[31] Holmes, like others, has also pointed to the absurdity of Freeman's claim that Mead blindly followed Boas' belief in "absolute cultural determinism," since Boas had no such belief: the refutation of any kind of determinism was central to his rejection of nineteenth-century teleology. Mead's own attitude to the nature/culture issue, I shall argue, had some questionable elements, but she was no simple cultural determinist: nor did she, as her feminist critics suggest, abandon her belief that gender is largely a matter of culture, though that does not mean she was in any unproblematic way a feminist.

The most disturbing, indeed sinister aspect of Freeman's book is the way in which, quite apart from his inaccuracies, he entirely wipes out the political resonances of Boas' struggle in the 1920s and 1930s against the tide of racist scientific theories, which Roy Rappaport has described as "one of the most vicious expressions of racism in American history," and which might, without the opposition he led, have come much closer to achieving in the United States the hegemony which they won in Germany.[32] Boas exemplified perhaps more than any other figure at this period the struggle to reconcile a libertarian belief in "universal human values," and a desire to "make the world safe for differences," as Ruth Benedict wrote in his obituary.[33] But a critique of racism is different from a denial of genetics, and in any case, far from embracing arbitrary theses, Boas showed the deepest reluctance to enunciate scientific theses at all. Mead's generation of anthropologists were much more ready to hazard hypotheses.

Mead saw herself at one with Boas in her moral opposition to racism, but if Boas remained committed, as he once put it, to the ideals of 1848, Mead herself was very much a modernist intellectual in her distaste for the mass. In spite of her liberalism and racial tolerance on the one hand, and her desire for widespread fame in democratic America on the other, she was an elitist. Mead, like Benedict, her friend and mentor, believed that any given culture encourages certain modes of behaviour, which are taken by that culture to be natural. Yet far from believing any culture completely determines behaviour, what interested them most were those people who do not fit in, whose innate temperaments were antipathetic to the cultural norm. Like modernist artists and writers, they valued the outsiders, the "deviants." This was how they each felt themselves to be in the context of American society, and it is "deviants" that attracted them most in their research. But if Benedict, shy, deaf, prone to depression, felt herself an outsider and a misfit, Mead was confident of her unique superiority.

Following Benedict, Mead interpreted cultures as "personality writ large." Their belief in the "wholeness " of primitive societies led them to think that the cultural patterns of each group could be analyzed in much the same way as Jung distinguished personality types, though Benedict's most famous distinction follows Nietzsche, between Apollonian and Dionysian societies.[34] They illustrated particularly vividly Levi-Strauss' depiction of the typical anthropologist as "a critic at home and a conformist abroad."[35] There was a tension in their work, between their respect and often admiration for what they saw as the organic cohesion of non-Western groups, and their opposition to bourgeois conformity, between their appreciation of the harmony of these societies, and their sympathy for the deviants. The theory of the deviant was in itself essential to the idea of cultural pattern. Mead's assertion that the Samoan pattern was harmonious, low-key, and anxiety-free was not shaken by the discovery of discontented, passionate and intense elements. These did not mean this society was more various than Mead had thought, or even that no society can be read as an autonomous icon, but simply that they were the unhappy outsiders, whose innate temperaments clashed with the cultural norm. Freeman is surely right to find Mead's reiterated description of Samoa as a simple society offensive and patronizing, though she was equally patronizing, in other terms, when she wrote about Americans.

Mead's exploration of gender, so radical in many ways, was part of this quest to understand the exceptional, and therefore herself, and, as well, to make sense, after her simultaneously Puritan and advanced upbringing, of the fraught debate over changing sexual mores of the 1920s and 1930s. In *Sex and Temperament* she specifically links gender roles to her concept of the deviant, whom she defines there— in terms which would apply to herself and all her colleagues—as "any individual who because of innate disposition or accident of early training, or through the contradictory influences of a heterogeneous cultural situation, has been culturally disenfranchised, the individual to whom the major emphases of his society seem nonsensical, unreal, untenable, or downright wrong."[36] Though in any culture personality types that go against the norm are disadvantaged, "any society that specializes its personality types by sex, which insists that any trait . . . is inalienably bound up with sex, paves the way for a maladjustment of a worse order."[37] In her famous formulation, "the personality traits we have called masculine or feminine are as lightly linked to sex as are the clothing, the manners or the form of head-dress that a society at a given period assigns to either sex."[38] To treat gender roles as normative, she argues, is to impoverish both the lives of individuals and society as a whole.

At the end of *Sex and Temperament* Mead contrasts the current Nazi enforcement of traditional Western gender roles, with the breadth of choice of lifestyles a free society should offer. Modern cultures, that is to say, multi-ethnic cultures like America, hetero-geneous and complex, are societies "in which hardly anyone doubts the existence of a different 'natural' behaviour for the sexes, but no one is very sure what that 'natural' behaviour is." As in the arts, what is needed, she argues, is "a recognition of genuine individual gifts as they occurred in either sex."[39] Yet, although she constantly attacks the way each culture, including hers, sees its own customs as natural, underlying the book, like much of her other writing, is the modernist nostalgia for authentic natural rhythms, undisfigured by the distortions of culture. In *Coming of Age*, the nostalgia is for the possibility of freely unfolding sexuality; in *Sex and Temperament* it is for parental tenderness. She makes it clear that she believes that a nurturing and caring culture is infinitely preferable to an aggressive and competitive one. Although she rejects the idea of natural gender roles, the qualities she most admires, "a willingness to cherish children" and opposition to war, are ones described in Western society as feminine.

By the time she wrote *Male and Female*, Mead was America's most famous mother, a celebrated exponent of natural childbirth and breast-feeding, endorsing even more explicitly her mother's and grandmother's belief in the superiority of the values which they associated with women. Mead writes in her autobiography that she, unlike her fellow career women, had always been interested in the things that engaged "most" women.[40] She had by now, to her apparent delight, finally become "culturally normal" and thoroughly American, while remaining, simultaneously, successful and exceptional. By this time, the postwar return to biology and traditional views of gender in the sciences, the social sciences and American culture at large had begun. Mead had always allowed for biology through her theory of innate temperaments, and, according to her daughter, ascribed her own "uniqueness" partially at any rate to genetics.[41] What her theory allowed her to do was construct an alternative myth of origin for herself, a narrative in which she was determined neither by her gender or her nation, yet still given a secure identity through her own exceptional gifts. She does, it is true, now make a pale concession to the possibility of innate gender difference—it may be, she says, the male sex has a slight natural tendency to more constructive activity, and the female to receptivity —but nothing like the way in which these qualities have been exploited by some cultures.[42] Significantly, the characteristic of human men which she here claims distinguishes them from other male primates is that human fathers help to nurture their young. The maternal qualities which her mother valued are not for her simply biologically innate to one sex, but best ideally for both. In spite of her use of a modified Freudian framework in this book, she contrasts cultural gender differences as vividly as ever. She discusses the role of bodily differences, but it remains the body mediated through culture. What she does for the first time is make explicit the assumption, present in her writing from *Coming of Age* onwards, that there are ways of life more in harmony with fundamental human needs than the mores of modern America.

What Mead consistently occludes, however, here and elsewhere, is any question of sexual inequality. She is interested in the misplaced individual, not the disadvantaged group. Until the war, Mead took no interest in politics, and certainly had no time for political feminism: in her biographical account of Ruth Benedict she notes with approval that Benedict was "bored" by women's suffrage.[43] For Mead, even more than for other members of the culture and personality school, outer structures are less potent than subjectivity. Changing laws are less important than changing thinking. She asks no questions about power, other than the power of custom.

One of the striking characteristics and limitations of Mead's writing is the way in which it keeps unpleasantness at bay. Her texts recount the existence of suffering and cruelty, but they rarely take account of it. *Coming of Age* is not the only one of her books in which the readers have remembered the upbeat ending, and forgotten the passed-over misery of the inner chapters. *Male and Female* gives, with little comment, a devastating picture of the American pattern of personal relations, whose grimness seems forgotten by the conclusion. Mead chose to work in the romantic South Seas, comparatively uncontaminated by modernity, rather than with the impoverished and acculturated American Indians. She was appalled by her one period of research with an American Indian group, the Omaha, demoralized, drunken, though highly sophisticated in bargaining information, and insistent on telling her their grievances: "I had the unrewarding task of discussing a long history of mistakes in American policy." They had lost, she writes, the homogeneity of a true culture. She returned to the South Seas, where, though she knew change would come, she would not have to "star[e] disaster in the face everyday."[44] Her pre-war work there has been criticized for her scant attention to the changes colonialism had already brought, and when she does to some extent admit the influence of colonialism, her response is telling.[45] Samoa she places, as Rousseau does his primitivist ideal, at a perfect moment when earlier brutal elements have been modified, but before the harmony of the whole has gone and the canker of choice has entered.[46]

Mead's occlusion of colonialism was typical of the anthropology of her day. While writing of her own society, however, she is ready to admit that others are oppressed on grounds of race. What she never acknowledges is that she herself belongs to a group disadvantaged on grounds of gender. When she describes Benedict's early project to write "the lives of restless and highly enslaved women . . . from the standpoint of the 'new woman,'" she significantly reformulates it as a desire to write about "famous women."[47] She, like other women anthropologists, never had the academic recognition she deserved, but as her colleague at Columbia Marvin Harris said: "She would sound off on everything else . . . but never on the under-representation of women in our department. If she had, it would be graven in one's memory. Margaret Mead was not the victim, ever, of anything."[48] Mead describes in her autobiography a memory she thought she had of her brother being locked and terrified in a cupboard: it turned out it had happened to her, and she comments that she tends "to erase small misfortunes from her mind. Later other people have to recall them to [her]."[49] Blotting out bad experiences and reascribing them to the other sex seems the pattern of her attitude to gender: as in that incident, she continually rewrites pain for women as problems for men. At De Pauw she was made wretched by her mistake in doing well academically in a co-educational group. Although she dealt with that by choosing a way of life in which she could fulfil her ambitions without competing directly with men, that humiliation keeps returning in her writing, reworked into pity for the male sex. The comments for which she has been most criticized by feminists in *Male and Female* are often examples of this. She describes the stresses of the young boy told that as a member of the superior sex he should never be beaten by a girl, while in practice competing with equally well-educated and faster maturing girls. In American culture, a boy learns he will have to be continually successful to defend his masculine identity. For the girl, the "desperate need for success remains," but "it is not as strong as for the boy, because for the girl success is demanded only as . . . of all human beings, and not with a threat that if she does not succeed she will not be regarded as a true female."[50] Life is hard for men, because they find it so difficult to reach the sense of "irreversible achievement" which women find in their biological role.[51] Mead's definition of American masculinity, precarious, driven, imperilled by the success ethic which defines it, is reminiscent of Lacan's notion of the fraudulent phallus, but unlike him she ignores the oppressive phallocentric symbolic order such an analysis implies. Yet this emphasis is not new in her texts. She had, it tends to be forgotten, made very similar points in *Sex and Temperament*: life is always harder for the male deviant, she com- mented there, because female interests, occupations and qualities, whatever they may be, have less status. The male deviant unlike the female loses prestige by indulging his aberrant temperament. The fact that this implies that all women, except possibly deviants, suffer from lower status than men is ignored.[52] She only concedes difficulties for women by insisting they are shared equally by men:

> Regimentation of one sex carries with it, to greater or lesser degree, regimentation of the other . . . There can be no society which insists that women follow one special personality-pattern, defined as feminine, which does not do violence to the individuality of many men.[53]

She is of course correct, and many of the points she makes have been taken up once more only very recently in discussions of masculinity. It is her evasion of women's disadvantages, not her understanding of men's, for which she should be criticized. Though she rightly insists that masculinity is as much a cultural construct as femininity, she never looks at the relation of these constructs to power.

Paradoxically, what was most radical as an anthropological text about *Coming of Age* was its attention to those without power, even if their powerlessness is passed over. It ignored the leaders, the men, and looked at the experience of girls and young women. In that sense, Derek Freeman's criticism of Mead for not consulting elderly men with authority in Samoan society about young people's sexual mores, for not writing more about Samoan hierarchy and exclusively male systems of rank, is reactionary and misplaced. Yet he is surely right to argue that her depiction of the ease of sexual relations owes much to the literary image of the South Seas, which focuses on women. As a literary text *Coming of Age in Samoa* is centrally in that tradition. In its contrast between the guilt-free sexual life of the Samoans and the fraught inhibition of modernity it is one of many modernist restatements of the primitivist myth. Unlike its contemporary European primitivist paradise, it is not a place of intensity and raw passion, as it would be for the Surrealists or Lawrence. This is modern primitivism US style, the escape from ambition, the escape from competitiveness, the escape into tranquillity, so praised by Mary Austin, Ruth Underhill, John Collier and other admirers of the cultures of the American Southwest. Significantly, the most disputed and universally criticized point in the book is Mead's far from romantic description of the Samoans as emotionally shallow and apathetic. This apparently arrogant judgement, shallow in itself, perhaps reveals something of Mead's own conflicts. It is the flaw she has drawn in this Eden: Mead cannot bring herself to admire wholeheartedly her picture of tranquil conformity and ambition-free passivity. As Theodore Schwarz put it, "while Samoa may have been Mead's Arcadia, it is not her Utopia."[54]

Mead was of course never a thorough-going primitivist. She acknowledged that what she called "simple" societies were always cultures, and not necessarily pleasant ones. What she valued about America was the possibility of choice, described in that first book as the one compensation for the instability and fragmentation of modern society with its "heterogeneous, rapidly changing civilization: . . . high proportions of crime and delinquency . . . conflicts of youth . . . ever-increasing number of neuroses . . . lack of a coherent tradition without which the development of art is sadly handicapped."[55] She never lost her enlightenment belief that democracy, science and education would, with her help, lead Americans to choose a better world. That was the intention behind the bland propaganda of her wartime book, *And Keep Your Powder Dry*. The dropping of the atomic bomb, coinciding as it did with her rejection by her third husband, shook her social and personal confidence. What disappears from *Male and Female* is the utopian dream of the end of *Sex and Temperament* of a future in which "No child would be relentlessly shaped to one pattern of behaviour, but instead there should be many patterns, in a world that had learned to allow to each individual the pattern which was most congenial to his gifts."[56]

For her to say, as she does in *Male and Female*, that changing women's roles in America may bring more distress than pleasure, is perhaps nearer defeat than complacency. Mead's picture of family life and sexual relations in the United States is bleak. In her sour analysis of American middle-class dating rituals, for example, she suggests they are little to do with sexual desire, but are instead deeply implicated in a competitive struggle for popularity and acceptability. Heavy petting is a ritual contest, between the boy, who must go as far as he can, and the girl, who must say no, but not too soon, and certainly never too late. No wonder, she says, so few American women can give themselves sexually after marriage. If Boas and Sapir criticized her for not distinguishing between romantic and sexual love in Samoa, neither seems present in her picture of the United States, or only there in the shallowest forms.[57] Yet, as usual in her texts, the bleakness is cocooned by what Clifford Geertz describes as an "upward and onward" introduction and conclusion.[58] Yet even there her rallying call to build "a world in which both sexes benefit" is tempered by her sense that American competitiveness is bound to make the progress of gifted women intensely difficult, because of the "devastating antagonisms that are likely to occur in America, where it is so hard to forgive any person who wins in the same race, although so easy to acclaim success in races one has not entered."[59] Change will be slow, though eventually brought about by exceptional individuals, one presumes like herself, who "have been reared with a light in their hand that can shine backwards as well as forwards."[60]

The conflicts which Mead negotiates in her work are not simply personal: they are, as Karen Horney would say, those of her time. As an American liberal intellectual of the interwar years, she was intensely critical of American ethnocentrism and conformity, yet also driven by her desire to be accepted and successful. This tension lies behind, on the one hand, her emphasis on individuality, her stance as an outsider, a role, as Levi-Strauss pointed out, the anthropologist can uniquely play. On the other hand, it informs her analysis of culture's power to shape, so invasive, yet leaving pockets (like herself, she hopes) of deviant resistance. She was aware of the devastating effects of American competitiveness, but unable to resist the lure of fame, or to admit to her consciousness anything which threatened her self-image of success. For all her innovatory work on gender construction, her assessment of American feminity is always distorted by her terror of admitting she belongs to a disparaged group. She falls back, as often in the history of American feminism, on a triumphalist account of the woman's role. She presents herself simultaneously, with all the strengths associated with women, yet untrammelled by her gender. Her autobiography, as James Boon says, "shapes a story by converting everything it remembers to personal advantage, a vector of a successful career."[61] Yet her dilemma is that there is no "culturally normal" place for a successful America woman. "Each step forward in work as a successful American . . . means a step back as a woman," she admits, though she adds quickly "and also . . . a step back imposed on some male."[62]

If many of the culture and personality anthropologists were either immigrants or women, Karen Horney was both.[63] She was one of the many intellectuals to come to the United States from Germany in the decade before the Second World War, though she had paid several earlier visits, and already had many professional contacts. Born in 1885, she was Ruth Benedict's generation rather than Mead's. Her family background—authoritarian, often absent father, bored unhappy mother, favoured elder brother—bred more radical rebellion in her than perhaps was ever felt by Mead. Like Mead, she owed her entry into higher education to her mother's support against her father. She trained as a psychoanalyst in Germany, being analyzed by Freud's disciple Karl Abraham until she broke off, frustrated and irritated by his conventionally Freudian approach to the female psychology. All her early essays combat Freud's negative definition of femininity—his belief that women's psyches are shaped by the discovery of their lack of a penis. In 1923 she attacked Karl Abraham's paper on the Castration Complex in women (in which among other things he suggests that the current demand for sexual parity was one of its symptoms), arguing that the idea that women regard their bodies as inferior is "masculine narcissism."[64] She developed these ideas further in 1926, suggesting that Freud and his fellow psychoanalysts were projecting male fears onto the growing girl, and that the desire for motherhood was not simply a sublimation of penis envy, but itself a powerful instinct. Womb envy was just as likely, if not more, to create dissatisfaction in men as penis envy in women.[65] At this stage Horney used arguments from biology that mirrored Freud's own, and indeed, by postulating different instincts for men and women, she found herself further along the road towards absolute sexual difference than Freud himself. It was a route she had to abandon.

Luckily, she found a more promising path. Even in these early papers, she was moving towards a theory of the psyche that included cultural influences. Following the social theorist Georg Simmel she argued that modern society was a masculine civilization, and women were taught inferiority from their earliest days. Because masculine attitudes have acquired the status of "objective" truth, women accept and internalize their culture's valuation of their relative worth.[66] As Simmel noted (some twenty-four years before Mead), "deficient performances in the most diverse areas are degraded as 'feminine,' while outstanding performances by women are celebrated as 'thoroughly manly'."[67] Though not a Marxist, Simmel believed that "cultural forms are conditions for the constitution of the individual personality and the formation of its identity," and that the development of modern society and urbanization, in its "masculine," "objective" form, led to alienation, isolation and the weakening of affective bonds.[68] Horney found in his work a cultural contrast between present and past, as well as a modernist questioning of the value of progress, at any rate as far as psychic contentment was concerned. Several of her articles at this period attacked traditional Western bourgeois marriage and monogamy—her own marriage was breaking down concurrently—and she became increasingly convinced of the ethnocentricity of Freud's views of femininity. Her friend, and at one stage lover, Erich Fromm, was also developing a model of psychic growth that took account of culture. She later cited an article of his written in 1930 as the first in German psychoanalysis to do so, an example perhaps of the feminine self-deprecation which she was so anxious to eradicate in herself and others, since she had clearly pre-empted him.[69]

After she went to the United States in 1932, her ideas matured with great rapidity. Her analytic practice convinced her that the neuroses of her US patients took different forms from those of her European patients. Moving in liberal intellectual circles where ideas of the culture and personality school were pervasive, Horney began to think in terms not just of the difference in psychic life between modernity and the past, but between Western and non-Western cultures. In her later book, *Our Inner Conflicts*, she describes how her growing conviction that Freud's view of gender qualities was culturally determined grew into a broader realization of the ethnocentricism of traditional psychoanalysis.[70] Freud's mistake, she believed, was to see his own society and its problems as universal. Although she always emphasized her indebtedness to Freud, especially to his ideas of the unconscious and repression, and to the technique of free association, she began to argue that Freud mistook symptoms for causes. The Oedipal complex is not an inevitable genetic stage but a neurotic response to certain cultural conditions: he was only describing "a certain part of the population of a certain culture at a certain time."

The problem for Horney, as to a greater and lesser extent it was for the culture and personality anthropologists who wanted to use some of his insights, was that Freud's theories rest on the nineteenth-century framework of cultural evolution with its assumption that white male civilization is the highest form of humanity. His later, more broadly cultural work drew explicitly on this framework, with the result that *Totem and Taboo*, for example, was sharply criticized by Boas and his followers, particularly for the idea that the "primitive" was comparable to a civilized child or to a neurotic. But this framework also underlies his claim for the universality of his purely psychoanalytic theories. The reason Freud can take it for granted that his analysis has universal validity is because he sees European culture as the forefront of human progress. Other cultural formations have yet to reach civilization, and represent forms of incipient rather than full, mature humanity. Like the nineteenth-century cultural evolutionists, he takes it for granted that patriarchy is the inevitable form of civilized society, and that a woman is less highly evolved and therefore less typically human, than a man. Although all the post-

Freudians, Adorno, Reich, Voloshinov, Marcuse, Klein, Lacan, have attempted to include in their revisions of his theories an extended dialectic between psychic development and social context, they have by no means always faced the problem of Freud's Eurocentrism.

Horney's first book, *The Neurotic Personality of Our Time*, published in 1937, cited a range of recent work by American anthropologists, including Benedict's *Patterns of Culture*, Mead's *Sex and Temperament in Three Primitive Societies*, and an essay by Sapir on "Cultural Anthropology and Psychiatry," to support the view that Western society does not represent a human norm. It is just one among many configurations. This book was, she later admitted, specifically an analysis of stresses within United States society, though, I imagine for reasons of tact, she never said so within the book. But one must also take its title "of our times" at its face value. She sees the United States as at the forefront of modernity, for good or bad, experiencing in more acute form the problems she already knew. Horney was continually aware of her own need for analysis—she had entered analysis in the first place because of depression, not in order to train—and the core of her theory is already present in an article she wrote in 1934, when she deals with the problem of a contemporary "feminine type," in whom she clearly sees herself as well as other educated women of her generation and the next.[71]

In this article, "The Overvaluation of Love," published two years after her arrival in the United States, she abandoned all residue of the quest for what Freud called the "psychical consequences of the anatomical distinction between the sexes." The "feminine type" she describes is formed by cultural pressures. Horney was acutely aware that educated working women of her day faced a conflict between incompatible expectations. Once a woman had entered the world of work, she competed on male terms for success and prestige. Yet her sense of her own worth still depended on how she was valued as a sexual being by men, and on how she succeeded in competing sexually with other women: she was still dominated by the "patriarchal ideal of womanhood, of woman as one whose only happiness is to love a man and be loved by him."[72] What went under the name of love for many was in fact the neurotic need for self-validation by another. The neurotic "feminine type" in this article was simply a woman in whom early experience had intensified this conflict. Such women were anxious and unhappy without male sexual partners, but having found one, each new relationship rapidly deteriorated. Conventional Freudian therapy told the woman her problem was accepting her feminine nature, that a husband and children would bring her contentment, and she should forget about her career: repeatedly, this analysis failed to help. For Horney such neurosis springs from insecurity and anxiety which goes back to childhood, when the young girl first experienced such conflicts: the psyche puts up defence systems which attempt to find compromise solutions, but in fact only exacerbate the neurotic conflict. This "feminine type" desires both power and love, and achieves neither.

In this essay, Horney was formulating her most central argument, that neurotics were not exceptional in their society but acutely typical of it. (Like Mead and Benedict she makes a clear distinction between deviants and neurotics.) Neurotics embody in an extreme form the central conflicts in the culture around them. The neurosis of the "feminine type" was a sharper, more accentuated version of the fears and defences found in her society in general. Reversing Freud's manoeuvre, which she had attacked so much, of interpreting women's psychic trajectory in terms of the masculine, Horney developed her view of the contemporary psyche from this analysis of the feminine type's conflict between affection and power. In so doing, she made a stinging attack on American capitalist culture. Although she never explicitly adopted Fromm's Marxism, her analysis of American society is close to his, and to the other exiles of the Frankfurt School. Both her biographers, mistakenly I believe, misread her and her work as largely apolitical.[73] She was cautious about making explicit political statements, though in response to J. Edgar Hoover's call to the American Psychiatric Association to follow their patriotic duty in revealing their patients' subversive activities, she said publicly and unequivocally that she would rather go to jail.[74] That the FBI listed her as a "communist or communist-sympathizer" perhaps proves nothing but their paranoia, but I do not find it surprising that they found her books in packets of communist literature they seized.[75] "Modern culture," she wrote,

> . . . is economically based on the principle of individual competition . . . The psychic result of this is a diffuse hostile tension between individuals. Everyone is the real or potential competitor of everyone else . . . It pervades school life. And most important of all, it pervades the family situation, so that as a rule the child is inoculated with this germ from the very beginning. The rivalry between father and son, mother and daughter, one child and another, is not a general human phenomenon but is the response to culturally conditioned stimuli. It remains one of Freud's great achievements to have

seen the role of rivalry in the family, as expressed in his concept of the Oedipus complex, and other hypotheses. It must be added, however, that this rivalry itself is not biologically conditioned but is a result of given cultural conditions and furthermore, that the family situation is not the only one to stir up rivalry, but that the competitive stimuli are active from the cradle to the grave.[76]

This hostile tension results in constant fear, of others' hostility, of retaliation against one's own hostility towards others, of failure in these competitive stakes, and of the resulting economic insecurity or loss of prestige: this fear, and the sense of emotional isolation it brings, leads in turn to an intensified need for affection:

> Because it corresponds to a vital need, love is overvalued in our culture. It becomes a phantom—like success—carrying with it the illusion that it is a solution for all problems. Love itself is not an illusion—although in our culture it is most often a screen for satisfying wishes that have nothing to do with it—but it is made an illusion by our expecting much more of it than it can possibly fulfil. And the ideological emphasis that we place on love serves to cover up the factors which create our exaggerated need for it. Hence the individual—and I still mean the normal individual—is in the dilemma of needing a great deal of affection but finding difficulty in obtaining it.[77]

The "neurotic personality of our times," though on the surface taking many forms, is, according to Karen Horney, fundamentally one torn between anxious competitiveness and a desperate need for affection—like everyone else, but more so. The added twist in American culture, is that "being popular has become one of the competitive aims."[78] It is striking what an apt analysis of Margaret Mead this is, with her compulsive need to succeed, to be unique, and her equally compulsive need to be loved, to be popular, to be a regular American.

For Horney, the neurotic psyche is always a battleground of contradictory desires and fears, and she goes on to elaborate what she sees as the three central contradictions in US society which give rise to them: the contradiction between an ideology of success and one of self-sacrifice and selfishness; the contradiction between an economic system which stimulates consumption through advertising to maintain a level of "conspicuous consumption" while making it impossible for the "great majority" to fulfil these fanned needs; a social philosophy which emphasizes the freedom of the individual, which in practice is deeply limited.

> These contradictions embedded in our culture are precisely the conflicts which the neurotic struggles to reconcile: his tendencies toward aggressiveness and his tendencies toward yielding; his excessive demands and his fear of never getting anything: his striving toward self-aggrandizement and his feeling of personal helplessness. The difference from the normal is merely quantitative.[79]

Horney, like Freud, believes neurosis is formed on the level of psychic rather than any "social," "external" or objective reality. Where she disagrees with Freud is that she sees him as positing a pre-social psychic dynamic, the libido, which is then frustrated by cultural circumstances—the price of civilization. For her, as for the anthropologists, culture is never absent. Problems may be caused, she says, by a dominant or indulgent mother, but the dominant or indulgent mother is the product of a particular culture. The neurotic personality is torn by conflicting compulsive trends, inner conflicts, but these are sown by cultural circumstances.

Unlike Freud, but along with her anthropologist contemporaries and indeed many modernist writers, Horney abandoned the primacy of the diachronic model for her therapeutic practice. Although she always maintained that "basic anxiety," or "core anxiety" as she later came to call it, was the result of experiences in early childhood, she did not see neurosis as simply the repetition of childhood traumas. Rather it was a cumulative and ever more complex system of conflictual and self-defeating defences. The present structure of the patient's personality had to be understood. If Mead had used Horney's analysis of personality to understand cultural patterns, instead of one based on Jung's personality types, she might have found a more useful model for the contradictions within Samoa. A Horneyan analysis would have seen the Samoans' excessive drive towards conciliation and social harmony as one bound to hide repressed aggression: so sporadic outbreaks of violence and fury would be expected, not inexplicable, or only explicable through a theory of deviancy.[80]

From her first book onwards, Horney, unlike Mead, never even mentions the possibility of any definite psychological differences between the sexes. Their trajectories are mirror reversals. The concept of womb envy in Horney's early work in the 1920s, written during the height of the feminist campaigning that went on in the

Weimar Republic, was taken up by Mead and made much of in her later work: Horney argued then for the positive joys of motherhood, as Mead was to do increasingly. Horney's early work considered the relation of biology to gender, which Mead came to after the war. In her last years Mead finally recognized with horror the negativity of the role Freud assigned to women, the subject of Horney's first essays.[81] Later all issues of gender disappear in Horney's texts. She writes extensively about the "dependent" type, who needs a partner for validation: *Self-analysis*, her bestselling book takes such a case-study as its centre, a patient she names as Clare, though it has been suggested that "Clare" is largely herself.[82] But she insists that although such types are much more often women than men in American culture, no neurotic formation is exclusively found in one gender. She argues against Freud's association of femininity with masochism or with jealousy, except in as far as he was describing a culturally specific pattern. (It is possible, she says, that in the Germany and Austria of Freud's day women were more often jealous than men.) In each of her works she posits three main neurotic types. The first, the conciliatory and dependent, is clearly associated with Western femininity; the second, the over-masterful/aggressive and the third, the emotionally withdrawn, are both associated with Western ideas of masculinity, a dominant and recessive version, one might put it. But she makes clear these gender associations cannot be taken for granted. "Self-effacement," she wrote in 1951, "has nothing to do with femininity nor aggressive arrogance with masculinity. Both are exquisitely neurotic phenomena."[83] By 1951 such denial of essential gender differences was deeply unfashionable, and I think the rigour with which she refuses to make those distinctions after the mid-1930s has much to do with her response to Nazism. Yet in her rejection of any sense of the naturalness of traditional gender characteristics, she ends by depriving herself of a language in which she can sufficiently specify the cultural gendering of subjectivity. If, as Mead wrote in 1935, there are cultures like the Arapesh, in which no-one "felt like a man," or "felt like a woman," in Western society gender identity is a crucial part of subjectivity.[84] In 1926 Horney had quoted Georg Simmel's words: "we do not believe in a purely 'human' civilization, into which the question of sex does not enter, for the very reason that prevents any such civilization from in fact existing, namely, the (so to speak) naive identification of the concept 'human being' [Mensch] and the concept 'man' [Mann], which in many languages even causes the same word to be used for the two concepts." She had agreed with him that "historically the relation of the sexes may be crudely described as that of master and slave. Here, as always, it is 'one of the privileges of the master that he has not constantly to think that he is master, while the position of the slave is such that he can never forget it'."[85] In her later work, that gendering of subjectivity (in both senses) is something Horney can only explore in oblique terms.

Horney's last two books develop the idea of the tyrannical "idealized self," similar in many ways to Lacan's pathological false ego. In both cases there is a terrified refusal to question the self-image, and a constant search for its validation from others. But for Horney this is still a neurotic formation produced by a competitive society, not a universal psychic pattern. As for Mead, and the modernists in general, for Horney fragmentation and alienation are the products of modernity, not in the nature of things but how things have become. This fragmentation is always set against a possibility of wholeness, in the work of art, in the primitive society, in the organic unfissured self. Just as Mead writes against an ideal—never to be found—of a way of life in touch with natural rhythm, against a vision of the wholeness of primitive societies in contrast to the fragmentation of the West, so Horney posits in her writings, though more tentatively, the conflict-free contrary of the neurotic self. Most of her work implies that in modern capitalist society such a self is scarcely possible; the difference between the neurotic and the normal, as she constantly says, is only a question of degree, not of kind. Only a few pages in each book deal with anything other than the exploration of the complex structures of the conflict-torn mind.

When Horney contrasts the false self with what she comes to call the "real self," she is speaking of something very different from the ego-psychologists' concept of the strong ego. She says herself she is not sure how she can define this real self, but it appears to refer to a mode of consciousness, not to the structure of the psyche, to potentiality rather than to essence. Under the influence of existentialism and Zen Buddhism (she had become friendly with both Paul Tillich and Daisetz Suzuki) she begins to use the concept of "wholeheartedness." If "neurosis" is to be driven to perform actions which hold terror at bay but never yield satisfaction, "wholeheartedness" is to be capable of absorption in creative and pleasurable enjoyment. "Wholeheartedness" is a concept which appears at odds with any kind of post-structuralism. Yet, although their language is in so many ways different, the person whose therapeutic aims she most closely shares is Julia Kristeva, for whom, as for Horney, the subject is always in process and for whom the role of the analyst is to help psyche to become an open system, responding to and creating art and love.[86]

Where Horney has been most criticized by more orthodox Freudians is in her absence of any developed theory of the genesis of differentiated sexual desire.[87] Although she sees gender characteristics as cultural constructs, she has little to say about the construction of sexuality. Gendered bodies have no more place than gendered subjectivity in Horney's later writing. Like Erich Fromm, she attacks sexuality's central role in Freud's theories. Sexual problems, in her analyses, are almost always the result of anxiety's disruption of inter-personal relations or intrapsychic balance. If she and Erich Fromm were writing now, they would see the centrality of the concept of desire in present psychoanalytically oriented theory as a sign of the culturally specific neuroses of late twentieth-century consumer capitalism. Fromm, indeed, attacked Marcuse's view of sexual revolution on the grounds that nothing was more a commodity in America than sexuality. Like T.S. Eliot, Horney was led by her dislike of capitalist materialism and consumerism to a non-Western religious and philosophical framework which eschews desire. What she lost was the central courageous leap of earlier theorists like Darwin and Freud and Marx, who wanted to understand humankind as complex animals, with material lives, not merely disembodied souls or minds. Yet, given the symbolic way in which the body has been used in this century to mark the possibility or the absence of power, her reluctance is perhaps at least as understandable as Mead's toying with the new biologism.

Horney's books largely consist of subtle, compassionate, witty accounts of the varieties of conflict-ridden psyches of modern society. Like Mead, who was described with horror by the British anthro-pologist A.C. Haddon as a "lady novelist," her discursive strategy is the construction of a plethora of vignettes.[88] Without endorsing Haddon's sexism (which neatly illustrates Mead and Simmel's comments on the assumed correlation between the feminine and the second-rate) it has to be acknowledged that Mead succumbs at times to the superficial and the stereotype, travel magazine perhaps, rather than novelette. Horney's accounts, however, combine clarity and depth, peeling off layer after layer of intrapsychic intrigue. On the other hand, perhaps Mead was attempting the harder task, representing the strange in familiar terms, not like Horney, revealing the strangeness in what her readers had thought was most familiar. Horney's work remained very much that of a Central European in its constant allusion to literature and philosophy: Goethe, Nietzsche, Stendhal, George Eliot, Rousseau, Ibsen, Schopenhauer, Flaubert, Dostoevsky, Sartre, and many more, all are called on to illustrate the psychic dilemmas and patterns she seeks to uncover, yet always in order to extend rather than restrict the accessibility of her writing. She and Mead both wrote, with great success, for a wide general public in a way few of their male colleagues achieved. As Deborah Gordon has pointed out of Mead and Benedict, this is in contrast to their comparative lack of professional or at any rate institutional recognition.[89]

Both Horney and Mead see modernity and modern subjectivity as a fractured melange of customs, values, codes. They see the qualities associated with gender in Western society as culturally specific, never absolute, natural or universal. But where they differ from present constructionists—postmodern constructionists—is that for them this fragmentation, these roles, hide the possibility of a more natural organic being, not for either of them natural gender roles, but a more natural way of being human. For both of them American competitiveness is the centrally destructive force. They are acutely aware of the disempowerment of women in that society, even though for quite different reasons it is not a problem they can directly address. Like Virginia Woolf, they produced their most significant contributions to feminist thought in the 1930s. The emergence of the motifs of "man the hunter" and the "mother-infant pair" in the post war years was clearly over-determined, but at one level it must be seen as an attempt to re-naturalize a Western civilization which now included Auschwitz and the atom bomb. Aggression had to be accepted as one aspect of normality, from which one could turn for solace to the other normality of maternal care. For Mead, the horror she felt at America's action in dropping the bomb (she appeared less disturbed by revelations of German evil) drove her further towards her affirmation of "womanly" values. For Horney's darker view of Western civilization, there is no need of new myths: of Hitler's attitude to the Jews, she says, "in more civilized and concealed forms we can observe most of these expressions of hate in everyday life, in families or between competitors."[90] The postwar revelations which were so devastating to some liberal humanists drove Horney further to an Enlightenment humanist position, in which gender becomes an unimportant marker in the psychoanalyst's quest to deliver the soul from the diseased culture of the West.

In their postwar work both Mead and Horney write as if any kind of political feminism is irrelevant. Yet because they both at different times and in different ways fundamentally question the naturalness of Western gender roles, their ideas undoubtedly helped to make possible the deconstructive work of modern feminism. And, perhaps in the very ways in which they might be accused of not being "feminist" at all, they make it clear that gender is not just a variable but a fissured, contradictory, and unstable category.

Notes

1. Cora Kaplan, "Feminist Criticism 20 Years On" in Helen Carr (ed.) *From My Guy to Sci-Fi:Genre and Women's Writing in the Postmodern World* (London: Pandora, 1989).
2. Kate Millett, *Sexual Politics* (Aylesbury: Sphere Books, 1971).
3. Henry Louis Gates discusses Homi Bhabha's attitude to Fanon in "Critical Fanonism" *Critical Inquiry* 17:3 (1991), pp. 457–70. Robert Young has recently given an account of Fanon as an anti-humanist, but only by attending to the later Fanon and evading the earlier. See Robert Young, *White Mythologies: Writing History and the West* (London: Routledge, 1991).
4. Millett, *Sexual Politics*, pp. 362–63.
5. Olive Banks, *The Faces of Feminism: A Study of Feminism as a Social Movement* (Oxford: Martin Robertson, 1981), p. 238.
6. Margaret Whitford, "The Feminist Philosopher: A Contradiction in Terms?" *Women: a Cultural Review* 3:2 (1992).
7. See Gayatri Chakravorty Spivak, *In Other Worlds: Essays in Cultural Politics* (New York: Methuen, 1987); Jonathan Dollimore, *Sexual Dissidence* (Oxford: Oxford University Press, 1991); Diana Fuss, *Essentially Speaking* (London: Routledge, 1990).
8. See Marcia Westkott, *The Feminist Legacy of Karen Horney* (New Haven: Yale University Press, 1986), for a feminist interpretation of her work as a whole. The feminist implications of her work up to 1934 were always obvious, though it has been criticized for its biologism. See Juliet Mitchell, *Psychoanalysis and Feminism* (Harmondsworth: Penguin, 1974), who appears not to know Horney's later work, and Dee Garrison "Karen Horney and Feminism" *Signs* 6:4 (1981), pp. 672–91, who sees her later work as an abandonment of her feminism. I have read Janet Sayers' largely unsympathetic and, in my opinion, often mistaken account of Horney's work only after completing this article, so will not be able to deal with it in any detail here: her misreading to some extent stems, I would want to argue, from a failure to see how important the cultural criticism is in Horney's work. Janet Sayers, *Mothering Psychoanalysis: Helene Deutsch, Karen Horney, Anna Freud, Melanie Klein* (Harmondsworth: Penguin, 1992).
9. Mead actually disliked being called a feminist: "In a sense," she said in the 1970s, "I never was a feminist. I made friends with women, I stood by women, and if I was asked to do something that might improve the position of women in general, I did it. But I don't believe all these women fifty years old who haven't tried anything but marriage and children, who talk about how they've been discriminated against, because on the whole none of them have done anything else." Jane Howard, *Margaret Mead: A Life* (London: Harvill, 1984), p. 362.

10. Jane Rendall, *Origins of Modern Feminism: Women in Britain, France and the United States, 1780–1860* (Basingstoke & London: Macmillan, 1985), pp. 304–5.
11. Banks, *Faces of Feminism* pp. 155–63.
12. Margaret Mead, *Blackberry Winter: My Earlier Years* (1972) (London & Sydney: Angus & Robertson, 1973), p. 20. Further references will be abbreviated to BW.
13. *BW*, pp. 103, 105.
14. In her account of Boas' lectures, Mead only records his condemnation of English anthropologists for their belief that England was the pinnacle of civilization. Given Boas's opposition to Morgan, I take it this is patriotic repression. See Margaret Mead, *An Anthropologist at Work: Writings of Ruth Benedict* (London: Secker & Warburg, 1959), p. 11. Further references will be abbreviated to *AW*.
15. *AW*, p. 14
16. Franz Boas, "An Anthropologist's Credo" *The Nation* 147 (1938), p. 201, quoted in Derek Freeman, *Margaret Mead and Samoa: the Making and the Unmaking of an Anthropological Myth* (Cambridge, Mass. & London: Harvard University Press, 1983), p. 24.
17. *AW*, p. 11
18. George Stocking (ed.) *Malinowski, Rivers, Benedict and Others: Essays on Culture and Personality, History of Anthropology Vol. 4* (Madison: University of Wisconsin Press, 1986), p. 6. See Ruth Bunzel's comment: "Some of us fled to the freer air of Paris . . . and eventually retired. Some of us joined radical movements and sold the *Daily Worker* on street corners, and some of us went into anthropology, hoping that there we might find some answers to the ambiguities and contradictions of our age and the general enigma of human life." Howard, *Margaret Mead*, p. 69.
19. Claude Levi-Strauss, *Tristes Tropiques* (1955), trans. John and Doreen Weightman (Harmondsworth: Penguin, 1976), pp. 502ff.
20. Edward Sapir, "Culture, Genuine and Spurious" in David Mandelbaum (ed.) *Culture, Language and Personality: Selected Essays* (Berkeley: University of California Press, 1949).
21. *BW*, p. 1.
22. First published in New York by William Morrow, 1928. References in this article are to the 1943 Penguin edition. Further references will be abbreviated to *CAS*.
23. *Male and Female: A Study of the Sexes in a Changing World*, first published in New York by William Morrow, 1949. References are to the 1950 Victor Gollancz edition. Further references will be abbreviated to *MF*.
24. James Clifford, "On Ethnographic Allegory" in James Clifford and George E. Marcus (eds) *Writing Culture: the Poetics and Politics of Ethnography* (Berkeley: University of California Press, 1986).
25. Marilyn Strathern, *The Gender of the Gift* (Berkeley: University of California Press, 1988), p. 70.
26. Margaret Mead, *Sex and Temperament in Three Primitive Societies* (London: Routledge & Sons, 1935). Further references will be abbreviated to *ST*.

27. Betty Friedan, *The Feminine Mystique* (1963) (Harmondsworth: Penguin, 1965), pp. 120–31, and Germaine Greer, *The Female Eunuch* (1970) (London: Paladin, 1971), pp. 96, 339, 340.

28. See Donna Haraway, *Primate Visions: Gender, Race, and Nature in the World of Modern Science* (London & New York: Routledge, 1989), especially pp. 126–27. Annette Weiner has said that Derek Freeman told her in 1980 that his work had been completed by 1965, but that he could not then find a publisher. Annette B. Weiner, "Ethnographic Determinism: Samoa and the Margaret Mead Controversy" *American Anthropologist* 85:4 (1983), p. 910. It is significant that it was not till the Reaganite, Moral Majority 1980s that his attack on one of the mothers of permissiveness could be launched.

29. James Clifford comments on this controversy in "On Ethnographic Allegory," and suggests that Mead and Freeman's work forms a "diptych," which can be seen as yet another manifestation of "a recurrent Western ambivalence about the 'primitive'" (p. 103).

30. "It must remain, as all anthropological works must remain, exactly as it was written, true to what I saw in Samoa and what I was able to convey of what I saw, true to the state of our knowledge of human behaviour as it was in the mid-1920s: true to our hopes and fears for the future of the world." Margaret Mead, "Preface 1973 Edition" in *Coming of Age in Samoa* (New York, 1973), p. 2, quoted in Freeman, pp. 113–14. Freeman interprets this to mean there should be no later accounts, while the context is clearly that of whether her original work should be revised by her in view of the later accounts which already existed.

31. Lowell D. Holmes, *Quest for the Real Samoa: the Mead/Freeman Controversy & Beyond*, postscript by Eleanor Leacock (South Hadley, Mass.: Bergin & Garvey, 1987).

32. Roy A. Rappaport, quoted in an unsigned editorial comment on the Freeman/Mead controversy in *Scientific American* 255:5 (November 1986), p. 58.

33. "Franz Boas: an Obituary" *The Nation* CLVI (2 January 1943), reprinted in *AW*, p. 420.

34. Benedict disliked the idea of a finite number of given personality types, such as Jung suggests: see *AW*, p. 206.

35. Levi-Strauss, *Tristes Tropiques*, p. 505.

36. *ST*, p. 290.

37. *ST*, p. 293.

38. *ST*, p. 280.

39. *ST*, p. 321.

40. *BW*, p. 196.

41. Mary Catherine Bateson, *With a Daughter's Eye: a Memoir of Margaret Mead and Gregory Bateson* (New York: Morrow, 1984), p. 139.

42. *MF*, p. 6.

43. *AW*, p. 5.

44. *BW*, p. 191. Mead wrote up this experience as *The Changing Culture of an Indian Tribe* (New York: Columbia University Press, 1932), where the Omaha appear as the "Antler" people. It is perhaps typical of her that while she is deeply critical there of Alice Fletcher (without naming her), she is lavish in her

public praise of Margaret Mead and Ruth Bunzel (eds) *The Golden Age of American Anthropology* (New York: Braziller, 1960), a book whose introduction also glosses over the considerable ideological differences between the work of the Bureau of American Ethnology and the Boasian school.

45. A useful account of some of these criticisms is given by Victor Barnouw in *Culture and Personality* (1963) (Homewood, I2.: Dorsey Press, 1979, 3rd edn), pp. 89–103.

46. *CAS*, pp. 216–19.

47. *AW*, pp. 6, 132.

48. Howard, *Margaret Mead*, p. 363.

49. *BW*, pp. 20–22.

50. *MF*, p. 318.

51. *MF*, p. 127.

52. *ST*, p. 302. Curiously, Millett's only reference to Mead is a quotation from the *Barnard College Bulletin* for April, 1969, in which Mead wrote: "One aspect of the social valuation of different types of labor is the differential prestige of men's activities and women's activities. Whatever men do—even if it is dressing dolls for religious ceremonies—is more prestigious than what women do and is treated as a higher achievement." I have not been able to read the full article so I am not sure whether or not this indicates a change.

53. *ST*, pp. 312–13.

54. Theodore Schwarz, "Anthropology: a Quaint Science" *American Anthropologist* 85:4 (1983), p. 921.

55. *CAS*, pp. 196–97.

56. *ST*, p. 321.

57. Boas' comment is recorded in *BW*, p. 121. Sapir made this comment more generally about modern morals, though with specific reference to "excited books about pleasure-loving Samoans and Trobiand Islanders" in "Some Observations on the Sex Problem in America" (1928) quoted by Richard Handler in "Vigorous Male and Aspiring Female: Poetry, Personality and Culture in Edward Sapir and Ruth Benedict" in Stocking, *Malinowski . . .* pp. 144–45.

58. Clifford Geertz uses the phrase of Ruth Benedict in *Works and Lives: The Anthropologist as Author* (Oxford: Polity Press, 1988), p. 106.

59. *MF*, pp. 369, 379.

60. *MF*, p. 384.

61. James Boon, "Between the War Bali: Rereading the Relics" in Stocking, *Malinowski . . .* , p. 240.

62. *MF*, p. 318.

63. Two of the women who graduated from Boas's secretary to anthropologist, Ruth Bunzel and Esther Schiff Goldfrank, came from German Jewish backgrounds: it was they who initiated the calling of Boas "Papa Franz" (*AW*, p. 345). Karen Horney was not Jewish, although the Nazis of course regarded psychoanalysis as "Jewish" science.

64. "On the Genesis of the Castration Complex in Women," paper delivered in 1923, first published 1924, reprinted in Karen Horney, *Feminine Psychology*, ed. Harold Kelman (1968) (New York & London: Norton library edn, 1973), p. 38. Further references will be abbreviated to *FP*.

65. Karen Horney, "The Flight from Womanhood: the Masculinity Complex in Women as Viewed by Men and by Women" in *FP*, pp. 60–61. She speaks of "the boy's intense envy of motherhood" and "the envy of pregnancy, childbirth, and motherhood, as well as of the breasts and of the act of suckling." Although she is often referred to as the originator of the concept of "womb envy" (for example, by Millett, *Sexual Politics*, p. 258) I have not been able to find the actual phrase in her work.

66. *FP*, pp. 55–58.

67. Georg Simmel, "Female Culture" (1911), p. 67, in *Georg Simmel: On Women, Sexuality, and Love*, trans. and intro. Guy Oakes (New Haven & London: Yale University Press, 1984).

68. Guy Oakes, "Introduction," *Georg Simmel*, p. 9.

69. Karen Horney, *The Neurotic Personality of Our Time* (New York: Norton & Co., 1937), p. 20. Further references will be abbreviated to *NPT*.

70. Karen Horney, *Our Inner Conflicts: a Constructive Theory of Neurosis* (London: Kegan Paul, Trench, Trubner & Co., 1946).

72. "The Overvaluation of Love" reprinted in *FP*, pp. 182–213.

72. *FP*, p. 182.

73. Jack L., Rubins, *Karen Horney: Gentle Rebel of Psychoanalysis* (New York: Dial Press, 1978). The Berlin Institute of Psychoanalysis, for whom she had previously worked, was in itself based on principles which acknowledged the link between poverty and neuroses, and treated many patients free: Susan Quinn quotes its Director, the socialist Ernst Simmel (no relation as far as I know), as saying that society "makes its poor neurotic and because of its cultural demands, lets its neurotics stay poor, abandoning them to their misery." (Susan Quinn, *A Mind of Her Own: The Life of Karen Horney*, London: Macmillan, 1987.) Jack Rubins mentions that in Germany she was a left-of-centre social democrat (p. 95): perhaps, writing within a Cold War climate, he did not see that as a political stance. Dee Garrison, who used Rubins as her source for biographical information, blames Horney's alleged lack of political commitment for her later avoidance of issues of gender.

74. Edward R. Clemens, "Karen Horney, A Reminiscence," p. 110–1, in Karen Horney, *Final Lectures*, ed. Douglas H. Ingram (New York & London: Norton, 1987).

75. Quinn, *Mind of Her Own*, p. 392.

76. *NPT*, pp. 284–85.

77. *NPT*, p. 287.

78. *NPT*, p. 116.

79. *NPT*, p. 289.

80. I have to say this is not a point made by Horney herself, who sees her own theory of the three dominant neurotic drives vindicated by anthropological findings: see *NPT*, p. 103.

81. In Jean Strouse (ed.) *Women and Analysis* (New York: Dial Press, 1975), quoted in Garrison, p. 672.

82. Karen Horney, *Self Analysis* (1942) (London: Routledge and Kegan Paul, 1962).

83. Karen Horney, *Neurosis and Human Growth: the Struggle towards Self-Realization* (London: Routledge & Kegan Paul, 1951), p. 247.

84. *ST*, p. 301: Strathern comments on this as an often forgotten insight, p. 61.

85. Horney, "The Flight from Womanhood," pp. 56, 69.

86. *The Kristeva Reader*, ed. Toril Moi (Oxford: Basil Blackwell, 1987), p. 14.

87. See for example Juliet Mitchell, *Psychoanalysis*, pp. 128–31 (although Horney does not, as Mitchell asserts, refer to women's "true nature"); Stephen Frosh, *The Politics of Psychoanalysis: an Introduction to Freudian and Post-Freudian Theory* (Basingstoke: Macmillan, 1987), pp. 177–78, and Jacqueline Rose, *Sexuality in the Field of Vision* (Brighton: Harvester, 1985), pp. 99–101 (the only one, apparently, to know anything of Horney's later work, though I think she is quite mistaken in suggesting Horney abandons the idea of the unconscious).

88. Howard, *Margaret Mead*, p. 124.

89. Deborah Gordon, "The Politics of Ethnographic Authority: Race and Writing in the Ethnography of Margaret Mead and Zora Neale Hurston" in Marc Manganaro (ed.) *Modernist Anthropology: From Fieldwork to Text* (Princeton: Princeton University Press, 1990), p. 147.

90. Horney, *Neurosis and Human Growth*, p. 1.

8

Erik H. Erikson's
Critical Themes and Voices
The Task of Synthesis

Lawrence J. Friedman

From the publication of *Childhood and Society* in 1950 through the 1970s Erik Homburger Erikson was acknowledged as a major influence in American intellectual life, a figure of great academic distinction whose views on American culture also commanded wide public attention. His wide-ranging approach helped make the immediate postwar decades an unusually hospitable period for interdisciplinary enquiry and maintained the vital role in America of the intellectual as cultural critic, and an examination of his engagement with American society helps throw many of his fundamental intellectual concerns into relief.

By the time he wrote *Childhood and Society* Erikson had built intimate ties with leading American personality theorists like Henry Murray and John Dollard, pioneering cultural anthropologists such as Margaret Mead and Ruth Benedict, and leaders within the international psychoanalytic community. If the book marked him out as perhaps the most significant post-Freudian thinker, in shifting psychoanalysis decidedly towards social concerns, its critique of American culture was subtle rather than severe. The criticisms deepened in subsequent years as Erikson confronted McCarthyism, developed close friendships with culture critics like David Riesman, Benjamin Spock and Talcott Parsons, came to engage Reinhold Niebuhr and Paul Tillich, and cultivated ties to innovative theorists in American psychoanalysis like David Rappaport and George Klein. In 1970 Erikson won the Pulitzer Prize and the National Book Award for *Ghandi's Truth*, a volume that looked to the non-violent Indian leader for alternatives to America's vast nuclear arsenals and its deepening role in the Vietnam War. His photograph appeared in publications ranging from the *New York Times* to *Newsweek*. He completed a decade teaching one of the most popular courses in the history of Harvard University, where he profoundly influenced a new generation of culture critics. Robert Coles, Robert Lifton, Carol Gilligan and Richard Sennett continue to see themselves in Erikson's debt. So does Vice-President Albert Gore.

From Geza Roheim in 1950 to Hetty Zock in 1990, intellectuals and scholars in both Europe and America have sought to explain Erikson's thoughts, to tell us what he "really" meant. Although most have acknowledged that Erikson was a very unsystematic thinker who constantly reformulated his ideas, they have felt compelled to "frame," "distill," or "explain" his contributions. For example, some have described him as a political-cultural "conservative" who insisted (like many other ego psychologists) on the subordination of the self to society and its traditions. Others have disagreed, maintaining that Erikson admired revolutionaries like Luther and Gandhi, who forged broad new identities for themselves and their societies. Most have placed Erikson firmly within psychoanalytic traditions (including an allegiance to drive theory), while others have asserted that he has gradually broken from psychoanalysis (the "Jewish science") in all of its essentials and become a Christian existentialist.[1]

Interpretations of Erikson's thought have tended to reflect the interpreter's need to explain him in clearer and more precise terms than he provided. There is a significant difference between the Erikson one reads and the Erikson one reads about, with virtually every Erikson interpreter resorting to some degree of reductionism in the interests of order and clarity. My recognition of this problem does not mean that I have been able to avoid it. When I have taught Erikson in my seminar on recent American intellectual history, I have assigned the essays in *Childhood and Society* to illustrate the pre-occupation of thinkers immediately after the Second World War with authoritarian-totalitarian social psychology, and his writings of the 1960s and 1970s to underscore the general intellectual pre-occupation of those decades with ethnic and gender differences and American militarism. These assignments produced a usable Erikson but also one that simplified the multiple, complex, and "layered" themes in his texts.

Perhaps it is impossible to avoid reducing Erikson's thought so that it serves our needs for order. However, let us make the attempt by underscoring three general topical areas—the nature of American society, the premises and applications of psychoanalysis, and the elements of the human life-cycle—that attracted much of his attention from the 1930s to the 1980s. In all three areas, his thoughts have evolved over time in subtle ways, and it is important to try to determine how he integrated them.

I

When I started a book-length study of Erikson in the spring of 1990, his friend Robert Jay Lifton urged me never to lose sight of his evolving visions of American society because it was among his foremost preoccupations. It was no small matter that when he was naturalized in 1939, six years after migrating from Europe, he changed his surname from Homburger to Erikson. Like Leif Ericson, the Norwegian discoverer of America, he was enchanted by America's possibilities. The severe economic depression that greeted Anna Freud's student when he arrived in Boston seemed less overwhelming than in Europe; he was exhilarated by the energy and hope that President Roosevelt seemed to inspire.

For this young immigrant, there was a fundamental difference between American and European responses to the international economic crisis. In essays of the 1930s and 1940s (revised as chapters for *Childhood and Society*), he compared America both implicitly and explicitly to the totalitarian tragedies of Germany and Russia. The United States was far more open to diverse ethnic and cultural groupings. With its flood of immigrants, America was a society of new beginnings and a more inclusive, pan-human identity. He anticipated Daniel Boorstin by asserting that America's traditions of democracy and social mobility promoted healthy compromise and non-ideological accommodation of disparate interest groups. To be sure, Erikson feared that this spirit of compromise could stifle some of the emotions requisite for healthy psychosocial development. This apprehension paralleled Louis Hartz's worry that liberal capitalist consensus checked political, social, and economic analysis. Like Richard Hofstadter, Erikson also worried about the intensity of American economic competitiveness, the country's work ethic, and its allegiance to productive efficiency over more enduring human values. Indeed, Erikson feared that American wives had come to embrace a puritan morality that provoked mistrust of life and healthy sensuality in their children; they did this to check the aggressive secular orientations of their husbands in the crude marketplace of industrial capitalism. But for Erikson, these ills of America were dwarfed by those brought on in Europe by Hitler and Stalin. He felt that these leaders exploited deep discontent that derived from the more socially stratified and culturally rigid character of the Old World with its capacity for dangerous ideological politics and imbalanced, sometimes gangster-like, youth rebellion. Whatever their problems, Americans could not produce a Holocaust.

A few months before *Childhood and Society* was published in 1950, Erikson resigned his first and much prized psychology professorship at the University of California. He saw shades of Nazi-like thought control in America's emerging McCarthyite climate and refused to sign the University's loyalty oath. The next year he joined the staff of the Austen Riggs Center in Stockbridge. He worked there with disturbed American adolescents and planned to write a book on them with a comparative chapter on a German adolescent, Martin Luther. That chapter became the book *Young Man Luther* (1958) and reflected Erikson's continuing need to compare New and Old World cultures. Until the early 1960s, though, he tended to characterize McCarthyism, homebound and puritanical "moms," disturbed adolescents, and other American deficiencies as serious blemishes in a relatively healthy national culture represented by the hopefulness and the pragmatic reform tradition of the New Deal.

By the time of the Cuban missile crisis, however, the negatives had come to outweigh the assets. Erikson became increasingly disenchanted with his adopted country. Above all, he became apprehensive that America's arms race with the Soviet Union could eventually lead to domestic turmoil and nuclear war. Invited by Hubert Humphrey to a private White House function shortly after the Gulf of Tonkin crisis, he warned that the economic and ethical costs of American involvement in Vietnam could destroy the New Deal-Great Society tradition of domestic justice and racial equality. Between 1965 and 1973, Erikson elaborated his concept of "pseudospeciation" as he observed a deepening American presence in Vietnam and a concomitant increase in domestic racial tension. "Pseudospeciation" signified the arrogant placing of one's nation, race, culture, and (or) society ahead of those of others; it was the failure to recognize universal mutuality—that all of humanity was of one species. Erikson spent much of the 1960s studying Gandhi's non-violent movement for Indian independence as he searched for a viable alternative to elements of "pseudospeciation" that he sensed were increasingly conspicuous in America.[2]

From a broader perspective, it was the combination of McCarthyism, the nuclear perils of the Cold War, the American presence in Vietnam, and the ebbing fortunes of the American civil rights movement that diminished Erikson's enthusiasms for the United States. By 1973, when he lectured before a National Endowment for the Humanities forum on Thomas Jefferson and American identity, he contrasted the national travesties of slave-holding and Indian killing with the fresh, flexible, hopeful, and protean qualities that had drawn him to America in the 1930s. Although there seemed, then, to be a basic shift in Erikson's perspective on America, it can also be characterized as a difference in emphasis. After all, many of the notions that he was advancing during the late 1960s and early 1970s had been implicit in *Childhood and Society*.

II

As Erikson's emphasis in his descriptions of America shifted, it was possible to discern changes in his perspectives on the psychoanalytic profession and its doctrines (his second long-standing topical interest). A wandering artist until the late 1920s, he received psychoanalytic training in Freud's Vienna that gave him a vocation and an orderly daily routine. He worked closely with Anna Freud, his training analyst, and spent time with her father, "the professor." As a result of this experience, Erikson identified firmly for the rest of his life with psychoanalytic tradition, including drive theory. He felt at home with most of Freud's essential formulations and never considered overt rebellion or deviation.

Still, even in his training period in Vienna, Erikson had a some-what different emphasis than the Freuds. He embraced the new focus on ego psychology but was always uncomfortable with Anna Freud's emphasis on the ego's defenses for coping with everyday problems. From the very start, he was more impressed than the two Freuds with ego strengths and self-confidence—the ways in which the normal, healthy self functioned successfully. Erikson also seemed somewhat more concerned than the Freuds with the effect of society and culture upon inner psyche. Indeed, aboard a ship with his family headed to the New World late in 1933, he showed fellow passenger George Kennan a draft of a psychoanalytic essay on Hitler and German youth that would later appear (much revised) in *Childhood and Society*.

As a research associate at Harvard, Yale, and the University of California during the 1930s and 1940s, Erikson deepened his interest in the psychological strengths of healthy children rather than pursuing the traditional psychoanalytic focus on deficits and defenses among neurotics and psychotics. Wherever he could, he chose to observe and work with children who demonstrated good coping skills. Moreover, his close contacts with Margaret Mead, Gregory Bateson, Ruth Benedict, and others in the early culture and personality movement led him to choose as his essential psychoanalytic focus the way cultural institutions and traditions shaped and were shaped by inner psyches. Sometimes he referred to this as a "configurational" perspective—a way of looking at phenomena like children's block constructions that suggested intersections between the outer society and the inner individual psyche. His shift from psychoanalytic orthodoxy went further. Whereas the Freuds and most of their close followers tended to view religion and other cultural institutions as neurotic crutches, Erikson showed how they could often be useful in promoting strong selfhood.

These differences in emphasis, and Anna Freud's insistence that she could not "understand" Erikson's writings, often gave him a sense of inhabiting the margins of the psychoanalytic profession. Perhaps to compensate, but also with genuine sincerity, he sometimes acted as a figure of the psychoanalytic establishment. In 1965, for example, he denied openly the legitimacy of the American Academy of Psychoanalysis because it was not approved by the American Psychoanalytic Association. At a national psychoanalytic meeting somewhat later, Erikson mocked Jeffrey Masson for his attack on Freud's revised seduction theory. Openly contentious alternatives to the APA and to "the professor" did not merit serious consideration.[3]

After the late 1950s, however, Erikson became more and more concerned with the way the individual found his place in the moral and ethical order of the world. Appealing less to clinical evidence or even to psychoanalytic theory, his style became increasingly evocative. Some characterized it as prophetic. For Erikson, the revolutionary insights of figures like Luther, Gandhi, Jefferson, and of course, Jesus, derived less from inner psychic or even psychosocial processes than from the decision of a person to take the full burden of his existence upon himself in its relationship to a higher essence. If Erikson continued to perceive that he was amplifying Freud's teachings under changing historical circumstances, he sometimes sounded more like the revolutionary existential prophets that he had researched.

III

With considerable assistance from his wife, Joan, Erikson spent the late 1940s working on the concept of an eight-stage human life-cycle. It overlapped with his two other topical interests, for it was rooted in his observations of American children and in his desire to elaborate Freud's developmental perspective. As his concept emerged, each of life's stages stood for a "crisis" in the developmental process, with a new psychic strength pitted against a new vulnerability. At the same time, each stage was psychosocial, for the crisis was acted out in encounters with other humans, beginning with the infant facing his mother. This mutuality expanded, as one aged, to a "widening radius of social relations."

In *Childhood and Society*, Erikson published the first detailed account of his developmental model: (1) Basic Trust vs. Basic Mistrust (infancy); (2) Autonomy vs. Shame and Doubt (early childhood); (3) Initiative vs. Guilt (play age); (4) Industry vs. Inferiority (school age); (5) Identity vs. Role Confusion (adolescence); (6) Intimacy vs. Isolation (young adulthood); (7) Generativity vs. Stagnation (adulthood); (8) Ego Integrity vs. Despair (old age). Unlike Freud, he emphasized neither infancy nor early childhood, but the fifth, or adolescent identity stage. The first four stages represented efforts to establish and consolidate a personal identity, while the last three stages signalled efforts to retain it in the face of aging and bodily infirmities. For the first time since G. Stanley Hall's 1905 study of adolescence, a major personality theorist was emphasizing that period in the life-cycle. Erikson retained this focus in *Young Man Luther* (1958) as he explored Luther's developmental crisis of adolescence in conjunction with the emergence of the Protestant Reformation.

Erikson continued to discuss adolescent identity issues in the 1960s, especially in conjunction with college-student protests (with which he tended to empathize). However, his major research of that decade, *Ghandi's Truth* (1969), focused on adult life. Erikson tried to explain how the middle-aged Mahatma organized a local labour strike in 1918 which launched his non-violent crusade against British rule throughout India. Because the adult stages of Erikson's psychosocial life-cycle were the least developed in his work, it is hardly surprising that as his interest in the middle-aged Gandhi developed (and he himself aged), Erikson made two major modifications of his eight-stage theory which (among other benefits) allowed him to gain greater insight into the meaning of adulthood.

First, he included within *Insight and Responsibility* (1964) a crucially important essay, "Human Strength and the Cycle of Generations." In it, he proposed a "schedule of virtues" to correspond with each of the eight stages of the life-cycle: Hope, Will, Purpose, Competence, Fidelity, Love, Care and Wisdom. These virtues were strengths inherent in the human organism that social environments (especially the conduct of adults towards children) could thwart or enhance. They were aspects of an evolving ethical character in the individual (coming into full fruition during adulthood) that was connected explicitly to psychological development. Erikson, with his increasing interest in the existential concerns of adult life, was linking ethical to psychosocial development in each of his eight stages.

In 1965, Erikson presented a paper ("Ontogeny of Ritualization") to the Royal Society of London. (Twelve years later he elaborated this paper in *Toys and Reasons*.) He related a social ritual form to each of his eight psychosocial-ethical stages. At each stage, he postulated, every society orients its members to ways of construing the world through a universal ritual element. At the first or infancy stage of Hope, for example, there was a ritualized *numinous* encounter between mother and infant, followed at each successive stage by the rituals of the *judicious*, the *dramatic*, the *formal*, the *convictional*, the *affiliative*, the *generational*, and the *integral*. The eighth or *integral* ritual saw the old person integrating or becoming living testimony to the wisdom of the society's entire ritual process.

By the middle 1960s, then, just as he was formulating the crucial strands of his biography of middle-aged Gandhi, Erikson had linked his schedule of ethical virtues and social rituals to his eight psychosocial stages. Through the completion of *Gandhi's Truth* and for at least the next decade, he focused on the seventh or "generative" stage when adults were ethically obligated to create and attend to younger generations. In terms of virtues, they were obligated to personally "care" for youth. From the standpoint of ritualization, adults became the "ritualizers" responsible for conducting the whole ritualization process in an authoritative and ethical, but not an authoritarian or moralistic, manner. Through their personal presence and words and deeds, they actualized and authenticated society's genuine, lasting rituals. Having worked out this perspective on the meaning of adult generativity, Erikson was able to articulate Gandhi's essential contributions to younger generations—the example of militant non-violence as an ethical obligation to redress social injustice and overcome ethnic, nationalistic, and often moralistic tribalism in favour of wider, more inclusive human identities.

Since the mid-1970s, reflecting his own shift from midlife to old age, Erikson focused increasingly on the eighth stage which involved the struggle for personal integrity, moral wisdom, and integration of the ritual process. In 1976 he wrapped up fifteen years of lectures in Bergman's film *Wild Strawberries* by publishing the extremely thoughtful article "Reflections on Dr Borg's Life Cycle." Focusing on the old man, Borg, in Bergman's film, Erikson described the quest of old age for integrity in the face of despair as a process of successfully reliving, integrating, and consolidating all of the prior seven life stages.[4]

Old age, then, was an active and vigorous period for the self, for society, and for the evolution of human ethics. In the late 1970s and through the 1980s, Erikson found himself in closer collaboration than ever before with his wife Joan as they jointly elaborated aspects of the eighth stage of the life-cycle. They portrayed "wisdom," the virtue of old age, as a phenomenon that involved more than self-integration and integrity. It was a "comradeship with men and women of distant times and of different pursuits who have created orders and objects and sayings conveying human dignity and love." Indeed, before he lost his capacity for sustained writing, Erikson had launched a biography and regular "dialogue" with a young man from a distant time and place, Jesus, who had also attempted to explicate "the last problems" of life.[5]

IV

By now, something of the complexity of Erikson's three long-standing general topical interests—American society, psychoanalysis, and the human life-cycle—should be apparent. Through the decades, there were certainly strong continuities in the way he elaborated each topic. But there were also marked shifts in his emphasis. In his initial quali-fied embrace and his subsequent relative coolness towards America, he was comparing it to other national cultures. From the 1930s through the 1950s, the comparison was largely to European societies, especially Germany. In the course of the 1960s, as he prepared *Gandhi's Truth*, India and Hindu culture also became crucial to his focus. Indeed, the book was in some sense a dialogue on the future of modern man between Freud the German Jew, Gandhi the Indian Hindu, and Erikson the Danish-German-American Jew turned Protestant. His extension of psychoanalysis into a perspective that dealt seriously with inner human strengths as well as deficits and outer culture as well as inner personality was so gradual and cautious that it is exceedingly difficult to show how it moved him to embrace questions of ultimate meaning and value. Changes in Erickson's developmental model for human experience were also slow and subtle. It was initially unclear that he was departing from Freud in emphasizing adolescence and adult life over early childhood and outer culture as the equal of inner psyche. A few suspected, however, that the more he amplified his developmental model, the less interested he was in traditional psychoanalytic issues.

It is no easy task to integrate the three aspects of Erikson's intellectual life. Consider the first. Although he embraced the America of Roosevelt as his promising new physical and political home during the 1930s, he continued to regard Freud's Vienna psychoanalytic circle of broad-ranging interdisciplinary thinkers as his intellectual and cultural base. His increasingly critical attitude towards America's warrior qualities in the 1960s and early 1970s may have correlated roughly with his development of a strong ethical dimension in his life-cycle theory and his increasing embrace of questions of ultimate meaning and value. However, elements of all of these were clearly discernable in his June 1950 statement against the loyalty oath to the University of California Committee on Privilege and Tenure. Surely, Erikson's increasing concern with existential issues after the late 1950s was compatible with his decision to explicitly couple ethical virtues with his stages of the life-cycle. Suggestions of this existential-ethical merger, however, could be detected in almost every essay in *Childhood and Society*. Logically, Erikson's deepened concern since the mid-1960s with the generative stage responsibility of adults for the well-being of youth (far more than the procreation of children) promoted his critical discussions of the dangers of nuclear war, bellicose tribalism, and the value of militant non-violence. It is also appropriate to note, however, that he and Joan formulated the life-cycle theory, in which generativity (and its ethical obligation of adults to children) was a stage, during the late 1940s as they reflected on their obligations to their three children in a world shaken in the aftermath of a devastating war and the Holocaust. In 1964 Erikson added a strong element of individual ethical choice and responsibility to each stage of the life-cycle. The next year, he amplified this addition by underscoring the importance of social ritual as the self sought to master the crisis of each stage. Although individual ethical decision is not necessarily incompatible with social ritual, ethical issues were more congruent with Erikson's increasing existential concerns after the late 1950s, while social ritual was closer to his cultural explorations of the 1930s and 1940s that produced *Childhood and Society*.

Clearly, Erikson's three areas of long-standing interest do not fold neatly into each other. In addition, he often had pressing interests that did not overlap clearly with his interests in American and other national cultures, his evolving psychoanalytic perspective, or his changing developmental model. Erikson's considerable historical writing, for example, focused on the role of the revolutionary leader in challenging increasingly untenable social-ideological premises and fashioning new identities for himself and the citizenry of his society. And though his discussion of the leader often involved national culture, psychoanalytic theory, and developmental considerations, Erikson, when he acted as historian-biographer, usually felt that he had another, more pressing task: to demonstrate deep clinical empathy for and understanding of the individual leader's life in the context of its immediate surrounding culture. He treated Luther and Gandhi, for example, in much the same way as he dealt with a hospital patient or an analysand. All else was subordinated to maximizing his clinical effectiveness. Similarly, when Erikson studied the Sioux in the late 1930s and the Yurok in the early 1940s, he was interested in marshalling the skills of anthropological field work through insightful social observations. Although he displayed modest interest in describing Sioux and Yurok ego strengths instead of psychic deficits, he did not consider psychoanalytic theory, national culture, or developmental stages to be his primary focus. One can cite other vital Erikson concerns—the sources of Einstein's scientific and Tagore's literary creativity, psychological issues in the Allied war effort during the early 1940s, or the American civil rights movement of the 1960s—which related only tangentially to his three long-term intellectual preoccupations. My point here is that Erikson had many and frequently changing if intense interests. Therefore, one cannot assess large portions of his writing in terms of his three general areas of intellectual preoccupation.

V

Is it possible to provide a meaningful overview of the ideas of a thinker with three general and evolving, if less than compatible, long-range intellectual concerns as well as a number of intense shorter-term preoccupations? When critics have been attentive to at least some of the incompatibilities in Erikson's thought, they have sometimes described him as an unsystematic and often exceedingly vague thinker. He was an artist, it is said, who never entirely made the shift from visual images to precise and logical scholarly writing. On the borders of several callings–psychoanalysis, history, theology, and anthropology–he never felt that he had to satisfy the methodological disciplinary obligations of any of them. It might be better to underscore the eclectic, vague, and often incompatible qualities of Erikson's thought, and to leave it at that, than to conclude (as many critics who recognize the lacunae and vagaries in his thought continue to do) by summing him up with reductionist clarity. However, perhaps we can do better than either the simplistic summations or the emphasis on Erikson's gaps and imprecisions. Neither does justice to the profundity and depth of his mind or the experiential, tentative nature of his language. The mind and the language worked in tandem with an evolving life and temperament. Attention to all four helps us to account for his long-term intellectual concerns as well as his inconsistencies and intellectual incompatibilities.

In 1959 David Riesman (with Talcott Parsons' support) wrote a letter to the dean of Harvard College, McGeorge Bundy, recommending that he hire Erikson as a professor. Riesman described Erikson as a man with

> a modesty so profound as to be trying at times to his friends and colleagues. A psychoanalyst without an MD, a social scientist without even an AB, an artist . . . he has felt a recurrent diffidence about what he could do outside the area of work with patients where he felt more secure and most widely appreciated. His decision that he is willing to come to Harvard indicates that he has attained . . . a greater confidence in his own powers as a teacher and colleague and fellow researcher.

Having come to know Erikson through a decade of summer visits in Bennington and Stockbridge, Riesman was underscoring Erikson's profound problem of self-confidence that appeared to be mending itself. This change was to the good, Riesman concluded, for Erikson would be able to "bring his way of working and his widening curiosities to a group of able and responsible undergraduates and graduate students."[6]

Riesman's appraisal of Erikson as a man with a profound and long-standing (if diminishing) problem of confidence that stood in the way of intellectual dialogue outside a familiar clinical setting was cogent. Erikson's personal papers at the Houghton Library and my interviews with dozens of his closest associates testify to his marked diffidence. It was often coupled with extreme political caution—a reticence to reveal his deficiencies by confronting or offending others. The diffidence and caution were rooted in many factors in his early life. Perhaps the most important were the circumstances of an adopted child who intuited even before he was told that German pediatrician Theodor Homburger was not his real father. He sensed that he had to learn more about his absent Danish parent to make himself whole. As he wandered about Europe as a part-time artist concerned with vague philosophic issues regarding the nature of existence, Erikson was (by his own subsequent admission) deeply disturbed and filled with self-doubts.[7]

It was not until he arrived in Vienna in the late 1920s that his life began to stabilize. He assumed a regular job as an art teacher in a school for the children of Anna Freud's analysands and others. She took him on in a training analysis and gave him the vocation of an early child analyst. At the same time, he married Joan Serson, a bright and creative student of dance and a daughter of devout Canadian Episcopalians. She had the self-confidence and "groundedness" that Erikson lacked. The marriage was an exceedingly close one, and he commenced a life-long habit of looking to Joan for stability and orientation.

With a vocation and the stability that Joan provided, Erikson found a measure of confidence. Before the Vienna Psychoanalytic Society, he chided Anna Freud for a mechanistic perspective on ego defenses that lost sight of the strengths and longings of the whole person. Believing, too, that he had the ability to practice child analysis more successfully and with fewer controls outside of Vienna, and feeling less than comfortable with Hitler coming to power in bordering Germany, Erikson moved with his family to Copenhagen, and then to America. After a spell in Boston he moved in 1936 to Yale.

At the Institute of Human Relations, for the first time since his arrival in America, Erikson came across an organized forum for broad interdisciplinary intellectual exchange. Anthropologists talked with sociologists, psychologists, and psychiatrists. He met John Whiting, Scudder Mekeel, and other interdisciplinary cultural anthropologists and took an interest in their field work. He was also introduced to Margaret Mead and Gregory Bateson and began to investigate Hitler's appeal to youth, American Indian societies, and, more generally, the relationship between psychoanalysis and culture. But Erikson sensed a constricted quality in Institute gatherings—an effort to somehow "tighten" and systematize psychoanalysis through behaviourist psychological assumptions and methods. Consequently, despite the exhilaration over witnessing for the first time sustained interdisciplinary dialogues, he was generally silent and exceedingly cautious politically. Indeed, he often felt like an outsider at the Institute seminar.

Erikson's confidence increased substantially in 1939 when he left Yale to become a research associate at the University of California's Institute of Child Welfare and to practice psychoanalysis in the San Francisco area. In the 1940s, he gained acclaim for published versions of some of the essays that became *Childhood and Society*. Anthropologists Clyde Kluckhohn and Alfred Kroeber, amazed at the depth of his insights into the Sioux and the Yurok, began extensive discussions with Erikson. Mead and Gregory Bateson liked the interdisciplinary culture and personality orientation of all of his early publications, visited with him regularly, and introduced him to Ruth Benedict. Benjamin Spock valued his writing on the connections between childhood and culture and became his close friend, as did the Jungian intellectual, John Wheelwright. By 1950, when his early essays on psychoanalysis and culture were brought together in his first book, Erikson felt more sure of himself as an intellectual among important thinkers than he had in the past. In recognition of the quality of his work, the university psychology department appointed him to a professorship. This meant a great deal to a man who had never received more than a German gymnasium diploma.

As the withdrawn and diffident young man Erikson grew older, gained confidence, and entered into a large array of serious intellectual dialogues, he simultaneously launched his three long-term intellectual preoccupations. *Childhood and Society* included essays on American, German, and Russian national character, an exposition of the eight-stage human life-cycle, and his cautious shift from psychoanalytic orthodoxy through emphasis upon culture and ego strengths, as well as other topics that captivated him.

It goes without saying that the substantial success of this first book at the age of forty-eight further reduced Erikson's timidity. Indeed, it opened rich dialogues with Riesman, David Rapaport, Reinhold Niebuhr, and other important intellectuals. If he tried to be cautious politically during the 1949–51 struggle against the University of California loyalty oath and refused to assume a leadership role, he still stuck out as one of the few in the faculty who risked their careers by continually refusing to sign the document. Although the university was still willing to continue his employment, he left on grounds of principle. When he did, his confidence received another boost, for he had seven impressive job offers from which to choose. He accepted

Robert Knight's offer to research, teach, and practice therapy at the Austen Riggs Center, where he quickly emerged with David Rapaport as the venerated intellectual co-leader of that premier facility. Rapaport ("Mr Metapsychology") detailed to the psycho-analytic profession the profound theoretical import of Erikson's work. By the time Riesman and Parsons recommended him for a special interdisciplinary professorship at Harvard in 1959, Erikson's self-confidence was higher than it had ever been. Moreover, he was eager to add to his circle of intellectual colleagues on the banks of the Charles River.

For Erikson, it is clear that self-confidence, intellectual exchanges, and innovative writing reinforced each other and made him less self-protective politically. As a very large circle of important thinkers and bright young graduate students conversed regularly with Erikson during his Harvard years, he expanded his life-cycle model by adding eight virtues and eight social rituals, became a serious student of the psychology of adult life, and completed *Gandhi's Truth*—the most ambitious of all of his writings.

If Erikson's enhanced confidence went hand in hand with his expanding intellectual dialogues and his innovative writing, these factors also help us to explain his intellectual inconsistencies. As the decades progressed, Erikson's initial diffidence became a joyous tolerance of different perspectives. Indeed, tolerance promoted wider and richer dialogues beyond psychoanalytic and anthro-pological circles, with theologians like Paul Tillich and Reinhold Niebuhr, historians like Bruce Mazlish and John Demos, and India scholars such as Suzanne and Lloyd Rudolph, Lois and Gardner Murphy, and many more. The American Academy of Arts and Sciences organized conferences to facilitate some of Erikson's discussions, and Robert Lifton established the annual Wellfleet meeting to provide additional dialogues for him. Erikson's corres-pondence in the 1960s and 1970s reveals that vast blocs of his time were devoted to a great diversity of intellectual exchanges, organized and spontaneous. Despite old age, he delighted in trading drafts of papers with other thinkers, commenting at conferences, and simply discussing ideas during long walks. In his many discussions, he maintained a language and a focus deeply respectful of the particular interests and experiences of his fellow discussant. Indeed, he openly acknowledged speaking "in different tongues to different audiences." Since he wrote against a background of this rich daily social-intellectual experience, it is small wonder that Erikson's ideas were rarefuly formulated systematically. It was inescapable, for example, that a work like *Gandhi's Truth* would reflect the existential concerns evident in his dialogues with Tillich, the apprehensions of nuclear war voiced in his discussions with Lifton and Brenman-Gibson, the joy for the colours and smells and sounds of India enhanced by exchanges with Pamela Daniels, Sudhir Kakar, and Kamla Chowdry, and the psychoanalytic interests of friends like Robert Wallerstein and George Klein. Since the language with which Erikson carried on each of his dialogues was nearly inseparable from the ideas exchanged, *Gandhi's Truth* consisted of many different tones, textures, and premises.

VI

In view of Erikson's expanding dialogues, it is not surprising that his writings often seemed vague and the three long-term concerns he addressed never folded into each other very well. Since only his unpublished private correspondence makes this fully apparent, one can understand why his ideas were often simplified, misunderstood, and attacked. Indeed, in the course of the 1970s and early 1980s, a guru of the American intellectual community became a somewhat peripheral figure. I shall conclude by offering some conjectures about why this happened.

Within American intellectual culture, widespread recognition often tends to provoke questioning and attack. By 1970 Erikson was perhaps the most sought-out speaker in academia. At this time, a series of attacks erupted. The first came from American feminists, including Kate Millett, Juliet Mitchell, Elizabeth Janeway, and his former teaching assistant Carol Gilligan. As part of his work at the University of California's Institute for Child Welfare in the 1940s, Erikson had observed the play constructions of normal Berkeley children. He found that the constructions closely paralleled the morphology of the sex organs, with boys making erect, intrusive, tall or long assertive structures while girls constructed low, enclosed, inner areas that were closely connected and readily permeable. In *Childhood and Society* and especially in a 1964 issue of *Daedalus*, Erikson developed a biological-psychological-social interpretation of his observations. Corresponding with their genital organs, boys built powerful outward turning and dominating structures while girls constructed more intricate inward turning structures which were more accessible. Boys patrolled and took charge of outer spaces; girls welcomed other people and objects within the inner spaces that preoccupied them. In an age when life was threatened by the projectiles of nuclear war, Erikson looked to the female disposition for survival, coexistence, and relational alternatives to male assertiveness. Women exhibited the qualities of peace and coexistence that men might choose to discover within themselves.

By the late 1960s and early 1970s, several feminist thinkers dismissed Erikson, as they had Freud, for portraying "deficient castrated womanhood," and for falsely describing learned behaviour in a sexist society as inborn. Gilligan's attack came later and was somewhat different. She charged that Erikson had subsumed women in what was essentially a male developmental model. However, the theme of Gilligan's widely heralded *In a Different Voice* (1982)—that men were more dominational and women were more relational—bore a striking resemblance to Erikson's ideas on inner and outer space. Erikson publicly held his ground. He claimed that he was stressing female differences as assets. Moreover, he was not arguing that biology was destiny; social and psychological forces were equally relevant. Still, Erikson smarted privately over the spirited feminist attacks.[8]

In March 1975, Marshall Berman, a political theorist at City College (CUNY), struck what Erikson regarded as a far more devastating blow. Reviewing *Life History and the Historical Moment* on the front page of the *New York Times Book Review*, he attacked Erikson for concealing his Judaism. Berman also mocked the "cosmic chutzpah of his claim to be Erik Erikson, his own father" by repudiating his legal name of Erik Homburger in 1939 and renaming himself as his own son (the ultimate self-made man). Although Erikson had established his reputation by emphasizing the need to face honestly all personal identity issues, Berman claimed he was actually insecure and arrogant and could not face the problem of identity in his own life. Erikson was not what he seemed.[9]

Berman's essay may have damaged Erikson's reputation like nothing before. Privately, Erikson wrote letters to friends countering Berman's account of his religious upbringing and his name change. Paul Roazen, a former student in Erikson's graduate seminar at Harvard in the mid-1960s, received one of these letters but saw validity in Berman's charge of duplicity. Indeed, Roazen totally rewrote his draft of *Erik H. Erikson: The Power and Limits of a Vision* to underscore Erikson's tendency to slide over complex theoretical issues and to revise significantly some of his early publications without indicating the change to his readers. Roazen also accused Erikson of a subtle conservative political bias where Erikson emphasized the "ingenious" adaptation of the self to the surrounding culture. Howard Kushner wrote two articles that accentuated Roazen's changes and echoed a claim that Joel Kovel had made even before the Berman review: that Erikson was an apologist for "the established order." But such a charge did not lead neoconservative intellectuals to embrace Erikson. On the contrary, David Gutmann scored him in *Commentary* for shifting from a favourable portrayal of America in the first edition of *Childhood and Society* to one unduly critical of its racist traditions and its role in the Vietnam War.[10]

Amidst these harsh attacks, Erikson had his defenders. John Munder Ross, Karolyn Gould, and Mark Gerzon wrote to the *New York Times Book Review* to criticize Berman. David Riesman urged Kushner to modify his attacks on Erikson's alleged conservatism. Others talked privately of the simplicities and overkill of the attacks. However, none felt obligated to wage the sort of systematic and prolonged defense of Erikson that had traditionally occupied followers of other leading psychoanalytic thinkers, and one can understand why. Unlike Freud, Heinz Kohut, or other major psycho-analysts, Erikson had never organized a movement to elaborate, propagate, and defend his ideas. Rather, he had simply maintained separate and highly idiosyncratic conversations with different creative thinkers. These associates never came together save for a gathering at Robert Lifton's Wellfleet cottage or an occasional American Academy of Arts and Sciences conference. Erikson's rapport with each always involved its own particular issues and its unique types of communication. His letters to Robert Coles, for example, differed fundamentally in content and style from those to Lifton. Because there was no cohesive Eriksonian movement like there had been a Freudian, Jungian, or Kohutian movement, it would have been difficult to conduct an organized defense or effective efforts to ostracize Gilligan or Roazen for their "infidelities." Erikson's close associates never even considered these traditional warfare techniques of the psychoanalytic profession.

Perhaps because there has been no Eriksonian movement, with specific followers assigned the task of precise and sustained doctrinal elaboration of his ideas, original Erikson publications have remained the major sources for his thought. As he aged and wrote less, dated and unrevised texts constituted his primary literary legacy. To be sure, there were developmental psychologists, psychoanalysts, educators, theologians, psychohistorians, and even a few literary critics who invoked Erikson's concepts to give theoretical shape to their own writings. But most of these works simplified, diminished, and transformed Erikson's richly multi-layered expressions and ideas into dull textbook-like lessons. It is difficult to believe that many of these publications, particularly the one-dimensional Eriksonian psychobiographies and the mechanical enumerations of the eight stages of his life-cycle, could draw bright young students to Erikson's original works.

Finally, it may be that Erikson's diminished reputation was partially grounded in the decline of those interdisciplinary values in academia that had helped to give his writings wide currency. He had gained prominence during the 1950s and 1960s, perhaps the high decades of interdisciplinary scholarship in recent American history. Much as *Childhood and Society* and *Young Man Luther* combined many disciplines, so did Riesman's *The Lonely Crowd*, Richard Hofstadter's *The Age of Reform*, David Potter's *People of Plenty*, and Leo Marx's *The Machine in the Garden*. By the 1970s and 1980s creative scholarship was being produced, more and more, by satisfying the tenets of specific academic disciplines. Even blatantly interdisciplinary work had to meet specific disciplinary-based criteria in traditional academic units. At Harvard, for example, there was no longer a Department of Social Relations to offer refuge to those, like Riesman and Erikson, who did not fit into a single academic speciality area. In the late 1980s, the Sociology Department into which Riesman had been moved had refused to tenure Paul Starr. Starr's monumental cultural, historical, and economic study, *The Social Transformation of American Medicine*, had failed to satisfy the department's specific disciplinary criteria. Thirty years after Riesman and Talcott Parsons had convinced McGeorge Bundy to hire Erik Erikson because he was different from most scholars and ranged broadly over many disciplines, it was difficult to believe that Harvard would do so again.

Notes

1. There are literally hundreds of publications and dissertations about Erikson. The fullest analyses of his work are Robert Coles, *Erik H. Erikson: The Growth of His Work* (Boston, Toronto: Little, Brown, 1970); Paul Roazen, *Erik H. Erikson: The Power and Limits of a Vision* (New York: Free Press, 1976); and Hetty Zock, *A Psychology of Ultimate Concern: Erik H. Erikson's Contribution to the Psychology of Religion* (Amsterdam: B.v. Rodopi, 1990). Coles praises heavily and places Erikson in the reform tradition of the revolutionary leaders he describes. Roazen is more critical; he underscores Erikson's inconsistencies and his political-cultural conservatism. Zock thoroughly delineates his increasing focus on existential concerns.

2. Erikson first used the term "pseudospeciation" in "The Ontogeny of Ritualization in Man" *Philosophic Transactions of the Royal Society of London.* Series B (1966) 251, pp. 337–49, 772. He elaborated it in *Gandhi's Truth* (Boston: Norton, 1969), and *Dimensions of a New Identity* (Boston: Norton, 1974). His "White House Notes" (1965) Erikson Papers, Houghton Library, detail his visit to the Johnson White House.

3. For the 1965 episode, see Jacques M. Quen and Eric T. Carison (eds) *American Psychoanalysis: Origins and Development,* (New York: Brunner, Mazel, 1978), p. 139; Jeffrey Masson, "The Persecution and Expulsion of Jeffrey Masson" *Mother Jones* IX: 10 (December 1984), p. 47.

4. Erikson, "Reflections on Dr Borg's Life Cycle" *Daedalus* 105: 2 (Spring 1976), p. 1–31.

5. For some of Erikson's most interesting reflections on old age, see "On Generativity and Identity" *Harvard Educational Review* 51: 2 (May 1981), pp. 249–69; Elizabeth Hall, "A Conservation with Erik Erikson" *Psychology Today* (June 1983), pp. 22ff; Erik H. Erikson, *The Life Cycle Completed* (Boston: Norton, 1982), Ch. 3.

6. David Riesman to McGeorge Bundy, 2 June 1959, Erikson Papers, Houghton Library.

7. Erikson's "Autobiographic Notes on the Identity Crisis" *Daedalus* 99: 4 (Fall 1970), pp. 730–59, is the fullest published account of his early years. Neither of two revised versions of this essay reveals as much. However, I have relied far more heavily for personal and professional biographical data on Erikson's unpublished letters and papers in the Houghton Library and on tape recorded interviews over 1990 and 1991 with Erik and Joan Erikson and their closest friends in the Cambridge-Boston area. Indeed, my entire appraisal of his confidence "problem" and the development of his intellectual dialogues in the rest of this section is based on these sources.

8. Jean Strouse (ed.) *Women and Analysis* (Boston: G.K. Hall, 1985), pp. 291–340, prints a somewhat revised edition of Erikson's 1964 *Daedalus* essay and his 1974 response to feminist criticism. Linda B. Hopkins, "Inner Space and Outer Space: Identity in Contemporary Females" *Psychiatry* 43: 1 (February 1980), pp. 1–11, provides an overview of the controversy over Erikson's theory and adds further criticism.

9. Berman's review of *Life History and the Historical Moment* is in the *New York Times Book Review*, 30 March 1975.

10. Howard I. Kushner, "Pathology and Adjustment in Psychohistory: A Critique of the Erikson Model" *Psychocultural Review* (Fall 1977), pp. 493–506, and Kushner, "Americanization of the Ego" *Canadian Review of American Studies* 10: 1 (Spring 1979), pp. 95–101; Joel Kovel, "Erik Erikson's Psychohistory" *Social Policy* 4 (1974), pp. 60–64; David Gutmann, "Erik Erikson's America" *Commentary* 58: 3 (September 1974), pp. 60–64.

9

Philip Rieff

Jerry Z. Muller

Philip Rieff has had his share of the honours which American academic life offers. In addition to a chair in sociology at the University of Pennsylvania, he has taught at Berkeley, Harvard, and Oxford, and has held prestigious lectureships at Yale, Princeton, and Columbia. But his renown is hardly commensurate with his intellectual achievement, and the work of one of the most profound conservative minds in America remains relatively little known among cultural conservatives. His influence, insofar as such matters can be traced, seems to be most evident on what might be called the anti-liberationist left, in works such as Christopher Lasch's *Culture of Narcissism*, or *Habits of the Heart*, by Robert Bellah and his associates. It is reflected also in the anti-liberal but otherwise not easily pigeonholed work, *After Virtue* by Alisdair MacIntyre. Some of Rieff's intellectual contributions may be vaguely familiar to those who have never read his work: a decade and a half ago, Joseph Epstein referred to the title of Rieff's *Triumph of the Therapeutic* of 1966 as "prophetic," and the term is now widely used in Rieff's sense by many with no sense of its provenance.[1] But even in the most learned of households, Philip Rieff is far from a household name. While Allan Bloom's *Closing of the American Mind* was a bestseller, Rieff's *Fellow Teachers*, which made many of the same points a decade and a half earlier with great poignancy, has remained a hot tip.

Rieff's limited readership may be regretted, but it is not entirely a mystery. To begin with, there is his style. My initial exposure to Rieff came with *The Triumph of the Therapeutic*, and my first reaction was that it was a fascinating work, which merited translation into English. Rieff's subsequent books and essays have on the whole been even more difficult. Yet this difficulty is neither incidental nor unintended. Beginning in his first book and with greater intensity over time, Rieff has conveyed to a cultured, educated, academic audience a series of messages which challenge the unquestioned assumptions of the dominant culture of the academy. Since few of his potential readers are likely to offer a respectful intellectual hearing to a direct assault on their assumptions, Rieff has adopted a style aphoristic, allusive, and ironic all at once. His Socratic approach leaves it for readers to discover his key insights, which are more often suggested by dramatic examples than stated outright. To most members of his intended audience, Rieff's essential message is scandalous. Rieff has warned repeatedly of the conflict between the dominant trends among modern intellectuals and the maintenance of moral decency. "If every limit can be seen as a limitation of personality, the question with which we may confront every opportunity is: after, all, why not?" he has written.[2] "Our smarts lead to more and more discoveries of exceptions to every rule. Such smartlichkeit cannot prevail over menschlichkeit without destroying it."[3]

Rieff's writings over the last four decades touch upon a remarkable range of subjects, while returning time and again to a few unifying themes. He is the author of three major books: *Freud: The Mind of the Moralist* (first published in 1959), *The Triumph of the Therapeutic: Uses of Faith After Freud* (1966), and *Fellow Teachers* (1973). Since 1979, the University of Chicago Press has reissued these three works in new editions which include important subsequent reflections by Rieff. More recently, thanks to Jonathan Imber, Rieff's readers can profit from a collection of his essays, first published in a variety of journals or as critical introductions to the writings of figures as diverse as the German Protestant theologian Adolf Harnack, the American sociologist Charles Horton Cooley, and Oscar Wilde.[4]

"The opening up of possibility, the liquidation of that which is 'not done,' represents the long revolution of modernity at its most basic level."[5] This quotation from Rieff's introduction of 1968 to a volume of essays by the black sociologist, Kelly Miller, conveys a central concern underlying his writings. For the source and first mention of Rieff's central concern, one can turn to his 1952 review of Hannah Arendt's *Origins of Totalitarianism*. In her book, Rieff found the notion that the mass murders in Nazi Germany and Stalinist Russia were "a revelation of the abyss of possibility." "Man emancipated from his particularity becomes not human but demonic," he wrote.[6] It is this presentiment — of the reality of what the rabbis called the "yetzer hara": the deeply-embedded human inclination to do evil—

that underlies much of Rieff's subsequent writing. The barrier which kept men from sliding into the "abyss of possibility" Rieff called "culture." "Everything is possible to human beings; we are members of a culture in the sense that everything is not permitted to us, nor even conceivable by us."[7] Thus Rieff's writings devoted to a "theory of culture" are anything but "academic." He regards his work as "ineluctably practical and moral," intended to "show the reader some little way toward the right conduct of his own life."[8]

Against the predominant emphasis of modern liberalism and left-wing radicalism on the desirability of liberation—from the past, from social mores—Rieff has stressed the typically conservative theme of the necessity for restraint and constraint. While many sociological theories have regarded shared understandings of what is morally desirable and morally undesirable as key elements of social cohesion, Rieff focuses on the latter, on what each culture *forbids*, or what he calls "interdicts," which are so often dismissed as "taboos." It is the very identification of the culturally forbidden with "primitivism" that he means to dispute: it is men without a firm sense of the forbidden who are most morally dangerous because ethically primitive.

While most contemporary theorists of culture have followed Clifford Geertz in stressing the aesthetic or symbolic nature of cultures, Rieff by contrast has insisted upon the centrality of *moral* demands in cultural systems.[9] According to Rieff, cultures are based on a shared vision of ideal moral behaviour, including behaviour which is forbidden. Following common usage, Rieff conceives of this shared culture in spatial terms: that which is most moral is "highest;" that which is absolutely forbidden is "lowest." The highest warrant for each cultural system Rieff calls its "god-terms;" forbidden behaviour he terms the culture's "transgressive depths." Given man's moral fallibility and frailty, transgressions are often committed, and each culture has "remissions" which allow the individual to live with having done what he ought not to have done. Remissions make it possible, in other words, to live with our frequent inability to live up to what is highest and to avoid what is lowest.

Rieff assumes that human beings acquire their sense of purpose and meaning from the cultures in which they live, and cultures unable to convey such a sense of meaning leave their members feeling empty or anxious. In successful high cultures of the past, this sense of personal order and meaning was provided by directing human instincts towards communal purposes. By attaching the self to some larger set of shared goals, and by requiring that man's asocial or evil urges be repressed or redirected towards higher, ultimate purposes, cultures provide individual purpose and collective cohesion. The culture's "god-terms," "transgressive depths," and "remissions" were articulated in systematic form by intellectuals, whose main task was to pass on these cultural creeds.

For Rieff, a morally desirable culture is one in which the system of moral demands is so deeply accepted by individuals that the evil instinctual possibilities of which men are always capable are generally felt to be repugnant: so repugnant that they are not even spoken of directly. Education is the process by which individuals internalize their culture's "consensus of shalt nots." The most important educational institution has traditionally been the family, where this cultural authority is first instilled.[10] Through creeds and institutions, men and women are trained in the necessary limitation of their possibilities. Depth of character, Rieff writes, occurs when cultural shalts and shalt nots become so much a part of us that we are disposed to fulfil them almost instinctively. Character in this sense leads to consistent action, and for just this reason it is the basis of social trust. The proper role of those most versed in the culture's creeds—of intellectuals—is primarily to aid in the educative process by which our culturally-acquired character keeps us from sliding individually or collectively into the "abyss of possibility." Where intellectuals regard their mission primarily as the opening up of possibilities rather than recalling the reasons why possibilities ought to be foreclosed, they pave the way for barbarism.

If much of Rieff's theory of culture sounds familiar, indeed recalls the wisdom of the ages, that, by Rieff's reckoning, is all to the good. "I am glad to say that I have never had an original thought in my life," Rieff writes with rhetorical overstatement, "I owe my every thought to some predeceasor."[11] It is part of Rieff's enterprise to recover— especially by a close reading of texts ranging from Plato and the Bible through Freud and Kafka—that wisdom which is too often forgotten in contemporary social theory and academic education. Indeed, it is precisely such wisdom about the nature of culture which Rieff asserts that his "cultured" contemporaries are least likely to have, and institutions of higher education the place that they are least likely to obtain it.

The ironic message which pervades Rieff's work is that modern culture has become not "higher" but lower, that much of higher education has a lowering effect, and that the spread of the characteristic assumptions of modern culture leads to barbarism. A cultural elite which disdains the need to resist what was once known as transgression and temptation as primitive "taboos" contributes to the spread of instinctual primitivism.[12] For it is Rieff's contention that past cultures based on political or religious ideals have been superseded in the nineteenth and especially in the twentieth century by a new culture based on diminishing our sensitivity to what is highest and increasing our acceptance of what is lowest.

In this process Freud plays a key if ambiguous role. For almost four decades, Freud has been the most frequent subject of Rieff's inquiries. Rieff is best known as an interpreter of Freud. His *Freud: The Mind of the Moralist* (1959) remains his best known and bestselling book; his second book, *The Triumph of the Therapeutic: Uses of Faith After Freud* (1966), picked up thematically and chronologically where the first book left off, and in between Rieff edited a ten-volume series of Freud's *Collected Papers*. The welcome many intellectuals accorded to Rieff's exegesis of Freud undoubtedly had something to do with their disillusionment with Marxism. This disillusionment had been chronicled and spurred by Lionel Trilling's novel of ideas, *The Middle of the Journey*, published in 1947. But there was no *Middle of the Analysis*, and indeed for those who placed their faith in Freud, analysis was interminable, a sort of permanent revolution in one ego. Rieff's work did for Freudianism what Trilling's had done for Marxism—but it did so in a highly subtle and ironic fashion. At a time when Trilling and other erstwhile radicals turned chastened liberals were touting Freud as an antidote to the psychological weaknesses of progressivist liberalism and as the high priest of a post-religious morality, *Freud: The Mind of the Moralist* was among the first works to interpret Freud as a moral and ethical theorist in the language of the humanities and social sciences. Rieff lavished on Freud the same exegetical attention traditionally reserved for the great texts of philosophy, and indeed he frequently compared Freud's views with those of Plato or Augustine.

There is no doubt that Rieff's work was a milestone in the acceptance of Freud into the American academic canon. Yet *Freud: The Mind of the Moralist* was an ambivalent work. On the one hand, the book asserted repeatedly that Freud was a great mind, and a rather conservative one at that. In contrast to a widely-shared impression of Freud as a legitimator of sexual revolution and instinctual expression, Rieff showed that Freud regarded the social repression of instincts as necessary and inevitable. On the other hand, the book contained learned and pointed critiques of the arbitrariness of Freud's interpretative method and of the fundamental misogyny within his intellectual system. And its deeper thrust was more critical still.

While Rieff's exegesis of Freud's texts in their cultural context was remarkable, Rieff's own interest was in Freud's significance as the catalyst of a new cultural sensibility which he saw as increasingly dominant among the American educated classes. He dubbed Freud "the first out-patient of the hospital culture in which we live," or what Rieff termed the culture of "the therapeutic." Central to the therapeutic sensibility and to Rieff's portrait of Freud was the "lowering" of authority, the premise that what men had regarded as high or ultimate was actually the expression of something lower, in this case of instincts and their sublimation. Freud's interpretation of culture and of human motivation, Rieff showed, was inevitably reductive. By interpreting all ethics of self-sacrifice and all religious belief as the veiled and distorted expressions of sexuality, Freud explicitly or implicitly deflated older, nobler aspirations. The feeling of parents towards their children became "parental narcissism," that of children towards their parents became oedipal desires, the bond between leader and follower became identification, and religion was reinterpreted as mass obsessional neurosis. Thus all social and religious goals were interpretively reconceived as veiled expressions of the instincts. For those steeped in the Freudian sensibility, to be rational was to be suspicious of all altruism, of public commitments, and of religious belief.

By defining all collective ideals as irrational veils of sexual instincts which led to unnecessary guilt, Freud promoted a standard of rationality which was distintegrative of group life. Above all, Freud taught the irrationality of guilt. To feel guilt was to demonstrate a lack of self-understanding, to be overly intolerant of instinctual demands. In the Freudian project, the rational development of consciousness would serve to increase the sense of well-being by diminishing the sense of guilt. Thus, while the previous dominant culture of the West, Christianity, had taught that a bad conscience was the result of the repressing one's higher, moral nature, Freud maintained that guilt was a result of repressing one's lower, instinctual nature. If Christianity thus encouraged man to look upward to resolve the sense of guilt, Freud directed his attention downward.

Freud, then, was what Rieff termed a "parodist" of previous political and religious cultures, who by creating "a science exhibiting the pathology of moral aspiration," offered an intellectually powerful rationale for self-concern in the narrowest terms.[13] Psychoanalysis delegitimated inherited cultural identities, while helping to create a new cultural ideal—what Rieff called "psychological man"— committed only to "his own careful economy of the inner life."[14] For psychological man, social relationships and cultural attachments were viewed as forms of therapy. Though psychological men entered into social relationships, they did so with deep suspicion, and with a constant attention to whether their investments were paying off in psychic health.

In *The Triumph of the Therapeutic* (1966), Rieff refined and rounded out the implications of the replacement of politics and religion by the therapeutic worldview. "The therapy of all therapies, the secret of all secrets, the interpretation of all interpretations, in Freud, is not to attach oneself too exclusively to any one particular meaning or object."[15] For what Rieff called "the therapeutic"—the man or women schooled in the analytic attitude—the highest wisdom was "to keep in touch with the options around which the conduct of his life might be organized; ideally, all options ought to be kept alive because, theoretically, all are equally advisable—or inadvisable, in given personal circumstances."[16] The therapeutic type was thus schooled against binding, permanent commitments; the bottom line of every social contract, for him, was the escape clause. This applied not only to personal commitments, but to cultural or intellectual commitments as well. It was not that he or she remained un-committed, but that commitment itself was viewed as a form of therapeutic self-enhancement, with each commitment to be abandoned when self-enhancement diminished. Therapeutics were "pro-choice" in the most profound sense: the possibility of choosing was the ultimate value, yet there was no compelling reason for making one choice over another.

The culture of therapy and analysis was therefore the antithesis of what Rieff regarded as high culture: by "deconverting" the individual from inherited religious and historical commands and under-standings, it made the mind open and pliable, rather than stable and trustworthy. The culture of therapy was a "remissive" culture, more adept at excusing or explaining away the "shalt nots" of the past than offering compelling reasons of its own for anti-institutional moral behaviour. It thus paved the way for a revolt against cultural restraints which Freud himself would not have applauded.

In Rieff's account, intellectuals were the first to adopt the culture of therapy, and have been most responsible for its diffusion into the larger culture. Far from their traditional role of articulating the necessity of the repression of desire for the sake of communal purposes and higher authority, intellectuals were increasingly devoted to demonstrating the arbitrariness of all restraints and authority.

Rieff's next book, *Fellow Teachers* (1973), explored (among a panoply of other topics) the links between the therapeutic revolt against authority once confined to the intellectual avant-garde, the diffusion of such notions through the university curriculum, and the popularization of these ideas in what had come to be called the counter-culture. "Those who already know what is not to be done seem weaker than ever before, especially in the universities," Rieff wrote. "We re-educated ones—we are the culturally deprived."[17] This most unusual of books originated in Rieff's response to questions about his work posed by the editors of the journal *Salmagundi*, and the pretence of addressing an audience of university professors of the humanities and social sciences was preserved throughout. A loosely-linked series of reflections which proceeded in part by reflections on texts by Kierkegaard, Pirandello, and John Barth, *Fellow Teachers* was an allusive, learned, and self-revelatory document, which sharpened many of Rieff's earlier themes and presented in aphoristic form the directions of his subsequent work.

To be truly cultured, in Rieff's sense of being imbued with the fact of ultimate truths, ultimate transgressions, and their symbolic expressions, meant to draw moral strength and identity from gratitude towards one's culture and a recognition of indebtedness to those from whom one had acquired it. From their teachers in the humanities and social sciences, students were likely to get the opposite of what they most needed. Rieff painted a painful portrait of university students who by the 1960s were often the children of parents who had themselves been imbued with the therapeutic ethos, and hence had left their children culturally disinherited, without a firm sense of historical memory or cultural authority. Those who came into the universities with a firm historical or religious identity were encouraged to abandon it for the sake of a critical culture which purported to be rational and universal but was capable only of demonstrating the arbitrariness of inherited authority. "A universal culture is a contradiction in terms," Rieff wrote. "Barbarism means the universality of those re-educated or brutalized out of membership in the binding particularities of their culture and, being able to entertain all, inhibited by no new god-terms."[18.] Instead of being taught the need for binding commands, students were being "transgressively educated; cart is put before the horse, criticism before loyalty to that which is being criticised."[19] Thus Rieff warned, higher education became a nursery in which students were taught to hop from one cultural order to another, while becoming inoculated against the possibility of binding authority and authoritative commands.

In *Fellow Teachers* and other writings, Rieff has traced the attempt of social science to replace religion, and of the social scientist to replace the priest or prophet.[20] This theme was sometimes explicit, as in the case of the French founder of sociology, Saint-Simon, who called his early attempt at social science the "New Christianity," and Freud, who viewed himself as a new Moses. A pervasive theme of modern social thought to which Rieff has called attention is the reductive explanation of religion, the assertion in a variety of forms that the divine is "really" something else. From Feuerbach to Durkheim, Rieff noted in an early essay, liberals treated religion as a form of social integration, while other theorists too exposed God as really "the dummy acting for social order and especially for the weakest in it."[21] For Marx, of course, religion was the opium of the masses; for Freud, God was really a projection of infantile helplessness, an interpretation which ultimately reduced all authority to the relationship of children to their parents. Related to this pervasive theme in modern thought is the denial that moral standards have any objective basis. As a consequence, Rieff notes, secular intellectuals often share the prejudice that the morally good person is unlikely to be very clever—the good are those who haven't caught on to the fact that their morality has no objective warrant.[22] Thus social scientists, wittingly or unwittingly, become the shock troops of "the long revolution of modernity at its most basic level, the opening up of possibility, the liquidation of that which is 'not done.'"[23]

The inculcation of these assumptions of social science, whether in its psychoanalytic or sociological form, makes the reappropriation of previous cultural traditions so difficult. In the preface to the re-issue of the *Triumph of the Therapeutic*, Rieff summarizes this theme: "At the end of the historical road taken by the Western spirit, there, waiting to waylay any founder of renewed faith and analyze away all festivals of divine recognition is the therapist . . . As actor-manager of his own indefinitely changeable identities, the therapeutic as therapist tolerates no revealed, eternal, and commanding truths."[24] For Rieff, then, contemporary intellectuals immersed in the critical culture of therapy can only teach one critique of meaning after another. They open the door to "liberation": and beyond the door lies the personal meaninglessness that comes from having to choose and choose again, without compelling grounds for choice.

In *Fellow Teachers*, Rieff portrayed himself as among those mired in the cultural contradictions of the critical/therapeutic world view, "stuck with our faith in criticism, only marginally different from popular versions of the endless expressional quest or liberated understandings."[25] The message of the book, therefore, was not prophetic, but rather prophylactic: a warning to those on the road to the culture of criticism of the dead end that lay ahead.

In Rieff's subsequent work—above all in a long epilogue to *Freud: The Mind of the Moralist* (1979), a new prologue to *Fellow Teachers* (1985), and several essays now available in *Feeling Intellect*—Rieff has made increasingly explicit a theme which was implicit, if ambiguous, in his earlier books. That message is religious, though not in any denominational sense. There *is* an ultimate warrant for moral action, and men have some intuitive sense of this which cannot be adequately described in rational or scientific terms, but which expresses itself in our sense of guilt at transgressing moral demands. That ultimate authority, in the Jewish and Christian traditions, is the eternal Creator who refers to himself in Exodus 3:14 as "Ehyeh asher Ehyeh," ("I am that I am"); and it is through our apprehension of this authority that, according to Rieff, we are able to repress the evil possibilities within us. Rieff asserts that much of modern critical thought is an attempt to deny or repress this reality, which he terms "sacred order."

Here Rieff has stepped outside the role of sociologist—who could at most assert the inevitability of "god-terms" for such historic culture—and into the role of religious apologist, to assert the reality of God, who is apprehended in a variety of ways in the historical cultures which recognize this reality. According to Rieff, guilt is the most tangible expression of the reality of sacred order and of our inclination to ignore, repress, or rebel against. For Rieff, the sense of guilt is not to be explained away, but to be cultivated: it makes it possible for men and women to develop that character that comes from recognizing the reality and power of the evil inclination, and deciding to act against it, rather than intellectualizing it away as "desublimating instincts" in need of appeasement. Recognizing rather than repressing the reality of guilt, Rieff maintains, is the first step away from the dead end of the culture of therapy.[26]

Needless to say, this message is literally incredible in the critical culture in which many of Rieff's potential readers live. Since their likely response is to laugh it out of court, Rieff must convince them they are laughing in the dark. This explains the peculiarity of his prose and of his pose. The prose has become increasingly poetic, expressing in metaphorical terms what Rieff believes is a reality which must be felt before it can be intellectualized and which cannot be reached from within the premises of a rationalist social science that does not provide a vocabulary to say what most needs to be said. The pose resembles the one described by Rieff himself in an essay of 1959 entitled "The Evangelist Strategy." The role of the modern religious apologist, he wrote, is to reach those outside the faith. The strategy of the religious apologist, like that of evangelist, is to confront his readers with a choice between "fatal meaninglessness and saving meaning," to make them confront the question, "How long can the misery and futility of life without faith be tolerated?'[27]

This has become Rieff's chosen role, to awaken his cultured readers to the limits of the therapeutic world-view. As Rieff knows, the audience for whom he writes is the one least inclined to heed his message; indeed they have a deep "resistance" to it, in that it challenges so many of their learned cultural assumptions. To arouse their initial interest, he often resorts to commentary and exegesis of the texts that are regarded as holy in the modernist canon. His evangelism is of a very subtle and intellectually demanding variety: far from threatening his cultured reader with the torments of future hell or the possibility of losing life after death, Rieff argues that the repression of moral sense in the culture of the therapeutic leads to a sort of spiritual numbness which is death in life. Hence Rieff's ironic dictum, *"You only live once, if then.* "[28]

Rieff also calls attention to the disastrous social and cultural effects of the denial of the possibility of transgression. "Every experience being, in modernity, worth having, an unprecedented cultivation of vulgarity has set in."[29] "In the mind of our remissive elites, there is always an excusing reason for everything," Rieff notes in the most recent essay in *Feeling Intellect*. "Or, worse, there is always some more or less elaborately rationalized indifference to the horror of a social offence in sacred order."[30] Once the human body is no longer regarded as the temple of God, how long will it be, he wonders, until rape is redefined as a "paraphilic coercive disorder"? As shamelessness becomes the idealized state of things, as recognition of the need to repress instinctual possibilities is contested by those "erotocratic movements of post-modernity" whose claims are now becoming enforceable codes at many of our leading universities and cultural institutions, who will explain what is not to be done and why?[31] "The remorseless criticism of everything raising in life" thus becomes the hallmark of culture, high and low.[32] In our public culture, as Rieff has been predicting for decades, "Why not?" has become the most unanswerable of intellectual questions. Rieff has tried to convey the frightening consequences of the inability to answer that query, and to hint at an adequate response.

The predictive capacity of Rieff's thesis that the culture of the therapeutic provides no downward limits appears borne out by subsequent experience. "The opening up of possibility, the liquidation of that which is 'not done,' represents the long revolution of modernity at its most basic level," he wrote in 1968.[33] By the summer of 1990, the dominant American cultural elites were unable or unwilling to explain why the exhibition of photographs of a man with the handle of a bull whip in his anus should not be subsidized by the national government. Indeed, those who insisted that this was not an achievement worthy of collective support were angrily and contemptuously characterized by most of the cultural establishment as intellectual Neanderthals, too primitive to comprehend the nature of culture, which, it was said, must necessarily be committed to the exploration of ever-new areas of experience. By the autumn of 1990, a jury in Broward County, Florida, found that the lyrics of the group "2 Live Crew" did not violate community standards. These lyrics included "He'll tear the [expletive for vagina] open 'cause it's satisfaction' " and "bust your [same expletive again] then your backbone . . . I wanna see you bleed." [34] The abyss of possibility, it seems, had now been absorbed into community standards.

Rieff's contribution to the understanding of modern cultural development can be appreciated even by those who do not share his conservative premises or the religious implications of his recent work. Others have offered more convincing explanations of the historical genealogy of the therapeutic ethic, but none has analyzed its inner dynamic or plotted its perils as powerfully as Philip Rieff.

Notes

1. Aristides [Joseph Epstein], "Incidental Meditations" *The American Scholar* (Spring, 1976), pp. 173–74. For other evaluations of Rieff's work, see Robert Boyers (ed.) *Psychological Man* (New York: Harper and Row, 1975), and Richard H. King, "From Creeds to Therapies: Philip Rieff's Work in Perspective" *Reviews in American History* (June, 1976), pp. 291–96.
2. All references are to the University of Chicago editions of Rieff's books, cited in note 4 below. Philip Rieff, *Freud: The Mind of the Moralist*, p. 328.
3. Philip Rieff, *Fellow Teachers*, p. xvii.
4. Philip Rieff, *Freud: The Mind of the Moralist* (New York, Viking Press; London: Gollancz, 1959; rev. edn, New York: Anchor Books, 1961; 2nd edn, London: Methuen, 1965; 3rd edn, with Epilogue, "One Step Further," Chicago: University of Chicago press, 1979). Rieff, *The Triumph of the Therapeutic: Uses of Faith After Freud* (New York: Harper and Row; London: Chatto & Windus, 1966; 2nd edn, with a new Preface, Chicago: University of Chicago Press, 1987); Rieff, *Fellow Teachers* (New York, Harper & Row, 1973; 2nd edn published as *Fellow Teachers/Of Culture and Its Second Death*, with a new preface: "A Pretext of Proof Texts," University of Chicago Press, 1984). Rieff,

The *Feeling Intellect: Selected Writings*, edited and with an introduction by Jonathan B. Imber (University of Chicago Press, 1990); this volume also includes a complete bibliography of Rieff's works through 1990. All subsequent notes refer to Rieff's works unless otherwise stated.

5. "Kelly Miller's *Radicals and Conservatives*" (1968) in *The Feeling Intellect*, p. 230.
6. "The Theology of Politics: Reflections on Totalitarianism as the Burden of Our Time" in *The Feeling Intellect*, p. 89.
7. "Toward a Theory of Culture: With Special Reference to the Psychoanalytic Case" (1972) in *The Feeling Intellect*, p. 324.
8. *Freud*, p. xxiii; *Fellow Teachers*, p. 133.
9. See especially *Triumph of the Therapeutic*, "Introductory: Toward a Theory of Culture," pp. 1–28; and "Toward a Theory of Culture," in *Feeling Intellect*, pp. 321–30.
10. See *Fellow Teachers*, pp. 38, 106; "The Cultural Economy of Higher Education" in *Feeling Intellect*, pp. 247–48.
11. *Fellow Teachers*, p. vii.
12. "By What Authority? Post-Freudian Reflections on the Repression of the Repressive in Modern Culture" (1981) in *Feeling Intellect*, p. 344.
13. *Freud*, p. 319.
14. *Freud*, p. 356.
15. *Triumph*, p. 59.
16. *Triumph*, p. 50.
17. *Fellow Teachers*, p. 165n.
18. *Fellow Teachers*, p. 39.
19. *Fellow Teachers*, p. 100.
20. See for example "Nineteenth-Century European Positivism" (1965) in *Feeling Intellect*, pp. 171–72.
21. "George Orwell and the Post-Liberal Imagination" (1954) in *Feeling Intellect*, pp. 155–56; *Triumph*, p. xii.
22. *Freud*, p. 279.
23. "Kelly Miller" in *Feeling Intellect*, p. 230.
24. *Triumph*, p. x.
25. *Fellow Teachers*, p. 88.
26. *Fellow Teachers*, pp. 100, 156ff; *Freud*, pp. 375ff, 417fnll.
27. "The Evangelist Strategy" (1959) in *Feeling Intellect*, p. 124.
28. *Fellow Teachers*, p. 111n.
29. "By What Authority" in *Feeling Intellect*, p. 345.
30. "For the Last Time Psychology" (1987) in *Feeling Intellect*, p. 362.
31. *Freud*, p. 381.
32. *Fellow Teachers*, p. xi.
33. "Kelly Miller" in *Feeling Intellect*, p. 230.
34. For a Rieffian analysis of the jury's decision, its cultural origins and social ramifications, see Charles Krauthammer, "Culture has Consequences" *The Washington Post*, 26 October 1990.

10

Hannah Arendt

Richard H. King

Burckhardt's reflection on Machiavelli's *History of Florence* applies equally to Hannah Arendt's *The Origins of Totalitarianism*: "Even if every line were demonstrated to be false, the whole would still present an indispensable truth."

Philip Rieff

My great dream was to live in a free German republic; lacking that I wrote the history of Rome.

Theodor Mommsen

If one were to write the intellectual history of our generation . . . in the form of the biography of a single person . . . this person's mind would stand revealed as having been forced to turn full circle not once but twice, first when he escaped from thought into action, and then again when action, or rather having acted, forced him back into thought.

Hannah Arendt

Before assessing the legacy of Hannah Arendt, one question must be asked: To whom or what does her intellectual history belong? Arendt's life was divided between thought and action; or, more accurately, between thought about thought, i.e. philosophy, and thought about action, i.e. political theory. In addition she straddled the transatlantic divide between America, whose political culture she admired but whose lack of philosophical capacity she regretted, and Germany, whose historical inability to think politically was matched only by its distinguished philosophical tradition. As Arendt wrote from America in 1949 to Karl Jaspers: "I often ask myself which is the more difficult: to teach Germans a political sense or to impart to Americans even the haziest notion of philosophy."[1]

If these are not ambiguities enough, Arendt's deep ambivalence as to whether she considered herself "German" was also a permanent personal as well as intellectual dilemma. She and Jaspers returned to this topic intermittently throughout their correspondence of over forty years. In 1953 she wrote "I will not deny your and Heinrich's [Arendt's husband] Germany, the tradition in which I grew up and the language in which I think and in which the poetry I most cherish is written."[2] But even before Hitler's rise to power and the ensuing catastrophe of European Jewry, Arendt insisted on distinguishing between Germany's intellectual and cultural tradition and the history of the German *Reich*.

The founding of the state of Israel presented her with yet another dilemma. The daughter of secular Jews, Arendt was the recipient of neither a religious nor a Zionist upbringing in Königsberg. She did however work for a Zionist children's organization in the 1930s while living in Paris after having fled Nazi Germany in 1933. But her Jewishness was not a self-conscious part of her identity until after the Nazi takeover and the beginning of systematic persecution of Jews. In the 1940s, she spoke out against the establishment of a specifically Jewish state in Palestine, preferring rather some sort of binational entity, and part of the reason why her *Eichmann in Jerusalem* (1963) aroused such controversy was her challenge to received Israeli and Jewish opinion on Israel's handling of the whole affair. Yet one of the central "lessons" of *Origins of Totalitarianism* (1951) was that a people required a political home where they enjoyed the "right to have rights."[3] Without ever suggesting that there was something inevitable about anti-semitism or the Holocaust, her position was that appeals to general human rights by or on behalf of stateless peoples had historically led to nothing—except tragedy.

In what follows I assume that the ambiguities and ambivalences in Arendt's own life mirrored much that was essential to the experience of modernity; specifically, her divided intellectual inheritance and multiple cultural origins meant that the experience of this proto-typical "good European" was on another level not at all unAmerican. The United States, Arendt always emphasized, was not a nation state in the European sense: "The principle of its [America's] political structure is, and always has been, independent of a homogeneous population and of a common past." In America "nationality and state are not identical," and thus citizenship did not depend upon cultural and social assimilation.[4] Yet these tensions in Arendt's experience were enabling rather than debilitating. She was one of the most original and creative political thinkers of this century, an indication of which is the continuing relevance of her political thought for the revolutionary upheavals of the late 1980s and early 1990s. What follows is a descriptive analysis of what made Arendt so important in her own time—and ours.

I

Certainly Arendt's historical and personal circumstances—being uprooted as a young girl by the First World War and then by the Nazis, internment in Vichy France and then flight across the Pyrenees (where her friend Walter Benjamin committed suicide), gradual establishment in the United States after arriving as a refugee with her mother and husband, Heinrich Blücher—go a long way towards explaining her intellectual preoccupations between 1940 and her death in 1975. But her experience of the quintessential twentieth-century phenomena she identified as "statelessness," "homelessness," and "worldlessness" subtly shaped the way she thought problems through and then conveyed them to the reader. Only the most obtuse reader could miss the deeply serious, restless and original mind at work in her writings. Ideas are put into motion and subject to relentless pressure; lines of thought pursued and conventional wisdom overturned. The results were—and still are—frequently exhilarating and often controversial.

In the 1920s Arendt studied philosophy and theology with Martin Heidegger, Rudolph Bultmann and Jaspers, the best Germany had to offer. Her intellectual homeland was, as she once said, "the tradition of German philosophy," which derived from the Greeks and culminated in the great modern tradition, beginning with Hegel and Kant and ending with Nietzsche, Heidegger, Husserl and Jaspers. Not surprisingly, academic philosophers in America and England were very wary of Arendt, a feeling she more than reciprocated. She thought the philosophers of language and logical positivists regnant in the postwar English-speaking world were third-rate. This opinion was a fairly predictable one. More surprising was the relative lack of influence of Marx and Freud on her intellectual development. Though her parents were social democrats, she remained apolitical until the 1930s. Her husband had been involved in the Spartacist movement in post-First World War Germany and one of her own political heroes was Rosa Luxemburg; but she was never tempted by Marxism and only seriously studied Marx in the 1950s.[5] She had even less time for the psychoanalytic tradition, so important in the intellectual life of Central Europe and of postwar America where its contributions to social, cultural and political thought were considerable. It is not surprising, then, that Arendt was largely indifferent to the Frankfurt Critical Theorists' attempt to combine Marx and Freud. Though she had some friends in common with the Frankfurt group, particularly Walter Benjamin and theologian Paul Tillich, her ideological affinities with other émigrés such as Theodor Adorno or Herbert Marcuse were minimal and her personal relations with them frosty to say the least.

One enduring moral Arendt drew from the *Nazizeit* was the political naiveté and the moral cowardice of philosophers and of academics generally. Surely the disgraceful behaviour of her one-time mentor Heidegger, who publicly supported National Socialism in 1934, contributed a great deal to her distrust of the political or moral capabilities of philosophers. She was later to take up the conundrum of the great thinker's relationship to the public world in her speculations about the relationship between thought and action, intellect and morality. Suffice it to say that Arendt's judgement of Heidegger focused on what she described as his "lack of character."[6] Arendt's understanding of the political experience of the twentieth century thus taught her that cant to the effect that philosophers spoke "truth" to the politician's "power" misconstrued the nature of both philosophy and politics.

II

Though Arendt ranged widely over modern European history and the tradition of Western philosophy, one basic historical assumption informs her entire oeuvre: that there had been a fundamental "break" in the history and philosophical tradition of the West. The foundation of her thought was, in other words, the modern loss of foundations. Arendt's lifelong project, begun during the war, can be divided into two phases. First was her attempt to understand what had led to the unprecedented extermination of millions of people in Nazi Germany and Stalin's Russia. Then, in the 1950s, she began to rummage through the ruins of the traditions of Western philosophy and political thought to discover what might be salvaged for a new beginning. Shaped by the German tradition that was suspicious of applying the methods of the natural sciences to the human sciences, Arendt eschewed what she considered pseudo-scientific explanations for historical phenomena. Moreover, unlike Karl Popper, she rejected the idea that ideas were the primary causal force in the emergence of totalitarianism; in her own words, she "proceed[ed] from facts and events" not "intellectual affinities and influences." She also insisted that the Marxist grand narrative, one that explained events in terms of constant historical forces, was wrong-headed. Such a conception of history denied the possibility of free choice or meaningful human action within history. Her intention in *Origins*, she replied to Eric Voegelin, had not been to construct a history of totalitarianism but to attempt an "analysis in terms of history."[7] The same approach might be ascribed to *On Revolution* (1965), where she sought to unearth a lost tradition of political freedom and to trace its vicissitudes in the modern world by offering contrasting (and highly contentious) characterizations of the American and French Revolutions.

Informing Arendt's approach to history was another contentious assumption—that academic historians were too enamoured of the idea of detachment to deal with what Hayden White has recently called the "historical sublime," i.e. those historical phenomena such as totalitarianism or the Holocaust—or manifestations of political freedom—that somehow escape the conventions of historiographical rhetoric and its modes of explanation.[8] When *Origins* was criticized for being "exaggerated," Arendt tartly responded that twentieth-century reality itself was "exaggerated." To do full justice to the totalitarian ethos in which "everything is possible" and a total transformation of human nature was intended, where "ideology" replaced reality and "terror" permeated the political ethos, it was necessary to convey not so much the experience of that ethos as its presuppositions and structures, as Arendt attempted in part III of *Origins*. Such an effort required an intellectual depth, theoretical training, and moral seriousness beyond the reach of most historians. To Arendt's way of thinking, when her work was compared not with the reality of totalitarianism but with what "other historians have said about the same topic while assuming that everything actually was as usual [*alles in Ordnung sei*], then of course everything appeared to be radical nonsense."[9]

In fact, as Philip Rieff shrewdly noted, there was a certain "theological" cast to *Origins*.[10] It would be a long and fruitless quest to find an academic historian (at least in the Anglo-American world) who would think it relevant to engage with questions about the nature of evil in a work of historical description and explanation; which of course Arendt insisted on doing in *Origins* and in *Eichmann in Jerusalem*. That she shifted her assessment of the nature of evil between the two works, emphasizing its radicality in the former and its banality in the latter, is less to the point than that she thought "evil" a relevant category of historical and political analysis at all.

Yet, despite her somber *topoi*, extraordinary energy radiates from Arendt's work, its vitality deriving, perhaps, from the opportunity, not just the burden, of re-reading and then rethinking the Western tradition in the light of the "dark times" of modernity. For Arendt, it no longer made any sense to speak of certainties and continuities, but at best of recapturing some of those fragments of the experience of political freedom found in the political history of the West. The results were often startlingly original—and, her detractors insisted, just as often historically skewed.

Perhaps it was because Arendt was so aware of the precariousness of thought or action that she felt more at home in America with intellectuals than academics, with literary people rather than with historians, philosophers or political scientists. Displayed prominently on one wall of the Arendt-Blücher apartment in Manhattan was a large photograph of Franz Kafka. Her friends included Mary McCarthy and Dwight Macdonald, Robert Lowell and Randall Jarrell, W.H. Auden and Alfred Kazin. Kazin later wrote: "she gave her friends . . . intellectual courage before the mortal terror the war had willed us" yet at the same time she was "arch, witty, womanly . . . I have never met a woman so reflective, yet so eager and gifted for friendship."[11] Arendt exchanged lessons in German and German poetry with Jarrell and Kazin for tuition in American literature and poetry from them; and Kazin records how much she infuriated novelist Saul Bellow by lecturing him on Faulkner and American fiction. She published primarily in Jewish periodicals during the war; then afterwards became a regular contributor to *Partisan Review*, *Commentary*, *The New Yorker* and *The New York Review of Books* until her death in 1975. She contributed to academic journals infrequently and only later did she accept a regular teaching position at the New School for Social Research. Most revealing of her contempt for conventional academia was that, with the exception of Jaspers, the intellectual profiles she collected as *Men in Dark Times* (1968) include no philosophers or academics as such.

Besides her thesis about the "break" in tradition, her categorical imperative, her guiding precept, was: "to think what we are doing." Referring both to epistemology and ethics, this injunction expressed her deeply held belief that thinking and conscience were intimately related. It was Adolf Eichmann's inability to think what he was doing, not just in his obedience to authority but also in his incapacity for expressing any but the most timeworn clichés of *Amtsdeutsch*, that so

astonished Arendt. Because Eichmann was so bereft of moral imagination and thus incapable of imagining things from any other point of
view, he could not do otherwise than he did. This was the important
and most profound meaning of Arendt's controversial phrase the
"banality of evil." Never did Arendt assert that there was a potential
Eichmann lurking in everyone; but she did suggest that without
constantly probing and evaluating our experience, we would be more
prey to behaving mindlessly and obediently. There was, as she also
wrote in *On Violence* (1970) and as was suggested in psychologist
Stanley Milgram's *Obedience to Authority* (1974), nothing to be gained
by positing an aggressive instinct or innate proclivity towards violence
to explain the extermination camps. Rather, as Dwight Macdonald
had already pointed out in his seminal essay "The Responsibility
of Peoples" (1945), it was in obedience not disobedience that the
greatest threat to modern survival consisted. Authority not anarchy
was most to be feared.[12]

Two characteristic features of Arendt's thought repay close attention. The first is the importance she placed on making distinctions.
This helps explain her hostility to Marx, Freud and the modern
"hermeneutics of suspicion," which assumes that reality is always
elsewhere than where we think it is. The proliferation of reductionist
and functionalist modes of thought, she observed in "What is
Authority?" (1956), exemplified the modern academic failure to
understand reality in its full variety and diversity. She objected, for
instance, to the functional equation of Marxism and religion simply
because they perform similar functions in certain contexts. More to
the political point, she felt that because historians and students of
politics failed to distinguish between authoritarian regimes, tyrannical governments and totalitarian rule, they would never understood
what totalitarianism had been about. Similarly, in *The Human
Condition* (1958) she insisted on distinguishing between labour, work
and action as forms of human activity, while *On Violence* contended
that the confusion between violence, power and authority both
reflected and encouraged a deep misunderstanding as to the nature of
politics.

Furthermore, the urge to make distinctions comported well with
her emphasis upon appearance *as* reality as opposed to the traditional
opposition between appearance and reality. For Arendt, an action
rather than what motivated it, an event not the law of history or
nature that explained it, was the proper object of intellectual address.
The problem, she observed in *The Life of the Mind* (1978), with the
unconscious or the biological as an explanatory entity is that it posits

the operation of unvarying laws that all but efface individuality and distinctiveness. To focus upon how things and people manifest themselves emphasizes the diversity of the world and the possibility of new beginnings; it is also to emphasize the public rather than the hidden or private. For these reasons, Arendt was uninterested in the psychological motivation for, or effects of, political action. She feared therapeutic and redemptive politics, a stance which both offers a valuable critique of much modern identity politics but also reflects a point of weakness in her understanding of what it has meant to be political in this century.

Her emphasis upon making distinctions and upon the primacy of appearances reveals yet another crucial facet of Arendt's thought: the assumption that the "world" is characterized by "plurality." We inhabit or have a "world" insofar as we are related to and separated by objects, loyalties, laws and institutions and thus have the space in which to distinguish ourselves by speaking and acting about matters bearing on the public realm. Totalitarianism destroys the world by so distancing people through terror that they have nothing in common or by compressing them together within "one iron band of terror" so that the distinctions among them are effaced.[13] Thus plurality and world imply one another and are prerequisites for action, the initial model for which is the creation of human life. The ultimate expression of free action is political speech and action, whose essence for Arendt is the preservation of a public space where we can appear before others and have a home in the world. Thus freedom is an attribute of action and a way of being rather than a legal status as such. For Arendt we should of course be free to act politically; but more importantly, we are free *in* acting politically.

Generally, Arendt affirmed Robert Frost's unsentimental view that "Good fences make good neighbors" rewritten as "good institutions make good citizens." Because friendship maintains a certain distance, a "space in-between," that love insists on closing, friendship—but not love—is a public, political virtue. By extension, neither the family nor the closeness of oppressed "pariah" peoples offers a proper model of the relationship among citizens. Inequality is the principle of family organization, while the lack of sufficient distance among members of an excluded group makes it difficult for them to form separate opinions or to tolerate disagreement amongst themselves.

Besides her insistence on making distinctions, Arendt also emphasized the political importance of re-telling the past in the form of stories. Her own forays into the past—the resurrection of the Greek *polis*, the apotheosizing of the American founding fathers, the evoc-

ation of the council system in twentieth-century European politics—
were narratives of those revelatory moments of human freedom when
the capacity for beginning again was revealed. Story-telling, narrating
the events of the past, is not just good in itself, a constant of human
existence; or at least a constant where a world exists in which to tell
stories. It is also the way that we, through our historians, novelists
and poets, maintain the world as a place worth inhabiting; or come to
terms with those historical phenomena that have sought to destroy
our world. Writing about the necessity in postwar Germany to
"master" the Nazi past, Arendt suggested the difficult work involved
in preserving public memory in a passage that reveals how close to,
yet also how very far she was from Freud, the great theorist of private
memory.

> Insofar as any "mastering" of the past is possible, it consists in
> relating what has happened; but such narration, too, which
> shapes history, solves no problems and assuages no suffering; it
> does not master anything once and for all. Rather, as long as the
> meaning of events remains alive—and meaning can persist for
> very long periods of time—"mastering of the past" can take the
> form of ever-recurrent narration. The poet in a very general
> sense and the historian in a very special sense have the task of
> setting this process of narration in motion and involving us in it.[14]

From this passage we can also see that Arendt's interest in
language had to do with its semantic and pragmatic rather than its
syntactic or structural dimensions. She was concerned with the
meaning of terms and the context of utterance. It is not hard to see
why she had little use for language philosophers and would, I suspect,
have rejected the systematic suspicion of language's capacity to refer,
so central to post-structuralist thinking. To those such as Arendt,
who had witnessed the bewildering power of totalitarian speech to
foreclose reality and create a kind of mind-numbing alternative
universe, it would have seemed politically indulgent, even foolish, to
question the possibility or desirability of some sort of common
reality, against which ideological assertions ("Jews are vermin" or
"Bukharin is a class traitor") could be tested. According to Arendt,
speech (*parole*) has a dialogic function and assumes a shared
"common sense" among those inhabiting a common world. If no
great thinker's work is without contradictions which "lead into the
very center of their work,"[15] this fact does not derive from language
itself. In particular, political speech has a persuasive function; and
Arendt would certainly have rejected the Foucauldian suggestion that

persuasion and coercion are scarcely, if at all, distinguishable. On such a distinction hangs her whole theory of politics. Finally, according to Arendt, "They [the language philosophers] are absolutely right; in the final analysis all problems are linguistic problems; they simply do not know the implications of what they are saying."[16]

III

Even in retrospect, Arendt's move from the totalitarianism theme to a concern with politics and freedom after *Origins* was hardly predictable. Students of Arendt's work disagree on the question of continuity between her first large work and what followed. But while no-one would claim an absolute break in her thought after *Origins*, it is also difficult to see how *The Human Condition* or *On Revolution* flowed inevitably from it.[17] What made Arendt relatively unique among her contemporaries in European or American intellectual life was that she drew the conclusion that one—though certainly not the only—factor in the rise of totalitarianism had been the apolitical nature of the German middle class and of European Jewry. While most European proponents of the mass society thesis and most postwar American liberals were distinctly cool towards participatory politics and felt that mass political involvement had been one of the vital ingredients of totalitarianism, Arendt attempted to resurrect the notion of politics as an autonomous sphere of practice, valuable in its own right. Above all else, her work returned politics and the political to political thinking. In this it was echoed by the work of American contemporaries such as Paul Goodman, C. Wright Mills and Sheldon Wolin. Along with these figures, Arendt's thought was much more prophetic and reflective of the "new politics" of the 1960s than was, say, Herbert Marcuse's.

But Arendt's developing conception of politics was—and still is—hard to place neatly on the spectrum of political thought. In her thought, politics, freedom and action are all but synonymous and thus her idea of freedom hardly comports well with the dominant Anglo-American idea of "negative" freedom, championed by liberal political philosophers such as Isaiah Berlin or implemented by libertarian conservatives in the 1970s and 1980s. Nor did Arendt develop a theory of "rights" or "justice," topics which have stood at the centre of the work of liberal political theorists, led by John Rawls and Ronald Dworkin, since the 1960s. In practice Arendt was an ardent defender of civil liberties in the McCarthy era and wrote a long essay in the early 1970s on the need to institutionalize "civil disobedience" as a protected constitutional right. Where "conscientious objection" had its source in private, individual motivation, civil disobedience was quintessentially collective and public. Though the public and private distinction was central to her political thought, she reversed the importance many liberal theorists placed upon the two spheres. Where liberals tended to see the protection and extension of the private realm as the point of politics, Arendt saw participation in political life as crucial not only to the health of a polity but to a conception of what it meant to be fully human.

Above all else Arendt firmly rejected the view that the essence of politics was the pursuit of self-interest and that the apogee of political wisdom was the party system, both consensus assumptions among postwar American political scientists and thinkers. The great failure of the framers of the Constitution, she contended in *On Revolution*, was the neglect of institutional encouragement for citizen participation, for public freedom. Instead, by entrenching representative government, they did more to discourage than enable citizen involvement in the life of the polity and contributed to the (modern) view that political institutions exist to maintain the economic or social welfare of society.[18]

It is hardly surprising that Arendt took this position. No-one who had been so concerned with the modern revolutionary tradition or with resistance to totalitarian domination could have agreed that self-interest exhausted the vocabulary of political action or that politics was essentially about the compromises and coalitions necessary for everyone to get a piece of the pie. In the 1960s she was to praise the New Left and civil rights movement for their "moral" orientation by which she meant that their political activity seemed to transcend mere self-interest. (Indeed, any political involvement that runs the genuine risk of injury or death or harm to one's family or possessions offers *prima facie* evidence against an interest theory of politics.) On this issue Arendt was not being utopian or unrealistic or sentimental. She was rather exposing the parochial nature of much postwar American political thinking and its lack of contact with historical reality, exemplified in its inability to understand not just the revolutionary liberation movements in the Third World, but also the startling emergence of the civil rights movement or the New Left.

Yet on one fundamental matter—her emphasis upon plurality and diversity—Arendt's views approximated those of liberal theorists such as Berlin's with his emphasis upon philosophical and value pluralism. Arendt's considerable wariness of the political implications of Western philosophy was based on its monistic search for one final truth, one standard of the good, one idea of beauty. Whenever any such unitary ideal provided the basis for a political order or movement, then politics itself became impossible, since those who possess the truth or know the good have no need to persuade other people to their positions. Their speech is dogmatic, even coercive, rather than persuasive—and potentially murderous. Political institutions must possess a certain authority or legitimacy; but the possibility of persuasive speech among equal citizens is the defining characteristic of authentic politics.

Arendt's reading in the late 1940s and 1950s also led her to suspect Western philosophy and theology for never having been concerned primarily with the "world." Philosophy and theology, Platonic Forms and the City of God, had devalued politics and preferred the *vita contemplativa* to the *vita activa*. It was to counter this un- and a-worldly tendency that Arendt made the "world" so crucial in her thought and once considered naming her second major book *Amor Mundi* rather than *The Human Condition*.

Interestingly, Alfred Kazin once referred to "the genuinely conservative Hannah Arendt."[19] As already stated, Arendt did share with conservatives (and many liberals and radicals for that matter) a deep distaste for transformational, redemptive, or therapeutic politics and no-one took the modern loss of tradition and authority more seriously than she did. But there were severe differences between her and genuine conservatives. She betrayed little or no nostalgia for the pre-modern Christian culture of medieval Europe. (As a Jew it would have been strange had she felt otherwise.) What she found worth remembering, then conserving, from the past were those moments when new beginnings had been hazarded: the founding of Rome, the creation of the new American republic, the French Revolution in some of its early manifestations and the Hungarian revolt of 1956. And however eccentrically Arendt expressed her democratic inclinations, she always insisted that, despite the real inequalities existing among human beings, all citizens are and must be political equals. Among citizens there are no superiors and inferiors, no masters and servants, no permanent rulers and ruled.[20]

One might say that Arendt was a modern-day republican, that is, a conservative revolutionary, centrally concerned with, though never writing at any length about, the institutionalization of freedom. Having made a revolution, how could its institutions acquire legitimacy or, as she would have preferred to say, "authority;" and, second how could those legitimate institutions preserve that spirit of public happiness and political freedom so central to, yet so evanescent in, modern revolutions? Arendt was horrified by the notion of permanent revolution or by a transformation of human nature through political means. Indeed her objection to modern capitalism was that it enshrined the impermanent and consumable and thus created or preserved no suitably stable world within which significant thought, action or creation could take place. Thus her thought was valuable in emphasizing the ways in which conservative concerns with the authority and stability of institutions are relevant to, indeed necessary for, any revolutionary vision.

But it is Arendt's relationship with the left, from Marx through to social democracy, that most resists any neat summary. Arendt's sympathies were generally with the left; she was thoroughly respectful of Marx and recognized his importance in returning philosophy to the "world." Moreover Arendt's thought, particularly in its early years, was decidedly hostile to the European bourgeoisie specifically and to capitalism in general. Flying a proto-Marxian flag in *Origins*, she accused the bourgeoisie of hijacking the nation-state in the nineteenth century and using it to advance its own economic and social interests. Indeed, the dichotomy Arendt set up between politics and society bore some resemblance to the Hegelian-Marxian state/civil society distinction.

But Arendt's most contested historical judgement cum theoretical move lay in her assertion that one of the pernicious facts of the modern age was the intrusion of "society" and the "social" into the public realm and the resulting assumption that the state had responsibility for the social and economic as well as the political/legal spheres.[21] Put another way, Arendt felt that the modern demise of politics and the fragility of the public realm could be traced back to the necessity for public authority to take responsibility for the operation of the economy and for solving social problems thrown up by the development of capitalism. These developments entailed the destruction of any meaningful distinction between the private and public realms and led to the emergence of the "social question"—poverty and misery—as *the* political problem.

In *On Revolution* she gave specificity to her abstract discussion of the "social" found in *The Human Condition* by distinguishing the American from the French Revolution. Where the former ignored economic and social oppression—white indenture or Afro-American slavery never appeared on the revolutionary political agenda—the Jacobins tried to address the suffering of "the people" through the instrumentalities of the state. That, according to Arendt, meant the fatal difference between the establishment of something like a constitution of liberty and the descent into terror, then reaction and the endemic instability that characterized French political life for more than a century. More importantly, it marked the point at which social equality replaced political freedom at the top of the revolutionary agenda of European politics. Though the destruction of slavery in the American Civil War would seem to undermine her point, it is important to note that former slaves were notionally guaranteed civil and political rights; but except for a few isolated examples, no fundamental changes in the distribution of land ownership, i.e. land reform, were implemented.

In the realm of thought, Arendt saw Marx as reflecting this decisive shift in revolutionary priorities by defining human beings as essentially "labouring" beings. The logic of this move was, according to Arendt, disastrous for the cause of freedom. Once biological survival became the primary revolutionary goal, the eradication of economic and social inequality began to take precedence over all other goals. And once that moral necessity had been given pride of place, then the point of political action and the destination of history itself became the abolition of social and economic inequality. Thus, history was moralized as the story of the implementation of a great biological necessity; economic questions triumphed over all others; and economic interpretations of individual and collective action were given explanatory privilege. Once the political realm became the site where necessity worked its will, once historical progress was incarnated in a class and a party, there was no longer in Arendt's terms a political realm of persuasive talk and free action.

Clearly, Arendt's challenge to Marx is quite controversial. Not surprisingly, there have been convincing challenges to her reading of Marx.[22] Yet I want to present a number of counter-claims that make her reading of Marx and the logic of modern left-wing politics more plausible. First, that we find Arendt's account strange, even perverse, illustrates precisely her point in *The Human Condition* and *On Revolution* about the great modern consensus—left, right and centre —that assumes the primacy of the social over the political. Moreover, Arendt is correct: the American Revolution has had relatively little influence on the modern revolutionary tradition inside and outside of Europe just because its great achievements were in the political and constitutional rather than in the social sphere. The implications of her description of the American Revolution are also broadly correct, for there would have been no war for independence or Constitution had slavery become an issue at the Continental Congresses or the Convention in Philadelphia in 1787. And though her reading of the

French Revolution and Marx gave historical and textual complexity short shrift, there is something about the logic of her position that is compelling and psychologically astute.

Finally, what seems perverse, even callous—the championing of political freedom over equality and the establishment of "lasting institutions" to protect that freedom—has a lot historically and morally to recommend it. First, Arendt enables us to see that Marx got the motivation for, and the cause of, revolutionary upheaval, wrong; at least, he drastically simplified motivation and causation. Marx's immiseration thesis doesn't come close to explaining the emergence or the success of revolutionary movements, while his presupposition of historical necessity as the motive force of history is metahistorical handwaving at odds with the capricious course of modern history and with the diversity of the classes or groups that have been the "carriers" of modern revolutions. Marx himself was too astute not to realize this at times.

Moreover, the blood spilled and the oppression justified in the name of one of the noblest of ideals—the abolition of human want and oppression—lends credence to the Arendtian claim about the murderousness of the moral/historical imperative to bring equality into human society and to abolish inequality by political measures. Where Western philosophy turned away from the world and Christianity murdered in the name of otherworldly ideas and transcendental faith, the Marxist regimes historically justified totalitarian rule in the name of abolishing human want and difference. But Arendt's great uniqueness lay in the fact that her hostility to certain aspects of the French Revolution and her critique of Marx did not lead her to dismiss all revolution as a disaster or to turn conservative. Instead, she proposed a different revolutionary tradition and a different revolutionary *telos*, whose historian and thinker she felt it her duty to become.

Arendt's critique of the primary of the economic and social was also aimed at non-Marxist movements, parties and regimes of the left. Understandable concern with economic and social welfare has meant that governments of the left, as well as those devoted to expanding the free market, posit self-interest and selfishness as the driving forces of politics. Either way, any strong commitment to the public interest or to the importance of acting in concert in public to preserve the public world has been relatively neglected or forgotten.[23] Parties of the left couch their programme in terms of the advantage of economic growth to individuals and groups. Government's role becomes one of economic management and social housekeeping, the primary purpose of which is to improve individual life chances.

Illustrative of Arendt's provocative thesis might be the fate of the Democratic Party in America. Over the years it has elevated the politics of economic growth (cum compassion for the downtrodden) above the politics of democratic participation, while trying to match Republican Party claims to be most competent managers of the economy. In the 1990s the British Labour Party has entered the debate about political and constitutional reform with extreme reluctance and bad grace, all the while claiming that its manifest lack of interest in the topic is justified by the lack of popular concern about such political issues, a fact—if it is one—which the neglect by the "people's party" of these same issues has helped create. Against all evidence, both parties of the left continue to think that economic issues are the only ones that garner votes, when both the Republican Party and the Tory Party have come to and remained in power by mobilizing the fears, often shamelessly and without scruple, of a sizable part of the population on issues concerned, however tangentially, with the common life of the polity. Ironically, it is not even in the long-term interest of parties of the left to pursue interest politics exclusively. If they are successful, they move their supporters out of a situation where they vote for the party of the left and instead come to see the party of the right as the party that furthers their (new) self-interest.

IV

Whatever defences one might mount of Arendt's elevation of the political over the economic and social, friends as well as critics have often wondered what, on her view, politics—party meetings, demonstrations, picketing, Congresses, Parliaments, legislatures and the like—was supposed to be about? What was all the talk and action in public to be concerned with if social and economic issues are excluded? It is a fair question and I want to conclude by trying to indicate several ways Arendt's position can be "saved" without dismissing economic and social issues as somehow irrelevant to politics properly so-called.

First, it is necessary to begin with a literalist Arendtian model of the relationship between the political and the economic-social before suggesting modifications. On this view, the common good or public interest would consist primarily in ensuring that the Constitution worked as it was intended. Political speech and action would be found primarily in legitimate executive, legislative and judicial institutions and at those times when constitutional structures are under pressure and subject to widespread debate. In recent years, the Watergate Crisis of 1973–75, particularly when the Senate Special Committee and the House Judiciary Committee were conducting televized hearings, would be a classic moment when the "political" re-emerged for the citizen body as a whole, when not just the question of "getting" Nixon but of returning to the first principles and spirit of the Constitution was seriously debated.

But Arendt never totally identified state institutions with the political: *res publica* was not for her synonymous with *raison d'état*. Thus Martin Luther King's "I have a Dream" speech, any of the large public gatherings of the civil rights or anti-war movement, or the grass-roots organizing engaged in by both movements would qualify as moments when the "political" re-appeared in public. Since the 1960s at least, the area of Washington D.C. between the Lincoln Memorial and Capital Hill has become a genuine political space, a place where all sorts of groups rally to speak about affairs affecting the public realm. Finally, collective civil disobedience, as already mentioned, was for Arendt a prime example of modern political action and a form of political freedom that, even as it violated the letter, upheld the spirit of the laws.

Turning to the economic-social realm, we find the orthodox Arendtian position hard to pin down. As already mentioned, Arendt was no champion of capitalism, though in republican fashion she did believe in the importance of genuine, not corporate, private property as one sort of guarantee of autonomy and privacy. Yet she had no systematic way to present an alternative. Strangely enough, she was not particularly interested in ideas of worker control or participation in management. In what was a strange echo of Marx's "withering away of the state" argument, she did suggest that since economic and social issues were inevitably governmental concerns in the modern era, they should be treated as matters best left to experts and technicians. The reason was that they were matters on which determinate answers could be given and about which public debate was inappropriate.

For instance, that everyone should have adequate housing was not a matter for debate and thus was a "social" issue. But, Arendt contended, whether that housing was to be integrated was a matter for debate and thus a "political" issue.[24] One sees what she means; but also sees, as even sympathetic critics have pointed out, that the distinction she drew was not such a simple one. Who supplies the housing (public authorities or private enterprise?) is surely a political issue, while some would say that the whole point of the civil rights revolution was precisely to depoliticize issues such as racial integration. Still I accept something like Arendt's argument here to the extent that at any given time and on any given issue, it is worth trying to decide what aspects are political, i.e. debatable and bearing on the general interest, and which ones are not, i.e. matters of technique, skill and expertise in furthering sheer human survival and normal functioning. More generally, such a position opens the way for an expansion of the purview of the political from an Arendtian perspective. Arendt's housing example suggests that, instead of seeing the political and social as separate spheres or realms, crucial public issues might be seen as having both a political and a social aspect. By extension governmental institutions should be seen both as sites of social housekeeping and political debate, according to the issue and the context. This in turn would imply, as Sheldon Wolin has suggested, that the political is a "mode" of thought and action not a specific place or institution.[25]

In addition, as George Kateb and others have pointed out, not all economic considerations bear just on special or private interests.[26] Questions of national debt and defence, inflation, distributive justice, especially allocation of resources for health and education, are all questions which are political and bear on the common good as well as affecting specific groups. Anti-poverty measures or special aid to certain communities or regions or groups can contribute to the general welfare of the citizen body and are thus political in any important meaning of the term. An Arendtian position should be able to grant that economic measures designed to increase the capacity of the citizenry to debate and deliberate on public issues are also political measures. For example, Lyndon Johnson's great "political" moment came in 1964–65 when he shed the role of the quintessential American broker-politician concerned with self-interest and the interest of his region alone and appealed to the public interest (and the judgement of posterity) in working for the passage of two civil rights measures and the war on poverty. Similarly, even when groups protest publicly by picketing or demonstrating for better jobs or higher wages, they re-enforce and illuminate the existence of a public realm where discussion of such issues properly takes place. That is, groups are being political even if their specific goals are economic. Finally, then, conceiving of the social and the political as "aspects" rather than "realms" allows a resolution to the paradox created from an Arendtian perspective when citizens chose to make social and economic concerns into political issues.

Arendtians are properly suspicious of large and permanent bureaucracies (what she called "rule by nobody"), both private and public. They create dependency and make new beginnings impossible. On the other hand, Arendt's view that "labour" is activity for the purpose of survival and the maintenance of basic functions alone sounds strangely archaic. Many workers, perhaps the majority, are no longer so enmeshed in the biological struggle that they are unable to reflect upon what they are doing, in part because of the development of universal education. Trade unions and professional organizations have also developed political expertise that their members make use of. The point here is that there is no reason in principle that more forms of worker participation and co-management could not be worked out.

Turning to a specific issue, Arendt would, I suspect, have considered the politicization of the abortion issue as a political tragedy, a prime example of the dangerous claim that "the personal is the political," ironically one of the left's (and the women's movement's) favorite slogans. The basic problem with the abortion debate is that for one side, perhaps now for both, there is no debate. Ironically, what Arendt noted about Marx is relevant here: the positing of the biological "fact" that a foetus is fully human creates a moral absolute—the preservation of that life at all costs—that allows no possibility of persuasion or accommodation between "pro-life" and "pro-choice" forces.

Still, trying to make Arendt's message compatible with the established practices of the left (not to mention the right) runs the danger of obscuring those moments of special insight in her thought. If anything is central to her thought, it is that lives bereft of concern for, and involvement in, the public world are incomplete, that freedom has to do not just with freedom from restraint but with political participation in public affairs. Above all else, it reminds us that economic questions are not synonymous with political questions and that a political culture which fails to recognize this is failing to be political in an important sense.

Finally, there is no doubt that Arendt, for understandable reasons, "essentialized" politics as always *this* rather than *that*. Perhaps we should cease talking of politics in the singular and recognize that at different times politics can refer to different sorts of activities. At times of foundings, such as the American Revolution, or of renewal and reconstruction, such as the American South in the 1960s and

Poland, Czechoslovakia, South Africa and in the Soviet Union in the 1989–90 period, politics comes close to matching Arendt's definition. Though it is easy to characterize such moments as pre-political or unpolitical, even by a figure such as Vaclav Havel whom Arendt would surely have admired, Arendt's work reminds us that these are political moments par excellence. But just as love affairs give way to marriages, ecstasy to friendship and affection, so Arendtian politics gives way to the "normal" politics of social housekeeping and economic management. Perhaps the best we can hope for is that the "lasting institutions" of a political culture will allow for, even encourage, periodic renewals of the spirit of public action and the re-emergence of the political freedom that has been obscured.

Notes

1. Hannah Arendt/Karl Jaspers, *Briefwechsel, 1926–69* (Munchen: Piper Verlag, 1985), p. 165, (my translation).
2. Arendt/Jaspers, *Briefwechsel*, p. 243.
3. Hannah Arendt, *The Origins of Totalitarianism*, 2nd edn (Cleveland, OH.: Meridian Books, 1958), p. 296.
4. Hannah Arendt, "Reflections on Little Rock" *Dissent* 6:1 (Winter 1959), p. 47.
5. That said, Arendt's work from the early 1950s to the mid-1960s can be seen as an ongoing debate with Marx. After *Origins* she intended to write a book on Marx and the origins of totalitarianism, in recognition of the fact that *Origins* had been much more "about" Nazi totalitarianism than Stalinism.
6. Arendt/Jaspers. *Briefwechsel*, p. 178. The term Arendt used was *Charakterlosigkeit*.
7. Hannah Arendt, Reply to Eric Voegelin, *Review of Politics* (January 1953), pp. 80, 78.
8. Hayden White, "The Politics of Interpretation" in *The Content of the Form* (Baltimore, MD.: Johns Hopkins Press, 1987), pp. 58–82.
9. Arendt/Jaspers, *Briefwechsel*, p. 212
10. Philip Rieff, "The Theology of Politics" in *The Feeling Intellect* (Chicago, IL.: University of Chicago Press, 199), pp. 86–97.
11. Alfred Kazin, *New York Jew* (New York: Alfred Knopf, 1978), pp. 195–96. Poet Delmore Schwartz less reverently once referred to Arendt as that "Weimar Republic flapper."
12. Stanley Milgram, *Obedience to Authority* (New York: Harper and Row, 1974); Dwight Macdonald, "The Responsibility of Peoples" in *Memoirs of a Revolutionist* (Cleveland, OH.: Meridian Books, 1963).
13. Arendt, *Origins*, p. 466.
14. Hannah Arendt, *Men in Dark Times* (New York: Harvest Books, 1968), p. 21.
15. Hannah Arendt, "What is Authority?" in *Between Past and Future* (Cleveland, OH.: Meridian Books, 1963), p. 25.

16. Arendt, *Men in Dark Times*, p. 204.
17. For a brief discussion of this issue, see Richard H. King, "Endings and Beginnings: Politics in Arendt's Early Thought" *Political Theory* 12:2 (May 1984), p. 235. To be sure, *The Human Condition* expanded on the "Ideology and Terror" chapter and *On Revolution* picked up and expanded on Arendt's "Reflections upon the Hungarian Revolution." But both of these chapters were added to the original text to make up the second edition of *Origins* (1958). See also Margaret Canovan's *Hannah Arendt: A Reinterpretation of Her Political Thought* (Cambridge: Cambridge University Press, 1992) for a strong defense of the continuity in Arendt's work.
18. See George Kateb, "Representative Democracy" *Salmagundi* 60 (Spring–Summer 1983), pp. 20–59, for this link between representative government and the politics of interest.
19. Kazin, *New York Jew*, p. 191.
20. See Sheldon Wolin, "Democracy and the Political" *Salmagundi* 60 (Spring–Summer 1983), pp. 3–19.
21. The "social" has many different meanings in Arendt's thought, but it is above all the realm of inequality, difference and discrimination. See Agnes Heller and Ferenc Feher, "The Pariah and the Citizen" and "Against the Metaphysics of the Social Question" in *The Postmodern Political Condition* (Cambridge: Polity, 1988), pp. 89–118, for a defense of certain aspects of Arendt's theory of the social and a rejection of others.
22. See for example Mildred Bakan, "Hannah Arendt's Concepts of Labor and Work" and Bikhu Parekh, "Hannah Arendt's Critique of Marx" in Melvyn A. Hill (ed.) *Hannah Arendt: The Recovery of the Public World* (New York: St. Martin's Press, 1979), pp. 49–66, 67–100. See also Heller and Feher, "Pariah" and "Against the Metaphysics."
23. For a thorough and insightful discussion of these matters, see Margaret Canovan, "Politics as Culture: Hannah Arendt and the Public Realm" *History of Political Thought* VI:3 (Winter 1985), pp. 617–42.
24. Besides Kateb , "Representative Democracy," see Arendt's response to questions in Hill (ed.) *Hannah Arendt: The Recovery of the Public World*, pp. 315–22.
25. Wolin, "Democracy and the Political," p. 18.
26. See Kateb's essay for a more thorough discussion of this point about the economic as a valid political concern.

11

Garry Wills

Stephen J. Whitfield

The belief in the moral sufficiency of the self-made man has commanded an allegiance and an authority in the last two centuries that no other cluster of American ideals has matched. The pursuit of wealth and opportunity—a pursuit not to be impeded by ancestry or tradition or government—has been, according to William James, "our national disease." It is fitting that one of the first doctorates granted in American Studies, to A. Whitney Griswold, was entitled "The American Cult of Success" (1933). Yet it has often been observed that, beginning in the 1960s, the consensus that had formed around liberal individualism began to unravel. When bank robber Willie Sutton got out of Attica State Prison after seventeen years, he complained to reporters that "people don't seem to want to work hard for anything anymore. Years ago, cons used to approach me in various prison yards and ask me to lay out a bank job for them. But not lately. These young kids don't believe in hard work."[1] Other young Americans blamed the dominant system of values for the failed promise to end poverty, to establish racial equality, and to maintain peace. By the end of the 1960s, when defendants in the Chicago conspiracy trial jeered at Judge Julius Hoffman for telling Tom Hayden, "Fellows as smart as you could do awfully well under this system,"[2] the fissures in the public culture had become too wide to ignore. An ethos seemed to be threatened with extinction.

One index of the vicissitudes of that ethos has been the work of Garry Wills. His first book described liberalism and conservatism as "the most misleading terms in the modern world;"[3] yet their imprecision has been not an impediment but an incentive to distinctive meditation on the American political experiment. Wills' writings deserve the attention of students of American culture because of the intelligence with which he has explored the meaning of liberalism, which is not limited to a particular location on the political spectrum, associated in this century with the extension of the welfare state, civil rights and civil liberties. In Wills' understanding, liberalism excludes religious transcendence and powerfully communitarian ideals; it sanctions positive law and the relatively free market. Because it has promoted the cult of the self-made man and the dream of success, few Americans have escaped its spell or ignored its importance.

One of them is Wills himself, and his work would exert its fascination if for no other reason than his struggle to challenge the tenets of so pervasive a creed. It is his *agon*. He has argued that liberalism is morally undesirable, logically indefensible and historically doomed. It is reductive, he claims, because it diminishes the human personality and depletes human possibilities. "How much is he worth?" is a part of the vernacular perhaps worn smooth by use, but it suggests the sovereignty of the marketplace values that Wills rejects. Nor does liberalism make sense even in its own terms. "The Lockean world of free agents bargaining to 'enter society,'" he wrote in 1970, "is as false . . . as the picture of a ghostly starting line at which all economic competitors somehow line up and begin the race of life with an 'equal start.'"[4] Liberalism has been historically implicated in the creation and distribution of unprecedented wealth, yet the charmed life that it has enjoyed in this country, he has asserted, is about over. That is an assumption Wills has barely altered in a writing career of more than two decades, during which he veered from right (*National Review*) to left (*New York Review of Books*). He has issued an invitation to re-examine what is still viable in the patrimony of most Americans, and the seriousness of his effort merits acceptance of that invitation.

He also represents something unprecedented in the interpretation of American experience. Lincoln Steffens made Walter Lippmann his protégé in order to prove that higher education was no handicap to journalistic accomplishment. Steffens' own reporting bore little trace, however, of the Berkeley, Berlin, Heidelberg and Paris where he himself had studied; and Lippmann, for all his ease with political thought, made few contributions to formal scholarship. The formal education of H.L. Mencken ended at the Baltimore Polytechnic School, and the splendid addition to learning that *The American Language* signifies did not prevent its author from including the academy among the targets of his satire. Across the Atlantic intellectual journalism has flourished more than in the United States, where its most admired practitioner, Edmund Wilson, kept fairly clear of academic entanglements after his undergraduate education ceased.

Like Wilson, Wills has largely avoided the pitfalls of journalism by doing his own thinking. He has read the original sources and the fine print; and even though the Eighth Commandment has rarely been considered applicable to the world of ideas, Wills' books are demonstrably his own, not pastiches of what experts have told him. The brains he has liked to pick have not often been his contemporaries' or even American, but those of St. Augustine, Samuel Johnson, Cardinal Newman and the subject of Wills' first book, G.K. Chesterton. Having taught classics, humanities, American Studies and public policy, in addition to his freelance journalism, Wills has closed the gap which, in different ways, the careers of Mencken and Wilson revealed. Wills is, at least figuratively, at home in the faculty lounge as well as in the press box; and it is hard to think of another American writer graced with such virtuosity. Covering Richard M. Nixon for *Esquire*, he cannot help asking the largest questions about the American political tradition. Speaking at a Princeton seminar, he can analyze the Second Continental Congress with the savvy of one of the boys in the backroom. Wills has been engaged in controversy in several scholarly fields, and is ingenious enough to propose solutions. Yet as a syndicated columnist and magazine writer, he brushes close enough to contemporary affairs to be both informative and insightful, providing commentary hard-boiled enough to be rolled on the White House lawn.

A pre-liberal environment once existed in America, which Wills reconstructed in *Inventing America* (1978) from Jefferson's draft of the Declaration of Independence—not to be confused with the document by which representatives of thirteen states proclaimed separation from Britain, or with the charter of freedom that Wills believes has become encrusted with romantic legend. A lesser journalist might have tried to ransack the American Enlightenment to illuminate the present, might have found some lessons for today in Jefferson's "expression of the American mind." But Wills' thesis is in fact the futility of such present-mindedness. His argument is that the Jeffersonian world is one we have lost, the Jeffersonian language a philosophically complex yet technically precise code, the Jeffersonian sensibility quite at odds with the images that his already diverse admirers and detractors have presented. In discovering that the commonsense moral philosophy of the Scottish Enlightenment is the key to Jefferson's thought, Wills could hardly have expected to convince his publisher that *Inventing America* would strike a popular nerve, since interest in Francis Hutcheson, Henry Home Kames, Thomas Reid and Dugald Steward is not widespread. In finding that key, however, Wills displays an agile mind, extensive reading, skill in dramatizing ideas, evocative power and formidable self-assurance.

A lesser scholar might not have tackled such a topic at all. Several historians of the period have recognized the importance of the Scottish thinkers and, to some degree, their influence upon the young Jefferson has been noticed. But Carl L. Becker's *The Declaration of Independence* (1922) was long considered important for its demonstration that Locke's justification for revolution was the model for Jefferson's justification for separation. In minimizing the impact of the *Two Treatises of Government* (though not the *Essay Concerning Human Understanding*), Wills inserted himself into eighteenth-century scholarship not as an interloper but as a peer. To advance his own claims, *Inventing America* criticizes in passing not only Becker but Daniel J. Boorstin, Julian Boyd, Winthrop D. Jordan and Merrill D. Peterson, among others, for their interpretations or scholarship. The response was mostly favourable. Professors David Brion Davis, Edmund Morgan and Gordon Wood were enthusiastic; and the book won the Merle Curti Award in American Intellectual History from the Organization of American Historians. Wills can hardly be expected to have the last word in an enterprise in which finality of judgement is notoriously elusive. But like Dr Johnson's dancing bear, what is remarkable may not be the quality of Wills's performance but the fact that it could be done at all.

His poise is also impressive, since *Inventing America* is neither hagiographic nor an act of debunking, neither a defense of Jefferson's *Weltanschauung* nor an explicit assault upon it. Wills does admire the intellectual elegance with which the Founder—and his alleged mentors in Aberdeen, Edinburgh and Glasgow—resolved some of the enigmas of moral conduct and explained the laws of nature and of nature's God. Whatever the role that the Whig tradition of rights played in the formation of Jefferson's politics, Wills sympathizes with Jefferson's allegiance to the school which inculcated "Reid's belief that all good sense is *common* sense, and that man in isolation is man insane; [Adam] Ferguson's belief that man is fully human only 'in groups'; [and Adam] Smith's belief that morality arises only from sympathy with others."[5] Jefferson is therefore placed outside the penumbra of liberal individualism instead of being commemorated as a Father whose wisdom still shapes the republic.

One result of this interpretation is to treat Jefferson's views on blacks less harshly than in other histories. In his two chapters on this topic, Wills does not, for example, use the word "racism." Jefferson favoured emancipation only if it coincided with deportation, Wills argued, because of "the need for a shared ethos . . . To ask men to overlook the kinds of wrongs inflicted by slavery, to enter into true brotherhood with the oppressor, would be an insult to the very feelings of humanity that bind societies together."[6] It was not because of hypocrisy or unresolved tension between holding slaves and advocating equality, but because of the commonsense philosophy, that Jefferson favoured the exclusion from the community of those held immorally in bondage. In highlighting the cohesiveness of such beliefs, Wills absolves Jefferson from the familiar charge of inconsistency, without valorizing the actual views that he espoused.

Even if this Founder was estranged from liberal atomism, he nevertheless typified facets of the political culture from which Wills dissents. For example, *Inventing America* asserts that the national past discloses the power of messianism—"our willingness to redeem men in blood. The heart of that urge comes from our dedication to a *proposition*."[7] The language here is, of course, an echo of Lincoln's, though the propositions have been Jefferson's. Nevertheless Wills does not explain how the Declaration of Independence in any way accredited the messianic impulse. He also implies that Jefferson was responsible for encouraging the national scrutiny of opinion, although the specifics of this indictment are not drawn up. Wills appreciates Jefferson's empiricism, his incessant effort to lend coherence to observable facts. But Jefferson also exhibited a penchant for mathematical solutions to political problems; this *esprit de géometrie* resulted in arid formulas to ensure that the earth belonged to the living. Such recourse to "political arithmetic," which Wills dismisses as folly, is depicted as intrinsic to Jefferson's intellectual style. Such politicians think too much, instead of seeking to tighten the bands that join the living, their ancestors and their posterity in a continuous civil society.

Inventing America therefore indicates an equivocal attitude towards the Jeffersonian legacy, truncated though it was by the popular worship of the "bitch-goddess" that William James identified. The philosophy that surfaced in the Declaration of Independence was an alternative to individualism, but Wills had no illusion that the Scottish Enlightenment is a usable past. That world remains lost, an Atlantis submerged beneath the culture that crystallized around the essays of Emerson, the fables of Horatio Alger and the metaphor of the competitive race.

Part of the effect that Wills' 1979 suspense novel, *At Button's*, achieves is derived from the discrepancy between the measured rationality of Addisonian sensibility and the violence endemic to modern intelligence agencies like the CIA. Wills has been attracted to the discontinuities and disjunctions of American culture, as though he were the journalist as eschatologist, a student of last things. Yet *Inventing America* offers no satisfactory account for the irrevocable abruptness with which the Jeffersonian world-view faded. It is puzzling and ironical that the language of the most articulate of the Founders is now most in need of decoding. Given the brevity of the American political tradition, such historical finality is rather unlikely. But the disintegration of an ethos is an especially compelling topic for Wills; and not even overstatement robs his argument of merit or, certainly, of interest.

Until he pursued his doctorate at Yale University, Wills was entirely educated in Catholic institutions, spending half a dozen years in the Jesuit novitiate. (As a seminarian he missed most of the Eisenhower years, "but I tended to believe people who assured me I had not missed a thing," he later wrote.[8]) Abandoning his plans for the priesthood was easier than jettisoning the influence of the Church itself, and it is reasonable to suspect an outsider's fascination with the Protestant ethic and with the spiritual athleticism that he associates with the pietistic version of Protestantism. "Something about laissez-faire individualism," he suspects, "is historically at odds with Catholic tradition;" and *Bare Ruined Choirs* (1972) opens with a memoir of the enclaves he later realized had resisted some of the pressures of liberalism. He reached maturity within "a ghetto, undeniably. But not a bad ghetto to grow up in." What he experienced was "shared, part of community life," rather than the fragmentation which he attributes to the rest of Christendom.[9]

In the 1960s, however, the faithful themselves called into question the durability of such enclaves. Instead of the eternal verities which the Church had preached, a commitment to "progress" emerged. Instead of the claims of authority, a spirit of self-reliance became manifest. Instead of the special vocabulary by which Catholics recognized one another, the argot of the *Zeitgeist* was spoken. And instead of piety, doubt seeped in, washing away the ancient barriers that had been erected against the flow of history. The doctrinal wisdom of the Church thus joined the competition in the marketplace of ideas; and even the faithful, Wills notes, have been unable to ignore the maxim, *caveat emptor*. So that a lifetime's sins might be forgiven, Chesterton had entered the Church. But, Wills writes, in the 1960s the Church itself entered society, championing reform instead of promising redemption. The culprit is liberalism: "The story of the Church's demise is not one of heretical betrayers, but of fatal insufficiencies in its very fabric; and this tale runs parallel to revelations of weakness in our society at large." Pope John XXIII and President Kennedy were the sorts of leaders liberals "thought would suffice, and found that this was not enough. The System, even given bright leadership, did not work. We are witnessing a basic failure in authoritative standards; they no longer convince, because they barely can stand."[10]

The problems afflicting the Church have become so familiar that the sly priest in a Broadway play, Bill C. Davis's *Mass Appeal*, nicknames them "the three C's—the current crisis in Catholicism." Yet *Bare Ruined Choirs* reaches for a special note in its blend of memoir, reportage, textual analysis and the logical repartee at which Wills is unsurpassed. Particularly noteworthy is his critique of the 1968 encyclical *Humanae Vitae*, in which Wills argues that the position adopted by Pope Paul VI undermined the tradition of virtual silence on the subject of birth control (thus endangering institutional continuity) and needlessly antagonized large segments of the faithful themselves (thus endangering institutional cohesiveness). Though not an explicit attack on liberal Catholics, Wills' analysis attests to his awareness that a once-unchangeable Church is a myth. Such a realization makes his objections to liberal adaptation seem unfair. In America, accommodation to the larger forces of the Protestant ethic and the spirit of capitalism only looks foolish if those forces are doomed. If not, adaptation is likely to enhance survival and preserve influence in a way that rigid resistance to liberalism cannot. In any event it would be astonishing if historically tenacious institutions like the Roman Catholic Church did not assume the coloration of the societies in which its believers have lived.

Although the dying fall of *Bare Ruined Choirs* is decelerated by an endorsement of the dramatic actions of priests like the Berrigan brothers, Wills himself anticipates no radical renewal of ecclesiastical energies. Nor does he consider a higher law of conscience—to which the Berrigans appealed—more important than the value of "convenience" (coming together). According to that priority, "the state exists to hold people together in peace," Wills proclaims, "not to enunciate 'raw justice'."[11] But by either standard the United States in the late 1960s appeared a failure. His report on the domestic arms race that escalated with the urban riots became the longest article until then published in *Esquire*. Entitled "The Second Civil War," his subtitle announced: "This time it's simpler, Black vs. White." Peering out from a patrol car, Wills concluded that these United States had become "two nations" and "an alien, armed place." A common history which had begun disastrously with "the kinds of wrongs [Jefferson knew had been] inflicted by slavery" led to the necessity for white America to meet the demands of black militancy. So Wills believed in 1968; and to fail to meet those demands was to flunk an intelligence test, "a final exam."[12]

The Second Civil War not only demonstrates the author's talent for interviewing. It also taps the anxieties of racial conflagration that are a subterranean current of American history, signalled by that nocturnal fire-bell that made Jefferson "tremble for my country when I reflect that God is just: that his justice cannot sleep for ever." The terrible "showdown between the white race and the former slaves," which Max Weber envisioned while visiting even the accommodationist Tuskegee Institute, had become "not a possibility, but present reality," Wills claimed in 1968.[13] As the 1960s ended however, the threat of apocalypse began to subside; but Wills still articulated his conviction that it was closing time in the museum of American political antiquities. The relics no longer had meaning; "the myth of the free market, the cult of the self-made man, social Darwinism . . . deadened the spirit." Covering the 1968 Presidential race for *Esquire*, Wills described its winner as the last consequential politician who could merchandise with sincerity "our self-flattering tenets—our individualism, self-regulation, discipline, achievement, 'markets,' Causes." It was time to say goodbye to all that, because Nixon was not intellectually or morally up to the demands that the preservation of such values imposed. "By embodying that creed, by trying to bring it back to life," Wills confidently declared, Nixon "has at last reduced it to absurdity."[14]

This thesis lends gravity to *Nixon Agonistes* (1970), but its aphoristic insight and intellectual pyrotechnics can be appreciated without accepting the larger argument. The book displays a mastery of the reportorial tradition as it has evolved from Mencken to Mailer. It includes some of the shrewdest observations ever recorded on the career and personality of Nixon, as well as wry and telling assessments of his rivals. Although Wills provides the reader with a ringside seat for an especially pugnacious campaign, the social and intellectual context is not neglected. He is, like Chesterton, especially adept in the use of paradox and continually manages to find the surprises lurking in reality. Thus President Eisenhower is presented as a cunning and efficient operator, fully aware of his own formidable skills, and fully in control of his administration. The Checkers speech of his running mate is shown to be a triumphant exploitation of television, rather than proof of Nixon's tackiness. Nixon is not identified as a conservative (because the vigorous capitalism he advocates tends to destabilize society), nor does labelling him a Republican moderate or centrist do justice to his politics. For Nixon's tactics have been guided, Wills claims, by a set of consistent moral and political assumptions. He has not been an opportunist or a chameleon or a Joe McCarthy with an extra coat of polish, as many Democrats charged, but a liberal whose hero is Woodrow Wilson. Though Wills was later honoured with inclusion on the White House "enemies list," the portrayal was quite different from the impression one receives on first looking into Herblock's Nixon.[15]

Unfortunately Wills does not seriously probe Nixon's understanding of the nature of Wilson's career. The parallel is strained beyond recognition because Wills' liberalism is a system that has historically overshadowed its alternatives. His book therefore exemplifies consensus history, though for the most part Wills avoids paying the price often exacted of that interpretation. He recognizes, for instance, the bitterness that has often marked political campaigns; and the 1968 campaign, with George C. Wallace as well as Nixon running, showed how readily emotions could turn rancid. Wills does not minimize the hostility that Nixon managed to arouse, nor "the denigrative method" that was his forte at least until 1968. For most of his career, he was Nixon "antagonistes." Yet the author shows how conflict is incorporated into the system as "the formula for resentment in America—the conflict between deference and competitiveness, both imposed as duties. Our individualism is both emulative (you must 'best' the next man) and egalitarian (without being better than the next man)." Wills adds that "one must achieve, yet remain common;" and such tension can generate the frustration and envy for acolytes of a soured liberalism to exploit. Consensus history has also tended to ignore the politically under-represented or excluded groups. But *Nixon Agonistes* fully acknowledges black grievances in 1968 and condemns the political failure to realize the promise of equal rights. The protests outside the Democratic National Convention are also taken seriously: "The true menace of Chicago [was that] these were our children in the streets—indicting us." And "a nation that forfeits the allegiance of its offspring," he warns, "is a nation that is dying."[16]

Even if a national autopsy report could be devised, it would not be necessary, since the past couple of decades have not confirmed such predictions of systemic death. So far no ideological alternatives to liberalism, as Wills describes it, have become widely accepted or adopted as viable. Militant black organizations were crushed or domesticated, with Panthers turning into tabby cats, or became nearly invisible. Even apart from the spectacular cases (like Jerry Rubin, who became a Wall Street analyst), most of the young whom Wills observed as a reporter grew up without endangering the system that they once excoriated. Though he claims that "the Market— the real Market where a man can *amount* to something—is disappearing,"[17] he does not spell out which forces within the polity have rendered the moral code of the nineteenth century obsolete. Wills nowhere indicates why liberalism could not adapt itself to the economic transformations that it has stimulated.

Even in its own terms, his argument might be more taut. If Nixon's career is supposed to portend the death of liberalism, his electoral *defeat* in 1972—rather than his landslide victory—would have strengthened the author's case. Nor did resignation two years later accelerate the decline of the creed, which none of Nixon's successors intended to subvert. An unconvincing determinism further weakens *Nixon Agonistes*. Had Robert Kennedy not walked through the service pantry of the Ambassador Hotel after his primary victory in California, had the Democrats held their convention in a city with a more conciliatory mayor than Richard Daley, or had Hubert Humphrey distanced his campaign further away from support of President Johnson's Vietnam policy, their party might have retained control of the White House. Then Nixon would not have become "the logical product of our recent history," but a victim of its contingency and caprice.[18]

Wills also overestimates the importance of logical coherence in accounting for the tenacity of belief. His analytical acuity can make some ideas seem so poor it is a wonder they were not buried in a potter's field of cultural history long ago. Yet they persist. With the singular exception of the Civil War, the American political system has managed to roll with the punches, to absorb the disaffected, and to heal some of the wounds on which adversarial figures like Nixon have been tempted to pour salt. In the consensus reading of the national experience, a liberalism that defeated the Confederacy, deflected the Populists, survived the Great Depression, and brushed aside the socialist movement that was so noticeable elsewhere in the industrialized world, need not have feared the Students for a Democratic Society.

Confessions of a Conservative (1979), a kind of summing up, at the age of forty-five, achieves a certain resolution of the tension in his writing between his consensus view (there has been no alternative to liberalism) and his conservative values (there should be an alternative to liberalism). Having begun on the right and moved to the left, Wills shifted to the centre, acknowledging the durability of the national habits of self-government. While the civilly disobedient are praised for revitalizing the democratic prospect, politicians are even more admirable for their skills in conflict management, for their efforts at accommodation. By knowing when to twist arms and when to hold hands, politicians make organized society possible. Their primary goal, he asserts, should be harmony, not justice, though these ideals can be compatible, as Lincoln realized in revising Northern war aims to eradicate slavery. These are the conservative virtues, for Wills honours community above self-reliance and social peace above the private conscience. *Confessions of a Conservative* prefers elitism to egalitarianism, and tries to take the long view.

But the harmony that the author wished to maintain has been the legacy of politicians committed to liberalism, and therefore his book vindicates a status quo which Wills has long criticized for its insufficiency. A career in dissent produced a profession of faith. The loyalties enunciated in this book testify to Wills' proximity to the very system which once alienated him. *Confessions of a Conservative* is a tribute to the resilience of the ethos whose doom he could no longer predict. As a conservative he cannot ignore the appeal of a creed that has managed to command such steady allegiance. And as a writer who has thrived on the sense of paradox, Wills apparently concluded that, even in the 1960 and 1970s, liberalism was far from dead; it was simply playing possum.

That sense has remained the pivot of Wills' oeuvre, which displays a taste for surprise that is both compulsive and supple. Indeed three recent major books exhibit so wonderful a flair for pulling frisky rabbits out of old hats that his stature has grown as one of the most resourceful and enlightening of contemporary American writers.

If the most glamorous yet doomed of all political families has generally benefited from an excellent, if not downright adulatory press, *The Kennedy Imprisonment* is custom-built to total the Kennedys' reputation. Every chapter in Wills' 1982 "meditation on power" manages to illuminate facets of a topic that should have been exhausted, and yet the book achieves its fresh effects because its manner is so thoroughly corrosive. If President Kennedy is the brightest, wittiest and most attractive of the brothers, he will be the most sharply criticized, whether for his position on Cuba or for his position in bed. If his intellectual credentials are easily the strongest of the brothers, an unanswerable assault will be mounted on *Why England Slept* and on *Profiles in Courage* (an attack drawn in part on the research of Professor Herbert Parmet). If the Bay of Pigs fiasco is blamed on Ike's CIA, Wills will show how the adventure had the bravado of a Kennedy operation instead, and that, far from learning lessons from that stupid misadventure, the administration became more reckless and less restrained in the Caribbean.

Yet the desire to debunk does not completely thwart the author's gift for paradox. If Edward M. Kennedy is the most disappointing of the brothers, Wills will summon resources of sympathetic understanding for the senator, who "inherited various simulacra of power, not its reality; he both was and was not 'a Kennedy' as his brothers had defined that political entity. And both being and not being like them hurt," Wills observed from a perch on the primary campaign trail in 1980. "He lives out of sequence with himself, the youngest child and oldest son alive; the kid brother who must father all his brothers' kids. Nearing fifty, he lives cramped inside the diminutive 'Teddy.'" The senator's plight is to be "allowed neither youth nor age, neither death nor fully living . . . Edward has no one but ghosts at his side, and they count more against him than for him, eclipse him with bright images from the past." Yet losing a whopping twenty-four out of thirty-four Democratic primaries that year, "Kennedy was being forced, every day, to demonstrate that he was not as good as his *brothers* . . . He could not make the counterclaim, that his brothers were not as good as his brothers, that Camelot had been a fabric of political unreality."[19]

Wills' originality, which can be so bracing, so rich in explanatory power, also enmeshes him in double standards, however. Take race, for example. In order to lash at Jack Kennedy, Wills contrasts him with Martin Luther King Jr, who never bore the compromising responsibilities of elective office. The agitator can indeed be more consequential than the politician, and can endow posterity with a more permanent monument. King "has no eternal flame," Wills writes, "and no wonder. He is not dead," for his speeches are studied and memorized in public schools; and the changes in human relations that he spearheaded "are so large as to be almost invisible."[20] Readers who may doubt the bounty of Wills' stylistic gifts should turn to his final pages, which achieve an exhilarating, lapidary eloquence in contrasting the president and the preacher. (The pair had in common a sexual compulsiveness that made them sadly vulnerable to the same unscrupulous adversary, J. Edgar Hoover. But Wills, who can demonstrate how Kennedy's character defect reduced his foreign policy options, fails to mention the perilous implications of King's adultery on the civil rights movement. *The Kennedy Imprisonment* was published nine years before the revelation of plagiarism in King's doctoral dissertation, surely as morally disreputable as Kennedy's cynical claim to have authored the Pulitzer Prize-winning book that he did not write.)

Wills ignores the actualities of Kennedy's record on civil rights, which was certainly inadequate by truly egalitarian standards, but far ahead of his immediate predecessor's. Eisenhower favoured even slower progress towards racial justice and never articulated the forthright case for integration, which Kennedy delivered in dispatching National Guard units to Ole Miss in 1962. That may be why so many blacks were visibly grieved when the eternal flame had to be installed at Arlington National Cemetery. Kennedy had championed a dramatic civil rights bill, which Ronald Reagan, like Republican candidate Barry Goldwater, emphatically *opposed* in the 1964 Presidential campaign, as did Reagan's future vice president and successor. Wills' 1987 biography of Reagan does not judge him by a standard of civil rights at all. The ex-actor's opposition to all civil rights bills in the 1960s is unmentioned in *Reagan's America*, which does show how little understanding Reagan cultivated of the historical forces and actions that defeated segregation, or sense of how black progress is still retarded. Of all blocs of voters, blacks were perhaps the least enchanted with Reagan's version of America and gained the least from its electoral success. "The Great Communicator" is not contrasted with King at all, perhaps because not even Wills can make Reagan a devotee of racial justice. Kennedy's purposes were more symmetrical to King's, and therefore must be shown to disadvantage.

Okay, Kennedy lied. But isn't that preferable to a politician who believes his own lies? Isn't it more dangerous to have a president who not only deceives others but who also deceives himself? Isn't it safer to elect a president who can distinguish reality from convenient but fictive versions of it? "*Nothing gets through,*" Leon Wieseltier complained of Reagan's 1990 autobiography. His "has been a life that, with the exception of some childhood 'insecurity,' has been lived without scars, without guilt, without shame, without anger, without doubt, without terror, without an adult day of feeling crushed . . . A lucky man. The problem is that nobody is this lucky. This is also a man who rewrites reality," which "comes to him already rewritten."[21]

The Kennedy entanglement in Hollywood had been treated rather acidly in Wills' earlier book. But what about the paradox of a two-term president who served as a part-time president? According to Lou Cannon of the *Washington Post*, Reagan lived in the dark in the White House; no activity took up more of his time than watching movies. Prior to the 1983 economic summit meeting in Williamsburg, he did not read the briefing book, even though it carefully respected his limited attention span, because, as he casually explained, "*The Sound of Music* was on [television] last night."[22]

Reagan's America not only delineates the bubble of illusion that its subject inhabited but indeed insists upon Reagan's impeccable skills of self-deception as clues to "an American life"—the title that a very atypical figure gave to his autobiography. Yet the outrage that animates Wills' portrait of the randy, manipulative and arrogant Kennedys is absent here, though both presidents pulled fast ones on the American public. In part this equanimity is due to Wills' sense of his audience, which is likely to condescend to Reagan and to romanticize the Kennedys. Their saga is hardly in need of further research, so his book on them is "a meditation on power," not research into its exercise and abuse (though Wills did use original sources in the Kennedy Library, plus gamy memoirs like Judith Campbell Exner's *My Story*, 1977). *Reagan's America* is by contrast the only Wills book that threatens to swamp readers in too much detail, to dazzle them with how much research was invested in it, especially in covering Reagan's early years.

Wills is adept in separating truth from falsehood in the presentation of self in political life, and scores direct hits again and again—from Reagan's misunderstanding of a student revolt at Eureka College to his misleading record of military service (in Los Angeles) to his misrepresentation of his duties at the Screen Actors Guild and the Music Corporation of America. Often Reagan's feats of imagination reveal his exasperating incapacity to distinguish movies from the rest of experience, but Wills also notes the complicity of his fellow citizens in this fantasy life: "No one has undergone a more thorough initiation into every aspect of American legend than Reagan has, and no one has found so many conduits—so many channels, open and indirect, associative, accumulative—for bringing that legend to us in the freshest way . . . Reagan does not argue for American values; he embodies them." By personifying "the Myth of the Market," he has been hermetically sealed against "the challenge of complex or contradictory evidence, from any test of evidence at all. That explains Americans' extraordinarily tacit bargain with each other not to challenge Reagan's version of the past. The power of his appeal is the great joint confession that we cannot live with our real past . . . Because of that, we *will* a belief in all his stories."[23] (This lament is a bit overstated. About forty per cent of those voting in 1980 and 1984 pulled levers for the opposition, and over half of those eligible to vote did not vote at all. Wills himself concedes that the 1980 election was more a repudiation of Carter than a mandate for Reagan, who still squeaked by with 51 per cent of the vote. A recession early in Reagan's term included the highest unemployment rate and greatest number of bank failures since the Great Depression.[24] Had the recession lasted until the 1984 election, how effective would those blithe anecdotes have been?)

Born six years before John F. Kennedy, Reagan "began his regular radio career the year Franklin Roosevelt delivered his first fireside chat," and has been inescapable in his fusion of past and present: "His life spans over a third of the history of Constitutional government" in the United States. Reagan is so dedicated to the uses of a past defined as the marketplace and the ethos of individualism that he countermands the death warrant that *Nixon Agonistes* signed for that belief system, which seems to be not only intact, but very popular, despite the contradictions that Wills detects: "According to the American myth he advances, capitalism is both individualistic and conservative, though the terms of that proposition are mutually contradictory. It is hard to understand why people should think capitalism is identical with, or even conduces to, individualism." Capitalism is corporate, superseding the yeoman and the independent artisan, and does not conserve tradition but overthrows it instead: "Capitalism is an instrument for change, for expansion, driven towards ever new resources, products, markets. It reorders life drastically."[25] Capitalism and individualism, which Reagan's conservatism was supposed to champion and revive, cannot be reconciled—not even politically, Wills asserts.

Indeed the evidence of Reagan's political failure and "voodoo economics" could be provided even more strongly than Wills does, especially because his treatment of the White House years is so patchy. An indictment of the Reagan presidency in terms of its own promises could easily be drawn. America was Back, yet in 1985 its national status was switched from creditor to debtor. Already by the end of Reagan's first term, the national debt had risen as much as all previous accumulations until then.[26] Despite his demand for a Constitutional amendment requiring Congress to submit a balanced budget, he never came remotely close to presenting such a budget himself. Despite a promise of reduced taxes, their burden became *more* onerous in the 1980s (except for the very upper strata). Even the inflation that got under control in the 1980s could be credited mostly to Paul Volcker, a Carter appointee whom Reagan kept on the job as chairman of the Federal Reserve Board. Not even the moral tone of the nation was much altered; the Reagans seem to have persuaded few Americans to say "no" to drugs, crime and pornography. Though Reagan promised (twice) that the laws be faithfully executed when he took the oath of office, the scale of corruption and criminality— from the Iran-Contra constitutional scandal to the savings and loan disaster (by far the costliest to taxpayers in all of American history), from the HUD rip-offs to huge Pentagon overpayments—has been unmatched. His administration marked another Era of Good Stealing.

Such catastrophes of public service and trust are barely adumbrated in *Reagan's America*, no more than the Watergate crisis could have been predicted from reading *Nixon Agonistes* in 1970. The reason may be the same: both books are designed to combat the disdain of intellectuals (and liberals), rather than reinforce their prejudices against Nixon and Reagan. Only afterwards does Wills' contempt for such betrayals of civic life become stronger, comparing the ostensible author of *An American Life* to "the cartoon character Mr Magoo, blind and optimistic, [who] loudly describes the happy things going on around him while the viewer sees him surrounded by perils, destruction and violence."[27] Wills does not explicitly revise the claim in *Nixon Agonistes* that the marketplace had become inoperable. But *Reagan's America* does acknowledge the passing of the Protestant ethic, with its imposed self-discipline, because the spirit of capitalism has stimulated yearnings too insatiable for "televangelists" to overcome:

> A dozen or so prominent preachers have become highly visible and affluent deploring these changes. Their very salience, however, is a confession of their failure. They are trying, from a few scattered rooftops, to shout back a flood that was once contained quietly, by the joint efforts of most preachers and their supportive parishioners. The few now deplore what the many once prevented. The TV evangelist's personal success, as an individual, indicates that his cause is lost.[28]

This is a view that collides with the thrust of one of Wills' most recent books, in which the few have become numerous enough to decide who occupies the White House. Virtually unnoticed, the victor in 1988 had elicited the support of these affluent preachers, whose language the losing candidate could not speak. *Under God* (1990) claims that the religion of America is . . . religion. This "illusion" has a future, and a past; and in making his case for the impact of piety on politics, the author exhibits his customary virtues: an amazing command of detail perceptively presented; a virtuosity in spotting a weak argument; a flair for offering unexpected yet engrossing interpretations; and an assurance so eerie that an admiring Whittaker Chambers nevertheless warned him in 1960: "You shall declare the truth, and it will set you into a straitjacket of most elegant trim and fit."[29] Wills remains as clever and prolific as a host of Huxleys. But this is a shapeless collection of essays that the 1988 campaign inspired, partly reportage intended to tweak secularist readers. It is not a comprehensive analysis of church-state issues. *Under God* devotes more space to fundamentalist R.B. Thieme Jr, the lone cleric it subjects to severe criticism, than to the Reverend Jerry Falwell, even though the former is apolitical. In an extended treatment of the Scopes trial, William Jennings Bryan is portrayed in unconvincing heroic terms; the sneaky agnostic, Clarence Darrow, is condemned. (Wills does not explain how Bryan, "the most important evangelical politician of this century,"[30] managed to lose all three of his Presidential races, two more than the hapless, worldly Michael Dukakis.) Although Billy Graham, whose career is studded with flattery of the powerful, praised President Bush for greater fluency with a "spiritual" idiom than any other chief executive he has known, *Under God* does not elucidate Bush's religious sentiments.[31]

The tenor of *Under God* is one of undue reverence for reverence, bereft of any critique of the shallowness of much of American religiosity. Nor is any explanation offered of the hucksterism and fraud that pervade evangelism. Wills misses how closely connected America's Christianity has been to its capitalism. Listening to preachers in a nation where "religious insanity is very common," Tocqueville found it "often difficult to ascertain from their discourses whether the principal object of religion is to procure eternal felicity in the other world or prosperity in this" (and he was there only nine months).[32] Full familiarity with Twain and Mencken should have enabled Wills to appreciate the aptness of their satiric jibes at organized religion.

He is right, however, to pay close attention to the durable features of American faith, from its "health-minded" and optimistic stress on salvation to its quickness to forgive the sinner who professes repentance. (Sixty per cent of the populace nevertheless profess to fear eternal damnation in Hell, according to a Gallup poll.)[33] The title of

Wills' book, a phrase lifted from the Gettysburg Address and inserted in the Pledge of Allegiance, reflects the self-image of the most observant of Western peoples. But the author is not skeptical or critical enough, for religion can too easily become a religiosity that distorts public issues and thwarts reasonable discussion. Even politics can be demeaned by submission to rituals of worship that candidates may not genuinely feel, and mere church-going can be an offence to the sublime and awesome spirit of prayer. Consider what made the God-fearing politics of Ronald Reagan so successful: "He *communicated* religious attitudes (despite his absences from church on Sunday); he *communicated* appreciation of the conventional family (despite his own family's messy interrelationships). He would pray at the drop of a hat—as when he prayed for a soap opera character's deliverance from the indignities imposed on her by the show's writers."[34] Such piety is not Augustinian, nor is such facile un-reflectiveness healthy for public life either. For all the absorbing information and insight packed into *Under God*, Wills might have pleaded for a less ostentatious engagement with the dilemmas of conduct and the mysteries of existence. A private space would be an excellent locale to (re-)read Matthew VI, 5: "When thou prayest, thou shalt not be as the hypocrites are: for they love to pray standing in the synagogues and in the corners of the streets, that they may be seen of men. But thou, when thou prayest, enter into thy closet, and when thou hast shut the door, pray to thy Father which is in secret; and thy Father which seeth in secret shall reward thee openly."[35]

(This is a revised and expanded version of an earlier article in *American Quarterly* 33, 1981.)

Notes

1. Quoted in *Time* 95 (5 January 1970), p. 31.
2. Mark L. Levine, George C. McNamee and Daniel Greenberg (eds) *The Tales of Hoffman* (New York: Bantam, 1970), p. 265.
3. Garry Wills, *Chesterton: Man and Mask* (New York: Sheed and Ward, 1961), p. 103.
4. Garry Wills, *Nixon Agonistes: The Crisis of the Self-Made Man* (Boston: Houghton Mifflin, 1970), p. 459.
5. Garry Wills, *Inventing America: Jefferson's Declaration of Independence* (Garden City, N.Y.: Doubleday, 1978), p. 301.
6. Wills, *Inventing America*, pp. 302–4.

7. Wills, *Inventing America*, p. xx.

8. Garry Wills, *Confessions of a Conservative* (Garden City, N.Y.: Doubleday, 1979), p. 81.

9. Wills, *Confessions*, pp. 37, 64.

10. Garry Wills, *Bare Ruined Choirs: Doubt, Prophecy, and Radical Religion* (Garden City, N.Y.: Doubleday, 1972), p. 262.

11. Wills, *Confessions*, pp. 57–59.

12. Garry Wills, *The Second Civil War: Arming for Armageddon* (New York: Signet, 1968), pp. 12, 14, 18, 156.

13. Thomas Jefferson, "Notes on the State of Virginia" in *The Portable Thomas Jefferson*, ed. Merrill D. Peterson (New York: Viking Press, 1975), p. 215; Marianne Weber, *Max Weber: A Biography*, trans. Harry Zohn (New York: Wiley, 1975), p. 295; Wills, *Second Civil War*, p. 153.

14. Wills, *Confessions*, p. 122; *Nixon Agonistes*, pp. 601–2.

15. Wills, *Confessions of a Conservative*, p. 106.

16. Wills, *Nixon Agonistes*, pp. 149, 334.

17. Wills, *Nixon Agonistes*, p. 185.

18. Wills, *Nixon Agonistes*, p. 15.

19. Garry Wills, *The Kennedy Imprisonment: A Meditation on Power* (Boston: Little, Brown, 1982), pp. 7, 8, 9, 11.

20. Wills, *Kennedy Imprisonment*, pp. 300–1.

21. Leon Wieseltier, "Reagan's Magical Mystery Tour" *M Inc.*, 8 (January 1991), p. 28.

22. Quoted in Lou Cannon, *President Reagan: The Role of a Lifetime* (New York: Simon and Schuster, 1991), pp. 57, 155; Garry Wills, "The Man Who Wasn't There" *New York Review of Books* 38 (13 June 1991), p. 3.

23. Garry Wills, *Reagan's America: Innocence at Home* (Garden City, N.Y.: Doubleday, 1987), pp. 4, 386.

24. Wills, *Reagan's America*, p. 368.

25. Wills, *Reagan's America*, pp. 1, 378, 381.

26. Wills, *Reagan's America*, p. 368.

27. Garry Wills, "Mr Magoo Remembers" *New York Review of Books* 37 (20 December 1990), p. 3.

28. Wills, *Reagan's America*, pp. 383–84.

29. Whittaker Chambers, *Odyssey of a Friend: Whittaker Chambers' Letters to William F. Buckley, Jr., 1954–1961*, ed. William F. Buckley Jr (New York: G.P. Putnam's Sons, 1969), p. 280.

30. Garry Wills, *Under God: Religion and American Politics* (New York: Simon and Schuster, 1990), p. 97.

31. "Preachers, Politics and Temptation" *Time* 135 (28 May 1990), p. 13.

32. Alexis de Tocqueville, *Democracy in America*, ed. Phillips Bradley (New York: Knopf, 1945), II, pp. 135, 142.

33. *Boston Globe*, 21 April 1991, p. 12.

34. Wills, *Under God*, p. 18.

35. Stan Lichtenstein, "America, By Religion Possessed" *American Jewish Congress Monthly* 58 (May–June 1991), p. 15.

12

Black Intellectuals Past and Present

Ross Posnock

In a 1987 essay Darryl Pinckney excoriates Steven Spielberg's cartoonish film version of *The Color Purple*. Adapted, he says, with "ruthless naiveté," it offers its dismal parade of black actors, "mugging and bugeyed," portraying "ridiculous pickaninnies, stern matriarchs, big brutes, noble sinners," images that have been part "of the American imagination since the abolitionist movement."[1] It is "not so much that Spielberg has revived these stock types," Pinckney continues "as that he has reminded us of how present these heirlooms of folly still are, how quickly and comfortably summoned, how great the pressure to conform to the familiar, the recognisable." Perhaps, he concludes, "Spike Lee's generation will escape these burdens and discover the freedom to be ordinary."

This freedom has been especially elusive for many black intellectuals, since traditionally they have been expected to play the heroic, even tragic role of exemplar. While a source of cultural power and spiritual communion, the role is also a cross to bear. To be in the vanguard of the race and to raise up the masses is how W.E.B. Du Bois defined the mission of the black intellectual in his 1903 plea for a "talented tenth."[2] This set the terms for a debate whose issues remain very much alive. Stephen Carter begins his widely discussed *Reflections of an Affirmative Action Baby* (1991) by declaring that "to be black and an intellectual in America is to live in a box" built by the assumptions of others that prominent black intellectuals "always and everywhere" represent the race and express a "single, genuine" black perspective.[3] Among important recent writers, Patricia Williams and Darryl Pinckney could be said to share something of Carter's frustration with the constrictions involved in being "exemplary," while Toni Morrison, one of the most distinguished representative intellectuals, accepts the burden. But the cost of being exemplary, the moral, intellectual, and stylistic choices it enables and disables, is the issue raised inadvertently but urgently by Morrison's recent critical book, *Playing in the Dark*,[4] and posed explicitly by Williams and Pinckney, both of whom meditate upon this venerable role and project alternatives.

The price of representative authority has often been weighed in black intellectual history. "That they were me and I was they; that a force stronger than blood made us one," is how James Weldon Johnson describes in his autobiography the awakening of his race consciousness in 1891.[5] Yet this unity will be belied when he soon notes that "we of the vanguard" look with "despair" at some of the "characteristics of the masses." The vanguard/masses hierarchy makes oneness precarious at best, and the cost of being in the vanguard often is repression of self and others. Johnson, one of the most distinguished "Race Men" of his time, describes this solidarity as a "deepening, but narrowing experience; an experience so narrowing that the inner problem of a Negro in America becomes that of not allowing it to choke and suffocate him." This sense of suffocation can also be deflected outward. So insistent has Spike Lee been in "promoting himself as the down voice of black life" who "speaks to and for black community," says the prominent black feminist who spells her name bell hooks, that he has shown "little interest in critical voices that he does not control, that do not unequivocally affirm his projects."[6]

That American culture now has a major black film-maker is one indication of a marked change in the status of black intellectuals since as recently as 1985, when Cornel West issued a dire assessment of what he saw as the stagnant condition of black cultural activity. Black intellectuals, he found, felt isolated and marginal, due in large part to the racial separatism that had deprived them of significant "institutional mechanisms" for building the "infrastructure" that can preserve and transmit traditions and stimulate exchange.[7] In the intervening years matters have significantly improved, so that bell hooks in a 1991 dialogue with West can speak of the "joie de vivre . . . of what it means to be Black intellectuals" now.[8] The single most powerful arbiter of bourgeois liberal culture, the *New York Times*, has been one catalyst of this resurgence by more or less anointing a quartet of black intellectuals—West himself, Lee, Morrison, and Henry Louis Gates Jr—as exemplary figures, both on the black and on the larger national scene.

Active both within and beyond the academy, these four have

performed the public intellectual's role—that of explaining the culture to itself—with notable success. As usual, the marketplace sets the terms of American success, and so—"the intellectual as star, celebrity, commodity," remains dominant, in West's words, an "individualist and elitist" bias that he regrets. But there has also been an impressive collective dimension to this ferment. The surge of activity among scores of black intellectuals has produced new journals, publishing projects, film and television companies, endowed chairs, and, with all of these, disciplinary innovations. In short, a number of the institutional mechanisms that West sought have begun to be set in place, and the terrain of American intellectual life has been permanently enlarged.

If in social terms the ascendancy sketched above is a remarkable chapter in the quarter-century growth of the black bourgeois professional class, any rapid transformation also produces anxieties and ambivalences in its wake. Not a little of this anxiety derives from the recognition that to be exemplary is also to be coerced, to exert authority over black experience is to make it conform to yet other stereotypes. In championing the right of black intellectuals to dissent from the traditional 1960s civil rights agenda without being branded neoconservatives, Stephen Carter hopes to preserve freedom of thought despite pressures to conform. He locates one source of conformity in affirmative action. For while affirmative action evolved from the corrective justice of the 1970s into a programme in the 1990s for representing the excluded, authentic black voice, it has meanwhile become, he argues, a project of enforced solidarity founded on the essentialist belief that "there is a black way to be." In a conclusion about affirmative action that itself has been attacked as reductive, Carter states that it has become one more device for society to insist "on rendering complexity simple, on squeezing people into preformed boxes."[9]

Complexity is the watchword of Darryl Pinckney and Patricia Williams, both of whom avoid "preformed boxes" by fashioning generically fluid literary forms. Pinckney's *High Cotton*[10] is a novel that at the same time is virtually an autobiography and an ingeniously allusive intellectual history; Williams' *The Alchemy of Race and Rights*[11] self-consciously blends cultural criticism, diary, and essay. Even if blurring genres has by now become conventional, it seems particularly apt in these instances. Both Pinckney and Williams assault (or at least interrogate) the received ideas abut coherence and identity that shape acts of social representation, particularly acts of allegiance to what Pinckney calls the "tribal code that said that I, as a black, had a responsibility to help my people, to honor my race." His novel largely concerns a young black intellectual's flight from that code as it is embodied in his Du Boisian grandfather, a minister and self-appointed "emissary from the Talented Tenth—Du Bois's elect" (p. 7) and "beacon to the unwashed." Although the narrator confesses to having once smugly believed that this grandfather "had not a clue as to how free and complex" his grandson was planning to become, the latter's efforts to renegotiate the terms of being black have produced little besides a deliberate "sinking into the lower classes" as a bohemian barfly after graduation from Columbia. By the novel's end his experiences have, nonetheless, yielded some wisdom: "Now I am sorry that I went to such lengths not to be of much use to myself just so no one would be able to ask anything of me. To have nothing to offer was not, after all, the best way to have nothing to lose" (p. 306).

On a number of levels, Patricia Williams also faces the temptation not to be free and complex and avoid the siren call of responsibility. As a black female professor of contract and property law, she is herself perceived, so she says as "an inherent contradiction," a condition she seeks to maximize both personally and professionally. Her transgression of the distinction between the personal and professional forms the virtual basis of her project. She recounts how her attempts to write law articles in her own voice rather than in legal jargon have placed her at "the center of a snarl of social tensions and crossed boundaries" (p. 6). This risky practice has exposed her work and teaching both to frequent criticism and notoriety ("self-indulgent," "anecdotal individualism," and "new-age performance art" are some of the responses she cites) but she prefers, indeed cultivates, this vulnerability. It is for her a way out of the sterile confines of a conventional law career with its sacrifices of subjectivity and complexity to the still reigning gods of neutrality, objectivity, and impersonality. Like the obligations of professionalism in general, law and legal writing repress the particularity and messiness of human motive and being by appealing to neutral, shared, universal beliefs; according to Williams, they seek to generate "a certain obeisance to the sleekness of a product that has been skinned of its personalized complication." Thus the professed colour-blindness of law and legal style partakes of the consumerist bias towards fungibility that animates commodity culture.

Williams is enough of a bourgeois and philosophical materialist (and property expert) to profit from her own marketplace status as a luxury, an exotic commodity: not only a female lawyer but, in the eyes of a race-conscious society, a credit to her race, an "experimental black," as she puts it. Being this "sleek product" is endless work, and she narrates the arduous labour of making such a self: "When I get up in the morning I stare in the mirror and stick on my roles: I brush my teeth, as a responsibility to my community. I buff my nails, paving the way for my race . . . I glaze my lips with the commitment to deny pain and 'rise above' racism . . . When I am fully dressed, my face is hung with contradictions; I try not to wear all my contradictions at the same time. I pick and choose among them; like jewellery" (p. 196). And even while she is assembling herself she is haunted by the opposite impulse: to refuse to "compose" herself "properly." As the reader first meets her, she is in dishabille, wearing an old terrycloth bathrobe in front of her TV, ready to "split at the seams" and return to the womb.

Stripped of its irony, Williams' insistence on dressing herself in contradictions, her experience of her "blackself as an eddy of con-flicted meanings . . . in which agency and consent are tumbled in constant motion" (p. 168) sounds remarkably Du Boisian. With the serene grandiosity that perhaps only his former professor Santayana could get away with, Du Bois begins his 1940 *Dusk of Dawn* with this self-description: "Crucified on the vast wheel of time, I flew round and round with the Zeitgeist . . . I did little to create my day or greatly change it: but I did exemplify it and thus for all time my life is significant for all lives of men."[12] Yet the significance of his example is predicated neither on the oneness with the masses that James Weldon Johnson describes nor on his own self-coherence. He describes his life as embodying a "whirlpool of social entanglement and inner psychological paradox." Du Bois's characteristic movement of mind is to revise and complicate all his assertions in accordance with his famous belief that black identity is inherently a problem, a "double consciousness" or "two-ness,—an American, a Negro; two souls, two thoughts, two unreconciled strivings."[13] Thus Du Bois's proclamation of his own exemplary significance and his general demand that the talented tenth serve the race inspire a project of racial unity founded on stable identity and at the same time make it problematic.

A Race Man who challenges its coercive terms of definition, Du Bois evades the labels historians have invoked to resolve his paradoxes: nationalist, assimilationist, pan-Africanist, Marxist social-ist, Hegelian and communist. Even a label like NAACP integrationist is too simple. It fails to do justice to Du Bois's strategically tense and often antagonistic relation to the organization he helped found in

1910. The mainstream liberalism of the NAACP would not countenance his advocacy of voluntary economic segregation in 1934. Du Bois's double logic conceived segregation not as an end but as a step toward the ultimate erasing of the colour line, and he urged it while fully aware that he was "touching an old and bleeding sore in Negro thought."[14] He was willing to expose his own painful vulnerability in order to shock the staunchly integrationist NAACP into changing its course, into admitting that Jim Crow remained the obdurate American reality. Acknowledging this would transform the identity of segregation from a traditional "badge of servitude" into a badge of self-respect: "If you do not wish to associate with me, I am more than willing to associate with myself. Indeed I deem it a privilege to work with and for Negroes."[15] Yet instilling racial pride was simultaneously a means of strengthening the prospect of integration. White America, said Du Bois, "will certainly never want us until we want ourselves."[16] And, finally, segregation was an opportunity to create a foundation of black economic power: "to make us," said Du Bois, "spiritually free for initiative and creation in other and wider fields."[17] Here glimmers the aesthetic utopianism in Du Bois's thought which he shares with Dewey. It seeks a world apart from capitalism's ascetic regime of compulsive consumerism. In attempting to unsettle from within the identity of both the NAACP and of segregation, Du Bois described his strategy as deliberately serpentine, forsaking the directness of frontal assault and instead combining forward marching with end runs and retreats. Not surprisingly, the NAACP refused to follow Du Bois's indirections and he resigned in 1934, having served for twenty-four years as editor of its magazine, *The Crisis*.

The most pertinent label for Du Bois's politics of non-identity would be pragmatist, since as a method it aimed to disrupt the compulsion to fix identity. In 1888 he imbibed at least an incipient pragmatism directly from one of its sources—his first philosophy professor at Harvard, William James, whom Du Bois revered as his "friend and guide to clear thinking." The incentive to pragmatist clear thinking is scepticism; John Dewey once described the pragmatist spirit as "primarily a revolt against that habit of mind which disposes of anything by tucking it away in the pigeon holes of a filing cabinet."[18] Doubtless James communicated to his student something of his love of the incorrigible, of the "unclassified residuum," the "more" that escapes assimilation into positivist systems. Fuelling Du Bois's prodigious career as a public intellectual was the logic of unreconciled twoness that usually left him "either too far ahead or too far behind, but out of step with mass thinking," to borrow Harold Cruse's rueful assessment.[19] What Cruse laments as chronic "incongruity" might also be taken as the imprint of Du Bois's genius. After reading *The Souls of Black Folk* in 1903, William James sent this "decidedly moving book"[20] to his brother Henry, who in that same year had used the phrase "double consciousness" (in describing Lambert Strether), and who, upon reading *Pragmatism* in 1907, discovered that all his life he had been "unconsciously pragmatising."[21] Henry James praised Du Bois's book in *The American Scene*.

The scepticism of identity and commitment to incongruity that William James shared with his brother and with Du Bois would influence another prominent Harvard-educated black intellectual, Alain Locke, who graduated in 1907. A "cultural cosmopolitan" and the first black Rhodes scholar, a black cultural nationalist and "socially Anglophile,"[22] a professor of philosophy at Howard University but best known as the self-described "mid-wife" of the Harlem Renaissance, Locke said his life was set in "the key of paradox," much as Henry James remarked that he and his siblings "ate and drank contradictions." Locke's appetite for paradox was likely stimulated by hearing William James' Hibbert Lectures, delivered at Oxford in 1908 and published as *A Pluralistic Universe*. In that work James gives up what he calls the logic of identity because reality, life, and experience exceed and overflow our logic, concepts and definitions: "When we conceptualize, we cut out and fix, and exclude everything but what we have fixed."[23]

In 1925, when Locke came to conceptualize "the new Negro" (he edited the landmark anthology of that same name) he seemed to heed James' critique of identity. For Locke sought to avoid offering "the new Negro" as simply another easily classified cultural commodity. A decidedly pragmatist logic informs his anthology's opening declaration that:

> in the last decade something beyond the watch and guard of statistics has happened in the life of the American Negro and the three norms who have traditionally presided over the Negro problem have a changeling in their laps. The sociologist, the Philanthropist, the Race-Leader are not unaware of the New Negro, but they are at a loss to account for him. He simply cannot be swathed in their formulae.[24]

William James would have cherished the existence of this elusive changeling, this defiance of categories, including separatism. For the new Negro affirms his Africanity as part of America's pluralist democracy, the "unique social experiment," says Locke, that is obstructed when any of its channels are closed.

Locke was also Zora Neale Hurston's teacher at Howard University in the early 1920s, and he might have helped transmit the pragmatist scepticism of identity that at least in part animates Hurston's contempt for representativeness, indeed for conventional modes of intelligibility, and her avidity for "disturbing . . . the pigeonhole way of life." Her iconoclasm was at once fierce and playful; it led not only to her notorious abhorrence of "Race Pride and Race Consciousness" but also to her challenging of Western assumptions that equate boundary and identity: "I do not wish to close the frontiers of life upon my own self. I do not wish to deny myself the expansion of seeking into individual capabilities and depths by living in a space whose boundaries are race and nation."[25] And later in the same text (her 1942 autobiography *Dust Tracks on a Road*) Hurston declares: "[There is] no *The Negro* here." Alain Locke used precisely this phrase that same year in his essay "Who and What is 'Negro'?" in an effort "to break arbitrary stereotypes." Although she taunts Du Bois (and other Race Men, Locke and Johnson) in *Dust Tracks*, Hurston is not as far from Du Bois as she would like to think. Both regret what he calls the "provincialism" of exemplarity, its inherent tendency to congeal. She regarded the Race Man or Woman as preoccupied with pigeonholing: "to him no Negro exists as an individual—he exists only as another tragic unit of the race," and in reaction Hurston empties her self of fixed coherence.

And she empties it of conventional political coherence. Logically her denial of inherent racial difference would seem to entail integration, a position she praises at times. But she is famous for her segregationist stance, including opposition to the Supreme Court's 1954 decision in *Brown* v. *Board of Education*. Like Du Bois, she hated to see blacks put in the position of forcing themselves upon whites: "How much satisfaction can I get from a court order for somebody to associate with me who does not wish me near them?" And her ethnic pride informs, of course, her research of Haitian and African-American oral folk tradition which she collected in two of her books. Hurston's segregationism, like Du Bois's, infuriated the NAACP; shortly after publishing *Dust Tracks*, notes her biographer Robert Hemenway, she went so far as to assert that "the Jim Crow system works."[26] Perhaps her mix of segregationist politics, profound race pride and (as expressed in her autobiography) universalism is meant not to be reconciled but to provoke. In this way she enacts her allegiance to intractability itself, a stance inspired by the folk archetype trickster's love of exaggeration and speaking from both sides of one's mouth. Her strategy forces the recognition that race relations are so complexly tangled that, as she announces in *Dust Tracks*, "none of the Race clichés mean anything any more." Neither white nor black "was one band of heavenly love. There was strain and stress inside as well as out."[27] And it should be recalled that Hurston cultivated this dissonance without a safety net, without constitutional affiliation to break her fall when, inevitably, her commitment to the precarious lost her any foothold she might have had in the literary marketplace. Having published more books than any other black American woman, she went unpublished in her last dozen years.

Although Patricia Williams doesn't mention Hurston, a measure of her anarchic spirit graces *The Alchemy of Race and Rights*. Lavishly, histrionically invested in transgressing bourgeois espistemologies and proprieties, Williams never surrenders to the predictably self-righteous gestures that this position often seems to inspire. Even as she spurns the moral purity of oppositionality, she performs a kind of immanent critique, a less tidy and self-flattering mode of cultural criticism. In other words, Williams scrupulously and vividly honours contradiction by living it. And if by now the exposure of capitalism's cultural contradictions has nearly become a bromide in cultural critique, she avoids the typical critical posture of the grim hanging judge arraigning the usual suspects from on high. This is not to say that some of these suspects escape sentencing. She is highly critical of the sheer hucksterism of a consumer ethos that preaches the pleasures of an enigmatic emptiness and turns products and selves into "floating signifiers." But she also invites this weightlessness directly to enter her text: "floating signifiers" is the phrase Williams uses to describe one of her own stylistic strategies, namely her sprinkling of recurring fragments of dream imagery throughout the work. Equally contradictory is her distaste for and suspicion of the culture of spectacle, which coexists with her own love of "dancing for display" and of shopping in department stores.

Indeed, the latter activity helps furnish a moment of communion with a stranger. Watching a funeral from her office window that overlooks a graveyard, Williams notices that:

> one of the mourners is wearing an outfit featured in the window
> of Bloomingdale's (59th Street store) only since last weekend.
> This recognition jolts me, and I am drawn to her in sorrow; the
> details of my own shopping history flash before my eyes as I

reflect upon the sober spree that brought her to the rim of this
earthly chasm, her slim suede heels sinking into the soft silt of
the graveside. (p. 231)

Such a delicate mix of absurdity and compassion could only be
achieved by an observer who has relaxed her political vigilance and
let her novelist's avidity for the detail of contemporary surfaces
disclose the terms of contemporary intimacy.

In her expectation that "fluid positioning" and an "ambivalent,
multivalent way of seeing" might be effective ways to resist culture's
pervasive reifications, Williams seems to share the language and
values of avant-garde cultural critique. Yet she rejects at least one
branch of this discourse—Critical Legal Studies. She dissents from
CLS's deconstruction of legal formalism, including that venerable
liberal abstraction, the rights-bearing subject. Rather than remaining
consistent to the left critical agenda, Williams finds postmodern legal
theory a luxury she cannot afford given the historical specificity of
black experience. Fluid boundaries have, for blacks, often meant not
"vistas of possibility" but helplessness, the "crushing weight of
total—bodily and spiritual—*intrusion*" (p. 164). Not having grown up
with the heritage of slavery and its legacy of trauma, white critical
theorists tend to be eager to liquidate formalism and embrace
informality. But, says Williams, she is "still evolving from being
treated as three-fifths of a human" and depends in her legal
negotiations on the formal protection of contracts and fixed identity.
"'Rights' . . . is still deliciously empowering to say," for their conferral
implies a respect that "elevates one's status from human body to
social being" (p. 164). Because her critique of Critical Legal Studies
affirms tenets of liberal individualism—distance, formality, and
identity—that she elsewhere seeks to dissolve, it is a striking instance
of Williams dressing herself in contradiction. By leaving unreconciled
her competing commitments to racial difference, left cultural
criticism, and literary experimentation, Williams explodes the
assumption that black intellectuals have a preordained politics.

From the start of her book and occasionally throughout, Williams
is tempted to relax the imperative of coherent identity, of "composing
herself properly," as if drawn to Hurston's seductive depiction of an
unbounded self that travels light, sustained by the barest minimum of
cohesion. ("In the main I feel like a brown bag of miscellany propped
against a wall," Hurston declares in the remarkable essay "How It
Feels To Be Colored Me."[28]) But Hurston is also a warning that such
radical dispersal of identity courts self-destruction, a possibility she

herself seems to acknowledge in her self-description (a "bundle of sham and tinsel, honest metal and sincerity that cannot be untangled"), which she calls a "corroding insight." Williams vows not to surrender her own bundled self; she must hold it tightly, she notes, "and never spill into the world that hates brown spills. I am afraid that everything I am will pour out into the ground and be absorbed without a word" (p. 183).

Her fear of spilling finds exemplification in the apparently inexplicable breakdown of black Los Angeles Municipal Court Judge Maxine Thomas, "a celebrated, savvy judge who presided over hundreds of mostly white male judges," who "one day just snapped and had to be carted from her chambers, helpless as a baby" (p. 192). As she gazes in the mirror, assembling her representative self, Williams realizes she is "very close to being Maxine," though the latter's more demanding job involved an even more onerous burden. Thomas' burden "was to wear all the contradictions at the same time, to wear them well and reconcile them" (p. 196). Refusing this impossible task, Williams saves herself from Maxine's fate but not without imaginatively entering it: "Standing in the mirror, I understand the logic of her wild despair, the rationality of her unbounded rage. I understand the break she made as necessary and immediate." Found by her clerk curled in a foetal position, the judge lay babbling fragments of "scattered wisdom," "giving birth to a thousand possibilities." Like Hurston, a predecessor in boundary transgression whose career ended in collapse and a return to the place of her birth, Maxine suffers an "ancient and incomprehensible restlessness" that finds peace by turning back to its origin in huddled helplessness. "Split at the seams," Maxine "returned to the womb," divested of the weight of contradiction, immaculately free and complex, purged of utility.

Yet Maxine's liberation from the role of exemplar comes, of course, at too high a price. Williams, in effect, must find a way to honour Maxine without becoming her, to find a way of appropriating the judge's rage against the pressure of roles and expectations while remaining the professional woman her mother implored her to be. "My only alternative," says Williams, recalling her mother's harsh binary, "was to 'die in the gutter.' There was no in-between . . . And so I became a professional woman" (p. 194), a role potentially as narrowing as that of Race Man or Woman. But *The Alchemy of Race and Rights* shows her mother was mistaken; for the book itself represents that "in-between." If the work of becoming a lawyer required, as Williams claims, repression of the "lonely, black defiled-female part of herself," and the projection of a competent, cool, masculine self, her book reveals that she has devised a self, a literary form, and a career that blurs these psychic dichotomies and defies labelling.

Williams' creativity is inseparable from her ability to turn everything to account. She makes use in her book, and in her law review articles, of her bouts of depression and nightmare (what she calls her schizophrenia), makes use of her slave ancestry (her great-great-grandmother at age eleven was purchased by a white lawyer and soon impregnated by him), makes use of being denied entrance into a Benetton's clothing store because of her colour. Through such acts of anecdotal appropriation she has advanced professionally in the very act of redefining what it means to be a law professor. Like Du Bois's troping upon the role of Race Man, Williams revises what being professional means by living not the stable identity of a representative but the tangled bundle of a "complicated oxymoron: a vain black female commercial law professor" (p. 210).

Williams is witty and disarmingly forthright about putting her biography to use: "Some part of me knows that it is intelligent for me to be schizophrenic. It is wise, in a way, for me to be constantly watching myself, to feel simultaneously more than one thing, and to hear a lot of voices in my head: in fact it is not just intelligent but fashionable, feminist and even postmodern" (p. 207). The saving self-irony of moments like this jostles against more serious, even anguished moments of self-indictment. Thus a blandly general conclusion, describing what the "hard work of a non-racist sensibility" must do, immediately follows an uncomfortably particular analysis of her own self-protective silence when she inadvertently witnesses a "casually jocular" anti-Semitic incident (p. 127). Here in a remark-ably intimate way she illuminates the insidious psychology of racism, how easily it spreads in an "encompassing circle" that can engulf even the most correct politics, even the most "fluid positioning." Williams' adroit juxtapositions produce a counterpoint that resembles nothing so much as her conception of justice itself, which she calls "continual balancing of competing visions, plural viewpoints . . . in pursuit of a more complete sense of the world in which we all live."

In pursuing completeness Williams, like Hurston and Du Bois before her, makes "provincialism" the enemy. Du Bois envisioned the "complete enjoyment of the possibilities of human existence,"[29] and the self-described "cosmic Zora,"[30] goddess of plasticity, scourge of definition, virtually becomes a Platonic ideal of being "gorgeously out of it." This condition, which tempts Williams, is craved by the narrator of *High Cotton*.

Darryl Pinckney's novel appropriates Hurston, along with Du Bois, William James, Alain Locke and others; it is constructed as a palimpsest upon which the traces of prior figures exert a continuous pressure, creating an intricate braid of cultural and literary allusion. Pinckney's imaginative energy is devoted more to his architecture of resonant allusion than to his novel's rather diffident *Bildungsroman* plot, the genre in which *High Cotton* seems a bit too complacently nestled. Characterization also is not a priority. Apart from the grandfather and a few others, most of the characters largely serve as occasions for witty social commentary. The narrator gives Pinckney the most trouble. An unnamed, ghostly presence, he is strangely bodiless and desexualized. One consequence is that *High Cotton* evades an interesting question, the fate of masculinity in a black society and in a more general American one that tends to regard being black, being male, and being an intellectual as colliding cultural codes. Although the recessive narrator exists virtually as pure voice, it is fortunately a brilliant one. And Pinckney's most impressive achievement is in creating a style of echo and inference that records in tensely coiled sentences how an intellectual hears the overlapping familial, historical, literary and cultural vibrations that comprise his experience. To achieve *High Cotton*'s allusive saturation, Pinckney's own *Bildung* has entailed a long apprenticeship, one which he has conducted largely in public. Since his early twenties he has been regularly publishing exceedingly acute reviews of African-American literature and culture, mostly in the *New York Review of Books*.

Pinckney narrates the first thirty years or so of growing up black after the "thaw" of *Brown* v. *Board of Education*, in the (relatively) easy living suggested by Gershwin's "Summertime" which echoes in his title. He feels "walled in on all sides by Negroes about to define themselves" (p. 23), and after his parents drag him to his first civil rights rally in the early 1960s, the narrator recounts his efforts to revise "what it meant to be coloured, Negro, black, Afro-American" and to become unburdened of race, of family, of identity itself. In effect, the narrator invents himself as a new Negro (the opening chapter's title). This is the book's second allusion to Locke; the first commences with the artwork under the novel's title page—a detail from Winold Reiss's illustration "Dawn in Harlem." Reiss is best known for his luminous portraits in *The New Negro*, so that when the reader of *High Cotton* turns the page to the first chapter, its title seems only apt. Like Pinckney's, Locke's project is generational—"if a 'New Negro' is not reborn every half generation or so, something is radically wrong"[31]—and it is meant to displace an earlier black commitment to racial uplift: "'Be representative' . . . was the underlying mood." Pinckney conceives his primary responsibility as aesthetic: "You want in your book to honor literature as an idea," he has said of his novel, "you want to write for literature, for other books."[32]

Resembling another nameless "invisible man" suspended in a state of elected hibernation, Pinckney's narrator is haunted by his grandfather: "I spent much of my life running from him, centripetal fashion . . . but he was forever rising through the waves of my denial . . . anxious to pass on that record of alienated majesty" (p. 6). Every morning his grandfather reminds him of "the problem that [he] would never, never get away from." However, the narrator escapes; "the burden of consciousness" is lifted, at least for a while. The allusions here, the thematic one to Ellison and the verbal ones to Emerson ("alienated majesty") and Du Bois ("problem" and "consciousness") announce his characteristic technique and initiate his novels' themes. Pinckney is drawn to both the exhilaration of dissolving selfhood in Emersonian transparency and to the liberating irresponsibility of Ellisonian invisibility: "Irresponsibility is part of my invisibility" declared the invisible man, who, we will recall, ends up hibernating after being groomed to be the "true interpreter of the people . . . the new Booker T. Washington."[33]

But Pinckney plays upon both modes of being "out of it" by asking what "being out of it" means in the 1970s and 1980s to an intellectual so saturated in texts that when asked if he knows Harlem, his immediate response is, "who hadn't heard of James Baldwin?" (p. 123). *High Cotton* resides self-consciously in the Barthesian world of the already read, where denotation is banished and connotation rules, where "the Negro capital of the World had moved, long before, to the rare-books desk of the Schomburg library" (p. 133). If, as Ellison once said in praise of Richard Wright and Baldwin, that they were as much products of their reading and of the library as of their painful experiences, then Pinckney is witness to the historic moment when the library becomes experience. Books don't even have to be read to function as useful tools in manipulating social codes: he carries "props" into the subway—"the latest *Semiotext(e)*, a hefty volume of the Frankfurt School"—to avoid being mistaken for "yet another young black prole, though I was exactly that" (p. 193).

Pinckney's life in New York coincides with those "embryonic New Wave days" when "access to your feelings, expressiveness of any kind . . . were social liabilities downtown." The generational divide in styles of affect is apparent in a witty, if ambivalent, homage to Ellison.

Pinckney cryptically mentions that his father's Uncle Ralph Waldo had "lived the blues so well that he wound up in a nuthouse without the sense he was born with" (p. 5), perhaps a cautionary tale against black soul and high-modernist pathos, two of the constitutive elements of *Invisible Man*. When Pinckney renders a predictable occasion for soulful pathos—the return to the ancestral home, the call of the "Old Country"—he portrays it as sedimented with cultural stereotype but not without poignancy. After his grandfather dies in 1985 the narrator goes to Sugar Creek, Georgia to say goodbye. He is moved by the hospitality and the visits to the graveyard and the church, where the gospel choir makes him feel the emotion he had "been looking for all those years." And he is also exhilarated by the chance to choreograph his *Roots* number. "I had the most dramatic conclusion in mind for my visit to the Old Country. I would walk over the bridge from Augusta into South Carolina, as a kind of humbling myself before history . . . I'd make noises, the way a child alone in a creaking room adds his own sounds just to scare himself" (p. 305). But the bridge is too long and he simply turns back, a "hydraulic whine" drowning out his footsteps and his planned rendezvous with destiny.

This refusal of pathos is also a refusal of the cultural cliché that Pinckney elsewhere has identified: the assumption that catharsis is the black artist's "major contribution to national life." The obligation to express noble suffering conflicts with the stubborn possibility that, as the narrator says, even when "you want to retain the past, as if through preservation its sufferings will have some meaning . . . sometimes suffering has no meaning, it's just suffering." Releasing himself from this racial typecasting, he enjoys the bourgeois freedom to select self-consciously among a variety of roles. Prior to his stint as Upper West Side bohemian, in the late 1960s he had distributed leaflets as "minister of information" for the "Heirs of Malcolm," a local radical cell. But his real passion is tucked behind his Angela Davis poster, where he keeps "Stanzas Written in Dejection Near Indianapolis." Poetry writing is part of his Anglophilia, which includes a penchant for "Byronic drag: frilly prom shirt, shoes and belts with big buckles." Flying off to London after high school gives him the opportunity to perfect an accent that sounds "like a blend of Katherine Hepburn and Godfrey Cambridge." This self-invention, a product of his groping efforts to become high-brow, inflates his Anglophilia to parodic extremes, with the salutary effect of relegating black experience to the ordinary, the realm of freedom.

Because he remains emotionally arrested ("there was a big hole in the middle of my heart that needed filling up") and professionally unfulfilled ("I'm wasting my life," he tells his grandfather shortly before resigning from a job in publishing), the narrator understands this freedom largely in negative terms, as a "comfortable resignation of the self that was also useful as a sort of certificate of exemption." But in his summing up the narrator at last moves beyond this escapism by coming to empathize with his grandfather: "One day—if it comes—I may be someone's old darky, exercising my fictitious birthright to run off at the mouth." And he imagines himself when lecturing a young listener who "will be suicidal to get away from [him]," just as the narrator recalls being "in the presence of grandfather, whose fear of forgetfulness I mistook as a wish to muddy my choices. I may elect myself a witness and undertake to remember." Only here, near the final lines, does the narrator end his flight from authority's various incarnations and assume what at the start he boasted of escaping: "the burden of consciousness." In electing this burden of "witness" and memory he pledges not exemplarity but the obligation to reinvent the freedom to be ordinary as something richer than adolescent lament. *High Cotton* itself counts as that pledge redeemed.

The freedom to be ordinary seems a modest enough goal, but in a society obsessed with skin colour blackness remains anything but ordinary. Instead it is a "problem," to use Du Bois's still relevant word from the beginning of *The Souls of Black Folk*. And "being a problem," Du Bois added, "is a strange experience." For one thing it seems to licence others to impose "solutions," be it by the necktie party, the cross burning, or the more mundane, daily acts of allegorizing blackness in endless permutations of the benign and/or demonic. Echoing Du Bois, James Baldwin wrote in 1951 that to be a black man is to be regarded as a "social and not a personal or a human problem; to think of him is to think of statistics, slums, rapes, injustices, remote violence; it is to be confronted with an endless cataloguing of losses, gains, skirmishes."[34] And when the individual emerges from the "jungle of statistics," a Rodney King, say, and somehow evades the protective allegories and assumptions, he shocks the public with the startling gentleness of his face and voice and words. In rebuking our expectations, King eluded all our definitions by becoming himself, to borrow Baldwin's words. Such escape is the only way, says Baldwin, of becoming a man or woman or artist, "For the Negro is not a statistic or a problem or a fantasy: he is a person and it is simply not possible for one person to define another. Those who try soon find themselves trapped by their own definitions."[35] A way out of the trap is discovered by Ellison's invisible man who declared that "the world's definition is possibility. Step outside the narrow borders of what men call reality and you step into chaos . . . or imagination."[36]

The equation of achieved selfhood with scepticism toward "narrow borders" of definition, indeed toward identity itself as a mechanism of social control and reduction, is a driving theme of Ellison's but also of Baldwin's essays. Like his revered Henry James, Baldwin has a distinctly pragmatic wariness of identity and of definition. Both are traps, stifling reifications erected in response to the terror of the disturbing particularity of human being. This scepticism forms the basis of Baldwin's particular sensitivity to the perils of that most monumentalized and static mode of identity, the artist as spokesman, what he called in reference to Richard Wright, the burden of being the representative of all black people. "It is a false responsibility (since writers are not congressmen) and impossible, by its nature, of fulfilment."[37] Many have noted the mordant irony of this admonition to Wright, for Baldwin went on to become the foremost exemplary intellectual of his generation while knowing full well the costs of doing so.

When the "burden of representation" (Baldwin's phrase) is rendered in the key of existential pathos it can doubly distort, for it tends to deflate all blacks to a single voice and inflate their representative to a grandiose omniscience. Yet this burden may be unavoidable in whatever key. Toni Morrison, in *Playing in the Dark*, argues that the black writer "is at some level *always* conscious of representing one's own race to, or in spite of, a race of readers that understands itself to be 'universal' or race-free." Hurston found this discrepancy intolerable, as we have seen, and in response at times urged a universalism that liberated the self from the confines of any representation: "the stuff of my being," she declared in *Dust Tracks*, "is matter, ever changing, ever moving." As a child she expressed this mobility in insatiable curiosity that made her incessant questions a nuisance to the "gods of the pigeonholes." As she grew up she discovered that in order to place themselves beyond the reach of interrogation, people "are prone to build a statue of the kind of person that it pleases them to be."

Statue building—authority's self-insulation—is the business of the exemplar, and *Playing in the Dark* can be regarded as an elegant small statue (of ninety-one pages) by the author Wendy Steiner has called "the closest thing we have to a national writer." This book bids to expand Morrison's domain into literary and cultural criticism, a genre to which she has contributed some influential essays but never a book. To call *Playing in the Dark* a statue is meant to suggest that these revised lectures first given at Harvard are most interesting for revealing how the pressure of being an exemplar shapes one's discourse, determining what things are sayable, and what are not. That the question of who is and is not granted speech and presence in critical writing is also the manifest subject of Morrison's text suggests its striking reflexivity.

This quality starts with an unnervingly theatrical cover which implicitly announces that *Playing in the Dark* is designed as a commanding performance. Reproduced front and back is the same photograph of a stunningly coiffured and dressed Morrison staring with impressive hauteur off into the infinite space of a vaguely lunar landscape. With the image of stark solitary grandeur established visually, her book proceeds to paint an equivalent critical scenario. Making virtually no acknowledgement of any critical predecessors, Morrison casts herself from the start as an explorer seeking to "map" and open for "discovery" the desolate terrain of American literary criticism, a terrain of "silence and evasion" (p. 3) regarding matters of race, the ignoring of which is "understood to be a graceful, even generous, liberal gesture" (p. 9). Evidently criticism is ill with a paralyzing gentility that has excised the "political from the life of the mind" and risks "lobotomizing" American texts, "immobilizing their complexities and power." According to Morrison, there is an eerie silence in the house of criticism, for the patient "remains too polite or too fearful" to speak of what is before its eyes: the "dark abiding" Africanist present (p. 33).

How has this strange impasse occurred? Morrison's answer is elaborate and deserves to be rehearsed before it is assessed. In explaining this "willed scholarly indifference," she reaches back to the very formation of American cultural identity which, she points out, simultaneously is formed and informed by a nation's literature. The new nation and its writers (most deliberately Emerson) self-consciously went about building "a new white man," and like any act of identity-making the project require repressions, omissions, restrictions, a demonizing of all that was not-me to sharpen the boundaries of the me. In short, establishing this new man in the new Eden of freedom required slavery. Who but the black slave, "with the dramatic polarity created by skin color," could so well serve as the not-me, serve as the vehicle, the "playground," the "staging ground and arena" by which "the American self knows itself as not enslaved, but free . . . not helpless but licensed and powerful . . . not a blind accident of evolution but a progressive fulfillment of destiny." Indispensable for "organizing American coherence," including its masculinity and individualism, was the "potent and ego-reinforcing presence of an Africanist population" (p. 45).

It would seem that academic study and criticism of American literature maintain authority in ways analogous to the formation of national and cultural coherence, by circulating as knowledge a basic set of imperial assumptions, the cornerstone being "that traditional, canonical American literature is free of, uninformed and unshaped by the four-hundred-year-old presence of, first, Africans and then African-Americans in the United States." Disguised in a rhetoric of neutrality, this alleged knowledge has robbed and impoverished the literature it studies, confining it to a cloistered "preserve of white male views, genius, and power." Mercifully, there is an exit from this monastery: "the writers themselves . . . the creators of American literature." Morrison rejoices in that literature as a "treasure trove," for it permits what is repressed to return and to disrupt works "with fear and longing;" the confrontation with the Africanist presence explains in large part why American literature is so marked by psychic and stylistic disturbances, so tempted and terrified by trespass. White authors appropriate blacks as "surrogate selves" for imaginatively acting out knowledge tabooed outside the text: that "Africanism is inextricable from the definition of Americanness." Often blackness is permitted to surface on condition that imagery of "impenetrable whiteness" (in Poe and Melville, Hemingway and Bellow) accompanies and immobilizes it. But in controlling black-ness, whiteness condemns itself to muteness and impasse, to selfhood frozen in solitude. Hence the fear and desire, the silence broken and repaired. "How troubled, how frightened and haunted" is our founding literature (p. 35).

Morrison's emphasis on "the parasitical nature of white freedom" (which seems most directly influenced by the sociologist Orlando Patterson, whom she mentions in passing) and the black presence as "surrogate and enabler" for the "elaboration of the quintessential American identity" is interesting and important. But it is a thesis that remains stillborn, not only because it is largely bereft of persuasive corroboration and critical context but, more important, because the larger argument which encases it blatantly misrepresents the state of contemporary knowledge in American literature. These enforced repressions wrap her book in a pristine solitude. The "dark" that Morrison plays in is filled with silence emanating from a number of sources, one being the absence of major works that her argument would seem to require as a test of validity. Minor works—Cather's *Sapphira and the Slave Girl* and Hemingway's *To Have and Have Not* and posthumously published *The Garden of Eden*—receive the most sustained analysis. This selection might have been less baffling had it been used as secondary evidence, to supplement a discussion, say, of Melville's "Benito Cereno" or Crane's "The Monster," seminal fictions that powerfully render and complicate the role of Africanity in the "process of organizing American coherence." The conspicuous absence of crucial primary texts mirrors a neglect of critical ones. Morrison seems determined to draw her new map as if from scratch, determined to play the rugged individualist going it alone.

The creation of this persona of intrepid pioneer may be the most impressive achievement of *Playing in the Dark*, which is to suggest that her book is as much about constructing exemplarity as about its announced subject. And its place on the *New York Times* bestseller list may have more to do with the clean lines of its exemplary narrative than with its literary criticism. For, like many bestsellers, it tells a heroic, if familiar tale: *Playing in the Dark* bears witness to an act of intellectual and moral courage as our great black novelist takes time off from her fiction to pursue a lonely quest for truth and singlehandedly expose part of America's racist cultural infrastructure, while putting the academy on notice that its genteel racism will not stand.

Yet what enables her exemplar narrative is a preposterous fiction depicting literary criticism as ruled by an apolitical, genteel hegemony. Moreover, she has fabricated this fiction in full knowledge of its falsity. Toni Morrison herself provides the best evidence for these assertions. To juxtapose *Playing in the Dark* with her other major discussion of American literature, her Tanner Lecture of 1988, provides a vivid glimpse into the process of her statue making.

"Unspeakable Things Unspoken," delivered at the University of Michigan and reprinted in the *Michigan Quarterly Review*, reveals a remarkably different Morrison, a well-informed, generously appreciative participant in the twenty-year-old debate that has transformed academic critical practices and pedagogy. So effective has the canon debate been, Morrison there argues, that "no-one believes the body of literature and its criticism will ever again be what it was in 1965: the protected preserve of the thoughts and works and analytical strategies of whitemen . . . it is to my great relief that such terms as 'white' and 'race' can enter serious discussion of literature."[38] Conveying her enthusiasm about how much has changed, Morrison warms to her task: "In such a melee [of debate on the canon] as this one—a provocative, healthy, explosive melee-extraordinarily profound work is being done." Citing the work of Edward Said, Martin Bernal and others, she speaks of "silences being broken": what was "formerly unspoken" is now "rendered speakable" and at least two generations of scholars are "disentangling received knowledge from the apparatus of control." Morrison also urges a continuing "wakefulness" regarding the canon, particularly the question of how the black has been a shaping but ghostly presence in nineteenth-century works. She then goes on to praise Michael Rogin's book on Melville for showing "how deeply Melville's social thought is woven into his writing." Morrison engages with both Rogin and *Moby Dick*, extending Rogin's thesis with readings of two of Melville's chapters.

The differences between the Morrison of 1988 and 1992 starkly speak for themselves. Whereas in 1988 Morrison seems at ease participating in an ongoing community of knowledge production, *Playing in the Dark* changes focus, as she declares at the start her interest in "what makes intellectual domination possible." And more than once Morrison tells us that her emphasis is on the master, "the racial subject," and not on the slave, "the racial object." Part of her look into what racism does to the "mind, imagination, and behaviour" of masters extends to (unnamed) "powerful literary critics" who blithely boast of their ignorance of black texts. Morrison is disgusted by the "wanton, elaborate strategies taken to erase" the Africanist presence from view. Moreover she notes that the pleasure and relish that these "arbiters of critical power" display in their ignorance seems not to have harmed them or eroded their influence. Her focus on how masters take unpunished enjoyment in the pleasures of wanton erasure provides a clue to her own strategies of suppression in moving from her Tanner lecture to *Playing in the Dark*. In linking cultural power with insouciant disregard, Morrison appears to replicate this wilful insulation from intellectual community and responsibility and thus is able to paint in the most melodramatic terms her own project of "organizing, separating and consolidating" her exemplary status.

Whether her narrative of exemplarity is worth this insulation is a question that evokes several considerations, if no unequivocal answer. A response must weigh her misrepresentation of the state of literary study against the fact that she is an inspiring exemplar with a vast readership to whom she speaks with nearly unrivalled authority. In this light *Playing in the Dark* can represent inspiring muckraking for some; for others, a trust violated. A statement from her Tanner lecture takes on new meaning here: she remarks on "the strategies one can be forced to resort to in trying to accommodate" the demands of different audiences. She was speaking then of black and white audiences, but here the division seems more between those within and without the academy. Perhaps one can regret her choice of strategies but be impressed by her audacious act of cultural power; after all, most power grabs involve not a little arrogance and bluff. The dirty game of cultural politics is no exception; she didn't invent the rules that she has brilliantly mastered.

A final consideration: if one sets aside the problems of suppression and distortion and judges *Playing in the Dark* on its own terms, what is most troubling is Morrison's uncritical attitude toward autonomy, authority, power, identity, individualism, coherence—the values her exemplar persona embodies and her analysis so insistently invokes. Immune to interrogation or even irony, these concepts are deployed as if they did not all contain their own perils, as if they are meaningful in themselves or can even be possessed in any uncomplicated way. And as if many of the great works of the American Renaissance did not subject these concepts to unsettling inquiry.

Playing in the Dark makes the various modes of irreverent scepticism found in Du Bois and Hurston, Williams and Pinckney, seem even more vital. The effort of the latter pair is not in representing but in renegotiating race, authenticity, and identity in our postmodern bourgeois moment. Yet to hold up their challenge to being representative as itself a model would be to fall into the trap of exemplarity. What is to be hoped is that this challenge will inevitably enter into debate with contrary views, as black intellectuals create a culture alive with options and combinations still to be fashioned.

(This is a slightly revised version of a review-essay which appeared in *Raritan* XII: 3, Winter 1993.)

Notes

1. Darryl Pinckney, "Black Victims, Black Villains" *New York Review of Books*, 29 January 1987, p. 20.
2. W.E.B. Du Bois, "The Talented Tenth" in *Writings* (New York: The Library of America, 1986), pp. 842–61.
3. Stephen L. Carter, *Reflections of an Affirmative Action Baby* (New York: Basic Books, 1991), p. 1.

4. Toni Morrison, *Playing in the Dark: Whiteness and the Literary Imagination* (Cambridge, Mass. and London: Harvard University Press, 1992).

5. James Weldon Johnson, *The Autobiography of an Ex-Coloured Man* (1927) repr. in *Three Negro Classics* (New York: Avon, 1965).

6. bell hooks, *Yearning: Race, Gender and Cultural Politics* (Boston: South End Press, 1990).

7. Cornel West, "The Dilemma of the Black Intellectual" in Cornel West and bell hooks, *Breaking Bread* (Boston: South End Press, 1991), p. 134.

8. West and hooks, *Breaking Bread*, p. 4.

9. Carter, *Reflections*, p. 2.

10. Darryl Pinckney, *High Cotton: A Novel* (New York: Farrar, Strauss and Giroux, 1992).

11. Patricia Williams *The Alchemy of Race and Rights* (Cambridge, Mass. and London: Harvard University Press, 1991).

12. W.E.B. Du Bois, "Dusk of Dawn: An Essay Toward an Autobiography of a Race Concept" in *Writings*, p. 555.

13. W.E.B. Du Bois, *Souls of Black Folk* in *Writings*, p. 364.

14. Du Bois, *Writings*, p. 777.

15. Du Bois, *Writings*, p. 1244.

16. Du Bois, *Writings*, p. 1248.

17. Du Bois, *Writings*, p. 711.

18. John Dewey, "Preface", *The Influence of Darwin on Philosophy* (New York: Peter Smith, 1951) p. iv.

19. Harold Cruse, *The Crisis of the Negro Intellectual* (New York: William Morrow, 1967), p. 176.

20. William James, *The Letters of William James* (Boston: Atlantic Monthly Press, 1920) Vol. 2, p. 196.

21. Henry James, quoted in R.B. Perry, *The Thought and Character of William James* (Boston: Little, Brown, 1935) Vol. 1, p. 428.

22. Alain Locke, *The Philosophy of Alain Locke*, ed. Leonard Harris (Philadelphia: Temple University Press, 1989), p. 16.

23. William James, *A Pluralistic Universe* (London: Longman's and Co, 1909).

24. Locke, *Philosophy*, p. 210.

25. Zora Neale Hurston, *Dust Tracks on a Road* (1942; repr. London: Virago, 1986), pp. 230 and 237.

26. Quoted in Robert E. Hemenway, *Zora Neale Hurston: A Literary Biography* (Illinois University Press, 1977), p. 289.

27. Hurston, *Dust Tracks*, p. 234.

28. Zora Neale Hurston, "How It Feels to be Coloured Me" (1928) repr. in *I Love Myself When I Am Laughing: A Zora Neale Hurston Reader* (New York: The Feminist Press, 1979).

29. Du Bois, *Writings*, p. 1060.

30. Hurston, *I Love Myself*, p. 155.

31. Locke, *Philosophy*, pp. 231–32.

32. Interview with Darryl Pinckney, *New York Times*, 18 May 1992.

33. Ralph Ellison, *Invisible Man* (1952: repr. Harmondsworth: Penguin, 1965), p. 16.

34. James Baldwin, *The Price of the Ticket: Collected Non Fiction, 1948–1985* (New York: St Martin's Press, 1985) p. 66.
35. Baldwin, *Price of the Ticket*, p. 181.
36. Ellison, *Invisible Man*, p. 464.
37. Baldwin, *Price of the Ticket*, p. 71.
38. Toni Morrison, "Unspeakable Things Unspoken" *Michigan Quarterly Review*, 28: 1 (1989).

13

Culture at Modernity's End
Daniel Bell and Fredric Jameson

Nick Heffernan

The sense was present—and still is—that in Western society we are in the midst of a vast historical change in which old social relations (which were property-bound), existing power structures (centred on narrow elites), and bourgeois culture (based on notions of restraint and delayed gratification) are being rapidly eroded. The sources of the upheaval are scientific and technological. But they are also cultural, since culture . . . has achieved autonomy in Western society. What these new social forms will be like is not completely clear. Nor is it likely that they will achieve the unity of the economic system and character structure which was characteristic of capitalist civilization from the mid-eighteenth to the mid-twentieth century. The use of the hyphenated prefix *post-* indicates, thus, that sense of living in interstitial time.[1]

When Daniel Bell made these remarks in 1973, his feeling that Western societies were entering upon a course of deep and definitive change derived from an evaluation of trends that were located in the technical-economic sphere. Bell's projection of these trends—at the centre of which he saw the wholesale reorganization of traditional industrial production methods and work practices under the pressure of an increasingly rapid pace of technological innovation—issued in his notion of the shift towards a "post-industrial" order. This became an important formulation in the social sciences with which to debate the nature of social and economic change and, more widely, to address the issue of historical transformation within which Bell's thesis was couched.[2]

At about the same time, however, another "post-" word was regaining a limited currency among analysts and practitioners of the arts. "Postmodernism," as the term re-emerged at the beginning of the 1970s, referred initially to certain novel stylistic departures in literature and in architecture. Yet twenty years later the term has so fully outgrown its early aesthetic field of reference that it is increasingly difficult to write or read cultural and social criticism without invoking or encountering it. In its now significantly expanded sense the idea of the postmodern has subsumed, if not displaced, the notion of the post-industrial. It has thus become the favoured term through which to speculate on the nature of contemporary social and cultural change and to describe that sense of culture-wide historical transformation identified by Daniel Bell above.

That this is so highlights the way in which change is now often seen and analyzed first and foremost in cultural terms. That is to say that change in, for example, its economic, technological or political particularity, is felt somehow to be more widely cultural in its significance; for culture is the level at which change is collectively registered, symbolized and given meaning.[3] Thus questions about all these other levels of social action and change are implicit within the issue of postmodernism and its assumption of a decisive historical turn within Western societies, especially the United States, towards a general condition of cultural postmodernity.[4]

Both Daniel Bell, one of the earliest to discuss postmodernism in an expanded sense, and Fredric Jameson, perhaps now the principal theorist of postmodern culture, have insisted in very distinct ways on the importance of taking a historical view of culture which must attend seriously to the economic and technological as well as to the social and political levels. Both concur on the pressing need to come to terms with the meaning and the consequences of those profound changes which each reckons to have transformed American culture in the post-1945 period and which each feels to be bound up with the question of postmodernism. Each in his own way (Bell perhaps less so, or less overtly so, than Jameson) encourages us to regard post-modernism less as an essence—that is, as a particular cultural or aesthetic style that can be defined and fixed in its meaning—than as a problematic, or an open set of questions about the nature and dynamics of contemporary culture.

I will consider some of these questions in the following sections of this chapter. For now, though, we might observe that what is at stake for both Bell and Jameson in the problem of postmodernism is precisely an evaluation of the validity and vitality of contemporary

American culture and of the possibilities it affords for meaningful collective and individual actions and satisfactions. Thus each is concerned to elaborate a particular politics of culture through which the problem of the postmodern can be articulated and an evaluation arrived at. For both, this involves the construction of a broad historical narrative of economic, social and cultural change within which the postmodern must be situated and of which it is, in some complicated sense, an effect or symptom. I will begin, then, by tracing these particular narratives in the work of each author.

Daniel Bell: Capitalism, Culture, Contradiction

In his shift from an early commitment to theoretical Marxism and the politics of socialism during the 1930s to an enduring but not always comfortable accommodation with the forms of postwar corporate capitalism, Daniel Bell is emblematic of a generation of American intellectuals which came to prominence after the Second World War. Like many of this generation, Bell's central concerns derive from what he holds to be the two great historical developments of the contemporary period: the "failure" of Marxism in both its intellectual and institutional manifestations on the one hand, and the "triumph" of capitalism in economic, political and ideological terms on the other. Yet unlike many of the same generation, whose interests were principally literary and aesthetic in focus, Bell's perspective on these developments was formed out of a sustained acquaintance with the structures of postwar American capitalism gained during his years as a labour affairs editor on Henry Luce's influential *Fortune* magazine, champion of the new style of corporate enterprise.

Indeed, it was through a collection of essays written whilst working on *Fortune, The End of Ideology* (1960), that Bell fully articulated a revisionist theory of American capitalism and its social and cultural framework which became influential with both intellectuals and policy makers of the period. *The End of Ideology* developed *Fortune*'s native theme of the adaptive dynamism of American capital and business organization, and elaborated on its central tenet: that although "Fifty years ago American capitalism seemed to be what Marx predicted it would be," subsequent historical transformations had instead resulted in "the formation of a kind of capitalism that neither Karl Marx nor Adam Smith ever dreamed of."[5] The capitalism of unregulated competition, social conflict and cyclical crisis had, it was claimed, been emphatically displaced by new, more rational, humane and socially inclusive forms of economic

organization. These had effectively resolved the sharp internal contradictions that had periodically threatened to destroy capitalism—
particularly during bouts of violent class struggle in the 1890s and
1910s, and the Great Depression of the 1930s—and inaugurated an era
of rapid growth, stability and widening prosperity based on the mass
consumption of goods and services and the emergence of the modern
corporation as the dominant economic unit. The new capitalism was
characterized by large-scale planning, state intervention and direction, technological innovation, and social cooperation or consensus.

For Bell, these developments rendered the Marxian grand
narrative of history obsolete. Invoking what he called "America's un-
Marxist revolution,"[6] Bell argued that capitalism had successfully
purged itself of those elements, particularly antagonistic class
relations and the tendency towards economic and social breakdown,
that made it amenable to such an analysis. Under modern corporate
forms, the ownership and accumulation of private property as the
foundation of social and economic power had given way to the
paramount importance of managerial control and technical expertise.
The social and economic basis for a capitalist ruling class had broken
up; this class power was now dispersed to a rising but essentially
classless stratum of socially mobile experts and professionals which
staffed the managerial and technical apparatus of the new capitalism.
Meanwhile, technologically advanced methods of production and
the spread of white collar administrative and service occupations
(developments Bell viewed as characteristic of an emergent post-
industrial order) had thoroughly recomposed the structure and
identity of the American working class. The promise (and, in some
measure, the reality) of unprecedented affluence had undermined
this class's social and spatial cohesiveness, extinguishing what remained
of its commitment to the politics of radical social transformation and
fully incorporating it and its institutions, particularly the trade unions,
into the operations and corporate ethos of the new capitalism.

Moreover Marxism, for Bell, was intellectually and morally
compromised by its association with Stalinism. From the particular
historical instance of "actually existing socialism" Bell argued that all
ideology (in his limited definition the infusion into political ideas of
systematic belief and a subjective moral "passion . . . to transform the
whole of a way of life"[7]) was totalitarian in tendency and socially
catastrophic. Though it persisted in degraded form in Eastern
Europe, ideology in the West was utterly discredited. There had
been, as the subtitle of Bell's book put it, an "exhaustion of political
ideas in the 1950s" in so far as no credible alternative to capitalist

liberal democracy remained. But this exhaustion was to be celebrated as a necessary consequence of the demise of economically determined class politics and the shift to an inclusive political pluralism of interest, status and symbol groups bounded by a general acceptance of the rightness and inevitability of corporate capitalism and its dominant business values.

In these circumstances, Bell argued, intellectuals should trade in the "naive and simplistic" utopianism of oppositional modes of thought for a "'mature' acceptance of the complexities of politics and existence."[8] They were to join the consensus as its moral guardians. This rhetoric of innocence and experience was the principal trope through which ex-radical intellectuals of Bell's generation explained their rapprochement with American capitalism and their adoption of some variant of the anti-communist liberalism espoused in *The End of Ideology*.[9] At its most self-serving, this rhetoric worked to rationalize the abandonment of critique for a more comfortable accommodation to institutionalized power and add an existential gloss to the fact that coming in from the cold of opposition ultimately meant enlisting for service in the Cold War. Bell's negative and very narrow definition of ideology in terms that applied only to Marxism (and, perhaps, to some of the emergent anti-colonialist nationalisms of the Third World) was itself clearly ideological in another, wider sense in that it rested on a set of assumptions about the desirability of liberal capitalism that were fully political in nature and served particular social interests rather than others. This was the sense in which Bell's thesis operated as an intellectual apologia for a new age of US economic and cultural imperialism based on militant anti-communism, and in which Cold War liberals were recruited as the cultural arm of post-1945 American foreign policy through structures such as the Congress for Cultural Freedom and the magazine *Encounter* (for both of which Bell worked) which were covertly linked to the CIA.[10]

Yet this wider sense of ideology, as explanation that "conceals a value,"[11] was in fact present as a secondary current in Bell's book where it was deployed to extend the dismissal of Marxism to other forms of European social theory, particularly classical sociology. For Bell, this school's resolutely pessimistic view of the destruction of traditional forms of social organization and cultural authority by economic and technological modernization sprang from a nostalgic hostility to cultural change and an anti-democratic distaste for the masses. Against it, Bell posited a theory of the historical exceptionalism of American culture which held that its freedom from pre-capitalist traditions and structures made this culture uniquely receptive to the transformations wrought by capitalist development. The exceptional capacity of the United States to undergo rapid economic modernization without succumbing to social revolution or some form of totalitarianism was, Bell argued, due precisely to this close historical articulation between capitalism and national culture: "the United States is the first large society in history to have change and innovation 'built into' its culture."[12]

While Bell used the term "culture" here in its widest sense to refer to the structures through which a whole way of life is conducted, he developed from it an argument about American culture in the more specialized sense of intellectual or artistic activity and achievement. If consensus capitalism and its soaring productivity resulted from the wider culture's historic openness to economic and technical modernization, then it was through the broad opportunities for education, leisure and personal consumption created by this productivity that, he claimed, culture in its narrower sense flourished as never before. For theorists of Mass Society and Mass Culture, affluence on top of economic and technical modernization produced a de-personalized, homogeneous and culturally impoverished mass of consumers socially disorganized and vulnerable to manipulation by the increasingly dominant communications and entertainments industries. For Bell, however, these processes enhanced social mobility and opened up a vast range of life-style and taste choices that worked against such massification while democratically increasing participation in cultural activities. Consumer capitalism thus generated a cultural and social pluralism which complemented and in some senses underpinned its political pluralism.

Bell's rejection of the Mass Society and Mass Culture theses sprang from a claim about the differentiated nature of audiences and social strata within modern capitalism and a respect for the integrity of popular practices and desires. Yet ultimately he subscribed to the same high or elite conception of culture as did his antagonists on this issue, arguing simply that "good" culture could be disseminated through the market and reinforced, rather than undermined, by consumption. His was a trickle-down or "progressive evolutionist"[13] version of cultural democratization in which bourgeois culture was put forward as the model of a universal culture. Consumers developed skills in the appreciation of this culture through leisure, education and, crucially, the leadership of a coherent and authoritative cultural elite which guarded and mediated cultural value on behalf of the wider public and its institutions. Drawn largely from the ranks of the politically disillusioned left and unified by a commitment to aesthetic modernism as the touchstone of cultural value, this elite testified to the "absorption of radicalism into the society" which for Bell characterized liberal culture and was central to the durability of consumer capitalism.[14]

This elite celebrated modernist forms for the trenchancy of their engagement with the so-called "human condition," defined as the isolation and alienation of the individual in modern life, and for the symbolic demonstrations of individual freedom they appeared to offer in the face of this condition. (That Hitler and Stalin had both suppressed modernism as degenerate and subversive made it particularly compelling to an American liberal imagination transfixed by the idea that individuality was about to be extinguished by one or another kind of totalitarianism.) It was a short step from here to the view that these forms flourished best, or only, in the "free world," and by extension, in the "free market" (despite, or even because of, the alienation often attributed to the latter). And it was through this selective interpretation that modernism was appropriated for American national culture, becoming in the process another medium for the conduct of the Cold War.[15] Bell was representative of the liberal cultural elite in making his case for the pluralistic vitality of American capitalism in terms of a notion of cultural freedom, constructed around this version of modernism, which effectively reconciled the interests of American intellectuals to those of US global power.[16] There was indeed an imperial ring to *The End of Ideology*'s central suggestion that, after two hundred years, the historic problems of modernity were being definitively resolved in the United States; for Bell's claims about the unique dynamism and social inclusiveness of American culture in both its general and specialized senses were underwritten by the geopolitical dominance of US capital and military force.

Not surprisingly, then, when this dominance was questioned Bell's arguments also began to unravel. The crisis of US imperial power in Vietnam in the second half of the 1960s was linked to an explosion of domestic social conflict and dissent, and a renewal of left theory and practice, which could not be accounted for in terms of pluralism, consensus or cultural inclusiveness.[17] Bell's presiding liberal culture was openly challenged by the formation of a "counter-culture" and the overtly conceived "cultural politics" of the New Left which sought to critique consensus capitalism, to expose its racism and its dependence on militarism and imperialism, through those very spheres and practices—consumption, lifestyle, education and leisure —that for Bell were keys to its stability. Moreover, the unforeseen return in the early 1970s of chronic economic crisis ("stagflation") now menaced the steadily rising productivity and prosperity crucial in Bell's view to the cultural and social vitality of consumer capitalism. The 1960s therefore mark a historical and theoretical break for Bell. The collapse of the hegemonic dream of an American Century of unrivalled US world leadership (to which the end of ideology thesis was implicitly attached)[18] precipitated the revision of his heretofore comedic narrative of capitalism and American culture into a tragedy in which capitalism undermines itself through its own success, liberal culture disintegrates through its very inclusiveness, and the problems of modernity reappear in the guise of postmodernism.

The roots of this tragedy lay for Bell in American capitalism's historic connections with individualism. In *The Cultural Contradictions of Capitalism* (1976) he argued that whilst capitalist economic and social forms were historically bound up with bourgeois individualism, the potentially corrosive and centrifugal impetus of the latter had been held in check by the common religious-cultural framework of Protestantism. The Protestant ethic of work, restraint and deferred gratification channeled the dynamic individualist energies of the bourgeoisie into economic activity and morally sanctioned the domination of natural resources and the accumulation of capital. Yet its very success in facilitating the rise of capitalism made Protestantism vulnerable to those forms of modern, secular rationality of which capitalism was exemplary. As the authority of the Protestant ethic weakened, individualism crossed over from the economic to the moral and cultural spheres and the bourgeoisie became internally divided. The majority, "radical in economics . . . [but] conservative in morals and cultural taste,"[19] came under attack from a dissident vanguard of intellectuals and artists which valorized expressiveness, experiment and the authority of the self. This increasingly powerful current of antinomian individualism—embodied for Bell in the aesthetic radicalism of modernism—substituted for capitalism's traditionally binding set of cultural legitimations and motivations an emphasis on the untrammeled self and its sensations. The culture of capitalism thus ceased to be a source of unifying values for the society as a whole. It severed its links with the economic and social structure and came into contradiction with this latter as "the discipline required by work was threatened by the libidinal energies diverted into culture."[20]

Yet on its way to achieving cultural dominance (indeed, as a condition for it) this adversary culture of modernism was co-opted by "the marketing system of business."[21] Its aesthetic individualism was translated back into economic and commercial terms and issued in vulgarized form as the hedonism and self-gratification of consumerism. In this respect "the Protestant ethic was undermined not by modernism but by capitalism itself;" and "the breakup of the traditional bourgeois value system . . . was brought about by the bourgeois economic system," in particular the "invention of the installment plan, or instant credit."[22] With its themes and forms appropriated by the advertising and entertainment industries, Bell argued, modernism lost its creativity and its critical purchase on capitalist society and became entirely a vehicle for the stimulation of insatiable consumer desire and infantile fantasies of liberation. The completion of this historical conjunction of economic and cultural individualism during the 1960s generated a new and, for Bell, destructive postmodern temper that was both cause and symptom of the social disintegration and spiritual impoverishment he now saw as endemic to American capitalism.

On one level, then, postmodernism refers to certain decisive changes that occurred or were completed during the 1960s and that define for Bell the current predicament of liberal capitalist democracy. It is, in this sense, as much a periodizing concept as an aesthetic-cultural one. It marks less a formal or stylistic break within culture (postmodernism being merely an intensification of the modernist emphasis on the autonomy and authority of the self) than an historic shift in the relationship between culture and the social formation as a whole. It signals for Bell that a culture now saturated at all levels with the hedonistic individualism of a degraded modernism can no longer function as a source of common values, motivations and rewards, and hence as the medium of social integration, for it contradicts both the disciplined rationality required for capitalist industrial production and the consensual spirit of restraint necessary to a non-ideological political pluralism.

On another level, in terms of its actual forms, postmodernism consists in an assault on those social and conceptual distinctions which for Bell underpinned liberal culture. Its transgressive impulse seeks to erase the boundaries between art and life, fantasy and reality, self and not-self in the name of that self's liberation from sensual and instinctual restraint. Although this same transgressive impulse had been constitutive of modernism in Bell's view, it had there been subject to the discipline of aesthetic organization and thus remained within the limits of imaginative control. In postmodernism, however, this impulse overflows its imaginative and aesthetic containment to be acted out in life in the anti-authoritarianism of the counter-culture and the hedonistic fantasies of consumerism alike. The destruction of boundaries therefore followed from the disintegration of that liberal cultural elite whose function it was to police them and authorize the distinctions they represented. For Bell, as for Lionel Trilling, transgressive modernism functioned positively as a symbolic bulwark against totalitarianism and a repository of cultural value only as long as it remained subject to the judgement and mediation of this elite.[23] When the modernist impulse became annexed to the commercial apparatus of mass consumption, the authority of this elite was undermined and postmodernism emerged precisely as a kind of market or mass version of modernism. The ground on which authoritative cultural distinctions between serious and inauthentic or high and low forms could be made disappeared, and the progressive-evolutionist project of a gradual raising of cultural levels collapsed. In this respect, Bell's conversion to the militant cultural pessimism of his latter period has been accompanied by the wholesale return of those Mass Culture theories he had previously derided as anti-democratic and anti-American.

Bell has conceded that the total colonization of culture by the market which postmodernism signifies was facilitated by liberalism's fatal attraction to individualism, by its "basic permissiveness," its inability to "define the bounds."[24] Indeed, the particularly narrow interpretation of modernism around which the Cold War liberals (with the endorsement of the CIA) constructed their vision of culture functioned, in its conflation of individual expression, cultural freedom and the free market, as a kind of Trojan horse for this colonization. Thus Bell's adoption of certain neoconservative positions during the late 1960s and the 1970s (among which was the defence of "traditional" cultural values and hierarchies) was linked to a crisis within liberalism which postmodernism did much to expose. Yet the principal offence of the postmodern ethos, and of the epoch it defines, is for Bell its disregard of the fundamental liberal distinction between the private and the public. On the one hand, the pop postmodernism of consumer culture represents the unseemly eruption of desire into the practices and rituals of everyday life. On the other, the more radical currents of postmodernism (especially those derived from the new political movements of the 1960s such as the New Left, black nationalism and women's liberation) deny any separation of the personal from the political and regard culture as unavoidably an arena and a vehicle for ideological struggle. Bell directs his fiercest invective towards those who would politicize culture thus. Yet these positions on culture are at least explicit about the interests they seek to serve in a way that Bell's, veiled by appeals to transcendent values and a universal human condition, is not.

Bell's discomfiture in the face of the collapse of bourgeois culture's universalist pretensions is registered by a number of instabilities in his theory of the cultural contradictions of capitalism. For instance, he veers between dismissing postmodernism and the counter-culture of the 1960s as, respectively, "a footnote to cultural history" and a puerile Oedipal revolt, and demonizing them as the twin assassins of enlightenment rationality, the bourgeois world-view and middle-class values![25] Similarly, he condemns modernism for being both anti-bourgeois and complicit with bourgeois society. Finally, he holds that capitalist culture has achieved a dangerous autonomy from the economic apparatus and, at the same time, become fully incorporated into it through the operations of the free market. The crisis of contemporary capitalism consists for him in the breakdown of the historic unity of bourgeois culture and economy. But it is equally apparent from his account that a postmodern culture of release complements and legitimates the capitalism of consumption and economic abundance in much the same way as a Protestant culture of restraint justified the earlier capitalism of production and scarcity. Indeed, Bell admits this much when he notes, "The one thing that would utterly destroy the new capitalism is the serious practice of deferred gratification."[26]

This final tension points to the ideological subtext of Bell's overall theory of "the disjunction of realms" in which his cultural arguments are situated.[27] For his insistence that culture, polity and economy have become thoroughly autonomous within modern capitalism, and that this latter does not therefore constitute any kind of totality, allows his militant cultural pessimism to co-exist with a technocratic optimism in his view of post-industrial forms of production. Bell is thus able to affirm capitalist modernization in economic and technological terms while repudiating its cultural and moral consequences. If the social formation is, as he insists, a series of discrete levels and spheres, then a total critique of capitalism (such as that provided by Marxism) is not required to address the crisis within it. Limited reform within the prevailing structures remains a possibility. Bell recommends, then, that culture be disarticulated from the relentless secular and individualist logic of capitalist modernization and returned to its origins in collective religious practices and beliefs.[28] Such a "return of the sacred" would set universally respected limits on the reach (both social and psychological) of capitalist market relations, balancing their creative-destructive dynamism with a counterweight of cultural restraint and continuity. It would thus serve to reconstruct the moral high ground upon which authoritative cultural judgement (and the elites who enforce it) could once again exist, and thereby revitalize those transcendent legitimations which in Bell's view secure the market's integrity as a mode of social and economic organization; for "what ultimately provides direction for the economy is the value system of the culture in which the economy is embedded."[29] In short, Bell argues that modernization should continue apace but disguise itself in the cultural costume of pre-modernity.

Bell seeks, then, to push the disjunction of realms further than he feels it has already gone. The theory is as much prescription as description. It functions as a device for the preservation of a liberalism that he concedes is "up against the wall," promising a methodological reinscription of those distinctions Cold War liberalism, with its attachment to a cultural version of the free market in its notion of modernism, was too feeble to sustain.[30] Bell's cultural conservatism and his professed socialism in distributive matters are in this respect servants of a dominant liberalism.[31] They are invoked to insure liberalism against the continuation of what he feels has been too deep an historical complicity with the individualist dynamic of capitalist modernity, the consequences of which threaten his vision of a meritocratic and market-driven post-industrial capitalism.[32] That this vision should be dependent upon a virtual counter-revolution in the cultural sphere, however, suggests that culture is in fact the determining realm for Bell, as the economic and social-political spheres derive whatever stability and popular consent they have from the cultural framework. It would appear, then, that for Bell capitalism indeed does (or should) constitute some kind of totality, integrated (or undermined) through its culture. I will consider what kind of totality this might be in the final section of this chapter. Now, though, I want to turn to Fredric Jameson for whom the relationship between culture and capital and the question of totality are also central to the evaluation of American capitalism at modernity's end.

Fredric Jameson: Marxism, Culture, Ideology

In many ways, Fredric Jameson's work stands as a reply to Daniel Bell's pronouncement of Marxism's historical demise and his conclusion that capitalism, despite its moral and spiritual vacuity, remains unassailable as a mode of social and economic organization.

For twenty-five years Jameson has argued for the indispensability of Marxism to an adequate understanding, and hence critique, of contemporary American capitalism and its culture. He has also recognised that this claim depends on Marxism's willingness to constantly renew itself with regard to the deep material transformations that capitalism has undergone since 1945, and to the new and competing varieties of intellectual response such change has provoked both inside and outside the Marxist tradition.

Jameson gravitated to Marxism as a way of extending, and then conserving in the decades of recuperation and neoconservative reaction that followed, the radicalism of the 1960s.[33] But in the absence of any flourishing Marxist tradition within the United States (partly the legacy of Bell's end-of-ideology syndrome) he turned to the writings of the European Marxist theoreticians of the 1920s, 1930s and 1940s to accomplish this shift.[34] This current of Western Marxism was congenial to Jameson as it arose out of a political conjuncture similar to that faced by the American New Left at the end of the 1960s—the fragmentation and defeat of a revolutionary movement, and the consequent rise, within a context of social and economic crisis, of powerful new ideologies of the political right. Moreover, it stressed, not just as compensation for political defeat but as an explanation of and response to it, the vital importance of the cultural sphere. This complemented both the peculiarly cultural nature of 1960s radicalism and Jameson's own overwhelmingly cultural interests.

The Western Marxist emphasis on culture had three main aspects. First, it held that capitalist societies were not simple mechanisms of domination: they depended as much on a certain degree of legitimacy or popular consent as on forceful coercion, and this was secured through public discourses (including art, literature and other kinds of representation) which were cultural in nature. Culture was thus rescued from its derivative status among vulgar or economistic Marxists for whom it was the passive, superstructural reflection of a determining economic base, and ensconced as the crucial sphere of ideological struggle and social reproduction. Second, given its constitutive role in normalizing and reproducing social relations, an understanding of culture, of its historical development and cognitive function, became central to fully understanding capitalism as a mode of production. Third, as culture's cognitive possibilities were no longer regarded as totally determined by the economic base, this sphere was felt to be more open to critical and oppositional currents than others. The analysis of aesthetics and culture therefore lent itself to a debate about the nature of those genuinely radical and popular forms that would contribute to the development of class consciousness and collective emancipation. The question of culture thus became the principal bearer of Marxism's utopian impulse.

For Jameson, however, the contemporary form of late capitalism is a far more technologically and spatially integrated, multinational and hence total system than that encountered by this previous generation of Marxists. Within it the central historical features which have traditionally concerned Marxists—the struggle of well defined ideologies and social classes at the level of production—have been occluded by the extraordinary postwar expansion of a global culture of consumption and media spectacle on the American model. As well as constituting a whole new sphere of commodity production in its own right, this culture presents radically novel forms of aesthetic and cognitive experience characterized by fragmentation and discontinuity. Any convincing extension of the Western Marxist narrative of the relationship between capital and culture had thus to account for "the coming of the whole new political and economic 'world system,' to which the older Marxist paradigms only imperfectly apply;" while the delineation of appropriate forms of radical cultural practice now depended on moving beyond the binary opposition of realism and modernism in which the debate on Marxist aesthetics had been deadlocked since the 1930s.[35]

These new conditions demanded what Jameson called a specifically Western, even North American, post-industrial Marxism adequate to the technologically advanced, socially differentiated and image-drenched nature of contemporary consumer capitalism. It would analyze and resist the tendency towards social fragmentation and historical discontinuity by stressing that capitalism constituted an historically developing totality, and its major task would be to pierce "the sticky webs of the false and unreal culture" and rediscover the "realities of production and work on the world" in which class struggle and the pressure of history could still be traced.[36] Indeed, the challenge was to demonstrate precisely how these two levels were part of the same social totality. The notion of postmodernism emerged as Jameson's response to these problems. But for a sufficient grasp of its implications we must first consider his complex, genetic approach to the historical development of cultural forms in which postmodernism figures as some kind of culmination.

In the earliest modes of human social and economic organization Jameson identifies an original and in some ways exemplary unity of culture and social life. Here, aesthetic or cultural activity (largely in the form of myth and ritual) is seen to be completely integrated into the practices and knowledges of everyday life. Just as importantly, it is fully collective in character, providing the society with a shared understanding of itself and the world it inhabits. In both these respects early kinds of cultural activity are for Jameson "socially functional" in a way that the increasingly specialized and marginal culture of modern societies is not;[37] and like Marx's notion of primitive communism this unity serves as a polemical point of reference or prototype for a utopian vision of the transformed cultural production of a liberated, classless society.

However, early cultural forms have an additional social dimension which remains constant in Jameson's view to all subsequent historical periods: they are always necessarily engaged in "inventing imaginary or formal 'solutions' to unresolvable social contradictions."[38] For the anthropologist Claude Levi-Strauss, even the most elementary or "primitive" cultural and aesthetic constructions are at some level sophisticated attempts to manage or compensate for potentially disturbing areas of tension in a society. In his famous example, the peculiar symmetrical-yet-diagonal design of Caduveo facial decorations is read as a response to the opposing claims of equality and hierarchy within a society that was unable to develop any institutional means of addressing this contradiction. For Jameson, Levi-Strauss' insight offers a way of grasping the profoundly ideological nature of cultural and aesthetic activity: the Caduveo face painting is not simply about the problem of power relations in that society; it is in a sense caused or structured by this problem. Yet it is also an active intervention into the problem which seeks to resolve it in symbolic or imaginary form. Thus for Jameson culture and ideology are not distinct categories which may, under certain conditions, impinge upon or inform one another; "rather the aesthetic act is itself ideological, and the production of aesthetic or narrative form is to be seen as an ideological act in its own right."[39]

If for Bell culture and ideology are antagonistic terms, the former standing as an ideal bulwark of unchanging existential themes and universal moral values against the transient concerns and sectarian passions of the latter, for Jameson they are virtually coterminous. This is particularly the case, Jameson suggests, in modern capitalist societies; for here the play of contradictory social and historical forces that constitute a genuinely collective "political unconscious" which motivates and structures every instance of cultural production, is especially complex and volatile. Marxist cultural criticism is therefore a form of ideological analysis which seeks through the interpretation of cultural texts to uncover the operations of this historically determined, and otherwise inaccessible, limit on conceptual thought and imagination. It does so by dismantling the symbolic resolutions proffered by cultural objects and reconstructing instead their underlying, and contradictory, social and historical conditions of production. This subtext is then understood in terms of a specific political tension or conflict which relates ultimately to questions of social class and class power. But the individual text is not only inhabited by the antagonistic or dialogical discourses of class, it is actively a part of this social sign system which, for Jameson, is in turn the index of a larger historical unity: the mode of production. Moving from the particular to the general through these various levels, Marxist cultural criticism takes as its ultimate object of analysis the social totality itself.

Different modes of production, though, generate distinctive sign systems appropriate to their organizational forms, to the play of social forces within them, and to the kinds of experience they make available. The cultural forms of pre-capitalist societies, myth, religion and types of what Jameson calls "magical narratives," are essentially pre-individualistic; the social worlds from which they emerge, being still more or less collectively based, do not provide the conditions necessary for the development of a conception of autonomous selfhood or individual, psychological subjectivity. It is only with the rise of capitalist social and economic organization, and of the bourgeoisie as the dominant class, that this becomes possible. And, Jameson argues, it is through the representational system of realism (particularly the novel with its concern for character and the integrity of individual experience and destiny) that the notion of the coherent individual subject is articulated and established.

The history of cultural forms, then, is bound not just to the development of modes of production but also to the construction of the various modes of human subjectivity. Indeed, by organizing and articulating experience in certain ways, a system of representation works to produce the kind of subjects required by a particular mode of production. The cultural apparatus or superstructure finds its "essential function" here "in the mediation of changes in the infrastructure."[40] This relationship produces what Jameson calls the "ideology of form." By tracing this ideology in his reading practice he seeks to illuminate the process of cultural revolution which is most evident at those historical and textual points where rival systems of representation (and hence modes of social organization and subjectivity) clash, the earlier ones becoming displaced by and incorporated into the later ones.

Jameson identifies three key moments in the capitalist cultural revolution. Each registers a further stage in the historical process of reification or rationalization, that is the "dismantling of the various traditional or 'natural' . . . unities (social groups, institutions, human relationships, forms of authority, activities of a cultural and ideological as well as of a productive nature) with a view to their . . . reorganization into more efficient systems which function according to an instrumental . . . logic."[41] The first, the moment of realism, corresponds to the rise of the bourgeoisie and the establishment of the "rational" structures of classical competitive capitalism. Here the construction in realism of the model of the autonomous individual is understood as a means of "reprogramming" the inhabitants of this new social world "to the 'freedom' and equality of sheer market equivalence."[42] The second moment, that of modernism, marks the extension of market relations and the deepening commodification of social and private life in the expanded system of imperialist monopoly capitalism. Modernism's fragmentation of realist form embodies the heightened pitch of reification in this new stage of capitalism and further retrains subjectivity to its demands, while its emphasis on psychological experience and the embattled interiority of private consciousness (particularly in its formal repudiation of the newly industrialized forms of low or mass culture) at once expresses and compensates for the self's increasing objective dislocation within this system.

The third moment of this revolution is the contemporary one of postmodernism, the cultural correlate of the thoroughly global or multinational system of consumer capitalism that arrives in the post-1945 period. Like Bell, Jameson sees postmodernism as a feature of the consolidation of this system in the 1960s and of the crisis of American economic and imperial power in that decade. But while for Bell postmodernism marks the disastrous triumph of the 1960s counter-culture, for Jameson it embodies this movement's co-optation and defeat. The radicalism of the 1960s was for Jameson an effect of the massive unbinding of social energies unleashed by the final and rapid expansion of capitalism into the remaining uncommodified enclaves of "Nature," achieved through the neo-colonialist exploitation of the Third World on the one hand and the media invasion of the unconscious on the other.[43] The counter-culture both protested this expansion and was necessary to it, in that its assault on prevailing bourgeois values and distinctions further cleared the way for the radically levelling effects of commodity exchange. The anti-authoritarian and anti-hierarchical forms of

postmodern culture are thus recuperations or aesthetic recontain-
ments of this radical energy which has been detached from the
project of social liberation and harnessed to the process of reification.

If "postmodernism is the substitute for the sixties and the
compensation for their political failure," then it is also a "new kind of
ideological hegemony" required to counteract the faltering of US
global economic and military supremacy since the mid-1960s.[44]
Whereas for Bell postmodernism is the cause as well as the symptom
of economic and imperial decline, for Jameson it embodies a shift
from overt economic and military forms of domination to a less
obviously coercive, and therefore more insidiously effective, system of
cultural domination, as "the moment American power begins to
be questioned, a new cultural apparatus becomes necessary to
enforce it."[45] Dissent and opposition are incorporated and defused
through the integration in postmodernism of cultural and aesthetic
production "into commodity production generally;" whatever free
play or relative autonomy previously obtained between economic
structure and cultural superstructure is extinguished by the logic of
late capitalism which "assigns an increasingly essential structural
function and position to aesthetic innovation and experimentation."[46]

This spells extinction for those cultural and aesthetic projects,
especially modernism, that sought to repudiate and hold themselves
aloof from the operations of the commodity. The collapse of the
distinction between high and mass culture in postmodernism has
serous implications for Jameson as it does for Bell, not, however, in
the collapse of bourgeois values and standards it undoubtedly entails,
but because it means that the ground on which effectively critical and
radical cultural practices might be constructed has been cut away,
and the very possibility of sustaining a "critical distance" from the
prevailing structures abolished.[47] This underlines the futility for
Jameson of the kind of moral denunciation of postmodernism offered
by Bell. For such gestures rest on the illusory and idealist belief that
it is possible somehow to "'step outside' actually existing reality into
some other space;" they thus deny and conceal the fact that the
"constriction of the total system, of its inescapability even for
the imagination" which must be fully felt if the necessity of its
fundamental transformation is to be grasped.[48] In contrast Jameson
posits a dialectical approach to postmodernism, a kind of internal
or immanent critique which, by rejecting the mirage of some transcendent "outside," seeks "the model of the presence of the future
within the present," much in the manner that Marx discerned the
elements of socialist society in the oppressive forms of capitalism.[49]

One trace of the presence of a more hopeful future in post-modernism is to be found for Jameson in the way that its radically fragmented or decentred forms enact the final breakdown of the kind of coherent and autonomous subjectivity articulated in realism, and then both problematized and reinforced by modernism. For Bell the unity of the subject, especially the golden age of bourgeois-Protestant character in the heroic phase of nineteenth-century capitalism, is a historical fact whose passing is to be denounced and resisted. For Jameson, though, this unity was always no more than a fiction, an ideological expression of the bourgeoisie's social dominance and its modernizing drive to shatter traditional and still largely collective social relations into the rational and individualized units of the capitalist marketplace. There can thus be no question of reviving the unified subject by, as Bell suggests, returning to bygone cultural mechanisms of restraint, for the notion was illusory and class specific in the first place. Moreover, the material conditions for its revival are lost. The discontinuous and depthless forms of postmodernism are as necessary for the education of subjectivity to the requirements of a post-industrial capitalism of media spectacle and the serial consumer high as were the bourgeois individualist forms of realism and modernism to capital in its *laissez-faire* and monopoly stages. To endorse, as Bell does, post-industrial capitalism while bemoaning the disappearance of bourgeois character is for Jameson wilfully to imprison one's thought in an irreducible and mystifying antinomy.

Postmodern forms contain a progressive moment, then, in their desiccation of the bourgeois subject; and in this respect they dimly foreshadow the kind of decentred subjectivity that for Jameson will characterize a genuinely collective radical culture and society. But, equally, the postmodern model of schizophrenic subjectivity cannot be accepted on its own terms, for it involves a breakdown of temporal and narrative modes of cognition which has serious implications for any such radical cultural or aesthetic practice. This is for Jameson part of a fundamental crisis of historical understanding in contemporary Western culture. Real history has given way to the simulation of history in media images and the voracious recycling of the past as so many meaningless styles, codes and fashions. Moreover, the temporal progressions of narrative, even of language itself, are broken down by postmodern forms into dissociated instants of affective intensity ("highs" and spectacles) which produce the sense of being adrift in an eternal present without past or future. This crisis is disabling not in the way that for Bell it involves a loss of the tempering influence of tradition and its hierarchical values, but because it undermines "our lived possibility of experiencing history in some active way," and thus of intervening in it by "fashioning representations of our own current experience."[50] The discontinuous forms and essentially spatial concerns of postmodernism—especially evident in architecture and contemporary narrative's fascination with the vast interlocking system of post-industrial communications technology—are inadequate to the task of representing the connections between individual experience and the impersonal, transindividual forces of history which, for Jameson, must be the function of any viable culture, especially one that seeks to be critical.

But this generalized crisis of representation is not simply a defect of postmodern cultural forms. Rather, it is a symptom of our current cognitive inability to grasp in its totality, either conceptually or imaginatively, "the whole new decentred global network of the third stage of capital itself."[51] The new and bewildering kinds of spatial experience embodied in postmodernism (Jameson's notorious example is Los Angeles's Bonaventure Hotel) are precisely partial or failed figurations of this network, and as such they contain a crucial, if incomplete, element of truth, even of realism in an unfamiliar form. Jameson proposes that this element be held onto and incorporated into a new cultural and aesthetic practice of cognitive mapping. In seeking to represent the system in its totality, this would overcome the gap between individual experience and the collective levels of society and history, and thus provide the cognitive materials for a renewal of political action and struggle aimed at social transformation.

It is in this possibility of a "new political art" which would foster "class consciousness of a new and hitherto undreamed of kind" that the utopian promise of culture persists for Jameson.[52] Yet it is nowhere clear in his account how such a practice might be forged or, indeed, what form it would take. He suggests that the strategy must be "to undo postmodernism homeopathically by the methods of postmodernism," and that a radical cultural practice must "try to use postmodern techniques . . . to go through and beyond" the present crisis of representation.[53] But, in his powerful characterization, postmodernism is so tightly bound to the commodity form and the process of reification, and the system it expresses so totally integrated, that it is difficult to imagine that there could be a "through" or "beyond," let alone what we might find (or, rather construct) by getting there. Jameson's insistence that to relinquish or condemn the concept of totality (as has become the norm in most postmodern discourse, as well as in some that oppose it such as Bell's) when late capitalism is a more total system than ever before remains crucial. However, there is a sense in which the conceptualization itself can be so total, so undifferentiated, that it defeats its own critical purpose and leaves no room for those points of tension and contradiction out of which change and resistance often springs. Jameson's theorization of postmodernism runs these risks and has been criticized from the left for doing so.[54]

Jameson's Hegelian stress on the "logic" of capitalist reification is problematic in this sense too. "Logic" suggests not just that the movement of history is guided by impersonal laws, but that its progress is also somehow automatic and its direction inevitable. Capitalism itself thus becomes the supreme and abstract subject of history with individual agency and, more importantly, the agency and struggle of oppressed classes being squeezed out of the picture.[55] While the scope for oppositional action is therefore somewhat restricted in this model, it makes it equally difficult to conceive how such action, if it did arise, could decisively alter the course of history.

These problems are bound up with Jameson's tendency to run culture and ideology into one another as forms of misrepresentation or misrecognition of real social and historical conditions. If culture is invariably a form of misrepresentation it is not easy to see how even the kind of radical mapping practice called for by Jameson could escape the cognitive and conceptual limitations of ideology. Jameson has stressed that there is always a utopian dimension to cultural production in its buried suggestions of more properly collective modes of thought and communication, and that it is only through the utopian impulse to imagine the present in radically different form that the vicious circle of ideology can be broken. But his tendency to locate utopianism in every kind of cultural product or discourse (including ruling-class consciousness itself) would seem to reseal the circle again forthwith. For it becomes impossible to tell ideology and utopia apart or to locate the particular social forces which embody and might best realize the utopian impulse. Thus Jameson's important insistence that Marxism combine the negative critique of ideology with a more positive elaboration of utopia in anticipation of collective liberation is weakened. However, this failure to elaborate satisfactorily a *specific* (that is socialist) utopia, rather than detect the vague shadows of a generic utopianism in any and every form of cultural or collective endeavour, is not only Jameson's; it is a major theoretical failure of the Marxist tradition as a whole.[56] Jameson's characterization of our own moment of postmodernism stands as a powerful reminder to the left of the necessity of addressing this aporia, and of closing it.

Postmodernism and Cultural Politics: Nostalgia or Utopia?

Both Bell and Jameson see postmodernism as the latest stage of the permanent revolution by which capital and the commodity extend their reifying reach further and deeper into all levels of existence. In particular, the once relatively autonomous sphere of culture becomes fully absorbed into the market, losing its capacity to provide the collective meanings and images by which we might orient ourselves in relation to our world and each other. For Bell this has entailed the collapse, first of religion, and then of high bourgeois culture as universal and unifying discourses which could legitimate the market system and limit its socially corrosive dynamic. The possibility ensues that the economic and social fabric of Western capitalist democracies will self-destruct through the absence of cultural legitimations and authoritative restraints on consumer hedonism. For Jameson the same development has made the prospect of constructing a critical and utopian cultural discourse, which could provide the resources for a radical political movement, more remote than ever. The possibility ensues that the economic structures of multinational capitalism will persist in their dominance through the absence of any effectively collective opposition. In both cases, however, the historical project or grand narrative of modernity, in which was contained the promise of a steady progress towards the rational, secular and enlightened organization of social life, is seen to be in crisis.

Bell's response is to reject the modern project in all but its technological aspects, to call for a partial re-enchantment of social life, and to situate this within a nostalgic vision of capitalism without modernity. Only by returning to sacred and religious forms can a universal and unifying culture capable of safeguarding capitalist economic production be established. While Bell might have shifted his allegiance over the years from bourgeois high art to the sacred forms of religion as the basis of a universal culture, the function of such a culture remains the same: to recycle the timelessly binding existential concerns of humanity, to secure assent to vested cultural authority, and thereby to reconcile a divided society to its divisions. In the Jamesonian sense, culture is to provide an imaginary or symbolic resolution of the historically specific contradictions of late capitalist societies. Thus despite the categorical opposition he seeks to maintain between culture and ideology, Bell's conception of culture is idealist, ahistorical and, precisely, ideological.

By contrast, Jameson holds on to the emancipatory project of modernity. Marxism and the aesthetics of modernism combine in his pursuit of the possibility of pushing through and beyond post-modernism, rather than retreating from it. The religious and potentially universal or unifying dimensions of culture are not denied in this perspective, but are held to be conditional upon the completion of the emancipatory project for their full realization. Until then, in a divided society, they must remain as buried utopian anticipations of a liberated future. Culture is not an anti-politics but a form of politics; therefore "a truly new culture could only emerge through the collective struggle to create a new social system."[57] The concept of postmodernism foregrounds this question of the politics of culture with appropriate urgency.

Notes

1. Daniel Bell, *The Coming of Post-Industrial Society: A Venture in Social Forecasting* (New York: Basic Books, 1973), p. 37.
2. Although *The Coming of Post-Industrial Society* was published in 1973, Bell had been writing about the "post-industrial society" since the late 1950s. The notion is not exclusively Bell's, however. Alain Touraine's *The Post-Industrial Society* (New York: Random House, 1971) was an important European perspective which differed significantly in approach and emphasis from Bell's.
3. This also points to a significant expansion in the sense and application of the word "culture," especially over the last 150 years. See the entry on "culture" in Raymond Williams, *Keywords* (London: Fontana, 1976), pp. 76–82.
4. Some commentators seek to maintain a distinction between postmoderni*sm* (a specific group of aesthetic and cultural styles) and postmoderni*ty* (the wider social, institutional and cultural condition of change in which such styles flourish). The distinction is useful insofar as it enables us to distinguish between particular instances of change and objects of analysis, but it should not imply any fundamental discontinuity between levels. Neither Bell nor Jameson insists on such a distinction and, for each, questions about wider social, economic and institutional change are inscribed from the start in the problem of postmodernism as a cultural style.
5. The Editors of *Fortune* with Russell W. Davenport, *USA: The Permanent Revolution* (London: Heinemann, 1952), pp. 62, 64.
6. Daniel Bell, *The End of Ideology; On the Exhaustion of Political Ideas in the Fifties* (Cambridge, Mass.: Harvard University Press, 1988), p. 449.
7. Bell, *The End of Ideology*, p. 400.
8. Bell, *The End of Ideology*, p. 300.
9. The classic example of this is Leslie Fiedler's *An End to Innocence: Essays on Culture and Politics* (Boston, Mass.: Beacon Press, 1955).
10. See C. Wright Mills, "Letter to the New Left" and Michael Harrington, "The Anti-Ideology Ideologues" both in Chaim I. Waxman (ed.) *The End of Ideology Debate* (New York: Simon and Schuster, 1968), pp. 126–40, 342–51. Also see Christopher Lasch, "The Cultural Cold War: A Short History of the Congress for Cultural Freedom," chapter 3 of his *The Agony of the American Left* (Harmondsworth: Penguin, 1973).

11. Bell, *The End of Ideology*, p. 34.
12. Bell, *The End of Ideology*, p. 37.
13. Alan Swingewood, *The Myth of Mass Culture* (London: Macmillan, 1977), p. 19.
14. Bell, *The End of Ideology*, pp. 313–14.
15. This included covert CIA involvement in the worldwide promotion of abstract expressionism through the New York Museum of Modern Art. See Serge Guilbaut, *How New York Stole the Idea of Modern Art: Abstract Expressionism. Freedom and the Cold War* (Chicago: University of Chicago Press, 1983). Also see Alan Sinfield, "Reinventing Modernism," chapter 9 of his *Literature, Politics and Culture in Postwar Britain* (Oxford: Basil Blackwell, 1989).
16. See Lasch, *The Agony of the American Left*, p. 97. It was precisely the attachment of many left-leaning intellectuals to these very notions of modernism and cultural freedom that caused them (however reluctantly) to rally to American capitalism as the best available social model in the 1952 *Partisan Review* symposium, "Our Country and Our Culture."
17. The signs of such conflict had been available to Bell, of course, in the struggles for black civil rights in the 1940s and 1950s. The absence of any mention of race or racism is therefore perhaps the most obvious gap in *The End of Ideology*'s account of cultural and political pluralism.
18. Daniel Bell, "The End of American Exceptionalism" in his *The Winding Passage: Essays and Sociological Journeys, 1960–1980* (New York: Basic Books, 1980), p. 272. The idea of the "American Century" originated with Henry Luce, Bell's employer from 1948–58 on *Fortune* magazine and the sponsor of that notion of the humane and socially benevolent dynamism of American capitalism which Bell placed at the theoretical centre of *The End of Ideology*.
19. Daniel Bell, *The Cultural Contradictions of Capitalism* (London: Heinemann, 1979), p. 17.
20. Bell, *Cultural Contradictions*, p. xxiv.
21. Bell, *Cultural Contradictions*, p. 84.
22. Bell, *Cultural Contradictions*, p. 21, and Daniel Bell, "The Cultural Contradictions of Capitalism" in Daniel Bell and Irving Kristol (eds) *Capitalism Today* (New York: Mentor, 1971), p. 50.
23. See Lionel Trilling, *Beyond Culture: Essays on Literature and Learning* (Harmondsworth: Penguin, 1967).
24. Bell, *Cultural Contradictions*, p. 79.
25. Bell, *Cultural Contradictions*, p. 52.
26. Bell, *Cultural Contradictions*, p. 78.
27. Bell, *Cultural Contradictions*, Introduction, and Bell, *The Winding Passage*, Preface.
28. Hence Bell's interest in a country like Japan which, he claims, has managed to modernize without destroying its traditional and collective cultural relationships and structures. Its ability to enjoy capitalism without individualism gives Japan, in Bell's view, its competitive edge over the United States and Europe. See Daniel Bell, "Models and Reality in Economic Discourse" in Daniel Bell and Irving Kristol (eds) *The Crisis in Economic Theory* (New York: Basic Books, 1981), pp. 47–79.
29. Bell, *Cultural Contradictions*, p. xii.
30. Bell, *Cultural Contradictions*, p. xi: "I am a socialist in economics, a liberal in politics, and a conservative in culture."

32. Bell, *The Coming of Post-Industrial Society*, p. 455.
33. See Douglas Kellner's introduction to the volume edited by him, *Postmodernism, Jameson, Critique* (Washington DC.: Maisonneuve Press, 1989), p. 9.
34. Jameson's first properly Marxist book was a sustained consideration of the cultural theories of the inter-war generation of European Marxists. See Fredric Jameson, *Marxism and Form: Twentieth-Century Dialectical Theories of Literature* (Princeton, NJ.: Princeton University Press, 1971).
35. Fredric Jameson, *The Political Unconscious: Narrative as a Socially Symbolic Act* (London: Methuen, 1981) p. 11. See also Fredric Jameson, "Reflections in Conclusion" in Ernst Bloch *et al. Aesthetics and Politics* (London: Verso, 1980), p. 211. The latter volume is a presentation of the most influential positions in the realism vs. modernism controversy in Western Marxism.
36. Jameson, *Marxism and Form*, pp. xix, xviii.
37. Jameson, *Marxism and Form*, p. xvi.
38. Jameson, *The Political Unconscious*, p. 79.
39. Jameson, *The Political Unconscious*, p. 79.
40. Fredric Jameson, "The Vanishing Mediator: or, Max Weber as Storyteller" in *The Ideologies of Theory—Essays 1971–1986, Volume 2: The Syntax of History* (London: Routledge, 1988), p. 25.
41. Jameson, *The Political Unconscious*, p. 227.
42. Jameson, *The Political Unconscious*, p. 221.
43. Fredric Jameson, "Periodizing the 60s" in *The Ideologies of Theory Volume 2*, p. 207. Jameson's source for his arguments about the expansion of commodification in post-1945 capitalism is Ernest Mandel, *Late Capitalism* (London: Verso, 1978).
44. Fredric Jameson, *Postmodernism, or, The Cultural Logic of Late Capitalism* (London: Verso, 1991), p. xvi, and Anders Stephanson, "A Conversation with Fredric Jameson: Regarding Postmodernism" in Andrew Ross (ed.) *Universal Abandon? The Politics of Postmodernism* (Edinburgh: Edinburgh University Press, 1989), p. 8.
45. Stephanson, "A Conversation with Fredric Jameson", p. 8.
46. Jameson, *Postmodernism*, pp. 4–5.
47. Jameson, *Postmodernism*, p. 48.
48. Jameson, *Postmodernism*, pp. 206, 207.
49. Jameson, *Postmodernism*, p. 206.
50. Jameson, *Postmodernism*, p. 21.
51. Jameson, *Postmodernism*, p. 38.
52. Jameson, *Postmodernism*, pp. 54, 418.
53. Stephanson, "A Conversation with Fredric Jameson", pp. 17–18.
54. See Fred Pfeil, "Makin' Flippy-Floppy: Postmodernism and the Baby-Boom PMC" in *Another Tale to Tell: Politics and Narrative in Postmodern Culture* (London: Verso, 1990), p. 107.
55. See Stanley Aronowitz's critique of "capital logic" theory in *The Crisis in Historical Materialism: Class, Politics and Culture in Marxist Theory* (London: Macmillan, 1990), pp. 216–22.
56. See Stephen Lukes, *Marxism and Morality* (Oxford: Oxford University Press, 1985), p. 99.
57. Jameson, *Postmodernism*, p. xii.

Index